THE PEOPLE'S RISING
WEXFORD, 1798

THE PEOPLE'S RISING
WEXFORD, 1798

DANIEL GAHAN

GILL & MACMILLAN

Gill & Macmillan Ltd
Hume Avenue, Park West
Dublin 12
with associated companies throughout the world
www.gillmacmillan.ie

© Daniel Gahan 1995
0 7171 2392 8 hard cover
0 7171 2323 5 paperback

Index compiled by Helen Litton
Print origination by *Deirdre's Desktop*
Printed by ColourBooks Ltd, Dublin

*The paper used in this book comes from the wood pulp
of managed forests. For every tree felled, at least one tree
is planted, thereby renewing natural resources.*

A catalogue record is available for this book
from the British Library.

5 7 9 8 6

*To my parents in Wexford
and to the memory of
Annie Gahan, 1903–1984
and my brother
Gerard 1970–1995*

CONTENTS

ILLUSTRATIONS

MAPS

Leading Participants

Rebels (residence and rebel rank indicated)

Gorey Barony
  Anthony Perry, Inch, Colonel/General
  Miles Byrne, Monaseed, Captain

Ballaghkeen North Barony
  Esmond Kyan, Mounthoward, Colonel
  Father John Murphy, Boolavogue, Captain
  Father Michael Murphy, Ballycanew, Captain

Ballaghkeen South Barony
  Edward Fitzgerald, Newpark, Colonel/General
  Morgan Byrne, Kilnamanagh, Captain
  George Sparks, Blackwater, Captain
  John Hay, Ballinkeele, Captain
  Thomas Sinnott, Kilbride, Captain

Shelmalier East Barony
  Edward Roche, Garrylough, Colonel/General
  Thomas Dixon, Castlebridge, Captain

Bargy and Forth Baronies
  Matthew Keogh, Wexford, Colonel
  Cornelius Grogan, Johnstown, Colonel
  Beauchamp Bagenal Harvey, Bargy Castle, Colonel/General
  Dick Monk, Wexford, Captain
  John Henry Colclough, Ballyteige, Colonel
  William Kearney, Wexford, Captain
  William Boxwell, Sarshill, Captain
  William Hughes, Ballytrent, Captain

Scarawalsh Barony
  Father Edward Sinnott, Kilrush, Colonel
  Father Mogue Kearns, Kiltealy, Colonel
  William Barker, Enniscorthy, Captain
  Thomas Clinch, Enniscorthy, Captain
  Luke Byrne, Enniscorthy, Captain

Bantry Barony
  John Kelly, Killann, Colonel
  Father Philip Roche, Poulpeasty, Colonel/General
  Thomas Cloney, Moneyhore, Colonel
  Matthew Furlong, Templescoby, Captain
  Michael Furlong, Templescoby, Captain
  Robert Carty, Birchgrove, Captain

Shelburne/Shelmalier West Baronies
  John Murphy, Loughnageer, Captain
  Walter Devereux, Taghmon, Captain

Government forces (rank and principal location during rebellion indicated)

Earl Camden, Viceroy, Dublin Castle
Gerard Lake, General, Commander-in-Chief, Dublin Castle
Francis Needham, Lieutenant-General, Arklow
Loftus, General, Arklow and Tullow
Lambert Walpole, Colonel, Carnew and Gorey
Henry Dundas, General, Kildare and Hacketstown
Sir James Duff, General, Kildare and Newtownbarry
L'Estrange, Colonel, Newtownbarry
Lord Ancram, Colonel, Newtownbarry
Lord Roden, Colonel, Tullow and Carnew
Charles Eustace, Major-General, New Ross
Henry Johnson, Major-General, New Ross
George Dalhousie, General, Duncannon
Sir William Fawcett, General, Duncannon
Sir John Moore, Brigadier-General, Fermoy and New Ross
Foote, Lieutenant-Colonel, Wexford and Duncannon
Maxwell, Colonel, Wexford and Duncannon

PREFACE

Every corner of the world is haunted by the past, but there are a few places where the ghosts are more palpably present than others. County Wexford is one of these. I grew up there, ten miles from its northern boundary with Wicklow, and was introduced, at a very young age, to the rebellion of 1798. The rising was, we learned, a valiant attempt by people in many parts of Ireland, but especially in ours, to overthrow the English yoke and to create an independent country. The cruelties of their oppressors were part of the legend of 'Ninety-eight,' and the bravery of the thousands of rebels who dared struggle against impossible odds lay at its very core. My family lived at the foot of Carrigrew Hill, about two miles from The Harrow and Boolavogue, places where, I soon learned, important things had happened in that momentous year, and no episode in the history of my country could possibly have matched the rebellion in importance in my child's sense of Ireland's bloody and glorious past.

Monuments to the men and the battles dotted the countryside, and every town of any size had a statue in its central square or on its main street, calling us to appreciate what 'our people' had once done. The most moving of them all were the two figures atop a high pedestal in the Market Square of Enniscorthy: one a young man in a loose shirt, the other an older man, apparently a priest, taller than the first, who stands beside him, with his arm over his shoulder, and points to some place in the distance, encouraging, urging. It was easy to be moved by such things.

Family lore added to the appeal. My great-great-great grandfather, Denis Gahan, had been 'out in '98', I was told, and had come home when the fighting was over to find the old farmhouse burned to the ground by the 'yeos'. Our family still owned the little farm from which he had gone to battle that summer, and the walls of the old cabin (rebuilt after 1798 but burned again by accident in 1947) were still there.

The ballads and the tales that still survived in the countryside, even after almost two centuries, did the rest. We learned many of the songs by heart, especially the more common ones, like 'Boolavogue', 'Kelly the Boy from Killann' and 'The Boys of Wexford'. A few of us listened to the snippets of lore the old people would share: how a man had shot a redcoat travelling the Gorey road from a rock on Clogh Hill; how the 'yeos' put people in barrels and rolled them down hills for sport; how a man who hated the rebels and heard that the rising had begun grabbed a slash-hook and went out of his house, declaring to his neighbours that the first 'croppy' he would kill would be his own son. Where these tales came from and how true they were I had no idea, and have no idea to this day. They were told with great conviction and complete acceptance by people like my Aunt Annie, who was born in Boolavogue in 1903, and who related them in the same matter-of-fact way over a glowing fire as she would something that had happened to her when she was a young girl.

The schoolroom confirmed it all. There the battles of Ninety-eight took on an even grander significance. There they were part of the great story of the redemption of our nation by men like Tone, O'Connell, Parnell and Pearse. In a time when pride in one's county counted for a great deal, it was a stirring thing to be reminded that we came from a county that had played no ordinary part in the great liberation.

Then, in the summer of 1972, at the age of seventeen, I read Thomas Pakenham's *Year of Liberty*.[1] The book was beautifully written and brought the rebellion to life in vivid detail. Like the novelist Colm Toibín, however, who must have been reading it around the same time in his home in Enniscorthy,[2] I too was disappointed by the image of the rebels I took away from its pages. Instead of the dashing amateur soldiers, fighting in gleaming linen shirts that I assumed them to have been, I encountered a desperate mob that was dirty, often drunk, frequently cruel, sometimes cowardly, and, always it seemed, far more numerous than their loyalist enemies yet strangely incompetent. The surprise was total and the disappointment shattering.

Perhaps Pakenham's book was needed. Perhaps it was time, in 1972, to show that the story was far less glorious than it had seemed. Certainly the propagandist nationalist versions which had appeared in large numbers in the previous hundred years, and which had, unknown to me, determined the bias of our history textbooks, needed a counterweight. Charles Dickson had taken the first step in this direction in 1955 with a well-balanced work on the rising,[3] and Pakenham might have followed his lead. What he did instead, unwittingly perhaps, was to provide us with a reborn version of the old loyalist interpretation, an interpretation which had appeared in many of the books on the rebellion that had been published in the four or five decades immediately after 1798, and which was also thoroughly biased; in this version, best exemplified by the work of Sir Richard Musgrave,[4] the rebels were an unruly mob, cowardly but cruel, and motivated above all by religious hatred.

No narrative of the rebellion has appeared since Pakenham's, but in recent years our understanding of 1798 has deepened markedly. Historians like Marianne Elliott, L. M. Cullen, Kevin Whelan, Nancy Curtin[5] and many others have begun to unravel the origins of the rebellion in Ireland in general and in Wexford in particular, and four years ago Nicholas Furlong, a native of Wexford, wrote a compelling biography of the most famous of the Wexford rebel leaders, Father John Murphy of Boolavogue.[6] What is still lacking, however, as we approach the bicentennial of 1798, is a comprehensive narrative of the rebellion in Wexford that incorporates modern scholarship and presents the story in as unbiased a fashion as is possible. The pages that follow represent my effort to provide this. I hope I have succeeded.

Several people have been of great help to me in the work I have done over the last seven years on this project. Most deserving of my gratitude is Dr Kevin Whelan, who kindly read earlier versions of this work and made many useful suggestions; errors in the text are mine. My thanks also to the staffs of the various libraries and archives in Ireland and Britain who played a crucial role, and to Ms Earlene Huck and Ms Melissa Powell of the University of Evansville history department, who both did a great deal of work for me. The University of Evansville gave its generous support to my research, and my colleagues gave unending encouragement, especialy Dr David Gugin and Dr Vincent Angotti. Special thanks go to my wife, Heidi, who suffered long and valiantly through the last seven years. The greatest debt of all is expressed in the dedication.

PRELUDE
14 JULY 1789 – 25 MAY 1798

AS DAWN BROKE ON 15 JULY 1798 A FEW DOZEN MEN WERE making their way southwards across the Irish central plain. They were scattered over miles of dark countryside, singly and in pairs or threes and fours, and unaware of each other's whereabouts. All of them were dressed in rags and had long matted hair and unshaven faces; a few were bloodied from wounds. To anyone who could have seen them at close range they looked half-starved, haggard and desperate. As they crossed over field after field in northern County Kildare and the western parts of County Dublin, swimming the canals and rivers when they came to them, they kept their eyes focused on the dark mass of the Wicklow mountains that began to appear in the grey early morning light on the horizon to the south.[1] In spite of their present dishevelled and undistinguished appearance, they were the last remnants of a great rebel army that had engaged in an extraordinary campaign to overthrow the government of Ireland by force of arms and to establish a republic modelled on the American and French examples in its place. Almost all of them were from County Wexford, the county that occupies the south-eastern corner of the country, where the rebellion had been most prolonged, most heroic and most brutal. Here men and women had witnessed at closest quarters the Irish version of that fierce struggle between monarchy and republicanism that shook all of Europe to its very foundations between 1789 and 1815.

The chain of events that led these few dozen men to the plains of Kildare in the middle of a July night went back at least a decade. Nine years earlier, when the French Revolution broke out, County Wexford was one of the most prosperous and one of the most anglicised parts of Ireland. It had benefited enormously from a generation of economic expansion, and its rich rolling farmland produced large quantities of barley and other commercial crops for markets in Dublin, Britain and parts of the continent.[2] It had several thriving towns, and most of the population spoke English.[3] It also had a sizeable Protestant minority, most visible in its northern half, where a few parishes were as much as one-third Protestant.[4] Although Catholics could not at that time participate in electoral politics, Protestants were sharply divided, as they were everywhere in Ireland, between a conservative faction that wanted to maintain the Protestant monopoly in political life and a liberal faction which wanted to extend full or almost full rights to Catholics.[5] In the decade immediately before the French Revolution the Irish liberals had managed to extend economic equality to Catholics, a move which was bound to be of special benefit to Catholics in a well-developed county like Wexford, but political emancipation was slower in coming.[6]

In 1789 liberal Protestants and politically aware Catholics in County Wexford watched events in France with interest and some sympathy.[7] Conservatives looked on in dismay, and in the parliamentary election of 1790 they rebounded and took both of the county seats, one of which was usually held by a liberal, and reduced the liberal voice from the county in parliament to a few members from Wexford town.[8] Not surprisingly, then, when a group of liberal Presbyterians and Anglicans, with some Catholic support, founded the United Irish Society in Belfast and Dublin in 1791 to press for reforms to make Ireland's exclusively Protestant parliament more representative, liberals from Wexford were among the first to form an affiliated group.[9]

In 1792, however, when liberals in parliament moved to grant full political rights to Catholics, a conservative from Wexford, George Ogle of Bellvue, became one of its most outspoken opponents;[10] and although the bill to grant the franchise and other rights to Catholic freeholders passed in spite of Ogle's efforts in early 1793,[11] the struggle between the two factions in the county only intensified as a result, and soon Catholics were drawn into the struggle to a degree that was unprecedented.[12] Then, to make matters worse, in the summer of that year, at the very time that the French Revolution was entering its most terrible phase, a half-organised protest against tithes and the expansion of the militia in the county led to a march on Wexford town by countrypeople from northern and western districts and culminated in a bloody riot in which troops fired on the crowd and killed as many as eighty people.[13]

Over the next three years there was relative quiet in Wexford in spite of the blood-letting of 1793, but events in the country at large raced towards crisis. In 1794, with the French on the march in Europe, the government banned the United Irishmen and unwittingly turned the society into a secret revolutionary organisation, dedicated to outright republicanism and independence in alliance with France.[14] It grew, a parish at a time, a barony at a time, until it was well established among the Presbyterians of east Ulster and among liberal Protestants and Catholics in north Leinster. By the autumn of 1796 it was creeping into south Leinster, parts of Wexford included, and into Munster, appealing powerfully to young artisans and farmers, young merchants or merchants' sons, teachers and clerks, and the occasional disillusioned aristocrat or member of the gentry.[15]

The reaction of the government and its conservative and moderate supporters was slow at first but became more urgent as time passed. In 1795 the Orange Order had emerged in southern Ulster as an Anglican secret society whose goals were initially local (its Catholic opposition was the Defenders), but in late 1795 and 1796 it spread southwards as a counterweight to the United Irishmen as well as to the Defenders.[16] In 1796 the government tried to formalise its own reaction by creating the yeomanry system whereby local landlords, in their capacity as magistrates, were encouraged to form companies of infantry and cavalry from tenants they knew to be loyal.[17] In Wexford the first yeomanry units were already organised on the northern border of the county by the end of the year.[18]

Just before Christmas of that year a French army of 12,000 men almost landed on the south-west coast of the country, failing only because of bad weather. They had been invited to invade by the United Irishmen in the expectation that thousands of their members would join in the overthrow of the Irish government.[19] Had they landed, Wexford and its neighbouring south Leinster counties would probably have played only a minor role in the ensuing war, since they were peripheral to the region of real United Irish strength,[20] but during the course of 1797 the United Irishmen declined steadily in Ulster and the movement gained recruits rapidly in south Leinster, Wexford included, and in Munster.[21] A sudden decline in grain prices, devastating to a granary county like Wexford,[22] and another victory for the conservatives in a general election that summer[23] contributed in part to this. The situation in Wexford became so serious that in November local magistrates declared sixteen parishes in the north and east of the county to be in a state of rebellion.[24]

The national United Irish leadership worked hard to bring about another French expedition in the spring of 1798.[25] In the meantime both the yeomanry system and the Orange Order continued to spread. The gap between liberal and conservative elements widened, and distrust between conservative Protestants and Catholics intensified.[26] The crisis came to a head on 12 March, when the government arrested most of the national and Leinster United Irish leadership.[27] The movement never quite recovered from this blow, but the organisation was fairly decentralised in its day-to-day organisation and managed to limp on through the next two months.[28] At the end of March the authorities in Dublin decided to impose martial law on the country selectively as the ultimate step in crushing the movement before the French could invade, and so in county after county in Leinster and Munster, where the revolutionaries were by now thought to be most numerous, magistrates and military authorities co-operated in the effort to uncover hidden arms, to identify and arrest United Irish members, and to extort from them, by torture if need be, the identities of their comrades.[29]

The campaign was less brutal in Wexford than in many neighbouring counties, principally because Lord Mountnorris, its largest landowner and a moderate in politics, tried hard to get local priests to encourage their congregations to submit before harsh military measures were imposed.[30] He had some success for a time, but martial law was declared on the entire county on 27 April despite his best efforts.[31] There followed a month of intense arms searches, arrests, house-burnings and judicial torture which affected all parts of the county but was most intense in its

County Wexford and Vicinity

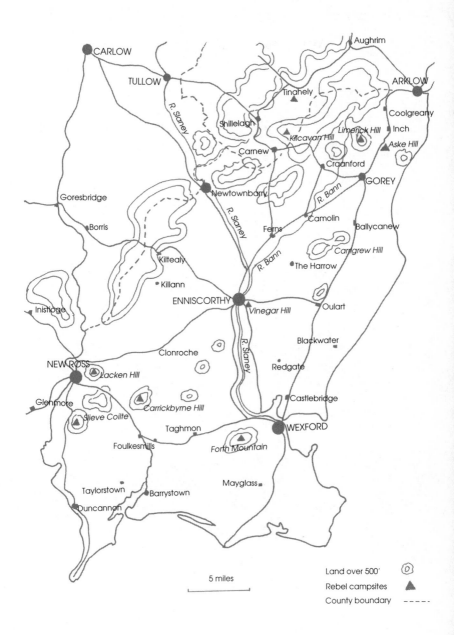

Aughrim

CARLOW

TULLOW

ARKLOW

Tinahely

Coolgreany

R. Slaney

Shillelagh

Limerick Hill · Inch

Kilcavan Hill

Aske Hill

Carnew

Craanford

Goresbridge

Newtownbarry

GOREY

R. Bann

Borris

Camolin

Ferns

Ballycanew

R. Slaney

Carngrew Hill

Kiltealy

R. Bann

The Harrow

Killann

ENNISCORTHY

Oulart

Inistioge

Vinegar Hill

Blackwater

Clonroche

R. Slaney

Redgate

NEW ROSS

Lacken Hill

Castlebridge

Glenmore

Carrickbyrne Hill

WEXFORD

Slieve Coilte

Taghmon

Foulkesmills

Forth Mountain

Mayglass

Taylorstown

Barrystown

Duncannon

5 miles

Land over 500'

Rebel campsites

County boundary

Wexford Baronies

northern half, where the revolutionary movement was strongest and where sectarian tensions were also especially high.[32] The fact that over the previous few months three Orange lodges were established in that area of the county, and that the North Cork militia, which came to Wexford town in April, brought a militia officers' lodge with them, did nothing to calm the situation.[33]

By the middle of May the national United Irish leadership (or what remained of it) resolved to make their move with or without a French landing. They were already badly disrupted by the arrests of March, and their only hope of success now seemed to be a pre-emptive strike. In an atmosphere of great confusion, they fixed the 23rd of the month as the moment of rebellion. The plan was for units in the capital to assemble that night and attack key points in the city and seize as many members of the government as possible. The mail coaches would be stopped, and this would be the signal to move for rebels elsewhere in the country. In the counties immediately around Dublin (Wicklow, Kildare and Meath) United Irishmen were to assemble and then move in towards the city to guarantee the success of the attack there and to cordon it off in case government forces in the provinces should try to move against the new regime. United Irish units in the rest of the country, County Wexford included, were to rise when they understood that the campaign was under way, and were to attack government forces locally and destroy them if possible or at least prevent them from marching against Dublin.[34]

These ambitious plans began to go wrong at an early stage. The government identified the main rebel officers several days before the 23rd and arrested them.[35] Then the plan of attack in the capital itself was discovered at a critical point, and when the Dublin rebels did try to mobilise, government forces in the city took possession of the streets first and defeated them.[36] In the counties around the city rebel units managed to launch their part of the rebellion, but there was great confusion among them too, and even though they captured a few small towns in the next day or two, they suffered several defeats and were forced back on the defensive very quickly. By the end of the 24th the rebellion had failed to spread beyond Wicklow, Kildare and southern parts of Meath.[37]

At that point United Irishmen in Wexford were probably unclear about both the details of the plan of rebellion and about the state of affairs in counties to their north.[38] The state of the organisation in the county at this juncture was probably similar to that in other southern counties. As elsewhere, each parish was expected to produce a company of thirty or so men, headed by a captain elected from their ranks, and these were in turn to form battalions by barony, each headed by a colonel.[39] In addition to its miltary organisation, the United Irishmen also had a parallel civil wing whose members were not directly involved with the military section of the movement.[40]

There is confusion about the identities of leading officers in Wexford, and it is difficult to distinguish between colonels and captains and even individuals who were not actually officers but who commanded respect locally and who rose into officer ranks later on. From the fragments of evidence we have, it seems the leadership included at least five prominent Protestants, all of them long-time liberals and supporters of Catholic political emancipation. These were Anthony Perry of Inch, a wealthy farmer from near the Wicklow border; George Sparks of Blackwater, on the east coast, another well-to-do farmer; Matthew Keogh of Wexford town, a merchant and former captain in the British army; and John Boxwell of Sarshill and William Hughes of Ballytrent, both farmers from the baronies of Bargy and Forth in the south-east. In addition, three liberal Protestant landlords from the south-eastern baronies, Beauchamp Bagenal Harvey of Bargy Castle, William Hatton of Clonard, and Cornelius Grogan of Johnstown Castle, were prominent in the civilian wing.

The Catholic officers came from a wide variety of backgrounds. Esmond Kyan of Mounthoward (near Ferns) and John and Edward Hay of Ballinkeele (a few miles south of Enniscorthy) were the sons of well-established Catholic landlords. Thomas Cloney of Moneyhore (a few miles south-west of Enniscorthy), Matthew and Michael Furlong of Templescoby (two miles to the west of the town), Miles Byrne of Monaseed (near the Wicklow border), Robert Carty of Birchgrove (south of Enniscorthy), Thomas Sinnott of Kilbride (a few miles from Oulart) and John Murphy of Loughnageer (six miles east of New Ross) were all from the ranks of well-to-do tenant farmers, many of them middlemen. Edward

Roche of Garrylough (just north of Castlebridge), Edward Fitzgerald of Newpark (just north of Garrylough), John Kelly of Killann (near the Carlow border), Luke Byrne of Enniscorthy and Dick Monk of Wexford town were all merchants or sons of merchants, several of them involved in various aspects of the grain trade. Prominent also was John Henry Colclough of Ballyteigue, on the south coast of the county, who was a doctor.[41]

Most intriguing of all were several priests, many of them under suspension for various reasons at the time, who became actively involved and achieved captain's rank or certainly had a great deal of influence by mid-May. Among these were Mogue Kearns of Kiltealy (on the Carlow border), Thomas Clinch of Enniscorthy, Philip Roche of Poulpeasty (half-way between Enniscorthy and New Ross), Edward Sinnott of Kilrush (near the Carlow border), Michael Murphy of Ballycanew (just south of Gorey), John Murphy of Boolavogue (just east of Ferns) and Thomas Dixon of Blackwater.[42]

The precise outlines of the command structure in which these and other officers fitted will never be known. It is likely that Perry, Kyan, Fitzgerald, Edward Roche, Keogh, Thomas Sinnott, Kelly and Cloney had the rank of colonel and were expected to lead battalions from their various baronies when the rebellion came.[43] The others were mostly of captain's rank. As for the rank and file of the Wexford movement, like elsewhere in Leinster and Munster they were a mixture of medium and small tenant farmers, tradesmen, clerks, teachers, and labourers, a cross-section of the county's population, certainly its Catholic population, although younger men for the most part.[44]

The opposition to the United Irishmen in Wexford was an interesting mixture too. For one thing, the Catholic bishop, James Caulfield, and the vast majority of his priests were well aware of the conspiracy and adamantly opposed it.[45] So too were several prominent Catholic laymen, including Harvey Hay, the father of John and Edward of Ballinkeele (his youngest son, Philip, was a yeoman).[46] Most Protestant landlords were fiercely opposed to the movement, although some, such as the Carews of Castleboro, the Colcloughs of Tintern, and Lord Mountnorris of Camolin, seem to have assumed that rebellion would not actually break out and pursued a moderate policy accordingly. Other less alarmist landlords included Isaac Cornock of Corbetstown (near Ferns), Solomon Richards of Solsborough (just north of Enniscorthy), Joshua Pounden of Daphne (just west of Enniscorthy) and John Grogan of Healthfield (south of Enniscorthy), who was Cornelius Grogan's brother.[47]

The main thrust of the drive to destroy the revolutionary movement in County Wexford came from well-known conservative sources such as the Rams of Gorey, George Ogle of Bellvue (south of Enniscorthy), the Loftuses of Loftus Hall (south of New Ross) and the Tottenhams of New Ross itself.[48] A few among the ranks of the staunch conservatives, such as the landlord James Boyd of Rosslare (south of Wexford Town), the middlemen Hunter Gowan of Mount Nebo (west of Gorey), Archibald Hamilton Jacob of Enniscorthy and Hawtrey White of Peppard's Castle (on the east coast), were especially fanatical.[49] Countless other Protestants and loyalist Catholics played a less prominent role but took their places in the various yeomanry corps and worked relentlessly to destroy the movement. Threats and torture were commonplace in the county in May, and most of the yeomanry corps had startling success in the week between the 15th and 23rd when they established collection centres for the surrender of arms in the main villages and arrested scores of suspects, among them many blacksmiths and the priest Thomas Dixon of Blackwater.[50]

Neither the authorities nor the rebels in Wexford were aware when it came that the 23rd was to be the day of rebellion in and around Dublin.[51] Two days earlier magistrates in Gorey, acting on well-founded suspicion, arrested Anthony Perry, imprisoned him in the market house there and had him tortured.[52] Through the next two days, as the rebellion developed in Kildare and Meath and spread southwards towards Carlow, he continued to endure brutal treatment but refused to talk.[53] His captains in the area around the town panicked when they learned of his arrest and went into hiding, thereby paralysing the movement in the northernmost barony of the county.[54]

In the meantime the fighting in the counties to the north had already produced several appalling atrocities. On the 23rd rebels at Prosperous in north Kildare killed several soldiers who surrendered to them.[55] On the 24th over thirty Catholic yeomen whose loyalty was suspect were picked out from the ranks in the village square in Dunlavin, in west Wicklow, and shot dead; and on the 25th, within hours of a failed rebel attack on Carlow town which resulted in hundreds of casualties on the insurgent side, the magistrate in Carnew, just across the Wexford/Wicklow border, had twenty-eight prisoners taken out of jail and shot in a ball alley.[56] It would only be a matter of time before reports not only of the rising itself but of these outrages reached United Irishmen in Wexford.

2

OUTBREAK
NOON, 26 MAY – 8 A.M., 27 MAY

IN THE AFTERNOON AND EARLY EVENING OF 26 MAY, WITH NEWS OF the rebellions in Kildare and Carlow and reports of the massacres at Dunlavin and Carnew beginning to filter southwards through the county,[1] the Wexford United Irishmen finally began to mobilise and follow the lead of the counties to their north. Some units appear to have begun to make preparations early,[2] but there was a great deal of confusion among them and most captains waited patiently for twilight before actually calling their men into the field.

To the outside observer the situation in the county changed little during the day. Hundreds of men continued to come into collection centres to surrender weapons to local magistrates and to get the all-important protections in return. The magistrates, who surely knew a good deal about the midlands rebellion by this point, continued as before, supervising the surrender of arms at the various villages where it was taking place and dispatching mounted yeomanry patrols out into the countryside to intimidate those who might still be holding out. At Camolin the young Lieutenant Thomas Bookey supervised the surrenders and had no trouble.[3] At Oulart the Catholic bishop, who was on his way back to Wexford after a visit to Archbishop Troy in Dublin, addressed scores of country people who were milling about in the street after handing in their weapons; he praised them for doing so and urged them to go home and encourage their neighbours to do the same.[4]

Amazingly, several very prominent United Irishmen continued to be involved in the disarmament as the day passed. Edward Fitzgerald's residence at Newpark was a collection point, and Fitzgerald himself and the magistrate Edward Turner of Newfort supervised the process there. It went smoothly all day, and

12

sometime that afternoon Edward Hay arrived from Wexford town to join them. When evening came, Turner took the collected arms back to his own house and bade Fitzgerald and Hay goodnight, still completely unaware of their membership of the United Irishmen.[5]

Bagenal Harvey spent the day collecting arms at his home, Bargy Castle, too. In the evening he loaded what he had gathered into carts and took them into Wexford town to hand them over to the authorities.[6] Since he was still only a civilian member of the United Irishmen, it is possible that he was unaware of the plans for a rebellion, and so his duplicity was not quite as dramatic as that of Fitzgerald and Hay.

The authorities in Gorey had finally tortured a confession out of Perry by this time, and they must have had a very different perspective on the situation. He had not revealed all the leaders to them, but he had named Harvey, Colclough and Fitzgerald as being prominent in the conspiracy.

The greatest danger lay well to the south of Gorey. The United Irishmen in and around Gorey and Arklow were in a very poor state now and presented little immediate threat to the authorities. Perry himself was in custody,[7] and the captains in the parishes along the border with Wicklow were still in hiding and effectively neutralised too. The experience of one of them, eighteen-year-old Miles Byrne from Monaseed, was probably typical. He had made his way into Arklow two days earlier and had hidden in the house of a friend. Terrified of being discovered, he and an associate had managed to link up with some recruiting sergeants and made their way out of the town on the evening of the 24th, travelling in the direction of Carlow, where the soldiers had been ordered to report. They spent the night in Hacketstown, and on the 25th they walked all the way to Carlow. They were still in Carlow on the 26th, surveying the damage from a battle that had been fought there the day before and trying desperately to make contact with rebels still in the field. All this time Byrne was out of touch with his comrades in north Wexford, and he had little hope at this point for effective mobilisation taking place anywhere in his own county.[8]

The organisation was in much better shape in central and southern Wexford. For a man like the High Sheriff, Henry Perceval, who must have received the details of Perry's confession in the late afternoon or evening, the capture of Fitzgerald, Harvey and Colclough was the most pressing task here. Harvey's involvement would have been especially disconcerting since he was well-to-do and a functioning magistrate.[9] Moreover, his membership of the organisation also seemed to suggest that the conspiracy in the county involved much of the liberal interest and was not at all limited to the radical elements among the Catholic and marginal Protestant populations. Perceval could only assume now that even if weapons were surrendered in vast quantities, as long as men like Fitzgerald, Colclough and Harvey were still free they might issue the call to arms and restore their weapons to rank-and-file followers as their first act.

The High Sheriff decided to have all three men arrested during the night and taken to the town jail. Harvey, completely unsuspecting it seems, obliged him by coming into the town that evening and going to his residence there to pass the night. The authorities arrested him quickly and dispatched him to the jail.[10] James Boyd and his trusted Wexford yeoman cavalry were selected to arrest Fitzgerald and Colclough; for reasons that are unclear, but which may reflect Perceval's sense of the relative importance of Fitzgerald, he decided to have him apprehended first.[11] As they finalised these plans and locked Harvey safely away in the town prison, Perceval and Boyd were well aware of how formidable the rebellion already was in the midlands,[12] and they must have speculated among themselves about the likelihood that a rising was planned for Wexford soon. What they almost certainly did not know was that at that very moment, as they made their move against what they thought was the heart of the conspiracy in Wexford, the United Irishmen were taking the field all across the north central part of the county. Those responsible for the maintenance of law and order in Wexford had made their move a fraction too late.

The United Irish leaders in the northern baronies of the county, Gorey excepted, had probably laid the groundwork for their mobilisation quietly as the afternoon and evening passed. The details of these efforts are largely lost to us, but the fragments of evidence available suggest that the centre of activity was the baronies of Scarawalsh and Ballaghkeen. The actual mobilisation itself took place at around twilight in a broad sweep of territory running from the parishes along the Carlow border near Newtownbarry, eastwards through places like Kilcormick, Oulart and Kilmuckridge, and on southwards as far as Castlebridge.

*

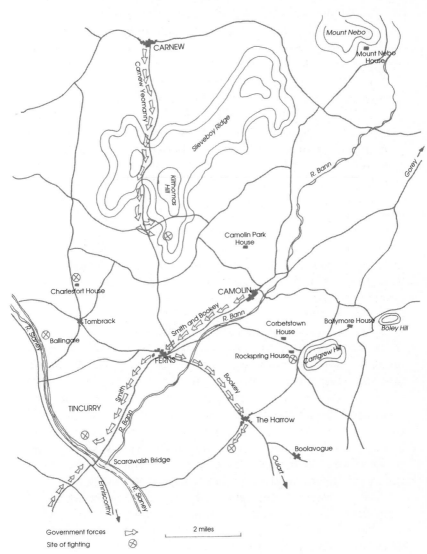

Government forces
Site of fighting

2 miles

Scene of Mobilisation of 26 – 27 May and Battle of Kilthomas

The mobilisation, when it did begin, took place at a frantic pace. There is some evidence that somebody lit a fire on Carrigrew Hill, one of the highest points in the northern half of the county, just before sunset.[13] Perhaps in response to this, (and/or to other communications), rebel units began to gather at various local rendezvous points.

Everywhere the pattern was broadly the same. Once the groups of thirty to forty men that were the building-blocks of the United Irish military structure[14] gathered together, they set about the critical task of acquiring weapons. Some of them had managed to hold onto pikes and guns throughout the yeomanry's disarmament campaign, but most had not, and they now therefore had to launch attacks on those places where the seized arms were being stored.[15] Many of them also looked forward to the chance to take revenge on local yeomen by burning their houses.[16] The yeomanry and militia were stationed for the night in the main towns; this meant that the rebels' best hope lay in attacking the homes of prominent magistrates and other well-known loyalists likely to have weapons in their homes. These raids had to be carried out quickly, certainly before dawn broke and the garrisons in the towns had a chance to launch a counter-attack.

The first violence of the rebellion took place at Tincurry, near Ballycarney and just to the north of Scarawalsh Bridge. At around seven or eight o'clock that evening a band of rebels attacked a farmhouse belonging to a family named Piper. Their objective was to seize arms, but in the struggle that followed at least one member of the family lost his life.[17] The attack was one of many that took place to the west of the River Bann as the night passed, and a young woman named Jane Barber who lived at Clovass, just to the south of Scarawalsh Bridge, spotted over a dozen houses on fire in the direction of Ferns from her window after dark.[18]

These 'western' rebels launched particularly determined and strategically significant attacks against three loyalist strongholds: Charles Dawson's house at Charlesfort (near Ferns), Francis Turner's house in Ballingale (near Ballycarney) and Lord Mountnorris's residence at Camolin Park, all of which were assumed to contain large quantities of arms. The attacks on Dawson's and Turner's houses turned out to be especially bloody affairs. Dawson had persuaded ten local loyalists to stand guard at his house through the night for fear that the large store of pikes he had collected would be taken. As dawn broke and no attack appeared imminent, the ten neighbours left to return to their own homes and families. Shortly afterwards Dawson learned that a rebel band was approaching his house. He had only enough time to call one of his neighbours back before the insurgents arrived. Having reached Charlesfort, the rebels demanded that Dawson surrender the house and its contents. He refused, and in the battle which followed they set most of the out-offices and the dwelling-house itself on fire. The buildings burned to the ground quickly, and Dawson's neighbour was killed as he tried to escape the flames. Dawson himself was badly wounded, although his wife and daughter had escaped through a window and fled to Newtownbarry, and he and his son eventually managed to get away to Ferns. The rebels almost certainly captured most of the weapons that were in the house.[19]

The attack on Ballingale followed much the same pattern. Francis Turner and several other loyalists had guarded his house successfully through most of the night, but early in the morning a large band of rebels approached it and demanded the surrender of everyone inside. Most of the defenders were well armed, and Turner refused to give in. The rebels then stormed the place, and he and several of the other loyalists were killed. All the women and children who were present escaped unharmed. The attackers again got away with at least some of the arms they sought and left the house in flames.[20]

At Camolin a rebel party formed sometime during the night or early on the following morning.[21] The village was completely ungarrisoned at the time,[22] and several loyalists, including the notorious local magistrate, the Rev. Roger Owens, fled northwards towards Gorey. The insurgents were able to advance on Mountnorris's residence at Camolin Park unhindered.[23] There was a huge supply of arms in the mansion, among them many of the pikes that had been handed in over the previous days and no less than 800 guns that had arrived recently from Dublin for the yeomanry. They seized this entire stock and set the building on fire. The local Catholic curate, Father John Redmond, went out and pleaded with them in vain not to harm Mountnorris's property.[24]

Around dawn and in the early hours of the new day the rebel bands that had been active for several hours in the area between the Carlow border and the River Bann began to converge on Kilthomas Hill, a shoulder of the Slieveboy range which jutted out to the south of the main mountain and gave an excellent view of the countryside to the east, west and south. It was centrally located between Camolin, Ferns, Ballycarney and Clonegal, and the steep slopes could be easily defended against an assault by government forces. Most of the rebels were still poorly armed, but some now wielded guns and pikes collected from the raids. Bands of men continued to climb up the slopes of the hill as the morning hours passed, and by about ten o'clock there were at least a thousand men camped on its summit, along with a large number of camp-followers.[25] Father Michael Murphy may have been there by that time, and he may even have taken command of the new-formed army, in the absence of Father Edward Sinnott, the man who would normally have commanded here but who had not appeared.[26]

As this dramatically successful mobilisation took place to the west of the Bann, rebels were taking to the field to its east and south-east too. Insurgent units mobilised simultaneously in the entire area from Kilbride parish down to Oulart and Kilmuckridge. The pattern was much like that in the west. It began with scattered bands of rebels forming into corps of thirty or forty men apiece and launching sudden attacks on nearby residences where arms were believed to be held. In some cases the targets were obvious ones since they were the homes of magistrates who had been actively collecting arms; in others they were merely the houses of Protestant farmers and were attacked because they might hold a gun or two or (and this surely happened in some cases) because of some private quarrel or sectarian rivalry.[27]

The process seems to have begun in Kilcormick before anywhere else to the east of the river, and it spread to adjacent parishes from there. There is little doubt, though, that rebel activity also began independently around Oulart, and perhaps around Newfort.

A rebel party formed at about sunset (which was at 8.30 p.m. that night)[28] in Kilcormick under the leadership of Father John

Murphy, the local United Irish captain. They were still assembling followers at about 10.30 p.m. when they accidentally encountered a yeoman cavalry patrol led by Lieutenant Thomas Bookey near The Harrow. There followed a brief skirmish in which Bookey and his deputy officer John Donovan became separated from the rest and were both killed, leaving the others to rush back to Ferns with news of the incident.[29] The brief struggle at The Harrow was typical of what was taking place all across central Wexford that night, and once it was finished, Murphy and his men concentrated on their main task for the four or five hours of darkness that remained to them—attacking houses where arms were stored. As the night passed they raided farmhouses in several townlands of the parish, including Garrybritt, Mullaunree and Dranagh. No lives were lost in these raids, but many of the houses were set on fire, either during the attacks or afterwards.[30]

In the parish of Kilbride, which bordered the River Bann near Camolin, a rebel band gathered around midnight and attacked Thomas Bookey's house at Rockspring, just at the base of Carrigrew Hill.[31] Bookey's servants fought the rebels off for much of the night, and several of the attackers died in the attempt to storm the house. Eventually, just before dawn, it caught fire and the defenders fled, taking at least some of the arms that were inside with them.[32] Immediately after this the rebel party marched a further mile westwards and attacked the house of Isaac Cornock, another magistrate, at Corbetstown, seizing any arms they could find there.[33]

Rebels in the parishes immediately around Oulart had mobilised by this time too and had begun to attack nearby loyalist strongholds. The residence of the notorious local magistrate Hawtrey White, at Peppard's Castle in Donoughmore parish, was an early target. White himself was spending the night with his men in Gorey, and so the attackers gained entrance to the house with ease. Once inside they conducted a largely fruitless search for arms, ransacked the place and threatened an elderly relative of White's who lived there; in the end they did her no harm and, curiously, left without setting the house on fire.[34]

In Kilmuckridge parish hundreds of insurgents were also moving about the countryside well before dawn. At Island House a loyalist named George Williams awoke to the sound of dogs barking in the early hours of the morning, and when he looked out across the country to his north he could see bands of men on the move in several places and a number of houses burning in the distance. His wife, who was spending the night in their own house at Ballyadam, a mile or so to the east, awoke to see the same thing and then spotted several of her servants perched on the rooftop and watching the whole drama.[35]

Men and women were on the move very early that night in and around the village of Oulart itself, a place which had long been a hotbed of United Irish activity. As with their comrades in Ballycarney or Camolin or Kilcormick, the first objective of the Oulart rebels was to attack houses in which they knew large quantities of arms were being stored. Among these was Kyle Glebe, just to the north of the village, the residence of the Rev. Robert Burrowes, a local Protestant clergyman. Burrowes was liberal by reputation, but his house had become an important repository for surrendered arms. At least ten local yeomen were spending the night there, and they had barricaded the entire lower floor. A local Catholic had come to the house sometime before sunset that evening (and so before the incident at The Harrow) and told Burrowes that his place would be attacked during the night. The clergyman and his comrades stayed awake all night, and as early as eleven o'clock (at about the time the fighting was taking place at The Harrow) they could see groups of rebels gathering around nearby cabins. At about 3 a.m., as dawn approached, a band of a hundred or more finally converged on the house and demanded that all inside surrender. The defenders refused, and a brief battle ensued. When it had ended, the house was in flames and Burrowes and most of his companions were dead. The clergyman died in front of the house, piked in confusing circumstances as he tried to negotiate with the attackers, and the others either died in the confrontation that followed or were killed after they had surrendered. A few of the men (and all of the women and children) who had been taking shelter in the house did manage to escape.[36]

Sometime around dawn (it is uncertain if it was before or after the storming of Kyle Glebe) rebel units from Kilcormick and Kilbride made their way southwards and joined up with those already gathered in Oulart.[37] The bands that had attacked the glebe-house had captured guns and a large quantity of pikes. With these in hand, and with the reinforcements from Kilcormick raising their numbers to around 400, they were now a force to be reckoned with.

At about 5 or 6 a.m. they marched south through Oulart village and went out into the countryside beyond. Their leaders were of no more than captain's rank, as the colonel for this area, Esmond Kyan of Mounthoward, had been among those arrested just before the outbreak.[38] Their immediate objective was to make a rendezvous with the units that had been forming in the parishes to the east and south of Oulart.[39]

They marched along the main Gorey–Wexford road for a mile or so and then turned eastwards for a short distance to Castle Ellis church, where they met several bands coming up from Kilmuckridge. From Castle Ellis they turned south in the direction of a little village called Ballinamonabeg, which lay two miles away. They expected that the battalions under the command of Edward Fitzgerald and Edward Roche would be there waiting for them.[40]

The mobilisation had not gone quite so smoothly in the parishes to the south of Oulart. The reason was the arrest of Edward Fitzgerald, which James Boyd's cavalry detachment had carried out at Newpark shortly before midnight. Boyd and his men were completely unaware of what was happening in the countryside to their north as they brought their no doubt shocked prisoner back towards Wexford. Edward Hay accompanied them, but he was still unsuspected of United Irish activity and was still a free man.[41]

At about that time, with rebel bands already on the move in many parishes to the north, a young man named Jeremiah Donovan rode southwards from Kilcormick and brought news of the action at The Harrow to places like Oulart and Garrylough. Donovan probably warned rebels who were already mobilising that the yeomanry were about and suggested a point of rendezvous for later in the day to the leaders in both the Oulart and Castlebridge areas.[42]

In spite of the setback of Fitzgerald's arrest (and perhaps with the encouragement of Donovan's mission), the rebel mobilisation took place in the area around Newpark and Castlebridge in the hours after midnight, a little later than may have been hoped, but fairly smoothly nonetheless. Edward Roche of Garrylough was still at large, as were the various captains of local corps, and they called their men into the field with considerable skill. There were some problems connected with the loss of Fitzgerald. For example, the Blackwater unit, led by George Sparks, had gathered as planned earlier in the night and waited in vain for the Newpark and Garrylough men just to the south of their home village for several hours. Eventually, with no sign of the southerners coming, they turned back in despair and returned to their homes.[43] Unknown to them, however, their comrades were taking to the field near Newpark and Garrylough by that time and were opening their campaign with an attack on Edward Turner's house at Newfort, where they knew arms were stored. Turner offered no resistance and fled, and the insurgents made away with what arms he had collected.[44] After that they gathered at some prearranged meeting-point and began to make their way northwards towards Ballinamonabeg with Edward Roche at their head.[45]

Turner himself rode frantically southwards to Wexford with news that the rebels were on the move in his district; he arrived in the town a few hours after dawn.[46] By that time Roche's force was already getting close to Ballinamonabeg, and the rebels moving down from Oulart and other points to the north were approaching it from the other side; the confused Blackwatermen had regrouped and moved eastwards and joined the Oulart column by this point too.[47]

The general rebel rendezvous finally took place in Ballinamonabeg sometime around seven or eight o'clock in the morning. The rank and file spread out in a field sloping above the crossroads that formed the heart of the village, and their officers met in a pub owned by a veteran of George Washington's army named Jeremiah Kavanagh and a prominent United Irishman himself.[48] The combined rebel forces in the village probably now amounted to close to a thousand men and women. Not all of them were committed United Irishmen (many were camp-followers, no doubt), and very few of them had firearms, but all told they constituted a formidable force.[49]

By 8 or 9 a.m. on Sunday 27 May, then, the Wexford United Irishmen had achieved a remarkable marshalling of their forces. In a matter of about six hours they had called perhaps 2,000 men into the field in a great stretch of country all the way from the

Carlow borderland to the county's east coast, a distance of twenty miles or more, and had begun to concentrate them in two sizeable armies, one at Kilthomas and one at Ballinamonabeg. They had attacked and in almost all cases overwhelmed groups of loyalists holed up in stone houses where quantities of arms were stored, and they had equipped themselves fairly well. By far the most important of these attacks was the one on Camolin Park, where they seized at least 800 carbines, but the Camolin band was too small to absorb this supply themselves, and it was impossible to get them to their comrades elsewhere in the county. For the time being they stockpiled them somewhere close by and awaited reinforcements from other parishes.[50] It must have been clear to all of them that if they could get these weapons into the hands of their fellow-insurgents, this alone might make all the difference in the coming struggle.

All this had happened even though the organisation in the parishes around Gorey had been paralysed by arrests and in spite of the fact that several important officers, including three colonels (Edward Sinnott,[51] Edward Fitzgerald and Esmond Kyan), had not been able to take part. All that was left for them to do now was to hold onto what they had taken and to keep local militia and yeomanry units occupied. This was certainly what the long-established United Irish blueprint had called for in Wexford and similar counties,[52] and at least some of the leaders gathered at Kilthomas and Ballinamonabeg that morning must have been familiar with this strategic arrangment.

For their part, the yeomanry and militia were thrown completely off balance by the suddenness of the uprising, and their response during its first ten hours or so very much reflects this. In fact, with the exception of those small groups that opposed rebel bands when they conducted arms raids, there was no real military response to the United Irish mobilisation in Wexford during those first ten hours at all. Even the various units stationed around the northern parishes of the county made no serious effort to respond until well after daybreak, giving the insurgents the vital time they needed to seize the initiative.

This ineffectiveness was partly a consequence of the strategy adopted by those in charge of government forces: as on previous nights, they had withdrawn to the safety of the main towns and villages until daylight returned, and so had left important strongpoints in the countryside, such as houses where arms were stored, to be guarded by only small companies of yeomen or by the owners of the houses themselves. Thus most of the yeomanry from Gorey and Ballaghkeen baronies spent the night in Gorey, and the units from Scarawalsh stayed in Enniscorthy, Ferns and Newtownbarry.[53] This left a large tract of territory between these towns completely unguarded, and it was in this open area that the insurgent mobilisation primarily took place.

There were a few halfhearted and confused efforts to respond to the first reports of trouble before darkness actually fell on the 26th, but these did nothing to stem the tide. The first commander to realise that the rising was beginning was Isaac Cornock at Ferns, who got reports of an attack on a loyalist house near Scarawalsh (probably Piper's of Tincurry) sometime early in the evening.[54] Not long afterwards news of the rebel actions in the same area reached Solomon Richards and John Grogan in Enniscorthy.[55] Cornock had no cavalry in Ferns,[56] and so he sent word to Camolin of the attack and asked the two young cavalry lieutenants there, Smith and Bookey, to come to his aid. Smith and his detachment had been patrolling the countryside off to the east all day, and they had not yet arrived back when Cornock's messenger got to Camolin. Bookey had to send a messenger of his own out to meet them and to tell them what was happening. Eventually Smith got back, but by the time the two detachments reached Ferns (leaving Camolin unguarded) Cornock was already getting reports of rebel activity around Kilcormick, several miles to his east. Accordingly, he decided to send Bookey and his men out in the direction of Kilcormick and to dispatch Smith's unit southwards towards Scarawalsh.[57] His plan may have been to have Bookey swing around to the south at The Harrow, a small crossroads hamlet in Kilcormick, and to join with Smith somewhere near Scarawalsh.[58] Instead Bookey's patrol ran headlong into the Kilcormick rebel corps outside The Harrow and, as we have already seen, were driven back with the loss of their leader and one of their men.

The authorities in Enniscorthy were beginning to react to reports of rebel mobilisation to their north by this time too.

Richards and Grogan rode out towards Tincurry with their cavalry to investigate the reports of attacks on loyalist farmhouses, and when they got there they discovered that the stories were true. Rather than ride further north in the gathering darkness and seek out the rebel band that had conducted the action, they decided to return to Enniscorthy and wait until morning[59] and probably made their way back unaware that Smith and Bookey were probing the area from the other direction.

As for Smith, when he reached Scarawalsh and made the same discovery that Grogan and Richards had done a short time before, he too became as wary of staying in the open country with darkness approaching and returned to Ferns for the night. While on his way he saw no sign of any rebels and arrived back in the village unaware that Bookey had run into serious trouble only a few miles to the east.[60]

On the arrival back in Ferns of Smith and his men and of Bookey's now leaderless unit, Cornock realised how serious the situation had become both to his east and south. He could hardly have been sure at this stage if a broad-based rebellion had actually begun or if this was localised violence, but, like Grogan and Richards six miles to his south in Enniscorthy, he was not prepared to risk having his cavalry wiped out and decided to keep them with him and wait for daylight before sending them out again, thereby giving the insurgents three or four crucial hours in which to organise themselves.[61]

Loyalist families living in areas where the rebels were now mobilising began to panic as soon as it became clear to them what was happening. Some remained where they were (including those who, like Dawson, Turner of Ballingale, and Burrowes, were eventually surrounded and attacked), but many fled from their homes when they had the chance, and as the hours of darkness passed scores of them began to stream towards Ferns, Enniscorthy and Newtownbarry.[62] Towards morning, as the panic spread further afield, refugees also began to arrive in towns more distant from the area of rebellion, including Wexford, Gorey and Carnew, bringing news of the rising with them to all these places, often in wildly exaggerated form.[63]

The commanders of government troops remained confused

about the whereabouts, size and intentions of the rebel forces well into the next day. Nevertheless, in the hours immediately after dawn detachments from Gorey, Carnew, Newtownbarry, Ferns and Enniscorthy ventured out into the countryside in search of them, undertaking what amounted to the first phase of the counter-offensive. Cavalry units from Enniscorthy and Ferns were among the first to move out. The Enniscorthy group, led by Richards and Grogan, went in the direction of Kilcormick. They had begun to hear terrifying reports of rebel attacks on isolated loyalist farmhouses in that area during the last few hours before dawn, and they decided that the main rebel concentration was somewhere nearby. They passed through several townlands in which loyalist houses had been attacked and pushed on as far as Boolavogue. By that stage they had concluded that Father John Murphy was the leader of the rebels in that district (either because they suspected him of United Irish membership long before the outbreak, or because eyewitnesses to the attacks had mentioned him), and they took revenge on the priest when they arrived at Boolavogue by setting his house and chapel on fire. They found his vestments and items for the celebration of mass hidden in the garden of his house, proving in their view that he had planned his departure in advance and thus implicating him in the attacks even more closely.[64]

Grogan and Richards allowed their men to begin take revenge on the ordinary countrypeople too. The developments of the night just ended had created a great stir around Kilcormick, and many people who had slept outdoors for several days for fear of attack had come out into the open out of curiosity.[65] The soldiers treated anyone they saw as a suspected rebel, and began to shoot at them indiscriminately as they rode along. They also took to setting fire to any empty houses they came across (of which there were a great many by this point), presuming that they were the homes of rebels. In doing this they spread a degree of terror through the area that at least matched anything the rebels had done an hour or two before.[66]

The mounted troops were unable to find the rebels themselves. When they left Boolavogue, Grogan and Richards turned westwards towards The Harrow, moving away from the direction the Kilcormick insurgents had actually taken. They may have done this because they had heard that two soldiers had been killed there a few hours before, or they may have been misled by those local residents who agreed to or were forced to talk. When they reached The Harrow they turned south, perhaps by way of returning to Enniscorthy, and found the bodies of Bookey and Donovan on the roadside, unmoved since their deaths. Both were badly mangled, but a sum of money and a valuable watch had been left untouched in Bookey's pocket.[67]

Lieutenant Smith and what was left of the Camolin cavalry had also ridden out from Ferns to The Harrow shortly after dawn. They were not aware that the Enniscorthy unit had gone in the same direction, but the two detachments encountered each other somewhere near the hamlet.[68] From there they turned north-westwards together and rode in the general direction of Camolin, moving even further away from Oulart, but searching the countryside on either side of their route for bands of rebels and continuing to shoot anyone they found whom they suspected of being a straggler. They also persisted with their policy of burning unoccupied houses and cut a wide path of arson across the valley of the Bann to the north of Ferns.[69]

At about 6 a.m. three other government detachments made their way out into the countryside in reponse to the reports of rebellion. The largest of these was a column of yeoman cavalry and infantry from Carnew amounting to about 300 men, which had received reports of the rebel mobilisation around Ferns and Ballycarney and which now pushed southwards, directly towards Kilrush parish.[70] A small cavalry force also rode out from Newtownbarry in the direction of Ballycarney at about the same time, but they encountered a sizeable band of rebels who attacked them with rocks and other missiles at Tombrack crossroads, and they quickly withdrew to the town and played no further part in the events of the day.[71]

The third force was a detachment of over a hundred cavalry under Hawtrey White which left Gorey and moved directly southwards towards Oulart at around five or six o'clock. White had received many reports of rebel attacks by that time, but he did not know exactly where the main rebel forces were, and so he moved cautiously and slowly. Like Grogan's and Richards's men, his troops took to killing anyone they found hiding in the fields near the road and began to burn houses indiscriminately as they passed.[72]

FIRST BLOOD
8 A.M.–MIDNIGHT, 27 MAY

A S THE EARLY MORNING HOURS PASSSED, THE REBELS AT Ballinamonabeg remained unaware that Hawtrey White and a column of a hundred cavalrymen was approaching them from the north, although they almost certainly expected some kind of opposition within the next few hours. At this time their leaders were more concerned with organisational matters. The loss of Fitzgerald seems to have created a leadership crisis, and many of the captains, including George Sparks of Blackwater, Morgan Byrne of Kilnamanagh, and Father John Murphy of Boolavogue, retained considerable authority,[1] even though Edward Roche was the only colonel present.

White and his men passed through Oulart at about eight o'clock and saw the bodies of Burrowes and his neighbours on the lawn of the glebe-house just to its north. In the village itself he learned of the whereabouts of the main rebel force and then led his men southwards directly towards them.[2]

The rebels had some lookouts watching the surrounding countryside, and these men spotted White when he was about a mile away. They spread the alarm, and the little army reacted quickly. Roche and the other officers realised they had a clear advantage in numbers, if not in weapons, and at Sparks's suggestion they decided to try to trap the approaching cavalry between the sloping fields that ran along the west side of the road and a marshy valley that ran parallel to it on the east side. To do this they sent several bands of men forward along the slope and along the other side of the road to outflank White's men once they came close to the main camp at the crossroads. The cavalrymen were armed only with sabres and pistols, so there was a good chance that they could be overwhelmed in close combat.

White noticed the movements on either side of the road once he got close to the rebel camp. He slowed his men down to a trot in response, and then, when they were just outside musket range, he halted them completely. At this point he realised what was happening and understood the likely outcome. After a brief pause he wheeled his men about and led them, at a gallop, back in the direction of Oulart. The rebels did not have an organised cavalry detachment, and so they could only watch helplessly as White and his men escaped without a shot being fired. The encounter may have encouraged them (White was, after all, widely hated, and his men had fled in panic), but the chance to capture vital sabres and firearms had been lost.[3]

White and his men stopped briefly at Castle Ellis. He had already concluded that the rebels would gain control of the entire district and that the loyalists of the area should be evacuated. He divided his troops into smaller units and ordered them to ride through the area around Oulart telling loyalist families to leave their homes and go northwards towards Gorey immediately.[4] In doing this he was relinquishing the whole area of the Ballaghkeen baronies, north and south, to the insurgents, presumably in the hope that the rebellion could be contained within that area once there was time for government forces to rally.

In many districts along the coast the rebel mobilisation was still taking place at this late stage, and this hampered White's efforts to get loyalist families away from the area. As his men scattered across the countryside with word to evacuate, he took a small detachment himself and went on eastwards to the residence of the Boltons of Island and told the family to leave for Gorey. He saw no rebels along the stretch of road between Oulart and Island, but when he turned westwards once again towards the Oulart–Gorey road and then swung eastwards towards his own residence at Peppard's Castle, he found the roads blocked by rebel bands in several places. Eventually he gave up the attempt to reach his home and made his way back towards the road to Gorey.[5]

One of his soldiers, a man named Darcy, was not so lucky. He tried to reach his home too, but a group of rebels spotted him in the townland of Ballynahown and killed him in a field near his house. As a yeoman in uniform they may have considered him fair game anyway, but the fact that he was related through his mother to the Loftuses and Tottenhams must have made him an even more inviting victim.[6] When the opportunity arose, White's men were merciless too, and they continued to shoot at anyone they suspected of being a rebel straggler. Within this category they often included men who happened to be near the road as they passsed by but who had nothing to do with the rebels.[7]

The flight of the loyalists from the Ballaghkeen countryside which now began was a panic-stricken affair. Entire families, especially landed families, threw armfuls of belongings into carts and drove northwards by any route that was open. While most headed for Gorey, fifteen miles away for some, a few, like the Williamses of Ballyadam, followed the advice of sympathetic servants and headed southwards to the 'Catholic country' of Ballyvaldon and Blackwater, where they expected loyalist–rebel tensions might not be so high. Some even made their way eastwards towards the seashore and waited on the beaches, hoping the turmoil would somehow pass them by. In several cases groups of rebels encountered these refugees as they fled, and in a few instances they threatened them; generally, however, they were left alone to flee as best they could, and few if any of them came to harm.[8]

White and his detachment of yeomen probably made their way back towards the Gorey road by eleven or twelve o'clock. They had scattered widely through the area, however, and it would take several more hours before they would have completed their rendezvous and be ready to withdraw.[9] In doing this they would be pulling back from the real epicentre of the rebellion, just as the Camolin and Enniscorthy cavalry had unwittingly done a few hours earlier. However, their part in the morning's drama was not quite over.

The garrison in Wexford town reacted even more slowly to the news of rebellion than did those further north. Edward Turner had crossed the bridge with word of insurgent attacks in the area around his home quite early in the morning, probably between six and eight o'clock.[10] At that point the garrison was short of cavalry since Boyd and his men had now gone out to Ballyteige to arrest Colclough.[11] Meanwhile the other cavalry unit, the Shelmaliers, had been decimated by desertions (including that of Edward Roche) and now numbered barely more than a dozen men.[12] The garrison commander, Lieutenant-Colonel Foote of the North Cork militia, was unwilling to risk the handful of mounted men he had by sending them into the turbulent country beyond Castlebridge, and so he waited for some time for Boyd's return.

Around ten o'clock, however, with Boyd still absent, he finally decided to take a detachment of infantry and what was left of the Shelmalier cavalry to investigate the reports of rebel mobilisation for himself. He selected about 120 men from the two units for the task, and had them prepare for the march. The Shelmaliers would function as his advance guard, and he left orders for the Wexford cavalry to follow him north as soon as they returned with their prisoner.[13]

Foote had no clear idea at first of where the rebel forces were concentrated but the loyalist refugees who had come into the town in the hour or two after Turner's arrival had suggested that they were gathering near Oulart, and this now became his destination.[14] The troops marched out in high spirits, and loyalists in the town seem to have watched them go with a sense of relief, confident that they would quickly crush whatever uprising had taken place.[15] The town's United Irishmen watched too, no doubt happy that the rebellion had evidently come, but confused about what to do, as they had not heard from their leaders and were very likely aware that Fitzgerald and Harvey had been thrown into prison.

At about the time that Foote and his men were crossing the bridge at Wexford and venturing out into the countryside to its north, the Carnew yeomanry force of 300 or more men was bearing down on the rebel camp at Kilthomas. Meanwhile the Enniscorthy and Ferns cavalry, under Grogan, Richards and Smith, was approaching the hill from the south. The fate of the rising in Wexford very much depended on what happened in the next few hours when the soldiers came face to face with the insurgents in confrontations such as this.

The first confrontation took place at Kilthomas, and the outcome was a disaster for the rebels. The Carnew detachment made its way through the Slieveboy gap and approached the western slope of the hill.[16] The sudden arrival of the soldiers may have taken Father Michael Murphy and his aides by surprise, although they must have expected some kind of response from nearby government forces by this point in the morning. The yeomanry were led by two prominent figures from the Fitzwilliam estate: the cavalry by Captain Wainwright, Fitzwilliam's agent, and the infantry by one of his tenants, Captain Bookey, a brother of Lieutenant Bookey who had lost his life the night before at The Harrow.[17]

With little hesitation the two officers decided to launch an attack on the ridge as soon as they had come close to it, even though the rebels occupied the high ground and outnumbered them heavily. The soldiers had the twin advantages of far better weapons and the benefit of the assumption that, when faced with men in uniform, an irregular force would always give way, regardless of its size.

The Carnew troops began their advance from the side of a broad valley to the west of the hill, and as they moved closer to its base the cavalry broke off to the left and began to climb towards its top along a narrow lane that ran up the slope beyond the rebel right. The infantry in the meantime formed battle-lines at the bottom of the slope and began a slow, steady advance across the fields and ditches towards the insurgents massed directly above them. Father Michael Murphy and the other United Irish officers no doubt tried to steady their men as the troops drew closer, but the rebels were facing organised troops for the first time and they began to waver early.

When the soldiers got to within a few hundred yards, they fired an opening volley at the rebel lines. This was the first volley almost every man on the hilltop would have heard, and the sound of it must have been terrifying to many of them. The troops were still out of range, however, and the bullets did no damage. They reloaded and pressed on up the slope. In a while they stopped again and fired a second volley, but they were still too far away and still did no damage. The rebel lines were holding steady at this point, perhaps in part because Father Murphy was planning a pike charge against the soldiers once they came close enough. His plans, whatever they were, were upset by a development he might have foreseen: the one hundred or so cavalrymen had by now reached the top of the hill to the right of the rebel lines and began to spread out across the ridge as if preparing to charge his men's exposed flank from level ground. The priest doubtless pleaded with his men to hold firm at this point, but they were heavily outgunned and the prospect of facing simultaneous cavalry and infantry charges disheartened them. They began to fall back and then to break, and in a short while many of them began a headlong flight, even before the advancing infantry could reach them.

The battle quickly became a massacre. The entire rebel army broke ranks and fled for their lives down the eastern slope of the hill and out into the countryside beyond. Some units stayed together, but many simply dissolved in the confusion. The yeomen, especially the cavalry, chased down and killed at least a hundred men, perhaps more, before they stopped. The Camolin and Enniscorthy corps joined in the pursuit at some stage as they came up from the south and added further to the toll. The cavalry and infantry devastated the countryside in the area around the hill through much of the rest of the morning, killing all the stragglers they found and burning scores of houses.[18]

The first open encounter between a Wexford rebel force and troops confirmed the loyalist assumption, certainly commonly held in the Wicklow/Wexford borderland, that the insurgents would collapse in the face of a resolute offensive. The battle was almost as great a disaster as the fiasco at Carlow two days earlier. Some of the rebels eventually rallied in small detachments once they had escaped from their pursuers, and during the afternoon hundreds of them started to drift in the general direction of Scarawalsh. Father Michael Murphy escaped and joined them there, and by evening they were rebuilding their army on Ballyorril Hill a few miles to the north of Enniscorthy.[19] Their fate now depended very much on what happened to their comrades to the east of the river, since it would be difficult for them to regain the momentum they had lost without help from elsewhere.

For the present at least, the Carnew forces retreated back to their base, and the smaller units from Enniscorthy and Ferns returned to their headquarters too.[20] The Camolin cavalry returned at last to their home base at around 3 p.m., but realised when they got there that the rebels had raided Lord Mountnorris's house and made off with its huge store of firearms. The cavalry's response was to abandon the village for the time being, and they made their way northwards to Gorey, which by now was the sanctuary for a large number of loyalist refugees.[21] The officers in charge of the garrisons at Enniscorthy and Carnew knew nothing of this sudden turn of events, however, and they undoubtedly continued to assume that the rebels had been defeated and destroyed and that the affair was as good as over.

Things went very differently for the insurgent cause around Oulart that day. The men of the rebel army at Ballinamonabeg kept their position for a time after White and his men fled, but when they realised that they had gone and were not returning, most of them broke camp and marched northwards. They halted briefly at Meelenagh church and then went on to the demesne of Island House, where they arrived not long after the Bolton family had left. They spread out on the demesne and waited there for other units to join them from the parishes further north and along the coast.[22]

Curiously, most of the rebel leaders decided to stay behind in Jeremiah Kavanagh's pub at Ballinamonabeg while this movement took place; they were apparently still puzzled by Fitzgerald's failure to appear, and in his absence they may have been trying to reconstruct the details of the campaign that lay before them, details which he probably knew much better than any of them. A small detachment of men stayed behind to guard the officers who were exposing themselves dangerously in remaining behind after the main body had gone north; apparently they assumed that there would be no immediate threat from the direction of Wexford town—an assumption that was very nearly a fatal mistake.

As the hours passed even more rebels poured into the makeshift camp on Island demesne, many of them from various points along the coast of Ballaghkeen. Among them was a band from the area around Morris Castle who had a bitter hatred of Hawtrey White and had very likely been involved in the attack on his house earlier. They were notorious as smugglers and so were a close-knit group already. They were an invaluable addition to the force for this reason and also because they were good marksmen and had brought with them some of the huge strand guns which they used to shoot waterfowl.

Oulart, Blackwater and Vicinity, 27 May

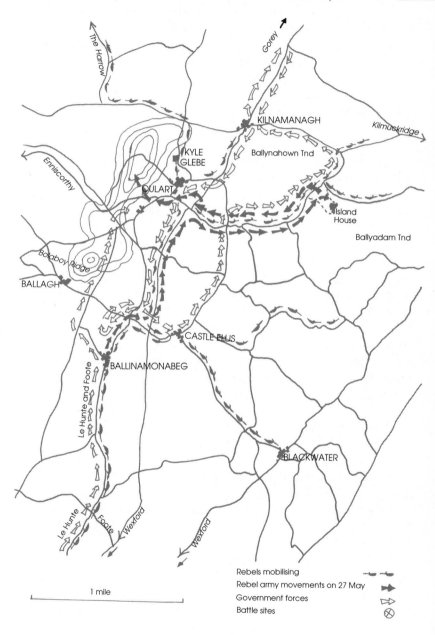

The Harrow

Gorey

KILNAMANAGH

Kilmuckridge

Enniscorthy

KYLE GLEBE

Ballynahown Tnd

OULART

Island House

Ballyadam Tnd

Bolaboy Ridge

BALLAGH

CASTLE ELLIS

Le Hunte and Foote

BALLINAMONABEG

BLACKWATER

Le Hunte

Foote

Wexford

Wexford

Rebels mobilising
Rebel army movements on 27 May
Government forces
Battle sites

1 mile

The army which was growing by the hour on Island demesne was far from stable, however, and a bizarre incident involving the Morris Castle group revealed how serious a problem discipline might be. At some point a rumour rapidly spread through the ranks that Hawtrey White and the cavalry were returning. A man named Redmond from Meelenagh volunteered to ride out along the road on which White was reported to be coming to see if the news was true. As he passed the Morris Castle contingent one of them, a man named Wat Lelis, accused him of trying to join White and intending to betray them. Redmond denied the charge, but Lelis and several of the other Morris Castle men suddenly attacked him, dragged him from his horse and killed him on the roadside. The real reason for the puzzling assault is unclear, but Redmond had formerly been a revenue commissioner, and the Morris Castle men may have run foul of him at some point in the past because of their smuggling and perhaps were seizing the chance to take revenge. The other men from Meelenagh did not see what happened, so the fracas that might otherwise have broken out did not develop, but one of Redmond's brothers left the rebel army in protest when he learned of his brother's death. (Significantly, Lelis was hanged for his crime by the government after the rebellion was over.)[23] The incident suggests that the rebel forces were far from being a united group at this early stage and indicates that given the right circumstances they might well break down into competing parochial factions.

Around midday, as White and his column approached Gorey and as the rebel army swelled at Island demesne, Colonel Foote and his militiamen halted at Castlebridge and tried to learn as much as they could about the situation in the country to their north. Loyalist refugees from that direction had already claimed that there were at least 5,000 rebels assembled near Oulart; others had declared that a second force had collected just a short distance to the north of Castlebridge.

Puzzled by these confusing reports, Foote now decided to conduct a sweeping movement through the countryside beyond the village, as much to reconnoitre the rebel positions as to attack them. He decided to take the 120 men of his own North Corks with him and to travel along a narrow road that led out towards the coast from Castlebridge, then ran northwards for a few miles close to the seashore, and then turned inland and met the main road to Oulart at Ballyfarnoge. Colonel Le Hunte and what was left of the Shelmalier cavalry (sixteen men) would ride parallel to him along the main road and meet him at Ballyfarnoge crossroads, which was no more than a mile south of Ballinamonabeg. Then they would push on northwards together and investigate the report of the huge rebel force that was supposed to be nearby. There was still no sign of Boyd, but Foote left orders for him to ride as far as Redgate, a hamlet a few miles to the south-west of Oulart, once he returned and to give him support from there if needed.[24]

The march to Ballyfarnoge went according to plan. The weather was warm,[25] making the journey tiring for the men, but Foote and Le Hunte met at Ballyfarnoge an hour afterwards without seeing any rebel units. By about that time Boyd and his men had finally arrived back in Wexford with Colclough, and they followed Foote and Le Hunte northwards, veering north-west towards Redgate once they got to the far side of the bridge.[26]

Everything was now in place for Foote's planned engagement of his enemy; it was a further advantage that the entire United Irish leadership was still meeting in Jeremiah Kavanagh's pub. A quick push northwards and Foote might decapitate the Wexford movement even more severely than Boyd had thus far done. The main rebel army, two miles further north at Island demesne, would then be leaderless and confused and might collapse by the end of the day.

The column of soldiers left Ballyfarnoge at around one or two o'clock and marched northwards along the narrow road directly for Ballinamonabeg. A rebel lookout posted just to the south of hamlet spotted them when they were no more than a mile away, and he passed the word quickly back to the crossroads pub. The officers inside were taken completely by surprise and rushed out, mounted their horses and galloped frantically northwards towards Island. Their guards and scouts followed, and in a matter of minutes the crossroads and the pub were completely deserted.[27]

Foote and Le Hunte arrived only minutes later. Le Hunte already suspected that Jeremiah Kavanagh was a United Irishman, since he had been among those who surrendered pikes in the previous days[28] (and his involvement in the American Revolution might have been enough to condemn him anyway),[29] and there were probably plenty of signs that a sizeable force had camped about the place not long before. To punish him, therefore, the colonels let their soldiers plunder the public house of its supply of drink. Many of them drank a great deal in a short time, and one, a drummer, got so drunk that he fell asleep by the roadside. After half an hour or so his comrades set the house on fire and pushed on towards Oulart, leaving the drummer where he was.[30]

By this time the rebel officers had reached the camp at Island with the news that government troops were approaching from the south. Somebody, probably Edward Roche, gave the order to hurry for the nearest high ground, Oulart Hill, the southern slope of which was clearly visible just two miles to the west; this was without doubt the best place to make a stand should the approaching soldiers attack.

The entire camp, now consisting of perhaps 2,000 United Irishmen, along with hundreds of frightened women and children,[31] marched hurriedly and in some confusion across the two miles of narrow roadways between the demesne and the hill. They got to the village and reached the foot of the hill beyond it without seeing any sign of the soldiers. Then they climbed up the hillside and began to deploy themselves along its southern slope, the women, children and other camp-followers on the flat summit, and the fighting men half-way down, with a large ditch as cover just a few yards behind them. Edward Roche took up a position close to the summit, along with most of the captains, and Father John Murphy had charge of the front ranks. The priest concentrated his gunsmen, who numbered one or two dozen, along the right flank of the line and placed pikemen and a few sturdy individuals with pitchforks and scythes along its centre and left. Roche had a good view of the entire scene and probably was the first rebel officer to discern the soldiers as they appeared at the top of Bolaboy ridge, a mile away across the valley.[32]

Lieutenant-Colonel Foote and Colonel Le Hunte no doubt approached their task all morning with the same basic assumption that had governed the behaviour of the Carnew yeomanry a few hours before: disciplined soldiers could overwhelm any mob anywhere, regardless of their numbers. Perhaps because he realised that the rebels he now faced were well organised and prepared for military action to a degree that common mobs were not, Foote stopped his advance as soon as he saw them drawn up on the ridge to his north. He conferred with his officers briefly, and then the column resumed its march and moved slowly down into the valley, ever closer to the village. Several of the men took off their heavy military boots and left them in a small cabin when they reached the floor of the valley, and when the first units reached the village Edward Turner of Newfort and a few more Shelmalier cavalrymen broke away and set several of its houses on fire. Turner's expectation was that the insurgents on the hill would come down from their position to protect the village, but they refused to move and watched silently as the soldiers moved back out of the village along the road to Enniscorthy and closer to them.[33]

Foote surveyed the rebel lines above him from this closer vantage-point and, according to his own account of the day, decided that he could not attack without reinforcements. His junior officers, however, disagreed, and, with or without his consent (it is not certain which), they got ready to lead a charge up the hillside.[34] As they prepared, Le Hunte and the Shelmaliers began to move along the foot of the hill and made their way slowly around to the rebel right as if they were planning to outflank them and come at them from behind. There was a narrow lane that ran across the hill from west to east some distance behind the rebels, and the cavalry was probably making for this.

The rebel camp-followers on the hilltop were terrified at this stage, and some of them, along with a few of the more faint-hearted rank and file, began to move away across the flat top towards the northern slope. As they did so, however, they caught sight of a cavalry force in the distance to the north. The detachment they saw was either a remnant of White's force still retreating towards Gorey and unaware of the drama now unfolding behind them, or it was possibly White himself, probing southwards once again and cautiously reconnoitring the rebel-held country. The frightened rebels and camp-followers could not tell much about them from such a distance, and they naturally assumed that the soldiers were approaching from the north for the purpose of trapping them. This was enough to send the crowds back towards the main rebel line on the southern slope, where Roche and Morgan Byrne continued to harangue them against any further retreat, Byrne making an especially impassioned plea for courage.[35]

Meanwhile at the foot of the hill the soldiers formed a battle-line and began to advance slowly up the slope. Foote was still behind on the floor of the valley, and a much younger officer, Major Lombard, was now in command of the charge. He rode immediately behind his men on their right flank, and the other officers, all young men too, rode or walked at other points along the line. The insurgents were still mostly lined up in the open about thirty yards in front of the ditch at this stage.

When they had proceeded some distance up the slope, the militiamen halted and Lombard ordered them to fire a volley at the rebel line. As at Kilthomas, this was the first volley most of the insurgents had ever heard. They were still out of range, however, and the shots hit no one. The soldiers fired a second time when they got a little further up the slope, and this time hit several rebels who were in the open ground. Immediately Father Murphy ordered the rest to fall back and take cover behind the ditch. It looked to the soldiers like the first stage of a rout, and they pressed on towards the top, eager for the chase.

The ditch the rebels sheltered behind ran across the slope and then turned downwards, running across the contours at the rebel left, and as the soldiers got closer they unknowingly moved into the V formed by the rebel line. Lombard stopped them yet again when they were only a short distance from the ditch and ordered them to fire another volley; the rebels were under cover now and the bullets had no effect. Moments later, however, a handful of shots rang out from the gunsmen on the rebel right, and several of the militiamen fell.

This was the rebel signal to charge. In a moment or two a great wave of men surged across the ditches in front of and to the right of the soldiers and raced headlong at them. A frantic hand-to-hand battle began immediately, bayonet against pike and pitchfork. The soldiers were outnumbered, half-surrounded and caught on the low ground. The rebels soon began to push them back, and then, in as critical a turning-point as the rebellion would have, the soldiers suddenly panicked and started back in headlong flight down the slope. The rebels, encouraged by this turn of events, gave chase and showed no mercy when they caught up with them.

In a matter of minutes the entire column was wiped out. Small groups were isolated and killed, many of them as they begged for their lives. A few managed to reload their muskets and fire shots back in the direction of the oncoming rebels, but to little effect. A handful even succeeded in reaching the bottom of the slope and fled into some boggy fields on the valley floor, but their pursuers caught up with them and killed them there. One man ran several miles to the south before a pair of rebels trapped him in a field and dispatched him.[36]

The Battle of Oulart, as it would subsequently be called, was over in minutes and was a complete disaster for the government side. Lieutenant-Colonel Foote and the handful of men who had remained behind with him had realised what was happening just in time and managed to escape, the privates riding pillion on Foote's and two other horses. The Shelmalier cavalry too got away relatively unscathed, although one of its members was shot dead by a rebel using a strand gun as they tried to round the hill.[37] Over a hundred men died on the slope and in the valley.

Foote and his little party of survivors rode due south without stopping, desperately trying to reach Wexford Bridge before any rebel cavalry caught up with them. The Shelmaliers gave up on their plan to round the hill and made a circuit out towards Enniscorthy and then went south towards Wexford by a different route. In the meantime Boyd's cavalry, which had ridden as far as Redgate, somehow got word of the disaster and turned about and made its way back towards Wexford. All these units were now abandoning the entire stretch of country between Wexford and Oulart to the rebels.[38]

The rebel army was exhilarated with its near-total victory. When the fighting ended, they immediately set to work stripping the bodies of the fallen soldiers of anything that was useful to them. The got at least a hundred muskets, cartridge boxes and military jackets, and in addition some swords and pistols. They may have captured some horses too.

In an hour or two the task was completed. The officers marshalled the army and marched them northwards from Oulart

to Carrigrew Hill, about five miles away. They arrived there by
sunset and formed a camp on the summit for the night.[39] In a
matter of a few hours they had gone from the disruption that the
loss of one of their principal leaders inevitably caused, to near-
disaster at Ballinamonabeg, to sweeping triumph at Oulart Hill.
Suddenly they had the initiative firmly in their grasp and were in
control of the entire area between the east coast of the county and
the towns of Gorey, Enniscorthy and Wexford.

News of the dramatic clash on the slope of Oulart Hill reached
Wexford town less than an hour after it took place. Henry
Perceval, the High Sheriff, had been posted at Castlebridge for
much of the afternoon, and when Foote and the other five
survivors of the North Cork detachment reached the village they
told him what had happened. He immediately mounted a horse
and galloped into Wexford with the news. Not long afterwards
Foote and the five privates rode slowly into the town themselves.
The militiamen's families had lived in Wexford while they
were stationed there, and they were among the first to hear of the
disaster. The wives and children of the men who perished were
devastated by the report, and some of them ran screaming through
the streets; one woman reportedly died from shock. The other
loyalists in the town were equally perplexed and no doubt
assumed that the rebel force that had gained such an incredible
victory would soon be on its way southwards.[40]
The United Irishmen in the town, remained quiet. With
Colcough, Fitzgerald and Harvey in jail, men like Matthew Keogh
and Dick Monk no doubt were anxious to conceal their real plans,
as were their rank-and-file followers. For the time being they
watched quietly and undoubtedly listened with great satisfaction
as news of rebel successes in the countryside to the north reached
them.[41]
As night fell on the first full day of the Wexford rebellion,
then, the insurgents were already in a strong position despite the
arrests of Perry, Kyan, Fitzgerald, Harvey and Colclough.
Government forces had had a decisive victory at Kilthomas, but
they had withdrawn to the towns once night fell, leaving the
countryside between Ferns, Newtownbarry and Enniscorthy open
to the rebels and so allowing them a chance to regroup. The

Kilthomas army was shattered for the time, but remnants continued to gather on Ballyorril Hill through the night, and from this core at least part of the army could be rebuilt.

It was the camp on Carrigrew Hill, however, that was by far the most important rebel rallying-point that night. By midnight it probably contained several thousand men, and units from other districts in north Wexford are likely to have joined them between then and dawn.

Government forces, confused about the situation they now faced, unwittingly played into the hands of the rebels. The abandonment of Camolin by its local yeomanry force earlier in the afternoon is one example of this.[42] The behaviour of the Ferns garrison was somewhat similar. Hundreds of loyalist refugeees had fled south from that village to the safety of Enniscorthy during the day, and much of the local garrison had followed them, reducing the outpost to a handful of North Cork militia and local yeoman infantry[43] and ensuring that a huge tract of territory embracing much of northern and eastern Wexford was either in rebel hands already or was effectively abandoned by government forces by nightfall.

By midnight garrison commanders in the nearby towns were too confused and too frightened about their own position to do the one thing that might have stymied the rising at this stage: conduct a co-ordinated attack on the Carrigrew rebels before they could link up with those at Ballyorril. As the night passed they huddled in their strongholds, waiting to see what the next day brought. In the meantime panic was beginning to grip Wexford town and Gorey, and increasing numbers of loyalist civilians in both places had begun to talk of evacuation.[44]

From the perspective of the rebel leaders on Carrigrew Hill, things had gone remarkably well on that first day. Edward Roche and his officers were probably still confused about the fate of Edward Fitzgerald and Edward Hay, but they had already achieved a morale-boosting victory without their help and now stood poised to strike out at any part of north or central Wexford they wished. It is not clear if by midnight they knew of the defeat at Kilthomas or that the units in the far north of the county, around Gorey, had not yet mobilised. Subsequent events would suggest that they had already agreed on a plan to join the other north

Wexford insurgent forces in the next day or so though and then to move against the central part of the county. It is very likely, therefore, that messengers went out from the camp to the west and north during the night to inform other leaders of the details of the next stage in the campaign.

To many of the rebels the first twenty-four hours of the struggle would have taught some chilling lessons, lessons which many of them were now mulling over. To all of them the great destruction that the rising was bringing would have been quite frightening, even if expected. We have no way to estimate casualties with reliability, but it is likely that at least 300 or 400 people had died in the county during that first day; this included the more than 100 soldiers killed at Oulart, the 100 or 200 rebels killed at Kilthomas, and the scores of civilians killed by both sides. In addition, both sides had burned hundreds of houses across the region affected by the fighting. Few people on either side would have predicted anything other than a very bloody struggle in the days ahead, regardless of who got the upper hand.

In Dublin the government's commander-in-chief, General Gerard Lake, knew nothing of the Wexford uprising at this stage. From his perspective, the planned insurrection in Dublin had been thwarted, and while there was always the chance that the rebels in the capital would make a second attempt, the main area of concern was now the counties of the midlands. Large areas of Kildare, Meath and Wicklow were in rebel control, and the authorities must have assumed that the situation in the counties beyond these three was potentially just as bad. In reality, of course, unknown to the Wexford rebel leaders at Carrigrew, the rebel cause was already in terrible trouble in the midlands that night. The Kildare and Wicklow rebels had achieved some victories and had taken possession of parts of their counties, but their successes were only partial and due to good fortune rather than military skill. More importantly, the defeat in Dublin itself had completely negated any chance of the orginal plan of rebellion being put into effect, and a setback at Carlow had destroyed the opportunity to spread the movement further down the Barrow valley.[45] Critical too was the fact that nothing had as yet happened in Ulster, and this failure was at least as important as the setback in Dublin.[46]

4

THE BATTLE FOR ENNISCORTHY
28 MAY

THE GOVERNMENT'S POSITION IN COUNTY WEXFORD DECLINED rapidly on Monday 28 May. The rebel army left Carrigrew Hill early in the morning and marched directly west to Camolin.[1] They met groups of rebels from the area around the village and from parishes to its north-west when they got there, among them Miles Byrne and others who had made their way from Monaseed during the night.[2] They seized and distributed the cache of arms at Camolin Park and then, after only a short delay, made their way southwards towards Ferns, three miles away.[3] By this point they numbered perhaps 3,000 or 4,000 men, and with the addition of the guns from Lord Mountnorris's residence, several hundred of them now had firearms.[4]

They got to Ferns at about nine or ten o'clock and found the place almost totally abandoned. Most of the population was loyalist, and these, along with other loyalists who had fled there from the surrounding countryside two nights before, had gone southwards to Enniscorthy. Isaac Cornock and his tiny garrison of infantry had apparently followed them as soon as they realised that the rebels were approaching.[5]

One detachment of the rebels broke off from the rest when they got to the village and ransacked the palace of the Protestant Bishop of Ferns, Euseby Cleaver. The bishop was a vehement enemy of the United Irishmen and had become notorious for drumming up sentiment against them.[6] They took revenge on him now by stripping curtains and carpets from his house to make tents and ripping the covers off of the books in his library to make saddles.[7]

Ferns consisted of only a single street, and when the main force entered it the place was eerily silent. One of the few people they found was a Quaker named Haughton who had remained behind when the garrison fled. Some of them, probably new recruits from the countryside around the village, remembered that a few days before Haughton had refused to sell a length of rope to an officer who was going to use it to hang suspected United Irishmen.[8] He feared for his life when the rebels first arrived, but after a short while realised that they intended him no harm. Like all Quakers from this point on, he would be regarded as a neutral rather than an enemy.[9]

Sometime before noon, after they had eaten food offered to them by Haughton, Roche and the other chiefs called their men to arms and marched out of Ferns along the road south towards Enniscorthy.[10] In about an hour they reached Scarawalsh Bridge and soon afterwards found Father Michael Murphy and a part of the Kilthomas group awaiting them on Ballyorril Hill, about half a mile to its south-west.[11] Rebel forces from both east and west of the Bann were now consolidated to make an army of perhaps 6,000 men or even more, and Father Michael Murphy joined the inner circle of leaders.[12]

The capture of Enniscorthy, only four miles to their south, was their immediate objective.[13] Were they to succeed, they would have taken their first town, and a strategic one at that, dominating as it did the entire central part of the county; should they fail, of course, the momentum might turn against them very quickly.

Enniscorthy was a viable objective now that their numbers were in the region of 6,000 men.[14] The garrison was under the command of Captain William Snowe of the North Cork militia, and his total force barely exceeded 300 men. Just over seventy of these were North Corks, twenty of whom had fled into the town from Ferns the afternoon before, and the rest were yeomanry, including 100 Enniscorthy yeoman infantry under Captain John Pounden and his brother, Lieutenant Joshua Pounden, of Daphne, as well as the Scarawalsh infantry under Cornock, and the Enniscorthy cavalry under Solomon Richards.[15] (Grogan and his unit had by this time gone to Waterford as an escort for an officer who was travelling there from Dublin.)[16] In all, then, Snowe had about 250 infantry and 50 cavalry. They were all well armed (though by this point so were the approaching rebels); however, their armaments did not include heavy artillery, and in the street fighting that would inevitably develop once the rebels attacked this might prove to be a critical weakness.

To add to Snowe's difficulties, Enniscorthy was, by its very nature, a difficult town to defend. It lay in a narrow gorge at a point where the Slaney was easily fordable and where its tidal stretch ended. By the 1790s it had sprawled up either side of the gorge, and some of its streets now stretched out towards the west beyond its rim. It had several large buildings which might easily be defended by concealed troops, including the castle and the market house, but it had no defensive wall. Besides, because of the topography its most vital point was the bridge linking its eastern and western sections, but a commander who chose to position himself here would have difficulty following developments at the far western and northern entrances, since all of them were well out of his view. To add even further to the problem, rows of cabins stretched out into the countryside at all the major entrances, and these would be very difficult to defend, not least of all because many of their inhabitants were sympathetic to the rebel cause.[17]

Up to this point, midday on 28 May, Snowe and the yeomanry officers had been confused about what was taking place to their east, north and west, and it is likley that they had no clear idea even as late as that morning from which direction an attack on them was most likely to come.[18] As soon as Cornock and his detachment arrived, however, the rebel intention must have become much clearer, and just after one o'clock Snowe had this confirmed when some of the lookouts posted out along the road to the north galloped in through the Duffry Gate and announced that a huge rebel force was approaching from that direction.[19]

Snowe had expected an attack soon, and his troops were already dispersed through the town in battle positions. He had placed the 100 men of the Enniscorthy yeoman infantry in front of the Duffry Gate, and they would now obviously take the brunt of the rebel assault. The yeoman cavalry and the Ferns infantry remained in the streets behind the gate as a reserve force, and there were small detachments of sharpshooters in the market house and the castle (where some United Irish prisoners were being held) who could sweep the nearby square and streets should the rebels get inside the town. A large number of armed loyalist civilians had taken up positions in upper-storey windows for the same purpose. The North Corks themselves were concentrated at the bridge, and Snowe decided to make this his centre of operations. His reasoning was that the most experienced men should be placed here to defend the line of retreat should the first defensive lines be overwhelmed. He decided to leave the cabin suburbs on the east bank almost completely undefended.[20]

The rebel force that Snowe's vedettes had observed coming towards them was led by a group of men who had given careful consideration to their plan of attack and whose strategy and tactics were well conceived, given their numerical advantage and the kinds of weapons they had. They would, they had agreed, drive directly at the town from the north and concentrate their gunsmen in front of the Duffry Gate and support them with some pike units. If the gunsmen failed to push the defenders back through the gate, they would drive a herd of cattle into their ranks and follow it up with a pike charge. In the meantime they would dispatch several large flanking parties to hit the town's defences at other points: one to swing around to the right and attack from the west, another to move to the left and drive at the defenders in Irish Street, just to the east of the gate, and yet another to cross the river, just above the bridge, and attack the east side of the town. The garrison could then be surrounded and would have no option but to flee or be destroyed.[21]

As the rebels approached the Duffry Gate, the yeomanry drawn up in front of it played into their hands by advancing slowly to meet them and taking up a new defensive line one or two hundred yards beyond it. The Pounden brothers evidently expected that they might intimidate the inexperienced insurgents by this ploy, and shortly afterwards Solomon Richards moved his cavalry out too and got ready to charge them and test their resolve. But just before he did this the rebels split into their three divisions, one heading off to the right, one to the left, and one, the central division with its lines of gunsmen, pikemen and cattle, moving straight at the yeomanry lines ahead of them.[22]

At a word from Richards the approximately one hundred men and horses of the yeoman cavalry thundered across the open ground in front of the new infantry lines and raced straight at the rebel centre. The rebel musketeers steadied, aimed at the charging horsemen and fired off a volley that swept several of them from their saddles. The rest of the cavalry, stunned by this, immediately lost their momentum and turned and galloped back to the infantry lines.[23]

The rebels pressed their advantage immediately. Their flanking parties to the left and right were making good progress, especially those moving to the right, and the musketeers in the centre began to edge closer to the infantry. When they got within range insurgents and yeomen began to fire concentrated volleys at each other and men on both sides began to fall. Lieutenant Pounden was hit by a rebel ball and fell mortally wounded, and his brother, Captain Pounden, ordered his men to retreat back to their original defensive position immediately in front of the Duffry Gate. They did this hurriedly, and the Enniscorthy infantry concentrated around the gate itself while the Ferns corps under Cornock moved over slightly to the right to defend the entrance to Irish Street. Meanwhile the rebel division that had moved off to the right was now all the way around on the western perimeter of the town and practically behind Pounden's men.[24]

At this point the rebel commanders ordered their men to stampede the cattle. The musketeers gave way and let hundreds of pikemen through, driving the cattle ahead of them and forcing them directly into the yeomanry's ranks. The cattle threw the soldiers into disarray, and the rebel pikemen seized the opening and charged directly at them themselves. Pounden's men held their line for a time, but then fell back into the streets leading down into the Market Square. Pounden quickly realised he could not hold on for long against such force, and he sent a desperate message to Snowe at the bridge, asking him to come up and help him. Snowe understood the danger and responded by leading his entire unit up to the square, leaving the bridge unguarded for the moment. When he got to the high ground, he tried to drive at the rebel units approaching from the west along the Daphne road rather than attacking the main rebel body pushing its way in from the Duffry Gate. Richards and his cavalry corps joined him in the effort, but they lost at least nine men in a futile charge, and after that Snowe fell back to the relative safety of the bridge and left the yeomanry to fend for themselves.[25]

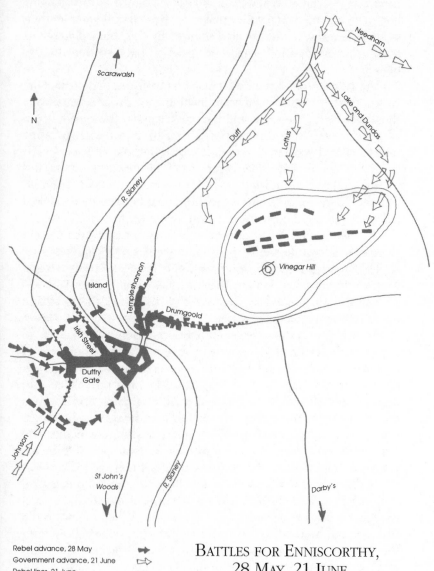

Scarawalsh

N

Needham

Lake and Dundas

Duff

Loftus

R. Slaney

Island

Templeshannon

Vinegar Hill

Drumgoold

Irish Street

Duffry Gate

Johnson

St John's Woods

R. Slaney

Darby's

Rebel advance, 28 May
Government advance, 21 June
Rebel lines, 21 June
From: Musgrave

BATTLES FOR ENNISCORTHY,
28 MAY, 21 JUNE

By this point, half an hour or so into the battle, the rebel centre, led on again by the gunsmen, had begun to force their way in through the Duffry Gate and soon pushed, house by house, down towards the Market Square. Loyalist snipers firing from windows along the street slowed down their progress for a time, but the Enniscorthy infantry were giving up ground steadily and the rebels pushed ahead in spite of the harassing fire.

Meanwhile the rebels who were attacking the Irishtown entrance were pushing the infantry before them too. Isaac Cornock was shot in the neck as he tried to rally his men, but in spite of his wound he continued to take part in the battle. His troops lost ground steadily, and the fierce musketry exchanges that took place along the street caused several thatched cabins to catch fire. The flames spread rapidly from roof to roof along the entire row and were very soon out of control.[26]

Off to Cornock's right a rebel detachment under the command of Thomas Sinnott of Kilbride made its way onto an island that lay just to the north of the bridge and tried to get across the river and to reach the eastern side of the town that way. Two detachments of the North Corks, one on the bridge and the other on the east bank of the river, opened fire on them simultaneously as they did so. There was no cover on the island, and the rebels were caught in a hopeless position. Several fell dead. Their comrades pulled back for a time and then made a second attempt to reach the far side of the river in the face of the deadly fire, but again they failed. In the end Sinnott led them back to the west bank, and from there they marched northwards along the river, looking for a shallow place that was out of the range of the militiamen. They found one less than a mile away at a place called Blackstoops, made the crossing safely and marched directly at the cabin streets on the east side of the river.[27]

On the other side of the Slaney rebel musketeers and pikemen began to make their way to the western and northern perimeter of the Market Square. The yeomanry withdrew to the entrances to the streets on its opposite sides and took cover behind makeshift barricades. The detachment in the market house still covered the open ground of the square from the windows, and other loyalists remained at upper-storey windows at various points around the square. Both sides had already lost large numbers of men, but the rebel losses were almost certainly considerably higher since in many instances they were the attackers and often had to expose themselves to deadly fire. Nevertheless, in spite of their inexperience as soldiers, they pressed on resolutely and gained a firm grip on the town, one building at a time.[28]

The fires that began in Irish Street spread quickly to other parts of the western sector of the town as the fighting continued. The Market Square and nearby streets soon filled with smoke. The rebels launched several charges across the square in an effort to dislodge the defenders at the barricades, but each time they fell back with heavy losses and the soldiers held their ground. In the meantime the flames continued to spread, and a huge area of the town began to burn furiously.[29]

The position of the garrison now became very tenuous. Thomas Sinnott's division forced their way into the cabin suburbs on the western bank of the river as soon as they reached them. Richards's cavalry made a desperate attempt to stop them, but for the third time in the afternoon the mounted yeomanry failed to repel advancing rebels, and soon Sinnott's men were threatening the bridge. A detachment of the North Corks pushed their way up the street leading to the bridge and stopped his advance at Lett's brewery. For a time there was stalemate, but the shooting caused a number of cabins to catch fire here too, and within a short while several buildings were ablaze. The flames leaped from roof to roof and raced along the entire length of two streets, Templeshannon and Drumgoold, destroying scores of houses.[30]

About two hours into the battle Snowe suddenly decided to abandon the town. His forces were still holding out on both sides of the bridge, but he realised that they could not do so indefinitely. With the thick smoke obscuring almost every street and giving him his only chance to get away, he quickly rallied his men by the bridge and led them out towards the road to St John's, passing the castle as he went. Many of the yeomen were still manning the barricades in the square when this happened and did not hear the retreat sounded, but eventually realised what was happening and abandoned their posts too. Several of them rushed into the castle to kill the prisoners inside before they left, but the jailer had already fled with the key and the plan was foiled. The rebels did not realise that a retreat was taking place and so made no effort to pursue them, losing the chance to capture hundreds of firearms.[31]

Loyalist civilians had been fleeing southwards to Wexford for several hours already when Snowe and his men headed out along that road, and some of them had already reached the town when the garrison began its journey.[32] The retreat quickly turned into a panic-stricken flight as civilians and soldiers mingled together along the road past St John's. The cavalry gave pillion rides to many of the refugees, but most of them had to complete the entire ten-mile journey on foot. Some, including the Mrs Pounden whose husband had died in the battle, waded across the river to join the main column, and others hid in the woods at St John's or in other places in and around the town and hoped to sneak away when darkness fell. The procession continued along the road towards Wexford all through the evening, and the last fugitives to reach the town did not arrive there until close to midnight.[33]

The rebels in the meantime made their way into the heart of the burning town when it became clear at last that the garrison and most of the loyalist population had fled. Without cavalry there was little hope of successfully pursuing the garrison, and so Roche and the other rebel officers soon decided to take most of their men out of the smoke-filled town and established them in a huge camp on Vinegar Hill. The hill overlooked the town and gave them a good vantage-point from which to watch for any counter-attacks that the garrison or other government forces might launch from the south.[34]

As the main force withdrew to the new camp, the situation inside the town itself became very chaotic. Small bands of men and women, some of them no doubt from the streets of cabins that had just been destroyed, began to seek out well-known loyalists who had failed to escape. They tracked down several of them and killed them in the streets, some in front of their families.[35] They also took to mutilating many of the bodies of soldiers that were strewn about in the streets, among them Joshua Pounden's, which lay in a field near the Duffry Gate.[36] To add to the horror of the battle's aftermath, scores of pigs and dogs, many from the burned-out cabins, began to roam the town freely and were soon feeding on the bodies of the dead.[37]

The Battle of Enniscorthy, as it soon would be called, was one of the most important engagements of the rebellion. In one fell swoop it gave the rebels command of the entire central section of the county and it provided their campaign with almost irresistible momentum. In addition, hundreds of men and women from the town joined their ranks or at least drifted towards the camp on Vinegar Hill, giving a strong urban component to a movement that up to this point had been exclusively rural.[38] The casualties in the battle were very high. The garrison lost close to a hundred men, one-third of its total, and the toll was epecially heavy among the yeomanry units that bore the brunt of the fighting, the Enniscorthy infantry losing half of its members.[39] Rebel losses were severe too, amounting to several hundred dead, perhaps even as many as five hundred, and including some of the best fighters they had.[40] The damage to the town was immense, and when the fires finally died down that evening hundreds of cabins on both sides of the river had been reduced to charred ruins and a large proportion of the 4,000 people who normally lived in the town were homeless.[41]

For a while after the fighting had stopped there were occasional rumours that the garrison was about to launch a counter-attack, aided by reinforcements from Wexford.[42] The reality, however, was that the garrison in Wexford was in no position to consider offensive action of any form at this stage. They had begun the day in shock from the disaster at Oulart the day before, and until well into the afternoon they had had no idea where the rebels were or what their intention was. Colonel Foote and a retired officer who had fought in the American war, Jonas Watson, had taken charge of the town's defences in anticipation of an attack during the morning, and they had sent the news of the Oulart defeat to General Sir William Fawcett at Duncannon and requested that he send reinforcements as soon as possible.[43]

It was not until the battle began at Enniscorthy that the Wexford garrison realised where the main rebel force was. At about 4 p.m. they saw the first plumes of smoke rising into the sky to the north, and at about the same time the first of the hundreds of fugitives from the town and the surrounding countryside began to arrive.[44] Many of them told of widespread massacre and destruction of property, and the rising pillar of smoke seemed to provide proof of this. By evening, with the arrival of the badly mauled garrison itself, the dimensions of this second disaster in as many days were becoming clear. Once again the rebels had killed about a hundred soldiers in an afternoon's action, and this time they had also practically destroyed an entire town. The inevitable boasts of the survivors of the garrison that they caused hundreds of rebel casualties themselves would have been cold comfort to a man in Foote's position.[45] When evening came he had still not received a response from Fawcett at Duncannon and had no clear sense of what the situation was outside of the south-eastern corner of the county. He very probably assumed that the rebellion had become widespread and that a rebel attack on the county seat was imminent. His only immediate options were to flee westwards towards Duncannon or to begin planning for a defence of the town against a massive rebel assault, an assault that might come as early as the next morning. By nightfall he had decided to stand his ground, and he used the hours of darkness to prepare his garrison for action.[46]

Wexford was an easier town to defend against an attack than Enniscorthy. It was larger (its population was around 10,000),[47] and between the local loyalist inhabitants and the refugees who had flooded into it in the previous two days, Foote had about 1,000 men at his disposal, many of whom could be called into service in some way. The garrison itself consisted of about 400 North Cork militia, plus about the same number of yeomanry, most of them infantry, and there were hundreds of civilians ready to act as supplementaries.[48] Some of these men, militia and yeomanry alike, had already had experience of fighting against the rebels, and this meant that complacency, such an important factor at Oulart Hill, was less likely to be a danger here. The Enniscorthy garrison had used a lot of ammunition earlier in the day, but Foote's men were still well armed and well stocked and, most important of all, had several pieces of artillery, something the insurgents had not yet faced.

Unlike Enniscorthy too, Wexford had a medieval wall, most of which was still intact. It ran around the northern, western and southern perimeter of the town and was quite high in most places, and it had several gates, all of which had been widened for modern traffic, but which could be barricaded easily. (See Map 11, p. 174) The rebels had no artillery to use against these obstacles, and their losses were bound to be very high should they attempt a frontal assault. Beyond this, Foote and Watson could expect reinforcements from Duncannon in a day at most.

Watson helped Foote plan the details of the town's defence that night. They decided to man the walls all around the town with musketeers and to block the gates with carts and any other materials readily at hand, leaving small passageways for mounted patrols to leave and return. They would guard against the danger of fire (having surely been warned of this by the Enniscorthy survivors), in part by forcing all the bakers to put out their ovens. In addition there was the problem of inflammable thatched cabins near the walls. These ran out from the town in long rows for quite a distance and would be almost impossible to hold in the face of a mass assault by an enemy numbering in the thousands. One of the rows, John Street, posed particular problems. It ran parallel to and very close to the wall along most of its western section, and many of its residents were sympathetic to the rebel cause (several of them were United Irishmen in fact) and might join the rebels as soon as they arrived. The only solution, Watson and Foote decided, was to demolish as many cabins as possible near the wall once morning came. In the meantime they kept their men at arms all night to watch for rebel movements and kept an anxious eye to the west for any sign that the reinforcements from Duncannon were on their way.[49]

As the insurgents rested in their camp on Vinegar Hill and as the Wexford garrison awaited the attack they now expected to take place within hours, the repercussions of the day's events were being felt in almost every corner of the county. In most places government forces went on the defensive and rebel units took quick advantage of the opening.

The most dramatic instance of this was at Gorey. News of the disaster at Oulart had reached the garrison there in the early morning. Hawtrey White and the yeomanry officers, apparently expecting that the rebels they encountered at Ballinamonabeg the day before would soon attack the town, had thrown up barricades at the southern entrances to the main street and kept their men at arms all night.[50] By morning, with the rebels encamped only three miles to the south at Carrigrew, an attack seemed imminent, and White and the others decided to abandon the town and withdraw to Arklow, ten miles to the north, just across the County Wicklow border. They chose this option unaware that the rebel army was actually headed towards Camolin, Ferns and Enniscorthy and posed no immediate threat to them at all. The entire garrison filed out of the town early in the day and made their way northwards along the road to Arklow, accompanied by hundreds of loyalist refugees. The local yeomen allowed themselves one last atrocity before departing: there were several suspected United Irishmen being held in the market house on Gorey's main street, and before they left they dragged half a dozen of these outside and shot them dead.[51]

News of the desertion of Gorey by the garrison spread quickly through the countryside of north Wexford and south Wicklow. In response, United Irish units, still paralysed by the loss of Anthony Perry up to this point, came out in the open and began to mobilise in the usual bands of twenty or thirty men. By evening this movement had spread all across the district and several very prominent United men were centrally involved in it, including Garrett Byrne of Ballymanus, his brother William Michael, and finally Anthony Perry of Inch, who had at last made his appearance, still bearing the severe scars from his torture.[52] Small groups of rebels were carrying news of the battle at Enniscorthy northwards by that time, and most of the units in the northern parishes began to move south in the hope of joining the camp on Vinegar Hill the next day.[53]

Rebels began to mobilise in the countryside to the west and south-west of Enniscorthy that afternoon too. John Kelly at Killann, Father Mogue Kearns at Kiltealy, and Thomas Cloney at Moneyhore were the central figures here. That evening, with the news of the victory at Enniscorthy being carried into the heart of the barony of Bantry by rebel horsemen, small insurgent bands began to gather at widespread locations. The earliest and largest gatherings were in the districts around Killann, especially near Killoughram Woods, but there were stirrings around Moneyhore before twilight too.[54] The only garrison that might have interfered with this process, that at Newtownbarry, was too small and too intimidated by what they knew of the extent of the rebellion across central Wexford to attempt to stop it, and so the Bantry and southern Scarawalsh rebels had a free hand as they mobilised that evening and night and made their plans to move in to Enniscorthy the following day.

The only area of the county in which the United Irishmen had not yet come out in the open was the extreme south. There, in the parishes to the south of a line from New Ross to Wexford town, government garrisons were still in a strong position, although they were under mounting pressure. In addition, in the south-east, in the baronies of Bargy and Forth especially, the rebel organisation was paralysed for the time by the loss of Bagenal Harvey and John Henry Colclough. The rank and file there may have known of the success of their co-conspiritors far to the north by nightfall, but their information was probably still sketchy; and so, with their own leaders in jail, they decided to follow the example of the rebels in Wexford town and await the arrival of the victorious northerners before participating openly in the rebellion. The few leaders in the area still at large, Cornelius Grogan at Johnstown Castle being the most prominent, also bided their time quietly for the moment.[55]

A similar situation prevailed in the south-west, in the baronies of West Shelmalier and Shelburne. The United Irish organisation was not, in any case, very well developed there,[56] and those units that did exist (there was a well-organised group at Rosegarland) were almost certainly awaiting the lead of their comrades in Wexford town before taking to the field. It is no surprise, then, that they were still lying low that Monday evening, two days into the rising, especially given the danger the government garrisons at Taghmon, Duncannon and New Ross presented to them.

As for the garrisons themselves, their positions had suddenly come to look very vulnerable. Reports of the rebellion in the northern parts of the county were reaching all of them by this point. At Duncannon Fawcett had received news of the disaster at Oulart during the previous night, along with the urgent plea for reinforcements from Foote at Wexford. The seriousness of the situation was now clear to him.[57] The garrison further north at New Ross was smaller and was made up almost exclusively of local yeomanry under the command of Charles Tottenham. Like Fawcett, he too began to receive confused but disturbing reports of events to his north by the evening, and for the first time came to realise that the government had lost control of much of the county to his north and east.[58]

5

THE ROAD TO WEXFORD TOWN
29 MAY

WHEN MORNING BROKE ON TUESDAY 29 MAY, DOZENS OF REBEL bands were already making their way towards Vinegar Hill from far northern parishes, especially from the borderland with County Wicklow. They arrived at steady intervals throughout the morning. When Garrett and Billy Byrne and Anthony Perry appeared, they immediately joined the leadership circle.[1] The entire leadership cadre of Gorey, Ballaghkeen and Scarawalsh baronies was now together, with the sole exception of Esmond Kyan.

The Bantry rebels reached the camp later in the morning. Mobilisation had gone on there throughout the night, and sometime early in the morning a general gathering took place at The Leap, a crossroads about three miles south-west of Enniscorthy, where there was a blacksmith's forge owned by a man named Duggan. Duggan was probably a United Irishman, and it appears that his establishment functioned as a gathering-place in much the same way that Jeremiah Kavanagh's pub did in Ballinamonabeg.[2]

The Bantry units attacked nearby loyalist houses in the early stages of their mobilisation in the usual effort to acquire arms and to neutralise those they assumed to be active yeomen, and by the time they gathered at The Leap they had captured a number of suspected loyalists. They forced these into a nearby quarry, and a company of pikemen surrounded the place to prevent them from escaping.[3]

By the middle of the morning most of the prominent United Irishmen in the barony had arrived, including John Kelly of Killann, Thomas Cloney of Moneyhore, and Matthew and Michael Furlong of Templescoby.[4] Sometime before noon the officers gave the word to march, and the long column began to make its way towards Enniscorthy, with the loyalist prisoners among them. They reached the outskirts of the town well before midday and marched from there directly to the camp on Vinegar Hill.[5] Their arrival added at least another thousand men to the rebel army, bringing it close to 10,000 by this stage,[6] and the leadership circle expanded even further now to accommodate men like Kelly, Cloney and the Furlongs. Two other important United Irish members, William Barker and Luke Byrne, Morgan's brother, had joined them sometime after the capture of Enniscorthy. Byrne, a maltster, was a prominent local figure and had a great deal of influence among the rebels from central parts of the county,[7] and Barker had been a member of the Irish regiment in the French army for several years and so had extensive military experience.[8] This was also true of John Hay of Newcastle, Edward Hay's brother, who had served for several years in France and who came into the camp that same morning.[9]

As this in-gathering was taking place at Enniscorthy, part of the rebel force concentrated its attention on the task of consolidating its grip on the town and its hinterland. During the night some of the rank and file had formed small reconnaissance bands, and these had gone out into the surrounding countryside to encourage the faint-hearted to come into the camp and to search out loyalists who were still hiding in the area. They had success in both tasks, though it is likely that at least some of the new 'recruits' who came to the camp that day did so as a result of intimidation. Any loyalists found by these roaming bands were marched into the town and placed in confinement in a barn (Beale's Barn, as it became known) near the southern foot of the hill.[10]

At some point during the morning too, probably at quite an early hour, a few of these bands renewed the vengeance killings they had carried out the afternoon before. They scoured the town and the area to its south, looking for loyalists who had not managed to flee with the garrison and who had spent the night in the woods or in other hiding-places.[11] They killed several of these when they found them, including on at least two occasions fathers and sons whom they found hiding together. In addition, one of the loyalist prisoners whom the Bantry men brought to the town with them was taken into Lett's brewery and killed by someone who suspected him of Orange sympathies just after he arrived.[12] Later in the day rebel guards brought several of the prisoners who had been held in Beale's Barn up to the camp and forced them into a windmill on the summit of Vinegar Hill. In the afternoon they dragged at least one of them, yet another Bantryman, outside and hacked him to death. They took several others out a few hours later in the day and shot them. It is unclear what role the rebel leaders played in these killings, but at least some of them must have known that they were taking place and did nothing to try to stop them, and it is even possible that they were carried out with their approval.[13]

That afternoon, as the campaign against loyalists went on around them, the leaders on Vinegar Hill began to discuss whether or not they should continue on the offensive and, if so, what town or towns they should attack next.[14] An argument could have been made at this stage against any further offensive at all. After all, they had now swept government forces out of the central and northern parts of the county and had pinned them into the extreme south, making it nearly impossible for those troops to come to the rescue of Dublin Castle. This fulfilled to all practical purposes the extent of the Wexfordmen's role in the rebellion as envisioned in the national United Irish plan.[15] The Wexfordmen might therefore justifiably consider returning to their homes at this point, and there is evidence that during the afternoon, in spite of the enthusiasm evident among the roaming 'recruiting' bands, some of them had begun to drift away.[16]

The situation was, however, complicated by the arrest of the three rebel leaders nearest to Wexford town. With Harvey, Fitzgerald and Colclough in jail, Cornelius Grogan, Matthew Keogh, Dick Monk, John Murphy of Loughnageer and the other southern leaders had made no effort to call their men into the field thus far. It was perhaps with this in mind that some of the Vinegar Hill leaders suggested that they now push on to Wexford and ensure the spread of the rebellion there. Others advocated further offensive action too, but called for attacks on other presumed government holdouts in the county, such as Gorey or Newtownbarry in the north or New Ross in the south-west. For a long time the debate was inconclusive, and it was still not resolved by the middle of the afternoon.[17]

*

As they argued the merits of the different proposals the Vinegar Hill leaders were unaware that a dramatic turn of events was occurring in Wexford town—a development which would have a profound impact on the direction of the rebellion. The day had begun favourably in Wexford for the beleaguered garrison. At dawn a column of about 200 troops arrived from Duncannon. These were mostly Donegal militia under the command of Colonel Maxwell, but among them were several officers from the regular army, including Colonel Colville. They had left Duncannon the evening before and had marched through the night and were exhausted when they arrived. But the addition to the garrison's manpower brought the total to about 1,200 men, including militia, yeomanry and civilian supplementaries, and, since Maxwell had also brought a six-pounder with him, the garrison's ability to defend the town was significantly improved. He also brought the welcome news that further reinforcements would be on their way by the following morning and announced that Fawcett had directed him to take command of the garrison.[18]

Later in the morning the Taghmon yeoman cavalry under Captain Cox also came into the town to reinforce the garrison even further.[19] Their abandonment of their home base left the entire countryside between New Ross and Wexford ungarrisoned, but their arrival compensated for the shortage of cavalry from which the Wexford garrison had suffered and added considerably to Maxwell's ability to reconnoitre the countryside at a distance from the town.

The situation of the garrison was still precarious in spite of these reinforcements, and as the morning advanced this became increasingly obvious to the officers in charge. For one thing, the soldiers were exhausted. Maxwell's own Donegal militia were fatigued from their night march, and the approximately 1,000 men under Foote's command had remained at arms throughout the night in anticipation of a rebel attack and were probably severely demoralised.[20] To make matters worse, the hundreds of loyalist refugees who crammed the town were panic-stricken and added constantly to the general fear of rebel atrocities with their exaggerated tales of insurgent outrage.[21]

The garrison remained on the alert all morning, watching for the attack they expected to come at any moment. By midday there was no sign of it, but Maxwell continued to keep the large force of armed men along the walls, and he set other units to work demolishing the thatched cabins nearby. Mounted patrols passed in and out through the barricades at the various gates, now guarded by the artillery pieces, and scoured the countryside for up to three miles in all directions; it was some comfort that, as the morning hours and then midday passed, these patrols saw no sign of the rebels.[22] By the afternoon, though, Maxwell was anxiously sending messages to his patrols in the west to watch carefully for Fawcett's men, now urgently expected from Duncannon. But as the hours passed and there was no sign of them, the safety of the garrison and the loyalist inhabitants became an increasingly important concern.[23]

All through the day Maxwell and his fellow-officers had to contend with the tremendous problems created by the crowds of loyalist refugees. At some point in the day, probably well before noon, some of these decided that the town was already lost and tried to persuade boatmen to row them out to the trading ships that were anchored in the harbour. They offered money to the oarsmen, many of whom complied and brought the fugitives out to the ships. Many of the ships' captains were United Irishmen, however, and were waiting expectantly for the rebellion to succeed. Naturally they refused to sail for Wales in spite of the pleadings of the loyalists, and to other refugees watching from the quayside this was all the proof they needed that they were trapped and doomed.[24] The rebel sympathisers among the population must have observed all this with great satisfaction.

Around the middle of the day, as the flight to the ships proceeded, there was yet another development which further undermined the garrison's morale. A small party of civilians had left the town at dawn that morning to go to Oulart Hill and retrieve the bodies of the officers who had died there. When they arrived back across the bridge, they had the bodies of Major Lombard and the other officers with them. The corpses were badly mangled and must have been a gruesome sight after two days. The widows and children of the dead men began to wail over the bodies, just as they had done three days before, creating a scene that must have had a devastating effect on those soldiers and loyalist civilians who witnessed it.[25]

By one or two o'clock many of the more prominent citizens had been infected by this general demoralisation, and they made moves to persuade Maxwell to sue for terms with the rebels before they could attack the town. Edward Hay, without question a United Irishman,[26] was still at liberty in the streets, and even before midday several local loyalists had asked him to go to Enniscorthy and persuade the rebels to disperse. They recognised that as a liberal Hay would be in a position to influence them, but he refused to ride northwards alone and insisted that a magistrate accompany him. No one would agree to do this, and the attempt to use him as a mediator fell through for the time.[27]

By the afternoon the clamour from the loyalists was becoming more insistent, and eventually, with James Boyd taking a leading role, they managed to persuade Maxwell to attempt a bold diplomatic move. First, he should send a messenger to Fawcett to let him know how serious the situation was to the north (Fawcett may not have known of the fall of Enniscorthy yet) and to ask that the reinforcements be sent immediately. Then he should dispatch two of the United Irish leaders he had in custody to Enniscorthy on condition that they promise to try to persuade the rebels to disperse. The plan had the disadvantage of requiring the release of two important rebel leaders who might break their word and simply join their comrades, but Maxwell decided to keep the third prisoner in jail as a hostage against such a betrayal. In addition, he asked five local gentry and the released prisoners themselves to pledge substantial amounts of money as surety for their behaviour. From a military point of view, Maxwell had little to lose by the plan—indeed, it might gain him some valuable time.[28]

There was a prolonged discussion at the jail involving all three prisoners and some of the town authorities before they agreed on the details of the plan. In the end Fitzgerald and Colclough both consented to ride to Enniscorthy and plead with the rebels there, while Harvey stayed behind as a hostage. George Sutton, a prominent loyalist citizen, volunteered to ride out to Duncannon with the request for immediate reinforcement. Sutton rode out through the John's Lane Gate around the middle of the afternoon, and the two United Irishmen rode out by the Selskar Gate for Enniscorthy at about the same time.[29] Bagenal Harvey was now the only United leader in prison, while elsewhere in the town Matthew Keogh and Dick Monk and their men watched and waited. In the countryside to the south of the town hundreds of rebels, including Cornelius Grogan at Johnstown, continued to bide their time too.

Colclough and Fitzgerald rode northwards along the west bank of the Slaney and reached the outskirts of Enniscorthy at St John's in an hour or two without incident. Somewhere near St John's they suddenly met a group of rebels who had come down from Vinegar Hill and were making their way homeward, possibly out of frustration at their leaders' indecision. As soon as they recognised the two horsemen, the rebels surrounded them and raised a tremendous cheer which could be heard as far as the town and Vinegar Hill itself. Then they escorted them as if in triumph back to the camp.[30]

We will never know what thoughts were in Fitzgerald's and Colclough's minds at this point, nor what they actually said to the other rebel leaders when they got to the summit of the hill, but circumstances suggest that they may have actually tried to persuade the rebels to disperse. Fitzgerald in particular seems to have taken this position, an extraordinary one for such a prominent United Irishman, and the reaction among the leaders who had brought the movement this far was predictable: they were very angry. In the end, after intense discussion, they decided to release Colclough and send him back to Wexford with the message that they would not disperse but would soon march south and demand the surrender of the town. Fitzgerald, on the other hand, whom they now treated practically as a traitor, was detained in the camp as a counter-hostage to Harvey.[31] The entire episode may have been an elaborate effort to deceive the garrison into thinking that Fitzgerald was loyal to his promise when he was not, but it appears that he did in fact try to carry out his instructions and, as a result, was kept virtually as a prisoner by his suspicious erstwhile comrades.

Colclough set off alone back along the road to Wexford as evening approached. When he reached the town, he rode directly to the Bullring, and there, with the garrison's officers and several prominent loyalist citizens gathered around him, he announced the rebel response. Then he asked that they let him ride out into the Bargy and Forth countryside to dissuade at least the United Irish units in that area from rising. The officers agreed, and after a brief consultation with Harvey, the subject of which we do not know (but the meeting itself is a suspicious circumstance), he left the town for his home at Ballyteige, some ten miles away on the south coast of the county. If he kept faith with Maxwell, he spent the evening visiting local rebel captains and persuading them not to rise; if he did not, his journey home may well have involved last-minute contacts with these men and hurried confirmation of a planned mobilisation in the next day or so.[32]

At about the time Colclough was making his way into Bargy and Forth the rebel army at Vinegar Hill, now well over 10,000 strong (Miles Byrne recalled it as amounting to about 16,000),[33] was breaking camp and beginning its march south. They took the road on the east bank of the Slaney, but then turned to the south-west at Ferrycarrig and made for the high ground of Forth Mountain as the twilight deepened and camped near Three Rocks, a group of outcroppings at its peak. The leaders had already decided to defer an attack on the town until morning, and the mountain was an ideal place to camp for the night. It was the highest point in the southern half of the county and lay two miles to the west of Wexford, over which it towered. Because of its height and position, it cut off the garrison from a quick retreat to the west and the safety of Duncannon or New Ross. It also functioned as an important rallying-point for rebels in the south-east who were now ready to join in the campaign.[34]

By the time darkness began to fall the rebels had encamped on the side of the mountain. Their camp-fires were clearly visible from the town, and the sound of the horns they began to use to communicate between one unit and another could be heard for miles in the summer night.[35] Maxwell's garrison was now trapped, and to loyalist and rebel alike a decisive showdown seemed imminent unless massive reinforcements came from the west soon.

In contrast to these dramatic developments in central and

southern Wexford, the third day of rebellion was remarkably uneventful in the far north and far west of the county. That morning Major Hardy, the commander of the Arklow garrison, held a regular inspection of the Gorey yeomanry and warned them that they should behave like soldiers from this point on. At around five o'clock that afternoon, as the rebels were preparing to leave Vinegar Hill for the Three Rocks, a small party of yeomen rode back into Gorey and took possession of the town once again.[36] The whereabouts of the rebels was probably still a mystery to them at this stage. At Arklow in the meantime the loyalist civilians from Wexford had suffered numerous indignities at the hands of the Antrim militia, and most of them passed the day taking what shelter they could in the streets, where they were forced to huddle for the second night in succession.[37] Major Hardy was clearly terrified by the possibility that there were insurgent fifth-columnists among them, and the merest suggestion of this must have led to real hysteria among the refugees.

At Newtownbarry and New Ross anxiety about the rebels increased too, but, as at Gorey, the garrison commanders were puzzled as to their whereabouts. Refugees were never numerous in Newtownbarry,[38] and the influx had probably abated there by this time, but at New Ross there were large numbers of them and these were augmented by new arrivals throughout the day, many coming in from Old Ross, the Palatine settlement four miles east of the town. There was nowhere for these people to find shelter, and Charles Tottenham allowed many of them to stay in a row of houses he had just completed building.[39] As of yet, though, in spite of many rumours about their strength and cruelty, there had been no sign of rebel units anywhere nearby, and for the time being, with the rebellion apparently confined to the central and northern areas, local loyalists are likely to have remained fairly confident about their ability to fight off an attack should one eventually come.

The reality, however, was that the rebels were in a very strong position by midnight. To Edward Roche and the other chiefs who were with him in the hastily constructed camp on Forth Mountain, things must have seemed to be going very well. In the space of three days they had driven their enemies from all of central and most of northern Wexford, and now the county town itself and its large garrison was almost within their grasp. The strange behaviour of Colcough and Fitzgerald was no doubt disconcerting, but once Wexford town fell to them, the task of liberating the rest of the county would surely seem a simple one. After all, they must have reasoned, if their comrades in the rest of Leinster were experiencing the same kind of success that they were enjoying themselves, then places like Gorey, Newtownbarry, New Ross and Duncannon would be taken with ease. What they did not know as they passsed the night on Forth Mountain, was that the rising in north Leinster had come to a tragic end that very afternoon in a massacre at Gibbet Rath in northern Kildare[40] and that no rebellion at all had broken out in Munster, Ulster or Connacht. As they prepared for their own grand triumph, then, they were unaware that the national cause was as good as lost and that in fact they were now completely alone.

They were also unaware, as they watched the town through the darkness, that reinforcements were on the way from Duncannon to relieve the garrison at that very moment and that these troops were headed straight for the western slope of the mountain on which they were encamped. George Sutton had reached Duncannon that afternoon without difficulty, and Fawcett had evidently listened sympathetically to his pleading. The general had decided to set out with about 200 militia himself late that afternoon, but he realised that he could not reach Wexford by nightfall and so chose to stop for the hours of darkness at Taghmon, six miles to the west of the town and just over two miles from the western slope of Forth Mountain. He had no idea, as he covered the early stage of the journey, that the rebel army was then marching south itself and would already be established on the mountain before he would get to Taghmon. He left instructions for a force of about a hundred men, mostly Meath militia but also including some members of the Royal Artillery, to follow him later and to join with him at Taghmon. This second column was critical to the operation since they were to bring several pieces of cannon with them.[41]

By midnight Fawcett himself and his small column had already reached Taghmon, just a few miles behind the rebel camp. The general found a place to rest until dawn and billeted his men in various parts of the village. The column of Meath militia and

Royal Artillerymen arrived an hour or two after midnight, but, amazingly, they saw no sign that Fawcett had stopped there. They were confused about what to do, and their young officers decided to press on towards Wexford, even though it was dark and they did not know the road. They had no idea that it would bring them along the northern slope of Forth Mountain and within yards of the huge rebel force.[42]

RUSE DE GUERRE
30 MAY

DAWN WAS BREAKING WHEN THE COLUMN OF MEATH MILITIA and Royal Artillery approached the western slope of Forth Mountain.[1] The road they were taking ran along the northern face of the hill for about two miles and then descended its eastern end.[2] The main part of the rebel camp was at the eastern edge of the mountain, overlooking Wexford town, but small detachments of insurgents were in various positions along the summit and there were a few units stationed at its western end. Most of these, especially the latter group, were there primarily as lookouts.[3]

The militia and artillery officers had stopped and asked some local people if there was a rebel force in the vicinity a short time before they reached the hill and had been assured that none were close by. When, having reached the top of the slope, they spotted several men on the hill above them, they concluded that these were just an isolated group of rebels and represented no threat. They stopped for a few moments to watch them, but then shouldered arms and pushed on.[4]

The rebel detachment had noticed the soldiers by this point, and one of them made his way along the summit of the hill and reported what he had seen to Thomas Cloney. Cloney in turn rushed further east and told Edward Roche of what was happening, and, after some confusion, they agreed that the bulk of the rebel army should stay where it was and that the Bantrymen, thus far uninitiated in combat, should attack the approaching column before it proceeded too far along the hill.[5]

Cloney and several of the other Bantry officers, Robert Carty of Birchgrove, John Kelly of Killann, and Michael Furlong of Templescoby among them, immediately got their regiment ready

on the slope at a point above the the road and waited for the
column of soldiers to arrive immediately below them. Meanwhile
Roche and the other leaders waited patiently to hear of the
outcome of the attack. The Bantry unit probably numbered at
least a thousand men, maybe more, and they had some firearms,
although probably less than the militia. However, they held the
high ground and would have the element of surprise on their side.[6]

The soldiers finally appeared, still pushing their way eastward
with no apparent suspicion of what their situation was, even when
they were almost parallel to the Bantrymen's position. The rebels
waited quietly until they got the signal to open fire, the raising of
a white flag on the slope below them. When the flag appeared,
several of the soldiers noticed it, but the rebels opened fire almost
immediately and threw the column into complete confusion.
There was a fierce musketry duel for a few minutes, but soon some
of the soldiers began to retreat back along the road towards the
west and others scrambled across the hedgerow below them in an
effort to escape. Cloney's men held their ground on the slope for a
while, but when it became clear that the column was giving
ground they made a headlong charge with bayonet and pike down
the hill. The force of the charge carried them across the fence,
onto the road and into the middle of the column. Hand-to-hand
fighting now broke out along the length of the line, and the
troops had no effective answer for the determined Bantrymen. A
few of the artillery gunners tried to spike the howitzers, but
insurgents got to the guns in time and saved them. In the
confusion a spark struck the powder and it blew up, depriving
them of an important prize, but the weapons themselves were
firmly in their control.[7]

The action was over in no more than fifteen minutes, and it
was a total rebel victory. The young artillery commander,
Lieutenant Birch, together with another artillery officer and about
half a dozen privates, made their escape westward along the road
and got back down the slope on the Taghmon side safely. Another
artillery officer and about a dozen gunners were captured. The
entire militia detachment, about seventy men in all, were either
killed, wounded or scattered, and the rebels seized almost all their
muskets, pistols and sabres, as well as the all-important howitzers.[8]

Fawcett only learned of the disaster when Birch and the other

FORTH MOUNTAIN, WEXFORD TOWN AND VICINITY, 29 – 30 MAY

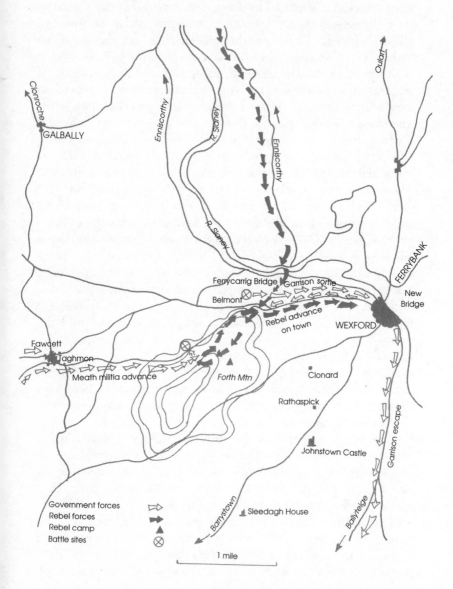

Government forces

Rebel forces

Rebel camp

Battle sites

1 mile

survivors got back to Taghmon and gave him the news. He saw immediately how exposed he now was himself should the rebels choose to make a drive to the west, and so he ordered his men to turn around and retreat to Duncannon, abandoning the garrison in Wexford town that he had come to reinforce and leaving the entire southern part of the county open.[9] Maxwell was now hopelessly cut off, and his one advantage, the fact that he had artillery and the rebels had none, was suddenly gone. (Curiously, George Sutton reached Wexford safely around dawn with word that reinforcements were on their way from Duncannon; it is unclear how he managed to get past the rebel camp on Forth Mountain.)[10]

The rebels were now in the strongest position yet, and Roche and his aides knew well how difficult it would be for the garrison to escape. Their confidence was boosted further not long after dawn when they suddenly noticed a column of smoke rising into the sky just beyond the town. The toll house on the northern end of the bridge had been set on fire by a crowd of rebels or rebel sympathisers from the countryside to its north. As the building burned, the crowd thronged the Ferrybank area on the north side of the river and prevented the garrison from making any serious effort to come out and save it. The flames quickly engulfed the entire building and then began to spread to the bridge itself. The ships that were anchored in the harbour were dangerously close to the long wooden structure, and most of their captains raised anchor and floated the vessels downstream to a point closer to the harbour mouth, a move which added to the fears of the watching loyalists, for whom ships were the only means of escape. Many of them had come out into the street, and some had begun to gather on the quays. A few now made desperate attempts to escape in spite of the report that help was on its way from Duncannon, some even jumping into the water and trying to swim to the anchored vessels. Most remained on the quay, however, and watched helplessly as the fire gutted the northern end of the bridge. Eventually a party of soldiers did dare to go out along the bridge. They tore up some of the planks when they got half-way across and managed to stop the fire from destroying it completely and from spreading to the town itself. But while this prompt action had averted an immediate crisis, it also ensured that any possibilty of escaping northwards in the event of a rebel atttack from Forth Mountain had now vanished.[11]

The United Irishmen in the town still watched and waited patiently. Whether based in the ships in the harbour, or in the cabin suburbs like John Street, or in the fishing villages at the Faythe and Oyster Lane, they realised they should not make their move yet. Their leaders likewise concealed their intentions for the time, but they must have watched the fire across the bridge and the panic it instilled among the loyalists with tremendous satisfaction and anticipation.[12]

As the sun rose higher in the sky and dawn turned into morning, Maxwell and his officers became increasingly anxious about the reinforcements from Duncannon. George Sutton had been back for some time and confirmed that Fawcett and his men should be reaching Forth Mountain soon, so the difficulty now was to get him and his column into the town safely in spite of the fact that thousands of rebels were in occupation of the mountain. Maxwell could either stay where he was and hope that Fawcett would find a way around the rebel camp somehow, or he could take some of his own men out towards the rebel lines and try to help him get through. The latter course would involve the risk of taking to the open country with a substantial portion of the garrison which might then find itself caught in a sudden rebel offensive; but in the end he decided to take this risk, and so, at around 8 or 9 a.m., he ordered his officers to get ready to march.

Maxwell took several hundred men with him when he rode out past the John Street entrance of the town towards the northern flank of Forth Mountain. Most of these were militia, among them all of his own Donegals, but they also included the Taghmon yeoman cavalry, and he asked Jonas Watson to ride alongside him; the latter's experience fighting rebels in America might now prove useful. The North Corks and most of the local yeomanry remained behind in the town.[13]

The insurgents had placed the two howitzers captured a few hours before from the Meath militia and Royal Artillery near their front lines on the eastern slope of the mountain by this time, and the guns covered the road along which Maxwell would have to pass. Those rebels who had had experience with artillery, including John Hay and William Barker, directed their operation.[14] Most of their comrades took up positions some distance up the slope but there were a few detachments at the bottom of the hill which functioned primarily as lookouts.[15]

The rebel leaders did not see Maxwell's column initially since a low ridge cut off their view of the John Street entrance to Wexford, but they spotted the soldiers once they had crossed this ridge, and at that point the front ranks of the approaching force were not much more than a mile and a half away.[16] Roche and his officers immediately prepared for the attack they thought was coming, and the gunners got ready to use their new prizes for the first time.

As far as Maxwell knew, Fawcett and his column of over 200 men were somewhere just beyond the high ground in front of him. He apparently assumed that the general and his men might get through if he could intimidate the insurgents into remaining on the hill. He had no idea, of course, that at this very moment Fawcett was making his way back to Duncannon as fast as he could and that well over a third of his force lay dead on and near the road just two miles ahead of him. As he got closer to the rebel positions Maxwell sent the Taghmon cavalry off some distance to his left to cover his flank on that side. Shortly afterwards the rebel gunners fired a shot from one of the howitzers which landed close to the front of the column, announcing the fact that the insurgent army had artillery and hinting that something had already gone badly wrong with the attempt to locate the reinforcements and escort them around the mountain.

As the rebel leaders watched from the hilltop and their gunners fired several more shots from the howitzers, they noticed that the Taghmon cavalry was coming closer to their right flank and that a small detachment of soldiers was riding forward from the main body on the road directly in front of them. The detachment in question was headed by Jonas Watson, who had persuaded Maxwell to let him take a few privates and ride closer to the rebel lines to reconnoitre. As Watson and his men came closer to the foot of the hill, one of the small rebel advance detachments spotted them. Then, when the party of mounted soldiers got within range, they suddenly fired several shots at them, hitting Watson. The men with him wheeled their horses about in panic and galloped all the way back to the main column, but their leader fell from his saddle and died on the roadside.

Now the rebels further up the slopes and to the right had began to move into position to attack the Taghmon cavalry. Captain Cox saw this happening and started to pull his men back, and Maxwell suddenly realised that he was in grave danger himself and that he could do little or nothing to help Fawcett at this stage. He quickly ordered a retreat, and in a matter of minutes this turned into a full-fledged flight. The rebels on the hillside watched with delight as the soldiers rushed back to the safety of the town and its walls, but the leaders resisted any temptation they felt to pursue the fleeing troops; with the succession of victories they now had behind them and with all signs good for a successful siege of the county town, there was no reason to take unnecessary risks. They stayed where they were for the present and left the next move up to the beleaguered garrison.[17]

As these dramatic developments took place in and around the town, Bagenal Harvey still languished in his cell in the jail. He was alone and frightened and at some point climbed up inside the chimney to hide.[18] His United Irish comrades outside, including Edward Hay, Matthew Keogh, Dick Monk and others, remained free. Ten miles to the south, on the other hand, John Henry Colclough had just spent the night at home with his wife, and at about the time that Maxwell made his ill-fated sally out towards Forth Mountain they left Ballyteige Castle together and began the journey back into Wexford in a phaeton. Colclough was voluntarily returning to jail and probably had turned his back on the rebellion at this point.[19] In the meantime his colleague in diplomacy of the previous day, Edward Fitzgerald, was still with the rebel camp on Forth Mountain, but he had lost most of his standing among his fellow United Irishmen and was playing only a marginal role, if even that, among the cadre of leaders.[20]

Soon after Maxwell and his column got back inside Wexford town the garrison suddenly began to collapse. A few of the yeomen had fled shortly before this, making their way in desperation westwards towards Duncannon, and trying to cross the south Wexford countryside without being noticed by the rebels. One of these was Archibald Jacob, who, according to rebel tradition, had also been one of the first to flee from Enniscorthy two days earlier.[21] He was followed soon after by Isaac Cornock's Scarawalsh yeoman infantry and the detachment of the North Corks under Captain Snowe. These had both been assigned to a barricade at Barrack Street, at the southern entrance to the town, but they suddenly abandoned their post and fled after Jacob's escape, making their way southwards towards Rosslare at first and then turning westwards and heading for the village of Mayglass, apparently hoping to make their way to Duncannon before the rebels even realised that they had gone.[22]

Maxwell may not have been aware of these departures,[23] but at about the time that they took place he and his fellow-officers began to confer with the prominent citizens of the town as to their next move. The mayor, Ebenezer Jacob, was among those he talked to, and since he was a liberal Protestant, Maxwell immediately assumed that he, along with Bagenal Harvey, might have some influence with the rebels. The colonel had evidently formulated a new strategy by this time, which was to use anyone he could to negotiate with the enemy but then to grab the opportunity to slip out of the town himself and make his own way, along with most of his men, to the safety of Duncannon. This necessitated betraying those who had agreed to talk with the rebel leaders, but he was evidently prepared to do this.

After talking with Jacob, Maxwell decided that the best course would be to ask Harvey to go out to Forth Mountain with the request that the rebels should not damage the town or take revenge on its defenders if they surrendered peacefully. This would give him the chance to slip away. A delegation of officers went to the jail, where they found Harvey hiding in the chimney. When they eventually managed to pull him down, he refused to have anything to do with the proposed mission. The rebels, he claimed, were from areas of the county unfamiliar to him and therefore would not listen to him. Maxwell and the officers took him at his word, although they did ask him to write a note to the rebel leaders on the mountain asking them to spare the town and its garrison.[24]

It was now around ten o'clock and Colclough had still not arrived back from his sojourn in Bargy and Forth, and so there was no option open to Maxwell but to find someone from the town itself that the rebels might trust. Initially a Catholic yeoman volunteered to take the message out, but Maxwell turned him down.[25] Then two well-known liberal Protestants, the brothers Loftus and Thomas Richards, volunteered to do it, and he agreed. So, at around ten o'clock in the morning, the two men rode out towards the rebel camp, taking some people from the cabins on the edge of the town along with them for safety.[26]

Maxwell set about mustering his men for the retreat as soon as the two delegates left. He passed the word quietly (the drums were not even used), and then he led almost the entire garrison, over a thousand men, out along the road to the south. Only one unit, Ebenezer Jacob's Wexford yeoman infantry, remained behind. Jacob may have elected to stay behind himself, but it is possible that Maxwell kept this entire unit in the dark about his plans and essentially abandoned them. He abandoned the vast majority of the loyalist refugees too. A few of the soldiers did take their families with them, but most of the rest were still going about the town or waiting on the ships in the habour as the garrison departed, and many may not even have been aware of the retreat.[27]

At about the time that Maxwell's rearguard got out of sight of the town the rebel leaders on Forth Mountain saw the Richards brothers riding towards their outposts with a white flag raised above their heads. The sentries let them pass on, and they made their way up the slope to where Roche and the other officers were gathered. One of the emissaries then read Harvey's note aloud. It promised that the garrison would hand over all their arms if the bargain were kept—heartening news to the insurgents. They were unsure as to whether they could trust Maxwell, however, and so before making a response they insisted that the Richards brothers ride west as far as Taghmon with Edward Fitzgerald to make sure that Fawcett had actually left for Duncannon. The brothers agreed and set out on their new mission at once; meanwhile the entire rebel army remained where it was.[28]

At least an hour had elapsed by the time the Richards brothers and Fitzgerald returned to Forth Mountain, and Maxwell and his men had made their way several miles into the Bargy and Forth countryside by that time. At one point John Hay suggested that a small detachment ride south to prevent the garrison from escaping; he was an experienced soldier and realised that such a move was one obvious option open to them. However, Roche and the other rebel leaders dismissed the suggestion, preferring to preserve the security that a unified force gave them; thus the chance to foil Maxwell was lost.[29]

The rebel leaders had finally concluded that they had Maxwell trapped and that there was nobody coming to his rescue, when the Richards brothers and Fitzgerald come back from Taghmon with the news that Fawcett and his remnant had long since left. Assuming that Maxwell had no escape, and certainly not suspecting that he and his men were already gone and were drawing further away from the town with every passing minute, they decided to send one of the Richards brothers and Fitzgerald into the town to insist on the surrender of all arms and to supervise the process. Then, shortly after the two had gone, they ordered the army to break camp and move down towards the outskirts. This move probably took some time, perhaps as much as an hour, but eventually, by around eleven or twelve o'clock, the insurgent army reached Windmill Hill, just to the east of John Street. There, on the very edge of the town, they halted and formed another camp, waiting, it seems, for the garrison to come out and lay down their arms.[30]

The garrison was by this time miles away and making rapid progress towards Duncannon. Archibald Jacob was moving fastest of all. He had been fleeing westward for an hour or more by now and had reached Barrystown, the point where a narrow causeway provided a passage across the head of Bannow Bay at low tide. The tide was in, though, and high, and he had to make the long journey north until he found a place to cross the Corock River. Then he was able to begin the last leg of his flight, the journey across the northern parishes of Shelburne barony to Duncannon.[31] The detachment of about 200 men under Cornock and Snowe, the second group to flee, was about ten miles behind him when he got to Barrystown, and they were making steady progress too.[32]

As for Maxwell and the larger column, they were probably two or three miles from the town when the rebel army settled down on Windmill Hill. This meant that a determined chase by the rebels might yet catch them, but as they did not have any organised cavalry companies, the chance of doing this was disappearing by the minute.

Inside the town, meanwhile, Ebenezer Jacob was desperately trying to come to terms with the new situation. Richards and Fitzgerald arrived shortly after the last of the garrison had gone, but by that stage the rebels on the northern end of the bridge had begun to place planks onto its burned section and were likely to break through to the quays at any moment. Apart from his own detachment of yeomanry and some of the armed civilians, Jacob had no troops and further resistance was impossible. He could not foretell what the rebels' reaction would be once they discovered that they had been duped, and his worst fear was that they would destroy the town and massacre the loyalists.[33]

The desperate mayor sensibly assumed that Edward Fitzgerald would have some influence with the insurgents from the countryside to the north of the bridge, and he persuaded him to go to the Custom House Quay and dissuade them from harming persons or property once they got across. Fitzgerald agreed to do this, but when he arrived at the bridge they were already making their way across and largely ignored any efforts he made to stop them. In a matter of minutes they spilled onto the quays and began to push up the narrow lanes and into the centre of the town, cheering as they went. The Wexford yeomanry realised the issue was decided, and they ripped off their uniforms and hastily donned civilian clothes and threw their guns into the water or hid them wherever they could.[34]

The rebels from north of the bridge made their way into every quarter of the town in triumph. One group broke into the jail and released Bagenal Harvey. Finally free, the most prominent United Irishman in this part of the county paraded back towards the centre of the town, as rebels from the town itself came out into the streets and celebrated the near-bloodless victory. The massive destruction of life and property that the loyalists had feared did not occur. Bands of insurgents attacked buildings that symbolised the old regime and its main supporters, such as James Boyd's house on George's Street and the Custom House nearby, but most of them simply milled about the streets. Some ran up green and white flags on a number of prominent buildings as a formal declaration that the town had been liberated.[35]

The sailors in the ships anchored in the harbour promptly answered the signal by running up their own white flags, thereby demonstrating their common cause with the country rebels and revealing how well organised the entire movement was.[36]

The main rebel army finally moved after the Ferrybank group had taken complete possession. They marched in in good order, and they too refrained from vengeance attacks. The townspeople signified their approval by hanging green flags and boughs from their windows and by bringing food and drink out into the streets for the famished men. Those who had been in the field for several days were by now very hungry, and they spread out all over the town taking advantage of the generosity of the citizens. The scene quickly became chaotic as thousands of rebels and country people thronged the crowded, narrow streets, but still the orgy of violence and plunder that so many loyalists had predicted did not take place; instead the atmosphere seems to have been one of celebration.[37]

It was only after they entered the town that the rebel leaders realised how they had been fooled by Maxwell. In response they organised an effort to ferret out any yeomen or other prominent loyalists who were concealing themselves. Small search parties of about half a dozen men began to go from house to house looking for them and for any firearms they were concealing.[38] At the same time, and for the same reason, the captains of the ships were given the signal to return to the quay. Two of them did not comply and sailed their vessels out of the harbour and made for the Welsh coast, but the rest obeyed the order, and when they docked large crowds were waiting for them. Once the loyalist fugitives came ashore, the rebels detained the men and marched them down the quays to the jail; the women and children were allowed to go free and fend for themselves in the crowded town.[39] By evening, as a consequence of the searches, there were close to a hundred prisoners crammed into the small jail; they were a mixture of yeomen and civilian loyalists, and, in view of the foreboding with which many of them had witnessed the rebel triumph, they may have greeted the confinement with some relief.[40]

John Hay once again suggested that a detachment march in pursuit of the the fleeing garrison later in the afternoon. However, the other leaders dismissed the idea yet again, probably because they assumed that the insurrection had triumphed as thoroughly elsewhere as it had in Wexford and so concluded that the garrison would soon be trapped anyway.[41] It was a reasonable assumption to make in the circumstances.

Meanwhile the various sections of the garrison were making steady headway in their retreat to the west. After they had passed through Mayglass the column under Cornock and Snowe headed directly for the causeway across Bannow Bay at Barrystown. Somewhere along the route, perhaps even before they reached Mayglass, they met John Henry Colclough and his wife travelling in the direction of the town. Snowe forced them to turn about and accompany him and his men as hostages. As they crossed the Bargy countryside small detachments of mobilising rebels occasionally appeared on ridges above them, but each time they did so Snowe forced Colclough to stand up and to plead with them to let the party pass. The tactic worked, and by the time they approached Barrystown there were no more rebel units to be seen. The officers were confident that they would not encounter any on the west side of the bay, and so they let Colclough and his wife go just before they reached the crossing-point; a friend of Colclough's named King lived nearby, and the young couple drove to his house to find shelter for the night.

Cornock and Snowe realised that the tide was in, making the causeway impassable once they got to Barrystown. Since their column numbered over 200, including some civilians, they had no choice but to go four miles due north and cross the bridge at Foulkesmills, which would bring them to within four miles of Forth Mountain and put them in real danger of encountering bands of rebels. They had no other option, however, and, after a short rest, set off on the roundabout journey.[42]

By this time the main column had also made good progress in their flight. A short distance outside Wexford town James Boyd and some of his cavalry passed them out and rode on ahead towards Barrystown (effectively abandoning them). Some cavalry units did remain with Maxwell to protect the flanks and rear, including Grogan's Healthfield corps, and one of the yeomanry units had taken some men hostage as they left the town and they used these as a further protection. When they got to Mayglass, some local rebels who had begun to mobilise blocked their passage, and there was a brief skirmish, following which the outgunned rebels broke and fled. In revenge for the effort to block their escape, the soldiers shot several men they found near the village, and they also put to death the two hostages they had taken with them from Wexford. In addition, they raped several women in and near the village, the first known instance of this outrage during the rebellion, and set the local chapel on fire. They continued to shoot at anyone they saw as they pushed on towards Bannow Bay.[43]

By evening they reached Barrystown and found the tide still in. James Boyd and his handful of men had got there before them and had persuaded some fishermen to row them across. Maxwell's column was too large for this, however, and so, like the detachment before them, they had no option but to risk a march northwards to Foulkesmills, where they could cross the Corock and then turn west. When darkness finally fell that night, they were still struggling to reach the safety of Duncannon Fort.[44]

General Fawcett had long since made it back to his base and immediately put his entire family on board the packet ship that was sailing that day from Waterford to London. Archibald Jacob arrived with news of the disaster at Wexford not long afterwards, and James Boyd and his small mounted band reached the fort sometime in the late evening. The going was much slower for the two columns of infantry. Maxwell's group eventually reached the fort in the early hours of the following morning. The smaller group, under Cornock and Snowe, fared less well. They were ambushed in the dark as they crossed Taylorstown Bridge, about six miles from the fort, by the Rosegarland corps of rebels led by John Murphy of Loughnageer. The column was caught on the bridge below sloping woods on either side, and well over a dozen of them, along with several civilians, were killed in the musket fire directed at them from the higher ground. Eventually most of them escaped the trap, but the detachment lost its formation and finally arrived at Duncannon in small groups and at intervals over the ensuing hours.[45]

In Wexford town, by contrast, the state of affairs was remarkably peaceful, considering what many loyalists had expected. Ebenezer Jacob had made himself the chief liaison agent between the loyalist population and the insurgents, and since he was a well-known liberal and on friendly terms with many of the southern leaders, he was able to do this effectively. For some time conditions in the streets were still too chaotic for it to be possible to impose any kind of order, but the vital contacts that would allow for an astonishingly smooth transfer of power appear to have been made by the time dusk came on.[46] Unfortunately the process was marred by two murders. One victim was John Boyd, the brother of James Boyd. He was recognised by some insurgents as he was taken off one of the ships, and was immediately attacked by them. He broke away and tried to escape by running down the quay towards the bridge, but they caught up with him there and several of them plunged their pikes into his body and left him lying on the ground bleeding slowly to death; nobody attempted to help him, and several hours later somebody gave the *coup de grâce* with a hachet. Another local loyalist, a man named George Sparrow, was dragged to the Bullring and piked to death by a group of rebels. There were many other cases in which threats and abuse were directed at loyalists, but these were the only murders.[47]

The rest of the county had remained relatively quiet throughout the day. At New Ross loyalist refugees continued to trickle in, and Charles Tottenham's garrison was still in a precarious position and hoping for reinforcements from Waterford or Kilkenny. He set a large body of civilians to work digging trenches along the eastern edge of the town and thus put himself in a better position to defend the place should an attack come, but he remained ignorant of developments to the east, and by nightfall neither he nor the local United Irishmen realised what had happened at Wexford.[48]

Further north the day passed quietly too. The garrisons at Newtownbarry and Carnew held their positions and probed the countryside to the immediate south and east, but remained unsure as to what was going on further south. More significantly, government forces re-established themselves at Gorey in considerable numbers, suggesting that they were now certain that, whatever else the rebels might be doing, they were not about to move against them. Civilians and yeomanry alike had been anxious to return to the town, and scores of non-combatants accompanied the soldiers on the three-hour trek back. Most of the United Irishmen who lived in and near the town had gone to

Vinegar Hill with Perry two days before, and so the loyalists found the place very much as they had left it. They learned on their arrival that at one point during the previous day a crowd of women from the countryside had approached the town with the apparent intention of looting it, but a band of prominent local Catholics, unsympathetic to the United Irishmen, had armed themselves and frightened them off.[49] As they re-established themselves in their former positions many of them may have assumed that government forces in the southern part of the county were easily capable of checkmating the rebels and that the affair would soon be over. They were, of course, unaware of the fall of Wexford town at this stage.

On balance, then, the day was one of triumph for the Wexford rebel cause. However, the fact that some of the more important members of the organisation were still missing was undoubtedly an ongoing concern. John Henry Colclough was passing the night at Barrystown, though the leaders in the town could not have known this; and Cornelius Grogan was still in Johnstown, a fact that might have eluded them too. The most worrying absence was that of Edward Fitzgerald; he had mysteriously vanished into the countryside to the north of Wexford Bridge at about the time the rebels took the town. He presumably went to his home at Newpark, but his reasons for doing so are not clear; it is possible that he felt so alienated from his comrades at this stage that he contemplated withdrawing from the rebellion altogether. This was a curious twist to the drama, considering the very prominent role which he had apparently held in the United Irish organisation before his arrest.[50]

In spite of this and a few other minor setbacks, however, the Wexford United Irish organisation appeared to have fully recovered from the arrests that had almost destroyed it a few days before. They had now captured the two largest towns in the county and had either overwhelmed or overawed their opponents. They had done all that was required of them in the United Irish plan, therefore, and had done it in three remarkable days. Leaders and rank and file alike could be forgiven for assuming that things had gone equally well elsewhere in the country and that the republic was already in existence. The only task that remained for them appeared to be to consolidate the liberation of their county and to await instructions from the provisional government which they believed to be already in place in Dublin.

FIRST REVERSES
31 MAY – 1 JUNE

THE NIGHT WAS EXTRAORDINARILY QUIET IN WEXFORD TOWN. Many of the rebels left once darkness fell and went to their homes in the surrounding countryside, while most of those who had come from the central and northern parts of the county returned to the camp on Windmill Hill.[1]

Once dawn broke the next morning, all those who had spent the night outside the town made their way back and crammed the streets once again. The searches for concealed loyalists and for arms and ammunition began again almost as soon as the darkness lifted. The outcome was disappointing: by midday the search parties had only found a small quantity of arms, some ammunition and three barrels of powder; the garrison had done a thorough job in depriving them of the spoils.[2]

At some point in the morning Cornelius Grogan arrived at the head of about 2,000 Bargy and Forth men. He was by far the oldest of the United Irish leaders and looked very stately riding a white horse. The additional manpower probably brought the strength of the rebel army up to at least 20,000 men and it may even have exceeded this by midday. Grogan's own presence brought the leadership circle very close to completion; only Colclough and the wayward Fitzgerald were now missing.[3]

Fitzgerald's behaviour the day before was probably still a mystery to many of the officers. However, he too arrived back in the town during the morning, and some kind of reconciliation took place. He had evidently spent the night at his home, pondering his future role in the affair, but by daybreak had decided to throw himself back into the campaign. When he rode across the bridge, several rebels challenged him and a few even threatened his life, such was their distrust of him. Eventually he persuaded them to let him pass, and he thereupon rejoined the army in the town. It would take him weeks to re-establish himself as one of the most important rebel officers, but re-establish himself he eventually did, and in the end his role would be a distinguished one.[4]

Sometime before midday the last of the rebel chiefs, John Henry Colclough, came in. He and his wife had passed the night peacefully at Barrystown, and during the morning hours had made their way back towards the town. Nobody interfered with them as they went, and by the time they reached the rebel camp they were very probably accompanied by rebels from the parishes to the south-west of Forth.[5]

Now it was time to think about consolidating their hold on the county and preparing for the official declaration of a republic. As the first step in this the rebel leaders ordered all the units that were still inside the town to move out to Windmill Hill.[6] Then, once most of them were settled on the hill, the officers held a council and began to discuss their next moves. The meeting lasted for some time and was contentious, but in the end they decided to split their forces into a southern division which would move to the west and deal with the government foothold at New Ross (and perhaps Duncannon), and a northern one which would attack the loyalist positions in Newtownbarry and Gorey.[7] This done, their task would be complete from a military point of view, and their only duty after that would be to keep order in the county and await word from Dublin.

They also had to consider the question of leadership. This was not a pressing issue, since any arrangements they made would be temporary and the provisional government in Dublin might well change them, but they agreed that the northern division, the one that would attack Gorey and Newtownbarry, would be commanded by Edward Roche, and that the southern force would be under Bagenal Harvey.[8] Harvey was also made commander-in-chief for the entire county, but it is clear that the office was largely symbolic, as it was decided that he would march west with the southern division instead of stationing himself in a central location from which he could direct both. This, along with the division of the forces itself, is consistent with their assumption that the only remaining task was to complete the liberation of the county.[9]

The meeting also had to consider the problem of governing the county until agents of the provisional government in Dublin arrived. The chief concern was Wexford town itself. As a sizeable settlement it would need to be provisioned now that the normal channels of trade had been disrupted; it was also necessary to devise measures to prevent a breakdown of law and order, which was a real possibility in the revolutionary climate that had so suddenly come to prevail. To deal with these problems they chose a governing committee made up of Matthew Keogh as governor, William Kearney as his assistant, Ebenezer Jacob as medical officer, and Cornelius Grogan as commissar. In addition, they made Edward Hay head of munitions manufacturing and seized a small press in the town to print proclamations and other documents, including vouchers for food and fuel. The makeshift town government was well chosen, and, significantly, it included the former mayor.[10]

The rebel leaders avoided any temptation to create a county-wide government or to declare a 'Republic of Wexford', and so no special provision was made for the government of the rural districts.[11] The implication was that the northern and southern divisions would establish military rule in these areas until such time as the provisional government could establish its authority.[12]

The first groups of rebels began to leave Windmill Hill to carry out their new tasks early in the afternoon. The northern division was the first to depart. Its leaders, Roche, Perry, Father John Murphy, Father Michael Murphy and Garrett Byrne, divided it into companies and brigades by parish and barony and then led them out to Forth Mountain, where they joined with Father Mogue Kearns and a group of his Scarawalsh units that had never come into the town. The combined force amounted to at least 10,000 men, and they covered the ten miles to Vinegar Hill in a few hours. There they divided once again into a column of a few thousand which pushed on to Carrigrew, about ten miles to the north-east, to be in position to attack Gorey on the following day, and another group numbering 1,000 or 2,000 which remained at Enniscorthy and was to storm Newtownbarry at the same time. The column which marched to Carrigrew was led by Roche, while Kearns took command of the one which was to move against

Newtownbarry; this detachment included Miles Byrne and the Monaseed corps. By the time Roche got his men to their final destination it was evening, and many of them, back near their homes now for the first time in five days, slipped away to spend the night with their families. Their officers could only hope that by morning most of them would return.[13]

The southern division passed the afternoon and evening of this critical day in a very different way. After the departure of the northern group Bagenal Harvey invited his fellow-officers and several of the more moderate loyalists of the town to a dinner in his house; in doing this he was probably trying to consolidate his own political position. As the northern division was pushing on towards Enniscorthy, then, the southern leaders moved back into Wexford town and gathered at Harvey's house along with men like Ebenezer Jacob and even Edward Turner of Newfort, the man who had brought the news of rebellion into Wexford in the first place and who had set the cabins on fire in Oulart village on the day of the battle there.

A crowd gathered outside Harvey's house as soon as it was realised what was happening, and some of them recognised Turner as he went in. Almost immediately they began to demand that he be sent back out to them, and in response several of the diners, including Harvey, Edward Fitzgerald and Edward Hay, went out and asked them to disperse. They would not relent, however, and in the end Harvey gave in and handed Turner over to them. They cheered in triumph as they dragged him down the street to the jail.[14]

It was nearing nightfall when the commander-in-chief and a few of his officers gathered part of the southern division and marched out towards the west. Many of the lower-ranking officers and their men had scattered by that point, and some, such as Thomas Cloney, had even returned to their homes, either unsure of when the march would take place or else so confident about its outcome that they were unconcerned about joining it.[15] Harvey began his march late, therefore, and made little progress, passing by Forth Mountain during the evening and only getting as far as Taghmon by the time darkness fell. He decided to halt there for the night to give the battalions that were still missing a chance to catch up with him.[16] In comparison with the lightning march of the northern divison, this was a poor achievement, but they were still well within a day's march of New Ross and would be able to attack the town by the next evening should things go well.

Meanwhile around the perimeter of the county there had been important developments during the day. To begin with, government forces at Duncannon and New Ross used the time to further strengthen their defences. At New Ross this meant improving the lines of trenches and other earthworks in front of the east wall and placing several cannon at strategic spots inside the town. Thus far the garrison still only consisted of a few hundred yeomen under Charles Tottenham, but messages had gone out to Waterford and other points beyond the Barrow asking for reinforcements. From Tottenham's point of view, it was essential that these should arrive before the rebels; with part of their southern division camped at Taghmon, only twenty miles away, the garrison was still in real danger of being overwhelmed before help came.[17]

On the northern border of the county, on the other hand, the government had already begun to make important moves. That very afternoon, as the northern rebels moved off Windmill Hill, a detachment of several hundred government soldiers arrived in Newtownbarry from Carlow. They were mostly militia from Queen's County and were under the command of Colonel L'Estrange.[18] They were the first significant reinforcement of government positions in the county since the rebellion began, and their presence suddenly made the little border town a far more formidable objective than it would have been with its original garrison of a few score yeomanry.

The government was making moves to stiffen its position on the 'Gorey front' too. One or two days before this, probably immediately after the 'Battle' of Gibbet Rath on the 29th, Lake had decided to send several small columns south from the midlands and east Leinster to deal with the Wexford rising. The rising was by then being contained to the west of Dublin, and he concluded that he could afford the diversion.[19] By the time the rebel regime was establishing itself in Wexford town a young courtier named Colonel Walpole was already in County Kildare collecting any troops that local commanders could spare for a quick march into northern Wexford along the west flank of the Wicklow mountains. He had little military experience and he owed the prominent role he had now assumed to his political influence at Dublin Castle. As he saw it, he was being given a chance to crush the Wexford rebels and to make a name for himself. In the end he managed to secure the command of a troop of several hundred men, and he was very confident that this would be enough to deal with the insurgents to his south; among other things, the poor performance of the Kildare and Meath rebels in the field may have led him to this conclusion.[20]

At about the same time Lieutenant-General Loftus was leaving Loughlinstown barracks, just to the south of the capital, with a column of several hundred men, headed for Arklow and points beyond. His objective was to make his way southward along the Wicklow coastal plain and to push on into Wexford and join Walpole somewhere in the northern part of the county.[21] General Lake appears to have decided that they should co-ordinate their movements with units coming into the county from the west and assumed that these combined forces could crush the rebels easily. He did not have any idea at this point how large the rebel armies were nor that they had captured Wexford town.[22]

By evening, as the northern rebels settled at Carrigrew and their southern comrades camped at Taghmon, these government columns were bearing down on the county. Loftus had made steady progress along the Wicklow coast and was setting up camp for the night in Wicklow town, a day's march from Arklow,[23] and Walpole in the meantime had collected his column in the midlands and was in southern Kildare, also about a day away from the Wexford border.[24] Most important of all, L'Estrange and his men had already spent an afternoon strengthening the defences of Newtownbarry, and by evening they were ready to fight off an attack.[25]

The position of government forces at Gorey, the only town they held well inside the county, had improved by that evening too. Several more yeomanry corps and civilian refugees made their way southwards from Arklow in the morning and afternoon, and the yeomanry who were already in the town became much bolder, several cavalry units riding quite far south on patrol. Two of them went as far as Camolin and Carrigrew and encountered a small band of rebels on the hill who were evidently not part of the large insurgent body that marched there from Windmill Hill later in the day. There was a brief skirmish between the two forces in which several rebels were killed and after which the rest took to flight. The cavalry was unaware at this point that a rebel army of several thousand was approaching from the south, and they rode back to Gorey confident that they were now getting a firm grip on the area.[26]

The day ended, then, with each side assuming that things were going well for them, though both were in fact ignorant of the real situation. From the rebel point of view, one more day, or at most two, should complete their task; after that, presumably, the greater part of the Wexford army could be disbanded and the leading members of the United Irishmen in the county would proceed to play their part in creating a new governmental structure in the country. For men like Roche, Harvey and Perry, such thoughts may well have included dreams of participation in a constitutional assembly of some sort and, after that, perhaps even membership of the new government.

The commanders of the government forces had a clearer idea of the situation in the country at large, but most of them, including Lake himself, were still not aware of how powerful a position the Wexford rebels now enjoyed.[27] Garrison commanders in places like Newtownbarry, Carnew and Gorey had the advantage of knowing that the rebels had failed in Dublin and that their own comrades were holding out in the midlands garrisons.[28] Lake himself knew that the midlands rising was crushed by this stage, but he must have worried about what might be going on in Ulster and Munster; so far there was no indication that rebellion had broken out in either province, but news from Munster had been cut off for four or five days and he had to be cautious in his response to developments in Wexford.[29] But from his point of view the situation, though still dangerous, had nevertheless begun to improve, and he must by now have begun to feel more confident that he could crush the rebellion unless there was a French landing. That was the great imponderable which was exercising the minds of everyone on both sides.

*

The rebel offensive against the garrisons on the periphery of County Wexford began early the next day, 1 June, at Newtownbarry. The column under Father Mogue Kearns set out for the town in the morning and marched along the west bank of the Slaney.[30] During the night a young woman had galloped into Newtownbarry and had warned L'Estrange that an attack was imminent. In response, he had kept his men at arms all night, and when morning came he sent several patrols out along the road towards Enniscorthy to look for signs of the rebels.[31] They saw no evidence of them at first, but eventually one of them spotted the rebel column as it made its way along the river valley; he returned and informed L'Estrange of what was happening. The commander immediately sent several mounted units out to skirmish with their vanguard, but these fell back after a short time, and as the main body of the rebels came closer to the town he concentrated all his men behind its defences.[32]

When they came within sight of Newtownbarry, the rebels moved off to the left a little and made their way up the slopes of a hill that lay just to its south. From there they could see down into the town and make out the elongated square that served as its main street and the network of roads that ran out of it. One of these, the road to Carlow which proceeded towards the northwest, was the only obvious route of escape for the garrison should they come under pressure, and, as the insurgents massed on the hillside and prepared to attack, Miles Byrne suggested to Father Kearns that he send a detachment to a hill just to the west of the town that would cut off their line of retreat. Byrne was a mere youth, and the priest dismissed him curtly and declared to all in hearing that they would launch a full-scale frontal assault. Byrne's idea may have made sense from a military viewpoint, but Kearns had two artillery pieces in his possession now (one of them a howitzer captured from the Royal Artillery) and he was convinced that the garrison could not withstand a frontal attack. Six days of rebel victories had made him supremely confident.[33]

Kearns launched his attack on the town at about nine or ten o'clock. His main force opened the battle with an artillery assault from the hillsides which the garrison could not possibly match because of the angle at which their guns had to operate. It became clear to L'Estrange that he could not withstand the pressure for long, and so, half an hour or thereabouts into the battle, he ordered his men to pull back from their barricades and to retreat along the Carlow road. Not long after that the rebels pushed down towards the entrances to the town and swept into the main square almost unopposed. The ease with which they seized the place must have amazed even their commander.

A few minutes after the insurgents burst into the square a group of loyalist civilians who had taken shelter in a house on its edge began shoot at them. A small band of men broke off from the rest of the rebels and tried to pin the snipers down but meanwhile the remainder of the force continued to range through the town. No one, it seems, paid any attention to the Carlow road, assuming only that the entire garrison had run for their lives and that the handful of men in the house would soon be forced to give up.[34]

L'Estrange and his men had retreated some distance out along the road to Carlow by this time. About a mile into their flight they met a reinforcement from the King's County militia coming to their aid. They could hear the sounds of the battle that still raged inside the town, and this inspired them to turn around and counter-attack.

Kearns had made no plans to guard against such an eventuality. The men in the square were not even watching as the soldiers pushed several cannon into firing positions on the Carlow road above them, and when the gunners hit them with several discharges of grapeshot and a volley of musketry they were thrown into complete disorder. The troops charged down into the square and attacked the surprised rebels with their bayonets; the rebels gave ground and broke into a headlong flight out along the roads into the countryside. The infantry and cavalry pursued the terrified men, chasing them over garden walls and into fields and ditches, and in the end the rout turned into a massacre. In an hour or less it was over and the rebels had lost well over a hundred men, compared with a mere handful of soldiers killed.[35]

The disaster for Kearns and his men was as complete as it was unexpected. The remnant of his column limped back towards Enniscorthy during the afternoon, grateful that the garrison did not keep up the chase and stunned that their apparent victory had been turned about so easily by an enemy that was supposed to be on the brink of destruction.[36] Here for the first time was a sign that something had gone badly wrong with the rebel cause in the counties to the north and west, and by evening the disturbing news of the affray and its outcome had certainly reached Enniscorthy and may have travelled all the way to Wexford and Taghmon.

Seven miles to the west of Newtownbarry, in the meantime, the Carrigrew Hill rebels were suffering a similar setback. When morning came, many of the men who had slipped away from the camp the evening before still had not returned, and but for this the entire division might have broken camp and marched on Gorey immediately.[37] Instead a detachment of 1,000 or 2,000 men led by Anthony Perry and Father Michael Murphy left the hill around the middle of the morning and marched west to Mounthoward and then turned north towards Ballycanew. Their plan was to move on from there and take possession of Ballyminaun Hill, a point which lay just two miles to the south of the town and would have been perfect as a staging-point for the final assault.[38]

Unknown to Murphy and Perry, however, the garrison in Gorey was being steadily reinforced from Arklow at that very time. The new additions included over a hundred men of the Antrim militia under Lieutenant Elliot, who now took overall command of the town. He sent several patrols out to his south during the morning, and one of these eventually approached the northern slope of Carrigrew Hill where their comrades had spotted some rebels the day before. As they got close to the hill they saw that there was now a huge rebel force on its summit. Some of the rebels responded to their sudden appearance by charging down the hillside towards them, and the cavalry retreated quickly along a road that skirted the northern slope and led towards Ballycanew. As they made their way towards the village they sighted the column under Perry and Murphy off in the distance to the south but heading northwards, and when they entered the village there was already a small rebel band there. They skirmished their way through and rode directly to Gorey and informed Elliot of the situation.[39]

The young lieutenant's response was bold. Instead of strengthening his defences in preparation for an attack, he collected a detachment of about 200 men and marched out to meet the approaching rebels. In less than an hour he and his men had reached the ridge of Ballyminaun and found that they were nowhere in sight. In fact they were making slow progress because they were searching for arms in known loyalist houses, some of which they set on fire, and had only got as far as Ballycanew when Elliot and his men reached the ridge.[40]

After a delay in the village the rebel column pushed on northwards without suspecting that a detachment of soldiers was nearby. They had reached Essex Bridge, half a mile to the south of Ballyminaun Hill, and were beginning to make their way along a road which rose slowly to its summit when they suddenly saw the 200 troops marching towards them down the slope. They were taken completely by surprise and had little time to prepare a line of battle. Their officers tried to create a line of gunsmen to hold the soldiers off, but they were no match for them in the musketry duel that soon developed, and they began to retreat before the pikemen could even join in the battle. This quickly turned into a general flight, and, as at Newtownbarry an hour or two before, both infantry and cavalry took full advantage of the panic and chased groups of insurgents across the fields for miles, cutting them down without mercy. Most of the rebel column survived somehow and retreated back in the general direction of Carrigrew, but they left well over a hundred men dead or dying in the fields. As at Newtownbarry, the losses on the government side were negligible.[41]

By evening the full extent of the setbacks at Newtownbarry and Ballyminaun was becoming clear at Vinegar Hill and Carrigrew. Scattered bands were still returning to the camps at that late stage, and the leaders in both places no doubt puzzled over why government forces that were supposed to be practically cut off would put up such stout resistance. Some may have speculated that the garrisons at Newtownbarry and Gorey were indeed trapped between themselves and the Kildare/Carlow/Wicklow rebels, and that this explained their desperate resistance. However, the alternative—and more realistic—explanation for the insurgents' unexpected reverses must have occurred to many in the rebel encampments; to them this was the day, the sixth day of the rebellion, when the first hint of disaster appeared.

*

While the rebel cause was suffering these astounding setbacks in the northern part of the county, its fortunes were suddenly experiencing reverses in the south too. At some point in the day, probably also in the morning, Bagenal Harvey and his army broke camp at Taghmon and resumed their march towards New Ross. When they reached Carrickbyrne, a high hill about six miles from their destination, they stopped and formed another camp. The reason for the halt is uncertain, but it seems that other southern units had not yet joined Harvey and he had no choice but to form a temporary camp and wait for them. Many of the missing detachments were still scattered around various parts of the south of the county and made no serious effort to join the commander-in-chief during the day. Thomas Cloney, for example, left Wexford town during the morning and went north to Moneyhore and spent the rest of the day there with his father and sister.[42] Other southern commanders are likely to have acted in a similar manner. Even Harvey himself seems to have shared their complacency; consequently, although a sizeable rebel force from Forth joined him in the afternoon, putting him in a good position to attack the town that evening, he decided to remain where he was for the rest of the day.[43] Unknown to him, however, the opportunity to assail New Ross while it was still garrisoned by only a small yeomanry force was slipping away with each passing hour. Like the rebel leaders in the north of the county, Harvey could not have known this, and as evening fell he must have settled down for the night still assuming that the Kilkenny rebels had the town cut off from their side of the Barrow and that storming it would still be easy.

As for the government forces, those in the northern part of the county spent the rest of the day consolidating their positions. At Newtownbarry L'Estrange sent a few more patrols out along the Slaney, probably as far as Ballycarney Bridge, but made no serious effort to press the advantage beyond that. Elliot adopted the same policy at Gorey. His victorious column returned to the town in the afternoon with hundreds of horses and cattle as booty, but for the rest of the day he kept his men behind the barricades and only allowed small mounted patrols to probe the countryside towards the south.[44]

Meanwhile in Dublin Castle General Lake was aware that the Kildare and Meath rebellions were waning by the morning and early afternoon of this crucial day, but he was still uncertain of the situation in Ulster and Munster; so far, however, he had heard nothing of rebellion in either place, and this persuaded him to continue with his plan to concentrate at least some forces on Wexford. He learned that reinforcements were on their way from England at this point, and this undoubtedly boosted his confidence.[45]

The plan itself was being implemented smoothly. By evening Walpole was camped in the foothills of south-western Wicklow, within a day's march of the Wexford border, and Loftus had continued his slow march southwards too and was only a few hours' march from Arklow when he stopped his men for the night. In addition, Lake had sent an express to Generals Johnson and Eustace at Waterford ordering them to move to New Ross with a sizeable force (close to 1,000 men) the following day and to push on into Wexford from there.[46] For the moment he was content to leave General Asgill with his large garrison at Kilkenny, but in time this force too might be brought to bear on Wexford. Lake was still working on the assumption that the rebels controlled only the central part of the county and that his three-pronged attack from north and west would trap them somewhere around Enniscorthy, but he showed his continuing concern by asking the viceroy, Lord Camden, for more infantry.[47]

The rebels who passed the day in and around Wexford town were completely unaware of any of these developments until at least the late afternoon or evening. They mostly spent their time consolidating the new regime. Keogh and his committee had several pressing concerns, including the defence of the harbour, the maintenance of law and order, and the establishment of a reliable provisioning arrangement. Wexford harbour was broad and would be relatively easy for a hostile naval force to enter, and to prevent this Keogh had four fishing boats fitted out as a small makeshift navy, each manned by twenty-five seamen, and directed them to patrol back and forth across the harbour mouth. During the day they intercepted and captured several ships loaded with grain on their way from Waterford to Dublin, thereby significantly augmenting the food supply of the town. He also had some boats anchored at the harbour mouth so that they could be scuttled to block it should British battleships approach, and sent out a small party of insurgents to dismantle some guns at Rosslare Fort and mount them at a spot overlooking the entrance.[48]

The maintenance of law and order was an even more pressing matter. The indiscriminate murders which had taken place two days before were not repeated, in part because the townsmen were encouraged to form volunteer companies which acquired arms primarily for the purpose of discouraging mob action. Looting was constantly a concern, and so also was the safety of the scores of loyalists now held in the jail. There were elements in the town by this point, especially among the sailors, who wanted to kill at least some of the prisoners; however, they were frustrated by the volunteer companies and by Keogh's efficient management of affairs, and accordingly there was no anti-loyalist violence.[49]

Food supplies, normally a serious problem in such circumstances, were adequate in spite of the vast numbers of refugees in the town. The stock of provisions was already substantial when the rebellion began, and the two grain ships captured by the gunboats augmented this; additionally, Cornelius Grogan set up an elaborate mechanism for transporting grain and livestock into the town from the countryside to its south. Merchants who were unsure of the status of banknotes in this revolutionary situation insisted on payments in specie for any goods they sold, but the governor's committee accepted scrip for the food they began to distribute themselves and thus averted the profiteering and food riots that might otherwise have developed.[50]

The Bullring, at the centre of the town, became a noisy open-air arms factory as Edward Hay went about creating an infant armaments department. He recruited blacksmiths anywhere he could find them and sent small parties out into the countryside to cut handles for the pikes they were making. At this stage, with most United Irishmen assuming that the struggle was practically over, the work was probably conducted in a fairly casual manner.[51]

The loyalist population now trapped behind rebel lines remained apprehensive about their fate throughout the day. The hundred or more prisoners in Wexford jail had been given food but knew little of what their captors intended to do with them. Rebel officers freed a few during the day on the grounds that they were wrongfully accused of being Orangemen, but small bands continued to search the town and the parishes around it for yeomen. They found a few of these and brought them in to the prison, but those they were most anxious to catch, such as James Boyd and Archibald Hamilton Jacob, were long gone.[52]

The prisoners at Vinegar Hill were less fortunate than those in Wexford. The killings that had taken place there on 28 May were repeated and were still taking place at this stage, two or three men being put to death each morning. The role of the rebel army in this is unclear, but the ritual of imprisonment in Beale's Barn, temporary confinement in the windmill on top of the hill and ultimate execution by pike thrust or musket shot had become well established by 1 June, and it would continue at intervals for the duration of the conflict.[53]

Most loyalists remained at large, however, and they tried to go about their lives as normally as possible. Things were still confusing for them, especially for the wives and children of yeomen and soldiers, but after the rebel victory many of them returned to their homes in the country and spent the 31st and 1st trying to re-establish themselves there. Most remained unmolested, and a few were even helped by neighbours who sympathised with the rebels, but all continued to be terrified of the possibility of violence being done to them in the future.[54]

The most disturbing development in this connection was the emergence of rumours that a massacre of Protestants was imminent. The reports, which were the work of a variety of people with little or no connection with the United Irishmen (many of whose leaders were Protestant themselves), were a total fabrication, but they convinced at least some loyalists in the area around the town to convert to Catholicism as a safeguard. Others refused to take any such action and placed their hope in the government's ability to stem the tide of rebellion sometime soon or, alternatively, in the rebel leadership's ability to control fanaticism.[55]

WALPOLE'S HORSE AND WALPOLE'S FOOT
2–4 JUNE

THE SECOND DAY OF JUNE WAS A TURNING-POINT IN THE Wexford rebellion. Until then the rebels had operated on the assumption that theirs was only a small part of a much greater national uprising. Their campaign had been marked by decisiveness and success at almost every turn. The insurgent armies had been responsible for some atrocities, most notably a number of murders in Enniscorthy and a few killings in Wexford town, but, generally speaking, the mass killings which many loyalists feared would follow a United Irish rising and victory had not taken place. More importantly, the leaders of the rebellion were determined to keep the movement fairly moderate in ideological terms and to avoid any appearance of sectarianism; Protestants were very prominent in the leadership circle, therefore, and the conciliatory gestures to men like Ebenezer Jacob and Edward Turner suggest that the 'new' republican elite would have room for many members of the old establishment. Among the rank and file there were hotheads and fanatics, of course, and these were responsible for many of the killings in the first hours and days of the insurrection; it is also more than likely that it was they who spread the terrifying rumours about the imminent massacre of Protestants. These elements were kept in check, however, and the general impression of the first six days of the rebellion is one of a well-organised and disciplined affair.

The entire situation began to change over the next few days as Lake's forces launched their counter-attack on the rebellious county. The campaign opened sometime in the morning on 2 June when Walpole and his column of 500 men got to Carnew. They stopped there and learned what they could of the situation to the south. In the afternoon Walpole himself rode out as far as the Slieveboy hills and observed the rebel camp on Carrigrew Hill, six miles away across the Bann valley. He concluded from what he saw that he could disperse the insurgents without any help from Loftus, and he was eager to attack the camp at once even though his instructions were to wait at Carnew for further orders. For the moment his better instincts prevailed, and he rode back down to his base and waited there for word from Loftus.[1]

Loftus and his men reached Arklow sometime that morning too. A dispatch rider from Lake who had come quickly down the coast road was already waiting for them with details of the plan of attack. The instructions were that Loftus and Walpole should combine their forces and drive at the rebel strongpoints in central Wexford from the north while other columns pushed into the county by way of Newtownbarry and New Ross, trapping the rebels somewhere around Enniscorthy. The plan was based on the assumption that southern Wexford was still in government hands, and since he had no reason to suppose otherwise, Loftus accepted it without hesitation. He wrote a hurried note to Walpole, ordering him to bring his entire force to Arklow as soon as possible and to leave only the local yeomanry to guard Carnew.[2]

Preparations for the offensive were simultaneously in progress along the western periphery of the county. Lord Ancram with at least 300 men of the King's County militia joined Colonel L'Estrange at Newtownbarry during the morning, giving the garrison there much greater offensive capacity. Ancram took over command of the post, but since he had received no instructions from Loftus up to this point, he had to wait patiently through the rest of the day to find out when he was to move out from his base and exactly where he was to lead his men.[3]

At New Ross the pieces fell into place more slowly, but government forces were moving steadily towards the town throughout the day in preparation for the offensive. The largest detachment was a column of several hundred men under Lieutenant-General Johnson which was moving up from Waterford, while Lieutenant-General Eustace was approaching the town from the north with a smaller group. Johnson and his men got a slow start in their march from Waterford, but both columns were on the way towards the town by the middle of the day and, if things went well, would be within only a few hours' march by nightfall.[4]

In New Ross itself in the meantime Tottenham and his yeomanry garrison watched the countryside to their east anxiously for any sign that the rebels were coming their way. The morning came and went without any such sign, and by evening Harvey's chance to attack the place while it was still defended by a weak yeomanry force was fast slipping away.[5]

In contrast to the decisiveness being shown by government forces (and to their own behaviour for the previous six days), the rebels now lost the initiative completely. Rather than gathering the force he already had and marching the remaining six miles to New Ross that morning, Harvey and his aides passed the entire day in camp and, incredibly, made no effort at all to move. At Vinegar Hill and Carrigrew Hill likewise there was a total halt to the rebel campaign. Nobody tried to organise a second, more determined push against Newtownbarry, and instead several units that had taken part in the attack the day before, among them the Monaseed corps, left Enniscorthy during the day and drifted northwards towards Carrigrew. The rebel force there was as immobilised as the others, and in spite of the arrival of units from the south, Edward Roche made no effort to push northwards in force and attack Gorey, the logical next step given the previous day's setback; instead he and his army simply remained on the hill throughout the day, waiting.[6]

It is difficult to account for this sudden paralysis. The insurgent leaders in the north of the county may have been reacting to the stiff resistance that the Gorey and Newtownbarry garrisons had put up the day before, and Harvey may have held his position at Carrickbyrne because he had learned of these setbacks the night before or early in the morning and was perhaps unwilling to risk making a similar mistake. It is also possible that he hesitated because several of his officers had still not arrived with their battalions, and he may therefore have decided to wait for them before moving; presumably he still believed that the Kilkenny rebels were in the field to the west of the town[7] and that he could be cautious without unduly affecting his chances of success.

All of these explanations for the sudden halt make a certain amount of sense, and they all may be relevant to some degree. There is another explanation, however, which fits the pattern just as well. On 2 June one of the vessels that made up the tiny insurgent navy at Wexford town intercepted and boarded a schooner that was approaching the entrance to the harbour. On board were found several officers of the North Cork militia, including the regiment's commander, Lord Kingsborough. He had come south with Loftus as far as Arklow, and when he discovered that the rebels were in control of all central Wexford (as he thought) he left the town by sea and sailed southwards to join his regiment, which, of course, he believed to be still in Wexford town. He only realised that the insurgents had captured the town when he arrived in the harbour.[8]

The rebel boarding party realised how important a prize Kingsborough and his fellow-officers were, and they made them all prisoners immediately and forced the captain of the ship to sail his vessel to the quay. When they landed, Matthew Keogh insisted that the colonel be held in a house rather than the jail, which was already overcrowded and where he might not be as safe.[9] The details of any conversation which took place between the two men are lost to us, but it is almost certain that they talked, and it is inconceivable that the militia commander would not have told the rebel leader what had happened elsewhere in the country. Keogh must have learned that the rising had failed utterly in Dublin and that the capital had been firmly restored to government hands by the time of Kingsborough's departure one or two days before, and also that the rebellion had largely failed in the midlands. Coming at the same time as news of the failures at Newtownbarry and Gorey, which would probably have reached him on the same day if not the night before, this must have been devastating to Keogh. Suddenly now, seven days into a struggle which was supposed to be over by this point, he and his fellow-Wexfordmen realised that they were all alone in their fight and, barring some extraordinary stroke of good fortune, were surely doomed to defeat. Keogh may have kept the information to himself, but it is more likely that during the day he sent dispatch riders out to Carrickbyrne and Vinegar Hill with the shocking news. This would explain the otherwise puzzling fact that the rebel armies, up to this point so decisive and so mobile, made no offensive moves whatsoever throughout this entire day.

By that evening it must have been clear to many that the initiative had shifted to the government side. Reports of the successes at Ballyminaun and Newtownbarry had reached Camden in Dublin Castle, providing him with the first good news from Wexford thus far.[10] The news was timely too, since earlier that day a ship had arrived from Wexford with reports of the rebel takeover of the county town[11] and intelligence sources had announced that a French landing in Wexford was likely.[12] At New Ross Tottenham was still holding on alone, but Johnson and Eustace were camped within a few hours' march of the town.[13] At Newtownbarry Ancram had a garrison of about 1,000 men and was unlikely to be overwhelmed by anything other than a massive rebel force. At Carnew and Arklow Walpole and Loftus were in position to move too.

But by this time an internal problem had begun to develop on that northern border of the county which might have the effect of undermining the chances of a successful drive against the rebel strongholds further south. A power struggle of sorts had emerged between Walpole and Loftus. Loftus had asked Walpole for a quick reply to his request that he join him at Arklow that afternoon. No reponse was forthcoming, however, and he sent out a second, more insistent dispatch to Carnew before evening came. By nightfall he had still not heard from Walpole and was left to wonder why the young colonel was being so reticent. As he and his men settled down for the night he could only hope that an answer would arrive early the next day, after which he could move on south to Gorey and prepare for the final attack on the rebels the day after that. For his part, Walpole was sulking. He had come south in the expectation that he would be given the leading role in the conquest of the rebels. Now, with Loftus treating him like an inferior, he was refusing to co-operate.[14]

The stalemated situation between rebels and government forces continued through Sunday 3 June, the eighth day of the rebellion. For the second day in succession the rebels held back from offensive action, as if still puzzled about their real position, and for the second day government forces closed in on the county but still held off from launching any major attacks on the insurgent positions.

The rebel southern division held its ground at Carrickbyrne for this second day, still assuming, it would seem, that they could take New Ross at will. Harvey did make serious efforts to rally the scattered detachments, and he sent an order out across the southern districts during the morning asking all available units to gather at Carrickbyrne on the following day. As the afternoon passed and the word to mobilise spread, some detachments began to move towards the camp, and the movement gained momentum as the day wore on, but by evening many of them had still not arrived and it was becoming clear that it would take several more hours to bring the division up to full strength.[15]

The situation was the same at Carrigrew Hill. Roche used the day to drill the men he had, and he called on all those who had scattered into the countryside to come back to the camp.[16] Sometime in the afternoon a detachment of several thousand arrived from Vinegar Hill and these brought the Carrigrew army up to at least 10,000 and perhaps as many as 15,000 men.[17] After two days of inaction they were building their strength once again, either in preparation for a new offensive or, just as likely, to meet the attack they suspected government forces would soon be launching at them.

Government forces were more decisive at this point, and they used the day to move into County Wexford and to get ready for what Lake's subordinates assumed would be the final assault. During the morning Eustace and Johnson both crossed the bridge at New Ross and entered the town, finally plugging the only remaining hole in the tightening net. They learned of the fall of Wexford town at once, and this persuaded them to abandon the idea of driving into the county in the next day or two; instead they decided to consolidate their hold on the town and to prepare for a rebel assault.

Johnson took command of the garrison and set his men to work reinforcing the defences. By the afternoon the government's grip on New Ross was much tighter: the town was even better fortified than it had been previously, and now it was defended by a force of 2,000 well-armed men, led by an officer who had faced American rebels twenty years before.[18] Whether he was aware of it or not, Harvey's chance for an easy victory on this part of the front was now irretrievably gone.

*

THE GOREY/ARKLOW THEATRE, 1 – 16 JUNE

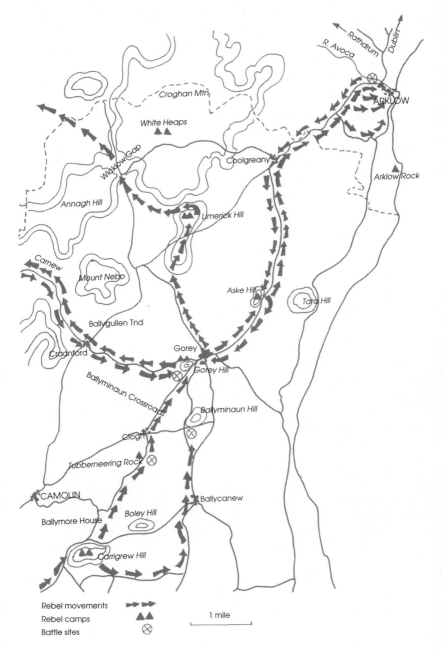

Rebel movements
Rebel camps
Battle sites

1 mile

At the other end of the county, in the meantime, Loftus was making steady progress. Early in the morning, still at Arklow, he finally received a response from Walpole. Incredibly, though, the latter refused outright to make a rendezvous and insisted instead that he attack and scatter the rebels on Carrigrew Hill by himself. Loftus fired off an angry answer, demanding that he comply with orders, but Walpole responded with a second refusal in the afternoon. By that time Loftus had already sent an advance unit of some 400 men south to Gorey and was preparing to take the rest of his column there himself before nightfall. He decided to press ahead with this plan regardless of Walpole's lack of co-operation and sent a final message to Carnew demanding that he join him at Gorey next morning with all the troops he had collected in the midlands.[19]

He reached Gorey without incident late in the afternoon and waited there, expecting that he would not see the troublesome colonel until the next day. That evening, however, Walpole finally rode in from Carnew at the head of about 400 men. He had at last obeyed the summons of his superior. But Loftus's problems with him were by no means over. For one thing, even though he had been asked to bring his entire column with him from Carnew, he had chosen to leave a detachment of about 100 men behind as a garrison. In addition, he still believed that he should be the one to break the Wexford rebellion.[20]

The immediate concern for Loftus was the rebel army camped just six miles to his south, and not his over-ambitious young subordinate. He learned of the fall of Wexford town as soon as he got to Gorey (the news had only reached the town the previous morning).[21] This information, which surely came as a shock to him, made the rebel position look very different. Before, working on the assumption that the insurgents held only Enniscorthy, Loftus could plan an attack from Gorey which would trap them between himself and the government forces at Wexford and New Ross. Now, however, the operation was bound to be more complex and would certainly last longer.

As he assessed his situation that afternoon, he decided that he was still in a fairly good position and that the offensive should go ahead on the following day as planned. The behaviour of the rebels themselves may have been one of the most important influences on his decison; from all he could learn, they were not a formidable force, in spite of their great numbers. The Gorey yeoman cavalry and Elliot's Antrim militia had already met and defeated them two days before at Ballyminaun, and their reports of the ease with which the rebels had been driven from the field certainly must have influenced him. In addition, cavalry patrols had gone out at frequent intervals in the time since that battle and had approached the northern slope of Carrigrew Hill several times with impunity. On this particular day, in fact, a detachment of the Camolin cavalry had ridden close to the north slope of the hill, but the rebels made no attempt to attack them, and they returned to Gorey with the same report on the rebel camp as the day before: that it was large but passive.[22] What they did not realise was that the camp was steadily increasing in size and that the men who composed it had spent the last two days drilling and training for battle.[23] They were not, therefore, the confused rural mob that the cavalry officers may have come to assume they were.

Loftus finalised his plans for the offensive during the evening. He assumed that a determined assault by his men would break the insurgent ranks and that he could sweep what was left of their army into the south of the county and trap them there. By nightfall he and his officers had agreed that four columns of troops would drive at the rebel position simultaneously: Loftus himself would march along the Ballycanew road with about 600 men and attack the hill from the north-east; Walpole would march at the head of another 600 through the hamlet of Clogh and drive at its northern slope; Walpole's men at Carnew would move down to Camolin and wait there in case the rebels should flee in that direction; and Ancram (who was to receive instructions during the night, it would seem) would move from Newtownbarry to Scarawalsh Bridge, to wait there for further orders and march to Camolin to join the Carnew detachment if he had heard nothing by three o'clock. The columns under Loftus and Walpole would be the main attacking forces, and the detachments at Camolin and Sarawalsh were to function as reserves and might be used to cut off any attempts on the part of the fleeing insurgent forces to escape to the west.[24] In formulating the plan, Loftus demonstrated high confidence in his men and what can only be seen as contempt for the rebels, whose success in the south of the county he was evidently prepared to discount completely.

There still were problems with Walpole even at this late stage. The young courtier insisted that he have the central role in the attack; this explains why he was selected to lead the column which was to drive directly at the rebel position, while the general himself was to be in charge of what amounted to a flanking operation. Beyond this, Walpole demanded that he be the one to chase the rebels into southern Wexford, where he would presumably annihilate them.[25] Obviously Loftus was unable to control Walpole (even though he had enlisted two militia officers to help him), and both men apparently assumed that the Carrigrew rebels were the only ones in the field, neither of them realising that another huge rebel army was encamped only a few miles from New Ross.

When darkness began to fall that evening, several of the soldiers and officers roamed about the streets of Gorey, drinking and relaxing. Full of confidence now, some of them talked openly of their orders for the next morning. Among those who listened was a rebel sympathiser. Once night came, this man slipped out of the town and made his way along the dusty roads to Carrigrew. The rebel leaders were sleeping in Ballymore House when he got there, and he awakened them and told them what he had heard. They hastily sent an order through the camp that all units should mobilise at dawn. Somehow a farmer from near Clogh who was a loyalist sympathiser heard of this development, and he in turn rode into Gorey with the news. He got a very different reception from the rebel informer: Walpole accused him of trying to demoralise his men and had him thrown in jail, completely ignoring his warning, and thereby giving the rebel army the upper hand at the outset.[26]

As a battle loomed in the far north of the county, there were some disturbing developments in Wexford town, now in its third day under rebel rule. Protestant loyalists decided not to hold any church services that day, despite the best efforts of the rebel leaders to persuade them otherwise.[27] Catholic masses proceeded as normal, attended in some cases by Protestants who had judged it expedient to make a hasty conversion to Catholicism.[28]

At some point before noon a small band of rebels under Captain Thomas Dixon, a cousin of the priest of the same name, exacted personal revenge on one of the loyalist prisoners held in the jail. The man in question was Francis Murphy, who was alleged to have informed on Dixon's cousin just before the rebellion. Dixon and his gang went to the jail while the town was quiet and seized Murphy and dragged him outside. They hauled him off to the Bullring and killed him without ceremony. Then they dragged his body down to the quay and threw it into the water.[29] Keogh and his aides only discovered what had happened when they came out into the streets themselves, but, significantly, they seem to have done little to punish Dixon and his gang for their crime. It was an ominous sign for the future.

As the day ended, then, the rebel leadership in Wexford town itself and in the camps at Carrigrew Hill, Vinegar Hill and Carrickbyrne must have still been quite puzzled about what was going on to their north and very apprehensive about the days ahead. There is no evidence that Harvey knew of the sudden reinforcement of New Ross by this point; it is clear that he was still planning on going ahead with his march on the town the next day. The leaders at Carrigrew had a more immediate concern. Not only had government forces stopped them in their tracks at Ballyminaun, but now they were on the point of attacking them in their current stronghold; more proof of the strong position of their enemies was hardly needed. Their own dilemma now was to decide whether to hold their position, to retreat, or to go on the offensive themselves. In the end, perhaps because they had such detailed information about Loftus's plans, they decided to go on the attack and to hit the army coming out from Gorey at its weakest point, the column led by Walpole.[30]

In Wexford town Matthew Keogh, William Kearney and the others could now only wonder what their fate might be. They could not have known of the build-up of government forces at Gorey, Newtownbarry and New Ross but they could surely have predicted that this would happen soon. Even more disturbing was the evidence that sectarian tensions were mounting in the town and that there were elements among the rebels, most notably Dixon and his followers, who still might have personal vendettas to finish with local loyalists.

The following day, Monday 4 June, was one of the most

decisive days in the entire Wexford rebellion and changed its character profoundly. It began quietly in the southern part of the county. When dawn broke, Harvey and the other southern leaders at Carrickbyrne were anxious to begin the march to New Ross, but, having ascertained that many units were still absent, agreed to wait for several hours for them to come up. Six miles to their west Johnson and Eustace remained in a defensive posture and waited for orders from Lake before making any effort to strike out at the camp. As the morning hours passed, the stalemate continued, and at noon the rebels were still at Carrickbyrne and Harvey had still not managed to assemble his forces for the two-hour march that would bring them to the edge of the town.[31]

In contrast, the morning saw dramatic developments in the northern part of the county. Not long after dawn the various government columns moved to their positions for the attack on Carrigrew: Walpole and Loftus mustered their men in Gorey's main street, Ancram led his column along the road from Newtownbarry to Scarawalsh Bridge, and the small detachment of troops Walpole had left in Carnew made their way to Camolin. At about nine o'clock the 1,200 men of Loftus's and Walpole's combined force marched out of Gorey. At the town's southern exit they divided into two separate columns, Loftus taking his 600 men out along the road to Ballycanew, and Walpole leading his group along the Enniscorthy road towards Clogh.[32]

The rebels on Carrigrew had been astir early too, and they were forming into companies and battalions on Ballymore demesne at about the same time that Walpole and Loftus were marching out of Gorey. They began to march directly northward along the road through the demesne, on towards Clogh and directly towards Walpole and his men. Their ranks took up over a mile of the road as they moved, and several small scouting parties moved ahead of them looking for signs of Walpole's approach.[33]

The two columns of government troops made steady progress for the first hour or so. At Barnadown crossroads, about three miles south of Gorey, a detachment of the Antrim militia broke off from Loftus's column and went a mile or so to the right to the crossroads at Ballyminaun Hill, where the battle had taken place three days earlier and from which they could go to the rescue of either column should they encounter difficulties.[34] As Loftus and

DECLARATION, RESOLUTIONS,

AND

CONSTITUTION,

OF THE

SOCIETIES OF UNITED IRISHMEN.

DECLARATION AND RESOLUTIONS.

IN the prefent great Æra of Reform, when unjuft Governments are failing in every quarter of Europe; when Religious Perfecution is compelled to abjure her Tyranny over confcience; when the Rights of Men are afcertained in Theory, and that Theory fubftantiated by Practice; when Antiquity can no longer defend abfurd and oppreffive Forms, againft the common Senfe and common Interefts of Mankind; when all goverments are acknowledged to originate from the People, and to be fo far only obligatory, as they protect their Rights and promote their Welfare:— We think it our Duty, as Irifhmen, to come forward, and ftate what we feel to be our heavy Grievance, and what we know to be its effectual Remedy.

WE HAVE NO NATIONAL GOVERNMENT.— We are ruled by Englifhmen, and the Servants of Englifhmen, whofe Object is the Intereft of another Country; whofe Inftrument is Corruption, and whofe ftrength is the Weaknefs of IRELAND; and thefe Men have the whole of the Power and Patronage of the Country, as Means to feduce and fubdue the Honefty of her Reprefentatives in the Legiflature. Such an extrinfic Powers, acting with uniform Force, in a Direction too frequently oppofite to the true Line of our obvious Interefts, can be refifted with Effect folely by the *Unanimity, Decifion,* and *Spirit* in the *People,*—Qualities which may be exerted moft legally, conftitutionally, and efficacioufly, by that great Meafure, effential to the Profperity and Freedom of Ireland—AN EQUAL REPRESENTATION OF ALL THE PEOPLE IN PARLIAMENT.

The Constitution of the United Irishmen.

Kyle Glebe. The house was besieged by the Oulart rebels in the early hours of 27 May. The Rev. Robert Burrowes was killed in the yard in front of the house.

Ballinamonabeg crossroads, looking northwards. Jeremiah Kavanagh's public house was here, and the rebels camped on the sloping field to the left; Hawtrey White and his men approached from the north.

United Irish badge.

A contemporary view of Duncannon, showing the fort.

Enniscorthy, looking northwards, showing the bridge on which Snowe established himself before the battle (the bridge in the foreground is a modern feature) and the castle in which prisoners were being held at the time.

The Duffry Gate, Enniscorthy, looking southwards. The yeomanry were drawn up at about the point from which the photograph was taken, and the rebels swept down into the town by this route.

Road across Forth Mountain, looking westwards. At about this spot the Bantry rebels who were drawn up on the slope to the left ambushed the Meath militia in the early hours of 30 May.

Taylorstown Bridge. On this narrow bridge the Rosegarland rebels, drawn up on the high ground nearby, pinned down part of the garrison fleeing towards Duncannon from Wexford town during the night of 30–31 May.

John Henry Colclough.

Carrigrew Hill, looking eastwards. The hill was the site of a rebel camp on perhaps four different occasions, and was the place where the hurried decision to abandon the county was made on 5 July.

Neville Street, New Ross, looking northwards into Church Lane, where fierce fighting raged throughout the battle on 5 June.

Father John Murphy.

his men made their way towards Ballycanew they saw no sign of the rebels and assumed that the same was true of Walpole, several miles to their right across the fields.

Events were not proceeding quite as smoothly for Walpole, however. When he and his detachment approached the little hamlet of Clogh, where the road to Carrigrew forked off from the main Gorey–Camolin road, some of them noticed a small band of men in the distance towards Camolin. The men disappeared quickly, but several of Walpole's officers expressed concern and asked him to send a rider to the Antrim detachment at Ballyminaun to let them know of the sighting. A road ran directly to Ballyminaun from Clogh, and this could have been done in a short time, but Walpole insisted on pushing on. The column thus renewed its march and made its way along the narrow winding road in the direction of Carrigrew. This road passed through a townland called Tubberneering.[35]

The small band of men that the soldiers had spotted were, in fact, part of the vanguard of the huge rebel army that was making its way towards Clogh at that very moment. They had turned back as soon as they had seen Walpole's men and spread the word of his approach among the first ranks. In response, a large rebel detachment left the road at Tubberneering, well before the troops came into view and climbed to the top of a high rock about a hundred yards to the west of the road. From there they caught sight of the troops through a field-glass and watched them as they came closer. In the meantime the main body of the rebel army was still moving along the road towards Tubberneering and was unaware of the discovery their advance units had just made.[36]

Some of Walpole's officers became very anxious about their position at this stage, and they finally persuaded him to stop and have the road ahead reconnoitred. A lone dragoon rode ahead to do this. As he did so the rebels on the rock only a few hundred yards to the south watched him and thought for a time that they had been spotted. Walpole's scout did not go very far, however, and turned around before he caught sight of the approaching rebels. When he got back, he reported that he had seen a lone man with a gun up ahead but nothing more, and, in what was to prove a fatal error of judgment, the inexperienced Walpole decided this was of no significance and ordered his men to resume the march.[37]

The road turned suddenly to the east for about fifty yards just to the north of the rock on which the rebel patrol lay concealed, muskets ready, and then veered to the south again and ran past the rock to its east. By the time the leading section of Walpole's column had rounded the second of these bends other rebel units had come up and had learned of the army's approach and had begun to make their way northwards inside the ditch running along the road on Walpole's right. The rebels on the rock held their fire and watched as this happened. Even at this stage most of the rebel army was still unaware of what was happening and was still marching briskly northwards along the road, but around a bend and out of sight.[38]

Just after most of Walpole's column had rounded the last bend the rebels hidden to his right opened a sudden attack. It was a combination of musket volleys, fired mostly from the rock, and a pike and bayonet assault launched from close quarters by the men who had crept along inside the ditch. The front ranks of the main rebel body then came around the bend to the south of Walpole and realised what was happening. Edward Roche quickly decided to move his men into the fields on his left and to try to link up with the men on the rock and to outflank the soldiers.

The government force was thrown into complete confusion by the sudden attack, and several men died in the initial hail of fire, including Walpole himself, who was hit a number of times and fell from his saddle to die on the roadside. In spite of this initial setback, however, the other officers rallied their men and held off the rebel assault, eventually even turning their artillery pieces around and opening fire on the rock. They also fired steadily on rebels trying to cross the open field between the road and the rock and inflicted heavy casualties on them too. The lines steadied in time, and the fighting became fierce. The stalemate that ensued was finally broken when Roche directed several rebel units to attack along the road itself and from the fields on its east side. For a time there was a desperate infantry battle for the cannon, with the insurgents capturing them at one point, only to have them recaptured by the troops, and then capturing them again and this time holding firm.

The militia officers directing the battle eventually saw that they were being surrounded on three sides and began to pull back their men. Some of the soldiers panicked at this stage and began to flee back towards Clogh. The rest retreated in fairly good order, but had no answer for the overwhelming numbers and determination of the rebels. At Clogh a part of the Armagh regiment made a brief stand, but the rebels drove at them once again and eventually they too were forced to join the general retreat northwards after losing an officer and a number of men.[39]

In spite of Loftus's well-conceived plans, no reinforcements arrived in time to help Walpole's men. The general himself heard the sound of the battle from his position on the Ballycanew road several miles away when it first began, but his initial reaction was simply to assume that Walpole had encountered a rebel outpost and was pushing it back. Eventually he realised that this was not the case and sent an express rider to the detachment at Ballyminaun crossroads with orders to go to Walpole's aid. The detachment complied, but by the time they made their way down to Clogh the battle was over and what was left of Walpole's force was retreating back along the road to Gorey. When Captain McManus and his Antrim militia approached the hamlet in the hope of saving the column, several rebel units spotted them and moved out to the right and left of the road from Ballyminaun and trapped them. McManus realised too late that he was surrounded. The rebels attacked him suddenly and in a matter of minutes had killed, captured or scattered almost his entire unit. The captain himself and Hunter Gowan, who was functioning as his scout, somehow managed to escape in the direction of Ballyminaun and made their way from there back to Gorey.[40]

The entire encounter in and near Tubberneering lasted between one and two hours, but by the time it was over the rebel army had punched a massive hole in the dragnet that was supposed to trap them. Now, with Walpole dead and his column retreating in disarray to the north, the other three columns were in real danger of being trapped themselves, partly because they were unaware for some time of what had happened at Tubberneering. The detachments at Camolin and Scarawalsh had remained at their stations through the morning, completely ignorant of the course of events, and as noon aproached Ancram moved to Ferns, three miles from the detachment at Camolin, where they were both very vulnerable should a sizeable rebel detachment move in their direction.

Loftus's situation was even more dangerous. He had led his men on to Ballycanew and then turned westwards to the road the rebels had taken to Tubberneering. When he reached the road, he was only a short distance south of the battlefield, but the fighting had ended by that time, and instead of retreating westwards and joining the outposts at Camolin and Ferns, he pushed back northwards towards Tubberneering. When he got there he saw dozens of soldiers lying dead along the road, including Walpole, and on arriving at Clogh he also discovered the corpses left from the action that had taken place there. Only now did he realise what had happened, but, in an incredibly reckless move, he decided to follow the rebel army northwards towards Gorey, thinking perhaps that he might still surprise them or might escape into Wicklow by circumventing them. He failed to realise that he was pursuing a force at least five times the size of his own.[41]

In Gorey in the meantime the rebels were establishing a firm grip on the town and strategic points around it as Loftus began his march back. When the first detachments of Walpole's fleeing column arrived there, armed rebels had already taken up positions at windows that looked out on the main street, and one group had built a barricade across it. The soldiers attacked and overwhelmed the barricade and then forced their way down through the street, firing through windows on both sides as they went and even breaking into some houses and bayoneting suspected snipers, many of them quite probably innocent people. One detachment unleashed a deadly volley at the windows of the market house, where Esmond Kyan and several other prisoners were held. Just in time Kyan shouted to all those inside the building to lie on the floor; this prompt action undoubtedly saved their lives. The soldiers were in too great a hurry to drag them out into the street and conduct swift executions as they had done a week before when the town was evacuated for the first time; as a result, the entire body of prisoners survived the evacuation unhurt. The hundreds of loyalist refugees, not long arrived back from their earlier flight to Arklow, joined the military in their retreat and streamed out along the hills that ran parallel to the road, hoping to avoid any fighting that might take place along it. Most of them got well clear of the town before the rebels arrived, and soldiers and civilians alike reached Arklow safely, although exhausted, later in the day.[42]

In the meantime the rebels from Tubberneering had reached Gorey not long after the last of the garrison and loyalists had left. Some of them went down into the street and took possession of the town, but most made their way up the steep slope of Gorey Hill, just to its south, and began to form a camp. The hill was high, and they placed several of their cannon on its eastern slope to guard the road from Camolin. They may not have realised at this point that Loftus was approaching from that direction, and he and his men may have spotted their camp on the hill before they noticed him.[43]

Loftus realised the danger he was in as soon as he got close to the hill. The rebels, however, showed an extraordinary reluctance to attack the exposed column and instead fired several cannon shots at them from the hillside. This gave Loftus the chance he needed. He sent a small cavalry detachment forward along the road to convince the rebel leaders that he was planning an attack, but he began to lead his men back towards Clogh as they were doing this. Some of the rebels moved out along the ridge to his west in response, and a few of these kept up a steady musketry fire on him as he marched. They did little damage, however, and eventually gave up the pursuit and returned to the main body, which showed no signs of moving.

By the time he reached Clogh Loftus realised that the rebels were letting him get away. A yeoman guide who was with him led the way along a winding route that went westward across the hills to Carnew, and he and his men spent the rest of the day and evening retreating towards the border town.

At about the same time or a little later the detachments at Camolin and Ferns began to make their way westward too, some towards Newtownbarry and others towards Carnew. By mid-afternoon all four government columns that had pushed their way into Wexford the day before or that morning were fleeing in panic.[44] The campaign that Lake had expected would end the Wexford rebellion one week after it had begun, and leave the government in complete control of the entire country, had unravelled completely, and the northern division of the Wexford rebel forces had regained the momentum after a three-day hiatus.

*

In the south of the county too, in the meantime, the rebels began to act in a more decisive manner. The swelling army on Carrickbyrne Hill remained in position through the morning, but sometime in the afternoon, as Loftus was retreating towards Carnew, the first battalions moved off in the direction of New Ross. Others followed at intervals, and by evening a sizeable rebel force had begun to form at Corbet Hill, a ridge that rose above the town and a mile or so to its south-east. The rebel leadership (consisting of Bagenal Harvey, Thomas Cloney, John Kelly and John Henry Colclough) made Talbot Hall, a large house on Corbet Hill, their headquarters as soon as they arrived. They may have hoped to attack the town before nightfall, but, if so, they changed their minds at some point in the evening and agreed to launch the assault the next morning. Their men, numbering at least 10,000, and perhaps a great many more, spread out along the hills above the garrison's defensive lines and waited for dawn and the attack that they had left Wexford town to make five days previously.[45]

Below them, as this took place, Johnson and his garrison held their ground. They were buoyed themselves during the day by the arrival of Lord Mountjoy and a column of the Dublin city militia, which brought the garrison's strength to well over 2,000 men.[46]

Patrols from both sides probed the small fields along the slope between the two lines during the evening. At one point Johnson took a detachment of fifty men and a cannon out into the no-man's land and fired several shells at the rebels, who responded in kind, but neither side showed any willingness to risk an attack with darkness coming on. As night fell an eerie quiet settled on the slopes, shattered now and again by a shot from one of the garrison's cannon. In New Ross itself things were equally quiet. Many of the loyalist civilians had already fled across the bridge into County Kilkenny by this stage, and those inhabitants who remained, many of them no doubt sympathetic to the United Irishmen, stayed indoors for fear of the soldiers who had treated them with real brutality over the previous twenty-four hours.[47]

Meanwhile far to the east, the town of Wexford had been quiet all day and remained quiet now as twilight approached. Matthew Keogh had maintained order in spite of the Bullring murder of the previous day, but he and his aides no doubt continued to ponder the significance of Kingsborough's information and to speculate as to what the future might hold for them should the rising actually fail. They may have still kept the intelligence to themselves, but it seems very likely that by this time they had relayed the news to the rebel encampments. Certainly the behaviour of the rebel leaders both in the northern and southern divisions on this and subsequent days makes perfect sense given that they were aware of at least the Dublin débâcle by this time.

The rebel position had nevertheless improved dramatically during the day. In the northern part of the county the government's position was at its lowest point yet as the day ended. The remnants of Walpole's column and the Gorey garrison had reached Arklow by the time darkness fell, and after briefly considering their situation, they and the entire Arklow garrison marched out along the road towards Wicklow, followed by many of the loyalist civilians, and thereby abandoning what had been the staging-point for their invasion of Wexford. They marched steadily through the night, effectively abandoning much of southern Wicklow to the rebels.[48] In response, dozens of United Irishmen who had remained concealed in the valleys of south-eastern Wicklow for a week now, came out in the open and started to make their way southwards towards the camp at Gorey. Meanwhile other detachments marching to the west, including that led by Loftus, arrived safely at Carnew by midnight. Evacuation became the order of the day there too as Loftus decided that as soon as dawn broke he would withdraw to Tullow, twelve miles to the north-west, leaving south-western Wicklow as yet another area open to rebel occupation.[49]

There had been one other development during this day which had no direct connection with the military struggles themselves but which would soon be of great significance. Sometime during the morning, long before the march from Carrickbyrne to New Ross began, a party of rebels left the camp there and marched several miles south to the little village of Tintern. There they arrested dozens of suspected loyalist sympathisers, along with their families, and took them back to the camp, where they joined other prisoners interned over the previous few days, most of them Protestants. The rebel party confined the prisoners in the dwelling-house and out-buldings of a farmer named King in the townland of Scullabogue, about a mile to the south of the hill. When the main rebel army moved off towards New Ross, a guarding party remained behind to take charge of them. The precise motive of the insurgents in taking this action is unclear, but they were evidently planning to use the prisoners as hostages should the need arise in the battle that was to come.[50]

By the end of the day, then, the situation had changed markedly. In the country at large Lake's position looked as good as ever. There was still no rebellion in Ulster or Munster, the midland counties remained cowed, and only the Wexford rebels were still in the field. Their position, however, had altered dramatically during the day. They had smashed the government counter-offensive and had swept government forces from the entire area of north Wexford and south Wicklow. The only government redoubts inside County Wexford now were at Newtownbarry, Duncannon and New Ross, and a large rebel army was in position to attack New Ross as soon as day dawned.

The seriousness of the situation probably became clear to Lake very late in the evening. An express rider reached Dublin with news of the disaster at Tubberneering that night, and the general probably learned of the fall of Wexford town from him too.[51] He may still not have known of the rebel advance against New Ross at this late stage, although it is possible that he had received some communication from Johnson by this point. Even without that, though, he is likely to have realised that the Wexford rebels now represented a grave threat.[52] If they were strong enough to seize their own county in its entirety, then they were strong enough to spread the rebellion outside its borders. From Lake's perspective, the prospect of this happening at the same time that rebellion broke out in Ulster and Munster would have been very frightening indeed. Suddenly now the Wexford uprising was no longer a local affair; it had become the centre of the national crisis. Critically, however, this was something of which the Wexford rebel leaders themselves were probably not aware.

THE GATEWAYS OF ROSS
5–6 JUNE

THE ARMY THAT BAGENAL HARVEY HAD UNDER HIS COMMAND on the hills above New Ross by midnight on 4 June was a formidable force. It probably numbered at least 10,000 men and may have been as large as 15,000.[1] It was armed mostly with pikes, but several hundred men, perhaps even 1,000 or 2,000 had firearms, and it also had half a dozen cannon which were perfectly positioned to hit the town. They suffered from one very important disadvantage, however: they were almost completely lacking in experience of battle. A battalion or two of the Bantrymen had conducted the attack on the Meath militia at the Three Rocks, and some of the Bargy and Forth units may have seen some action at Mayglass, and the Rosegarland corps had ambushed Snowe at Taylorstown, but, apart from these small engagements, the vast majority of the force had not been involved in any real fighting. The spirits of the rank and file were high that night, but it was difficult for Harvey or any of the other officers to predict how well they would perform in hard combat.[2]

Harvey and his officers discussed their situation in Talbot Hall during the night.[3] They eventually agreed to give General Johnson the chance to surrender without a fight before committing themselves to a full-scale assault; doubts they had about their own forces or concerns about the strong position of the garrison may have prompted this. Harvey drew up a letter to Johnson demanding the immediate surrender of the town, and at about 3 or 4 a.m. Matthew Furlong of Templescoby volunteered to take it down the hill to the goverment outposts. He carried a white flag in one hand as he rode down the steep slope in the dim light, but as soon as he got close to the first group of soldiers they opened fire on him without warning and shot him dead. The rebel rank and file reacted with fury when they realised what had happened, and Harvey and the other leaders had trouble restraining some of them.[4] The leaders realised now that a full-scale assault was the only option, and they spent the next hour or two preparing to launch it.

Harvey and his aides had agreed upon a plan of attack by 5 a.m. They decided to throw their forces at three points in the town's defences simultaneously and to have them drive straight for the bridge once they got inside.[5] The main part of the attack would be against the Three Bullet Gate at the south-eastern corner of the town, directly in front of Talbot Hall. They chose the Bantrymen to conduct this part of assault, which John Kelly of Killann would lead. His instructions were to take the gate itself and to hold it until other battalions joined him; only after that was he to push on into the heart of the town. In the meantime another group would have swung around towards his left and attacked the Priory Gate, which lay at the southern entrance near the riverbank, and a third would have swung to his right and attacked the Market Gate, near the north-eastern corner; William Boxwell was to command the men on the left and John Henry Colclough those on the right. If all went according to plan, all three divisions would be able to force their way into the town at about the same time, and the garrison would have no option but to retreat across the bridge.[6]

Central to Harvey's plan was the assumption that United Irish units from Kilkenny would be in place on the west bank of the Barrow by early in the day and that they would trap the garrison as it tried to escape. The role of the Kilkennymen in the affair is unclear, but the evidence suggests that there was some kind of communication between the Corbet Hill camp and areas in the south-east of the neighbouring county. As a result, by dawn some small, scattered groups were gathering around Glenmore and Inishtiogue, and these were planning on taking some part in the struggle that was expected at New Ross.[7]

The garrison in the town was expecting the attack and was already well dug in and in quite a strong position. Johnson had placed most of his troops in a long crescent from the Market Gate around to the Three Bullet Gate, and the Clare and Dublin militias, two units in which he had a lot of faith, occupied either end of the line (the Clares at the Market Gate, the Dublins at the Three Bullet Gate). Other trusted detachments occupied important positions inside the town, including the barracks, which stood a short distance from the Three Bullet Gate, and the Main Guard, an imposing building just to the west of the all-important bridge. There was also a force of cavalry on the quays to protect the bridge should any of the rebels break in by way of the Priory Gate.[8]

As a battlefield New Ross presented severe challenges to both sides. The streets of the town sloped steeply down to the riverbank, giving some advantage to the attackers, but they were winding and narrow and so were ideal for soldiers equipped with muskets and cannon who were determined to defend them.[9] Anyone could have predicted that a battle in such a place would be enormously destructive, particularly for those who had to take the offensive.

The rebels launched their assault on the town's walls an hour or so after dawn, at around 5 a.m. In the first minutes Colclough and his battalions moved off towards the Market Gate, Boxwell swung to the left, aiming for the Priory Gate, and the Bantry units under Kelly and Cloney drove straight ahead. For reasons that are still unclear, but perhaps because they had never faced fire before and were thus inclined to panic, the units led by Colclough faltered at the beginning of the advance and soon afterwards fled the battlefield altogether, followed by their leader.[10]

Only the centre and left were intact, and they were now suddenly exposed to an assault from the garrison's left and, for this reason perhaps, began to falter themselves. Boxwell's men had not encountered much resistance and were pressing on, as were the front ranks of the Bantrymen under John Kelly, who were closing in on the garrison's outposts at the Three Bullet Gate. The battalions behind Kelly's unit, however, were slowing down, and, like Colclough's division, they soon stopped too and began to retreat back up the hill, leaving both Kelly's and Boxwell's men isolated and in real danger of being destroyed should Johnson realise this and launch a counter-attack.[11]

Johnson was not the kind of soldier to fail to notice

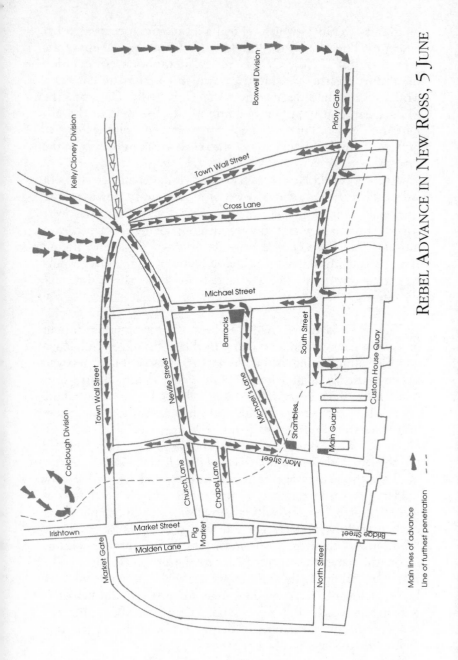

REBEL ADVANCE IN NEW ROSS, 5 JUNE

Main lines of advance

Line of furthest penetration

such things. When he saw what was happening, he called a detachment of cavalry up from the quays and ordered them to move out to his left, then swing around to his right and trap the forward rebel divisions against the defensive lines. The dragoons in question numbered about a hundred men, and they rode quickly out through the Market Gate and passed along the face of the hill towards the right flank of the rebel centre, frozen just above the Three Bullet Gate. But as the the cavalry made their way along a narrow roadway that ran across the face of the hill, the Bantry rebels who had retreated further up the slope suddenly turned about and charged down at them. At the same moment Kelly's men also turned around and attacked them from the other side, so that in a matter of moments the dragoons were trapped between the rebels above and below them. Johnson's infantry units at the bottom of the hill watched helplessly as this happened, since their officers did not dare lead them out from behind their cover. The rebels quickly overwhelmed the cavalrymen and killed more than twenty of them, including their commanding officer. The rest managed somehow to escape and fled back into the town by the way they had come.[12]

The action restored the momentum to the insurgents, and the Bantry forces drove down towards the Three Bullet Gate for the second time and now with renewed enthusiasm. Kelly was still leading them. He ordered them to halt when he saw a militia officer ride out in front of the trenches and approach them. The officer was Lord Mountjoy, commander of the Dublin city militia, and he wanted to persuade them to abandon the attack. By this time, however, the rebels were unwilling to entertain any such suggestion, and several of them attacked Mountjoy as soon as they got close to him and killed him on the spot.[13] For many of them, no doubt, this was just retribution for the shooting of Matthew Furlong an hour or two earlier.

It was clear to both sides that it would be a fight to the finish now, and a fierce musketry duel opened almost simultaneously in front of the Three Bullet and Priory Gates. The soldiers held their ground for a time, but some of the cabins behind the Three Bullet trenches caught fire and began to burn furiously. Once this happened, the soldiers gradually began to lose ground. Kelly and the Bantrymen pressed the advantage, and when the soldiers finally broke and retreated back into the town, abandoning this critical section of the line altogether, they made their way to the gate and then, in spite of their orders, pushed on down the street as far as the barracks. Kelly and his battalion were suddenly deep in the heart of New Ross and far ahead of the battalion under Cloney, which had stopped at the gate as they were supposed to.

Instead of retreating now, Kelly led his men in an attack on the barracks. The troops inside opened fire on them as they did so, and, since the rebels were in exposed positions in the street, several of them were hit, among them Kelly himself, whose thigh was shattered by a bullet. Suddenly demoralised, his men picked him up, carried him back to the gate, and for the time being gave up the attempt to take the barracks. It was obvious immediately that the young colonel could take no further part in the battle, and he was carried out to safety beyond the gate. His loss was a severe blow, and Thomas Cloney would now have to take command of the Bantry division.[14]

By this time Johnson was trying to react to the sudden collapse of the centre of his line. He realised quickly that he had to establish a new one somewhere inside the town. By now though, the rebels under Boxwell had forced their way in through the Priory Gate, and so Johnson's grip on the southern part of the town was in jeopardy. To meet the threat, he decided to leave the Clares where they were and to have cannon and musketmen placed at strategic points on the main streets running in a north–south direction, especially Neville Street, Michael's Lane and South Street. He decided to keep the cavalry on the quays, to prevent an attack on the bridge from that direction. When this redeployment was completed, the general had effectively surrendered the southern third or so of the town to the rebels, but his new line was a strong one and would be very difficult to overwhelm.[15]

The rebels renewed the attack when they had had a chance to reorganise themselves. It was now about 7 a.m. or perhaps a little later, and Harvey had moved his headquarters down to the Three Bullet Gate itself and was ready to direct the drive into the heart of the town from there.[16] The various units drove along Neville Street from the Three Bullet Gate and travelled quite a distance before meeting any opposition. Some detachments broke off and pushed down Cross Lane, into the other end of which some of the units that had come in through the Priory Gate were now making their way. A detachment of troops was trapped in the lane for a short while by this movement, but they eventually escaped through a connecting alley, partly through the efforts of a flamboyant local yeoman in a brass helmet named McCormick. Their retreat gave the rebels firm control of the southern perimeter of the town.[17]

Progress was more difficult further up the hill, along Neville Street. Here the soldiers met the rebels as they pushed towards the upper part of Mary Street, and over the next hour or more there were fierce musketry duels and running battles in that part of the town. Over and over again the attackers charged militia and yeomanry positions, only to be driven back by concentrated musketry and cannon fire, and their losses were now very heavy.[18] In time, perhaps after half an hour or even an hour of this fierce struggle, some rebel units finally broke through to the upper part of Mary Street. Now they were poised to cut off the Clare militia at the Market Gate if they could take possession of the Pig Market and Market Street behind them. They were also in a good position to drive straight down Mary Street itself and attack the Main Guard. If they were able to take that building, the entire garrison might be trapped inside the town.

There were especially fierce struggles in the small lanes that connected Mary Street and Market Street as the rebels tried to force their way through; the fighting was most intense in Church and Chapel Lanes. Somehow the soldiers managed to hold both these lanes, however, and the rebel losses were appallingly high, dozens of men losing their lives as they tried to storm barricades in the narrow spaces where almost every bullet fired at them ricocheted in a deadly pattern.[19]

Fierce struggles went on in several other places at this stage in the battle. Rebel units made their way down Michael's Lane and threatened the central part of Mary Street from there, and other units, mostly Boxwell's men from the Priory Gate, began to make progress in spite of intense fire and heavy losses along South Street.[20] The rebels were taking the town one building at a time, and as eight o'clock approached, three or four hours into the battle, they had gained possession of its southern half.

At around eight o'clock, with smoke from the streets of burning cabins beginning to fill the town, some of the garrison began to pull back and make their way towards the bridge. Units of the Dublin militia, among them those who had been stationed at the Three Bullet Gate earlier, were the first to do this. Others soon followed, and in time large numbers began to make their way across the bridge to the Kilkenny side of the river.[21] As this happened some of the rebels forced their way closer to the northern end of South Street and got within sight of the Main Guard, while others began to push down Mary Street, also making for that strategically important building. Still others began to force an approach to the Pig Market along Chapel and Church Lanes.[22] The dwindling garrison had now been pushed back to a defensive line that ran from Market Gate, through the middle of Church and Chapel Lanes, down to the Main Guard; only the northern quarter of the town was still in their hands, therefore, and even this was on the point of being lost. This was a remarkable achievement on the part of the rebels, especially considering the setbacks they had suffered earlier and the heavy losses they continued to sustain.

The turning-point came not long after eight o'clock. At that point a large rebel band made its way down Mary Street and came around a bend just up the hill from the Main Guard (probably beside the jail in the Shambles). There they were suddenly hit by a huge discharge of grapeshot from a cannon which had been pulled out into the street by the militiamen at the Main Guard. The explosion did terrible damage, felling many in the front ranks and driving the others back up the hill.[23] The rebels rallied and tried to make their way slowly down the street, using the doorways and windows for cover, but as they did this loyalist snipers in upper-floor windows opened fire on them and killed many. Combined with the musketry fire kept up by the militia from the bottom of the street, this made it impossible for them to get any further than the junction of Michael's Lane and Mary Street.[24]

The rebels attacking along South Street were checkmated at about this time too. They had pushed close to the Main Guard, but here again the soldiers unleashed intense cannon and musketry fire on them and caused severe losses. In a short while the remaining rebels began to pull back out of range and established a new position further down the street.[25] At the Pig Market too the Clare militia held on and kept the rebels from breaking through to the little square.[26]

The rebels now found themselves beset by problems of many kinds. For one thing, Bagenal Harvey and the officers immediately around him had difficulty following the course of events inside the town. From their vantage-point at the Three Bullet Gate they could have seen only part of the way down Neville Steet, and the fighting that was taking place in parts of the town like the north end of South Street or near the Pig Market was out of their view completely.[27] To add to their troubles, many of the fires that had caught hold by this time were burning close by, so that there was probably a thick pall of smoke hanging over the entire southern third of the town.[28] Those rebel units that were struggling so fiercely against militia positions at the other end were most likely doing so without any direction and thus could not co-ordinate their efforts.

To add even further to the rebels' troubles, the rank and file were not well situated to carry out a final push for victory by this stage. They had come this far without at least one-third of the original army, and the effects of the battle were beginning to show. Hundreds had died already, and huge numbers, certainly hundreds and maybe even thousands, had been wounded. Those who had not fallen had been fighting hard for at least three or four hours and for much of that time had been trying to operate in thick smoke. They were exhausted and confused, and even though they were within sight of victory, many of the most active units needed to rest.[29] Not least of all, they had been using gunpowder that was of low quality all this time, and even that was now running low.[30]

Then, to compound the problems, there was the matter of the Kilkenny rebels. They had not shown up, for reasons that were never to be explained but that seem to have included a lack of co-ordination among their own captains.[31] This meant that the soldiers who retreated across the bridge could rest there without concern for their safety and watch the town for signs of what might be happening.

Shortly after eight o'clock, with the two armies in these positions, there was a lull in the fighting as the rebels halted their offensive and tried to regroup.[32] While they were thus engaged, the soldiers held onto their vulnerable positions in the northern section of the town, and Johnson took advantage of the sudden lull in the fighting to go across the bridge and try to stem the tide of retreat that had already taken most of the garrison over to the west bank of the river. He had a difficult time persuading them to turn about, but eventually they began to listen to him and to consider making an effort to retake the streets that had been lost.[33]

As the rebels tried to regroup for their own attack, some of them went about the streets picking up the wounded; they carried most of those who had fallen near Mary Street to a four-storey building at the top of the hill that they now turned into a makeshift hospital. There was little they could do immediately for these men, many of whom were very badly injured, but they laid them on the floors of the building and tried to make them as comfortable as they could for the present time. Presumably they decided that they would receive proper medical attention as soon as the conquest of the town had been completed.[34]

At about 8.30 or 9 a.m. General Johnson came to realise that the rebels were not going to force their way across the bridge after all. He used all his powers of persuasion to convince the troops sheltering on its western side that this was the situation and that they should counter-attack and save the men who were still holding out at the Main Guard, the Pig Market and the Market Gate. The first detachment to respond were the Dublin militia, which had been one of the first to retreat. Major Vesey, their commander now that Mountjoy was dead, led them back across the bridge, and they moved in behind the Main Guard and waited for the word to go further. After a short interval other units came across and joined them, and within about half an hour the entire garrison was back on the east side of the river and getting ready to attack the rebel positions in the town and enlarge the bridgehead that had been held for them by the Clares and Donegals.[35] The rebel leaders, unaware of these developments because of the smoke from the burning cabins, did not realise what was about to take place and made no provision for defensive action. Their numbers had dwindled considerably by this point as a result of losses and desertions, and they may have had as few as 4,000 or 5,000 men at their disposal.[36] Furthermore, with their powder supply now seriously low, they would be in a bad position to hold the streets against soldiers who were still well supplied.

*

Johnson's counter-attack probably began around 9 a.m. or shortly afterwards.[37] The rebels were caught completely by surprise, and the soldiers quickly overwhelmed them in the eastern and southern parts of the town. They retook all of Mary Street and then pushed their way southwards, driving up along Neville Street, Michael's Lane and South Street with fierce determination. The rebel counter-charges were costly and had little effect.[38] Because the soldiers gained control of the northern sector with such speed, several rebel units found themselves suddenly cut off from their comrades. Among them were the seventy or so men in the makeshift hospital, and these now became the victims of the worst atrocity to be committed in the war so far. As soon as it was discovered what the building was being used for, a detachment of soldiers surrounded it. Then somebody, perhaps several men at the urging of an officer, perhaps a lone individual, set a fire in the ground floor. The building was dry inside, and flames spread quickly to the upper floors. When they realised what was happening, the helpless men inside began to scream so loudly that they could be heard all over the town. The soldiers in the street below watched unmoved as the entire building became an inferno and as the shrieks inside gradually died away. One man somehow managed to escape and ran through the smoke and confusion back towards the rebel lines. Everyone else inside died.[39]

As the soldiers in Mary Street destroyed the rebel hospital, their comrades were behaving just as ruthlessly elsewhere in the town. They fought their way further southwards until they had regained control of almost the entire town, except for a small area around the Three Bullet Gate. Rebels who lay wounded along the streets were shown no mercy by the advancing soldiers but were bayoneted or shot without hesitation. Those who surrendered were given the same treatment, as were countless non-combatants, many of them inhabitants of the cabins that had been burned down and who had no option but to take to the streets.[40]

Harvey and his officers were caught completely by surprise. With Colclough and Kelly both gone from the scene, Boxwell and Cloney became the commander-in-chief's principal aides. They tried to organise at least two major counter-charges along Neville

Street to turn the tide, but their numbers had dwindled even further now and ammunition supplies were practically exhausted. Their efforts became increasingly desperate, and each time they were driven back with great loss.[41]

At about one o'clock Harvey finally realised that the day was lost, and he pulled what remained of his army back from the Three Bullet Gate and retreated in fairly good order up to Corbet Hill.[42] Cloney made one last effort to rally the demoralised remnant when he persuaded a column of about fifty men to follow him and attack the Clare militia position at Irishtown. They made their way succesfully to within the last open field by the cabins, but the assault failed when the Clares began to pick off the exposed men as they charged across the open ground, and the entire unit fell back in disarray.[43] After this it was clear even to Cloney that the day was lost.

A few insurgent officers briefly considered one more drive against the town when they reached the ridge of Corbet Hill and realised that the soldiers were not pursuing them. At that moment, however, they caught a glimpse of a small government detachment across the Barrow valley to their west, and this changed their minds. (The column in question was on its way from Waterford to New Ross and, ironically, was actually in the process of turning around, thinking that the town had fallen to the rebels.)[44]

The rebel defeat was devastating. The army of at least 10,000 men which had moved against the town eight hours before was reduced to a tattered remnant of 2,000 or 3,000.[45] As they retreated back towards Carrickbyrne they left over a thousand men dead in the streets below them.[46] They had used up immense amounts of ammunition and powder and had lost hundreds of guns and pikes.[47] All but one of the six artillery pieces they had brought with them were left behind, and but for heroic efforts of a woman named Mary Doyle even that gun would have been lost.[48] Besides all that, they now had ample proof, if any was still needed, that the government was firmly in control of the regions beyond the Barrow and that its forces were very far indeed from collapsing.

But the tragedy of the day was not yet complete. During the morning groups of rebels fleeing from the initial stages of the fighting had passed by Carrickbyrne, and some of them told the guards at King's farm at Scullabogue to kill the prisoners because the soldiers were murdering captured rebels in New Ross. The guards ignored these demands, however, and the prisoners remained safe.[49] Later in the morning reports of government atrocities became more chilling and the demands for revenge more insistent. Eventually, probably around 10 a.m. but possibly as late as 11 a.m. or noon,[50] the guards gave in to the demands for revenge and conducted a massacre that more than matched the horrors of New Ross. They took about thirty of the loyalist men who had been held in King's farmhouse out onto the lawn and shot them all, a few at a time. Then they locked the rest of the men, along with the women and children, about eighty people in all, into a barn and set it on fire. They let no one escape, not even the children, and in minutes the building was engulfed in flames with the trapped screaming victims inside. The terrified prisoners almost forced the door open at one point, but the rebels outside hacked at fingers and hands with pikes and bayonets and forced it shut again. One child is said to have crept out under the barn door only to be piked by a rebel and flung back into the flames.[51] In all, over a hundred people died in the massacre, and when Harvey and the main part of the army arrived back at Carrickbyrne they were greeted with the sickening sight of bodies strewn about the lawn in front of the dwelling-house and the even worse spectacle of the gutted barn inside which the charred corpses were still standing upright because they had been so tightly packed in.[52]

In a matter of a few hours the southern front had produced two appalling atrocities that made the terrible things done by both sides up to this point pale into insignificance. Nothing could be the same again for either of them.

There was considerable confusion about events at New Ross all across southern Wexford during the afternoon and evening. Small bands of rebels drifted eastwards all day, bringing reports of the battle with them: some claiming a spectacular rebel victory, others a defeat, others a stalemate that would be decided in the coming days. Some reports may have reached Wexford town well before nightfall, including the official dispatch sent by Harvey to Keogh,

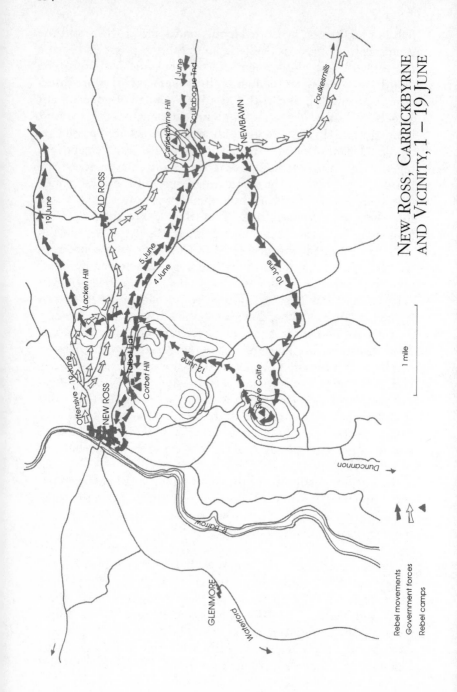

New Ross, Carrickbyrne and Vicinity, 1 – 19 June

1 mile

Rebel movements
Government forces
Rebel camps

but people in many parts of the south-east outside the town were still unaware of what the outcome had been when night fell.[53]

By nightfall the fires along the cabin streets of New Ross had finally burned out, but the town still reeked of smoke and roasted bodies, and, as at Enniscorthy a week earlier, pigs and dogs began to eat the flesh from the corpses. The soldiers continued to hunt for rebels and showed no mercy on those they found. On one occasion a group of soldiers even shot a young man who was probably a loyalist, simply because he dared to say that their behaviour was outrageous. Afterwards they threw his body into a burning cabin. Some rebels did manage to conceal themselves in cabins and other places about the town and remain undiscovered to the end of the day; these were few in number, however, and they must have realised that it would be difficult to remain hidden for long. Johnson made some effort to control the troops, and he made them empty their guns at one point in the evening, but they continued to kill prisoners and by nightfall many of them had even begun to loot shops and private houses.[54]

Several miles to the east the rebels were trying to recover as best they could from the disaster. Harvey and his army settled for the night at Carrickbyrne. However, the great majority of the units he had commanded that day were nowhere to be seen. Some had fled eastwards, others had slipped away to pass the night with nearby relatives. Even Thomas Cloney was among these. He fell asleep in his saddle on the retreat and woke up towards the end of the day to find himself alone on the roadside where his horse had stopped. He made his way to the house of a relative and spent the night there, leaving the task of regrouping the Bantry battalions to another day.[55]

In contrast to the fateful and tragic events that took place in the south of the county on 5 June, the day passed relatively quietly for the rebels in the northern part of the county. The leaders on Gorey Hill were still unsure where the government forces that had evaded them the afternoon before had disappeared to, and they had kept several detachments of men on patrol around the town throughout the night to guard against a surprise counter-attack. Just before dawn, at about the time that Harvey was getting ready for his move against New Ross, bands of

Wicklow United Irishmen began to arrive in Gorey and brought the news that the army had abandoned Arklow.[56] Somewhat surprisingly, there was no rush to take possession of the undefended town. This hesitation was probably because Arklow was outside the county and its capture was therefore not originally part of the Wexford United Irish plan. Although they were surely fully aware that the government was holding out to their north, the principal objective of Edward Roche and his fellow-commanders was to maintain their position for the time being and to replenish their supplies of food and ammunition, both of which were now low. As the early hours of the 5th passed, therefore, he dispatched foraging and reconnaissance patrols out into the countryside around the town[57] and sent a messenger southwards towards Wexford with an urgent request for gunpowder.[58] He and his officers knew they could not risk any further moves until this arrived, and they must also have known that it could take at least a day before that happened.

For Roche and his officers, finding out as much as they could about what was happening to the rebellion elsewhere was as important, and as difficult, as any other task. Most of the recruits who had come to them during the morning from County Wicklow were not in a position to give precise information about the situation beyond the Wicklow mountains. They had, however, witnessed the survival of the government forces in the early days of the rising in their own county, and they had seen the reinforcement of places like Arklow during the ensuing days. Regardless of how vague their sense of the bigger picture was, therefore, their reports would almost certainly have confirmed the fact that the government had survived and had counter-attacked in some force in the east Leinster counties. With this information to work from, and considering the gunpowder problem, it is not surprising at all that the Gorey leaders decided to hold their position for the day and wait for news either from the north or the south.

The rank and file of the Gorey camp was nevertheless not entirely inactive during the afternoon and evening. They had considerable success in replenishing their food supplies, since many of the patrols that went out into the countryside in the morning returned with sizeable herds of cattle they had seized from loyalist-owned farmlands. They also rounded up individual loyalists when they found them and confined them in the market house, which they now in turn used as a prison. In addition, they conducted three significant acts of revenge against their enemies when they burned the residences of the Rams at Clonattin and Ramsfort Park and of Hunter Gowan at Mount Nebo. Significantly, they made no attempt to conduct a systematic arson campaign against the hundreds of other Protestant-owned houses in the parishes around the town.[59]

Government forces in the northern theatre spent the entire day attempting to regroup. The Arklow garrison and its civilian entourage had reached Wicklow town early in the morning. The commander there was incensed at what he regarded as their cowardice and ordered a small detachment of the troops to march back and retake the town that afternoon. Such a detachment did leave for the south in the afternoon, but as evening fell it was still on its way, and so an entire day passed with Arklow completely undefended.[60]

In Dublin in the meantime General Lake spent the day reacting to the collapse of the offensive against north Wexford. The Wexford rebellion had come to look very serious now that it embraced the entire county; indeed, from his vantage-point, New Ross and Newtownbarry may have looked as if they were on the point of falling to the insurgents too. However, there still was no definite news of rebellion in Ulster or Munster, and this encouraged him to continue to focus primarily on the Wexford threat. Early in the morning he ordered Lieutenant-General Francis Needham to muster a force of about 1,000 men at Loughlinstown camp, just south of Dublin, and to take them south to bolster the garrison which he still believed to be holding out at Arklow. Needham comandeered dozens of carts and began his journey south during the afternoon, probably around the time that the battle at New Ross was reaching its final stage. He got as far as Wicklow by evening and learned of the abandonment of Arklow from the garrison there. With night falling, he decided to stay where he was for the time being and to start again once daylight broke. He was earnestly hoping, no doubt, that he would get to Arklow before the rebels did.[61]

Meanwhile, twenty miles to the south-west of Wicklow town, Loftus was conducting himself very differently. He led the entire force at Carnew (including the yeoman garrison) out of the town that morning and spent the rest of the day marching them across the hills of south-west Wicklow towards Tullow. The column reached Tullow in the afternoon, and in the evening Loftus sent a small detachment of troops eastwards to occupy Tinahely, just inside the Wicklow border.[62] This move plugged an important gap in the defensive line that now ran from Wicklow town across the central part of the county to Tullow, but it also meant that government forces had for the moment abandoned practically the entire southern half of the county.

Wednesday 6 June saw little action anywhere in Wexford, but it was a decisive day in the struggle. In the southern theatre Harvey made no attempt to regain the initiative, and there now began a stand-off that would prevail between the rebels and the government forces dug in at New Ross for two weeks. The rebels at Gorey remained in their positions too, letting slip their one real chance to take full advantage of their stunning victory at Tubberneering and establish themselves at Arklow.

In contrast, Needham and his column set out from Wicklow on the ten-mile march to Arklow early in the morning. The small detachment which had left to reoccupy the town the evening before had arrived by that point and had established a token government presence there. Since he was still using the commandeered carts, Needham and his men travelled in some comfort, but the bulk of the old Arklow garrison accompanied them, and this slowed their progress down considerably. Among these were many of the militia units which had escaped from Tubberneering and also various north Wexford and south Wicklow yeomanry corps. These men were thirsting for revenge against the rebels, and the yeomen in particular began to devastate the countryside on either side of the road as they marched, burning houses and shooting almost anyone they saw. Needham attempted to stop them, ineffectively for some time, but eventually he placed several of them under arrest and this finally put an end to the depredations.

The column came within sight of Arklow well before noon in

spite of the delays. As the troops approached the bridge they noticed scores of people in boats in the harbour. Needham was unsure of what this meant, but later discovered that these were townspeople who were so terrified at the prospect of the soldiers' return and the massacre they expected to follow it that they fled to the water. Eventually, after he had settled his men in the town and was satisfied that no rebel attack was imminent, Needham was successful in persuading these people to come back.

By the early afternoon he was in firm possession of this vital point on the coastal route from Wexford to the capital, and he set his men to work on fortifications which would help him defend against any attack that the rebels might launch. From this point onwards any attempt by the rebels to initiate a thrust along the coastal plain would be certain to be very costly to them.[63]

Ten miles to the south at Gorey Hill, the rebels were still making no move and were oblivious to what was taking place in Arklow. As on the day before, they sent several search parties out into the countryside to look for fugitive loyalists; those they arrested, almost forty in number, were confined in the market house. The search parties continued to acquire provisions for the camp too, mostly beef, and large numbers of animals were butchered and their carcases boiled in and around the camp.

The shortage of ammunition was by far the most serious problem they faced by this stage, and the day came and went without any sign of a new supply arriving from Wexford. Thus far they knew nothing of the battle and defeat at New Ross, and so they could not have realised why the leaders in Wexford town were so slow to meet their request. Until the powder arrived, of course, they were unlikely to take any offensive action of their own.

However, they continued to reconnoitre the surrounding area. Miles Byrne was with a patrol that rode out towards Carnew during the morning looking for information about the enemy in that direction. They skirted around the town to the north and eventually came to within a few miles of Shillelagh, where they suddenly encountered a mounted government patrol. The loyalist cavalry faced them for a short time, but then turned about and fled westward. Byrne's group decided not to give chase, perhaps because they feared an ambush, and so they learned little about the local situation. The cavalry in question were probably from Tullow and were probing eastwards for Loftus, but the rebels did not realise this and returned to Gorey Hill later in the day still largely ignorant of the disposition of the garrison forces to their west and, incredibly, still assuming that Carnew was in government hands.[64]

In south Wexford, by contrast, the rebels had completely lost their former momentum. Bagenal Harvey spent the day trying desperately to rebuild his demoralised army and to impose some kind of order on a situation that threatened to get out of control. To lessen the tensions that had now begun to develop, he raised a subscription among his officers for the burial of the victims at Scullabogue; then he issued a proclamation declaring that all able-bodied men should report to the camps at once and that any man guilty of desertion, the murder of prisoners or looting would be shot.[65] Most of his army was still missing, including Colclough's entire regiment, but Harvey was letting it be known that from now on the southern rebel division would be a citizen army and would be disciplined.

The rebel leaders in Wexford town and elsewhere in the south-east of the county were still managing to preserve order. Many of them must have begun to realise that the defeat at New Ross and the sudden deterioration of the movement meant that the cause was lost and that they would face a fierce loyalist backlash once the end came.

General Johnson was now in a very different position, and he spent the day consolidating his position at New Ross and sending detailed reports of the battle up the Barrow valley to Dublin Castle.[66] He was satisfied that the rebels had no intention of attacking him again, but he was unwilling to risk marching out against them. He sent out some of his soldiers to continue the seach for rebels hiding in and around the town, and, as on the day before, most of those they found they shot immediately, although they hauled a few off to prison.[67] The most pressing tasks now were the repair of damaged fortifications and the burial of the hundreds of corpses that had begun to decompose in the summer heat. James Alexander, a veteran of the American Revolutionary War, organised a corps of auxiliaries from among the town's artisans and labourers, many of them quite possibly United Irish sympathisers or even members. Their purpose was to stockpile provisions, repair trenches and bury the dead. They set about their work early in the day and made steady progress. The task of burial was particularly gruesome. They dug huge open pits just to the east of the wall and threw hundreds of mutilated and half-burned corpses into them and covered them with quicklime to lessen the danger of disease. They carted hundreds of others, most likely those who fell in the fighting inside the town, down to the riverbank and tossed them in the water. For days they floated down the Barrow and eventually reached the open sea. By evening, according to his own account, Alexander and his men had disposed of at least 2,000 bodies.[68]

In Dublin Castle Lake was beginning to realise that his forces had regained the initiative in Wexford. By this time he knew of the checkmating of the rebels at New Ross and was probably aware that Loftus's troops had established a new defensive line at Tullow and Tinahely. More importantly, he also realised that Needham had reached Arklow and was digging in there with a garrison of 1,500 men.[69] With no reports of rebellion elsewhere in the country, it must have been increasingly clear that the wholesale uprising he had feared would not now develop. Unknown to him, though, and to the Wexford insurgents too, on this very day the Ulster United Irishmen had initiated their uprising in south Antrim and north Down. Reports of this would not reach Lake for another day or two, but once they did, his perspective on the Wexford threat would change considerably.

As night fell on 6 June, then, the Wexford rebel leaders faced a very uncertain future. The officers at Gorey Hill still did not know of the defeat at New Ross and were most immediately concerned with the fact that their gunpowder had still not arrived, even though it had been two full days now since they had broken through the government chain at Tubberneering. They had essentially completed the task assigned to them in the United Irish plan, but since the plan had so obviously failed, this was of little consolation. We do not know what was going through the minds of men like Roche, the Murphys or Perry at this stage, but they must surely have been very confused and very worried about the chances of ultimate success.

Similar thoughts must have passed through Bagenal Harvey's mind. From his perspective, the rebellion had completely changed from what it had been in its first days. It was no longer the easy task it must have seemed at first, and it had produced unspeakably cruel atrocities on both sides. Like Roche at Gorey, he could not have had any illusions about the fact that it was all up to the Wexfordmen, with only a slender chance remaining at this stage that the Ulstermen and the French would be of any assistance.

A FOREST OF PIKES: CARNEW AND ARKLOW
7–9 JUNE

By 7 JUNE THE REBELLION IN WEXFORD HAD BEGUN TO SHOW ALL the signs of an uprising whose leaders realised that their backs were to the wall and who understood that they had to prepare for a long and perhaps desperate struggle. The quick sweeping victory the United Irish movement had expected was simply not to be, and now they had to adapt or face certain defeat.

Up to this point the Wexford leaders had made little attempt to create a centralised command structure, but now they set about establishing one. In part the effort was motivated by strictly military concerns, but it also had the hallmarks of an attempt to legitimise their uprising and to rekindle the morale of their followers.

The central figure in the reorganisation was Edward Roche. He left the Gorey Hill camp and rode south to Wexford either during the night of the 6th or during the morning of the 7th. Once he arrived in the town, he devised and implemented what amounted to a complete overhaul of the leadership structure.[1] He himself took over from Bagenal Harvey as commander-in-chief, but he remained in Wexford, since the town was a useful base from which he could stay in touch with both armies, instead of going out to Carrickbyrne. The southern force would be led from this point on by Father Philip Roche, who was from the north of the county and who was a close confidant of the new commander-in-chief; and Anthony Perry, who was also a close acquaintance, would command the northern one. Harvey in the meantime would be asked to return to Wexford town and to become president of the administrative council there. This position was superior to Matthew Keogh's, at least in official terms, but Keogh remained on as governor of the town and was still its most important official.[2] The restructuring amounted to a northern takeover of the United Irish movement in Wexford and saw the moderate and more politically oriented southerners lose considerable ground; from this point on men like Harvey and Colclough would play a secondary role in the south, while military leaders like Philip Roche and Thomas Cloney took control.

That afternoon Roche sealed the reorganisation (and reorientation) of the rebellion by issuing a proclamation addressed to 'the People of Ireland'. Significantly, this was the first such document to be issued by the Wexford rebels, and while not actually declaring a republic, it nevertheless implied that they saw themselves as the most important bearers of the revolutionary standard at this point. Its preamble was a classic example of republican language and sentiment:

> Your patriotic exertions in the cause of your country have hitherto exceeded your most sanguine expectations, and in a short time must ultimately be crowned with success. Liberty has raised her drooping head: thousands daily flock to the standard: the voice of her children everywhere prevails. Let us then, in this moment of triumph, return thanks to the almighty ruler of the universe, that a total stop has been put to those sanguinary measures which of late were but too often resorted to by the creatures of government, to keep the people in slavery. At this eventful period, all Europe must admire, and posterity will read with astonishment, the heroic acts achieved by a people strangers to military tactics, and having few professional commanders: but what power can resist men fighting for liberty?[3]

The intent of the document clearly was to renew support for the struggle, to justify the rebellion by appeals to liberty, and to remind all that defeat would mean a return to oppression. It is significant too that Roche reminded the rebel rank and file that it was 'all Europe' that was watching, and that, in true Enlightenment fashion, it was 'posterity' that would be the final judge. From this point on we can almost speak of a 'Wexford Republic', created out of necessity as the spearhead of what amounted to a second phase of the United Irish rebellion.

*

Not surprisingly, 7 June saw little significant military activity. The Carrickbyrne rebels remained at their camp throughout the day, and Harvey, who was still with them at this stage, attempted to entice those who had left two days before to come back to the base. He had little success, and with no more than a remnant of his former force at his disposal there was no chance of launching a second attack on New Ross.[4]

Meanwhile, to the east of the camp, there were some serious threats to the safety of the loyalist prisoners in Wexford town. At one point in the day a party of rebels made their way into the building where the captives were lodged and took about twenty-five men outside with the intention of shooting them. They had already made the men kneel down on the ground when somebody brought Father Currin, the local priest, to the rescue; he persuaded the would-be executioners that their intended victims were from the town itself, that they had never shot at the people, and that they ought to be spared.

The rebels desisted and returned most of the prisoners to the jail. They handed about half of them over to a party of rebels from Enniscorthy, however, and these men took them to Vinegar Hill, where many of them were eventually executed. For the moment, though, the effort by extremists to begin a bloodbath in Wexford town itself had been thwarted.[5]

Similarly, the military situation in the northern part of the county changed little during the course of the day. The rebel leaders on Gorey Hill were still unsure if there were garrisons at Carnew and Arklow as the day began. They sent yet another patrol out in the general direction of Carnew early in the day. By late afternoon the scouting party had still not returned from the west, and the leaders in the camp were still unaware of the situation in Arklow. Nevertheless, for reasons that are not entirely clear, Perry and the others decided to break camp and to march on out towards Carnew. At the very least they might have a chance to take revenge on the property of some of their most hated enemies in that area, and there was also the chance that they might capture some more arms.[6]

They marched out towards the west as evening was approaching, and before they had gone very far they met their patrol returning from the countryside. When they had learned all they could about the whereabouts of Loftus and his men, the chiefs urged the men on to Carnew, and they entered the town without incident a few hours later.

Almost immediately some of the men began to set fire to the houses and property of known loyalists. The flames spread quickly, and soon other houses began to catch fire, and in half an hour or so most of the town was burning, with the exception of a few stone buildings. The soldiers in Loftus's outpost at Tinahely, only four miles to the north, almost certainly saw the smoke from the fires, but they made no move to oppose the rebel sack of a famous loyalist stronghold, and the northern rebel army occupied the streets of the town with impunity for several hours.[7]

When they had finished searching the town, Perry led them out to Kilcavan Hill, a high point about a mile to the north which dominated the countryside for miles around, and they set up camp there for the night with the intention of marching back to Gorey when morning came. During the evening, however, someone rode out from Gorey with news of the regarrisoning of Arklow. This immediately sparked a debate over the question of attacking the town. Arklow was not part of the territory for which the Wexfordmen were responsible, but it was vitally important to the south Wicklow battalions under Garrett Byrne that had been with the Wexford army for a week now and had played an important role in the capture of Wexford town and in the battle at Tubberneering. The debate lasted over the next several hours and developed into the more general argument over strategy which was inevitable sooner or later, given the changed circumstances in which they now found themselves. Garrett Byrne suggested that about 8,000 men from both counties should now push north into the heart of the mountains and harass the government positions along the Wicklow coast, presumably in anticipation of a French landing taking place soon. Other officers, Father John Murphy perhaps foremost among them, advocated a return to Gorey and a more cautious and defensive approach which would enable them to defend the one liberated county they knew of; this argument also must have been based on the assumption that a French force was on its way. The debate became quite intense and eventually ended in defeat for Byrne's position; it was agreed that the army would remain intact and march back to Gorey when daylight came.[8]

The Kilcavan debate testifies to the difficulty of the rebel position now. The fact that such a dispute occurred at all indicates that few of the insurgents had any illusions about their situation at this stage. Those who saw their best hope in a conventional war against the forces then closing in on them (and who at present appeared to have the upper hand) evidently assumed that there was still some hope for insurrections in other parts of the country, especially Ulster, and were willing to remain faithful to the finer points of the original plan of rebellion. Garrett Byrne's alternative was more imaginative and reflected the need, obvious at least to him already, to adopt a guerrilla approach.

The various government forces ranged around County Wexford spent 7 June strengthening their positions and holding their ground. At New Ross Johnson kept Alexander's battalion of auxiliaries busy digging more trenches and continuing to bury the dead. His soldiers were still busy searching the town for rebels, and they continued to shoot most of those they found. The officers put many of the captured rebels on trial, found them all guilty and condemned them to be hanged a few days later. Apart from the occasional cautious patrol, however, Johnson did not risk any kind of move towards the east and was satisfied to leave the rebels at Carrickbyrne in control of the surrounding region for the time being.[9]

The government garrisons elsewhere maintained the same kind of defensive posture. There was a token force at Duncannon that simply watched events from afar but which had not come under any pressure from the rebels up to this point. The relatively small garrison at Newtownbarry was not under any immediate threat either, and it confined its offensive actions to small patrols and raids down the Slaney valley towards Enniscorthy, none of which ventured much further than Ballycarney Bridge.

Loftus too held his position at Tullow and Tinahely, even though the rebel attack on Carnew, of which he must have been aware by midnight, might have appeared to be the prelude to an offensive against him. He is almost certain to have sent word of this development northwards to Dublin during the hours of darkness, but in the absence of any instructions to attack the enemy, he was content to remain where he was and await events.

At Arklow Needham also spent the day, his second in this border outpost, consolidating his position. He had restored some discipline to the yeomanry by his actions the previous day, and he mobilised much of his force to level ditches and to create a long crescent of trenches and earthworks along the southern perimeter of the town. The trenches ran from its western end (approximately where the Catholic church stands today) to the fisheries at the seashore. Most of the troops camped between these two points and the defences began to look formidable by the late afternoon. A small detachment of dragoons rode in from Wicklow to further reinforce his position and they brought the strength of the garrison to over a thousand well-armed men. Now that they had a good system of fortifications to protect them, they were in a strong position to withstand a sizeable rebel force should one choose to attack; for the moment, though, neither Needham nor his men were aware of where the rebels were camped or what their intentions were.[10]

In Dublin in the meantime Lake was keeping his attention focused on news from Ulster. At this stage it was unclear what was happening there, so for the moment he was perfectly happy to keep the Wexford rebels contained behind the chain of garrisons he now had in place and to send limited numbers of troops southwards to reinforce the Arklow section of the line. That morning, in fact, he had allowed the Durham Fencibles to leave the capital and to move southwards to join Needham; like Needham himself, they used commandeered carts to speed their journey, and by evening they were just a few hours away. They decided not to stop for the night, but pushed on and arrived at the town just after 1 a.m.[11] Behind them yet another regiment of British fencibles, the Dumbartonshires, were also making their way south in commandeered carts. They had left much later in the day and stopped for the night in a Quaker meeting-house in Wicklow.[12] Lake realised that when all these units reached Arklow the garrison there would amount to about 1,500 men, creating a formidable barrier across the coastal route to the capital and, along with Tullow, Newtownbarry and New Ross, trapping the Wexford rebels inside their own county.[13]

When morning broke the next day, Friday 8 June, some local

Protestants came to the rebel camp at Kilcavan and requested that a young loyalist named Effy Page whom they had captured the previous day be released. The rebel leaders eventually agreed to do this on condition that the delegates do all in their power to secure the release of a rebel who was then in the hands of Loftus's men. After these discussions they abandoned their one-night camp and began to make their way back towards Gorey. The negotiations over Effy Page delayed their departure, however, and owing to this and to the problems some units experienced in keeping their formation on the march, it was well into the day by the time they finally reached Gorey Hill.[14]

There was a messenger from Wexford awaiting them when they arrived. He had brought the long-requested gunpowder supply with him, as well as the news that Father Philip Roche was to leave immediately and take up command of the rebel army in the south. He also informed them of the defeat at New Ross three days before, and of the atrocities that the government troops had committed. It is not certain if he told them of the the killings at Scullabogue, but the news of the battle was surely further confirmation of their isolation and must have caused some of them at least to waver in their optimism.[15]

The report of government atrocities at New Ross sparked an angry response from some elements in the camp, many of whom had become anxious to take reprisals on loyalists whenever they could. The day before, while the main army was at Carnew, some of those who had remained behind in the town had taken two yeomen out of the market house and shot them dead in the main street. Now, in the wake of the news from the south, a party of them went down to the market house, where thirty-eight loyalists were being held, and took several of them back up to the hill with the intention of shooting them. Just then, however, another messenger arrived from the south bearing Harvey's proclamation banning the killing of prisoners and other atrocities, and this proved enough to stop the massacre before it began.[16] The two executions of the previous day and this barely averted massacre nevertheless showed how easily even the northern rebels might resort to revenge killings, and how unstable the situation was now becoming.

Once they had restored calm, Perry and his fellow-colonels had to consider their next move. An immediate attack on Arklow was an obvious option, but they were divided on the wisdom of this move, with Father John Murphy still apparently its main opponent. In the end those in favour of an attack prevailed but even at that stage Murphy still did not accept the decision.[17] It was by this time late in the evening, and rather than risk a march with night approaching, they decided to wait until the next morning.[18]

The position of the government forces in Arklow had, however, improved steadily as the day passed. The Durhams had rested in the early hours of the morning and then set to work on the trenches and other earthworks during the day. They had brought several valuable pieces of artillery with them, and Needham had these placed near the right of his defensive crescent. By the middle of the day his only pressing problem was the yeomanry. They had remained as undisciplined as ever, some of them taking to racing their horses up and down the main street for entertainment. In response, Needham decided to issue instructions that they should appear for inspection every morning, just as the militia were required to do.[19]

The day was largely uneventful for the other government strongpoints around the periphery of the county. At New Ross Johnson and his auxiliaries were completing the task of reinforcing the defences and burying the dead, but there was still no sign of a rebel move against them, and thus they saw no action for the third consecutive day.[20] The outposts at Tullow, Newtownbarry and Duncannon also remained quiet, and their commanders all waited patiently for instructions from Lake.

Lake's own perspective on things had changed dramatically by now, since the news of the Ulster rebellion had finally reached him and none of his commanders in the south-east could have been unaware of this. As had been the case with the Leinster rising in its early hours, the reports were confused and exaggerated, and the reality was that the Ulster rebels had only managed a partial mobilisation. The Castle authorities were nevertheless constantly worried about what might happen in the capital itself were they to send too many men south to deal with Wexford before reinforcements came from England; the need to maintain a defensive posture in the south-east must have seemed more obvious now than ever.[21]

*

The Wexford rebels had already decided to force the issue themselves in their own northern theatre, however, and the camp on Gorey Hill began to stir early the next morning. By nine or ten o'clock the insurgents had formed into battalions and companies and began their march down through the main street and on towards Arklow. They raised immense cheers as they passed along the street, and when they came abreast of the market house the guards inside forced some of the prisoners whom they had pitch-capped the night before to stand where they could be seen and show their scorched scalps. This caused the loudest cheering of all.[22]

The march to Arklow should have taken two to three hours, but instead it took closer to five or six. Part of the problem was that the battalions crowded in on each other several times and brought the entire force to a halt in the confusion, much as had happened on the way back from Carnew the day before. At one point Garrett Byrne tried to leap his horse across a ditch to sort out the trouble and fell from his saddle as he did so. Reports that he was badly hurt (which he was not) spread along the column, causing even more delay. Then, when they arrived at Inch, about half-way to Arklow, most of the units insisted on raising a cheer as a salute to Anthony Perry, since his house at Perrymount was only a short distance away.[23]

At Coolgreany, the last village before Arklow, they stopped yet again. The halt at Coolgreany was taken for several reasons. One was the fact that it was a very hot day and many of the men needed to rest. More important, however, was the fact that the dispute between Father John Murphy and the rest of the officers over the wisdom of attacking Arklow in the first place seems to have broken out again. The issue had not been resolved the night before, and Father Murphy's group had come along unwillingly. The debate ended with the priest from Kilcormick falling out with the other officers and refusing to let his men go any further at present, thereby depriving the attacking force of one of its most experienced corps for the early stages of the struggle.[24]

The situation was further complicated by an argument over strategy among those who wanted to attack the town. A young rebel who was familiar with the area suggested outflanking the town altogether and later ambushing the garrison while it was fleeing back towards Dublin. As the officers debated this proposal, a deserter from the Antrim militia who had slipped out of Arklow a short while before came into the camp and assured the officers that his entire regiment would come over to them if they had the chance and implored them not to attack that day in order to give his comrades the chance to get away under cover of darkness and join them. The rebel chiefs discussed this possibility for a time too, but in the end they rejected both suggestions and decided to make a full-frontal attack at once.[25]

The main body finally moved out along the road to Arklow at about 3 p.m., and by that time some of them, probably the less disciplined recent recruits, had become intoxicated by whiskey they had looted out of the lone tavern in Coolgreany. It was an inauspicious start to what was always going to be a difficult undertaking.

At Arklow in the meantime Needham's position had improved even further while the rebels were marching from Gorey. Early in the afternoon, at about the time the rebels were in Coolgreany, the Dumbartonshires arrived. They too moved to the line without delay, stopping only to wolf down some loaves of bread that Needham had arranged to have specially baked for his men. This latest addition brought the garrison's strength to close to 2,000 men, all well armed and and well dug in and aided by at least six pieces of artillery, making the rebel task now a very formidable one indeed.[26]

At around three or four o'clock cavalry units which Needham had on patrol duty near Coolgreany and Arklow Rock galloped into the town and announced that a rebel army was approaching. By that point Needham had his garrison in their battle positions. He had for some time assumed that the main thrust of any rebel attack would come from the west, along the Coolgreany road; accordingly, he placed the Antrim militia, a unit he trusted, at a barricade at the western entrance to the main street and positioned the Durhams and Dumbartons in the line of trenches to its immediate left to blunt the assault there. Other militia units, many of them veterans of Tubberneering, filled out the rest of the crescent of trenches that ran around to the eastern entrance to the town. At the eastern end lines of thatched fisherman's cabins ran out into some sandhills from the main street, and Needham ordered most of the cavalry to take up positions there. He placed a few other mounted units at either end of the bridge and immediately behind the trenches on his right and centre. In addition, he had a small detachment of Antrim militia marksmen occupy the upper floor of the barracks, which was half-way down the main street. Their job was to cover the street, so that, in event of the rebels breaking through at its western end, he would be able to retreat in good order across the bridge. His sole outpost was a small cavalry detachment which he sent to a crossroads about a quarter of a mile west of the Antrim barricade (where the roads to Coolgreany and Woodenbridge met).[27]

As they came closer to the town the rebel leaders sent a large column across the open country off to their right. Their instructions were to go all the way to Arklow Rock and then to march against the eastern end of the town. The rest of the army pushed on along the Coolgreany road towards the crossroads where Needham's cavalry outpost was waiting, but just before they got within range of it a large group of them broke away from the main body and made their way down the avenue of a local loyalist named Bayly and attacked and ransacked his house. This held up the advance for a time and gave Needham even more time to prepare.[28]

Once they renewed their march, the rebel vanguard spotted the cavalry outpost at the crossroads up ahead of them and sent a mounted detachment forward to attack it. The government cavalry made no attempt to resist and simply fled back behind the defences after a very quick skirmish. This left the rebels in possession of the crossroads, and of a small building housing the Charter School that stood nearby, and placed them within range of the Antrim barricade at the western extremity of the main street. For their part, the Antrim soldiers stayed at their posts; many of them may have wished they had had the chance to join the forces that were now preparing to attack them, but the chance to do so had vanished.[29]

As Perry readied his men for the attack on Needham's right, the column that had moved off towards Arklow Rock was making steady progress towards the first cabins of the fisheries. For reasons

that are not clear, he decided to send other units out to join them at
this stage. Among these were the Monaseeds under Miles Byrne,
and they made their way across several fields to the south of the
town in an effort to catch up with the groups moving in on the
fisheries before they got too far. The move was a risky one, and they
were caught in open ground and within range of some of Needham's
musketmen at one point. The soldiers opened fire on them as soon
as they saw their chance and hit several of them. Eventually they
reached the safety of the sandhills and joined the larger column, but
because of their commander's mistake they had lost many of their
best men before the battle had even properly begun.[30]

Perry eventually got all his units in place, and by that stage his
army formed a huge crescent that stretched from the Charter
School around to a point close to the fisheries. Esmond Kyan,
serving as commander of the artillery, had his gunners place the
two cannon that made up his entire battery on a gently sloping
hill opposite the Durham position. At around four o'clock he
ordered them to open fire on the Durhams. This action was
effectively the beginning of the battle.

The thousands of rebels massed opposite the garrison's lines
watched the exchange of cannon fire for some time and made no
attempt to throw themselves at the entrenched soldiers. Initially
Kyan's gunners fired too high, and their shots smashed into the
roofs of houses well behind Needham's men. When they lowered
them, the balls began to rip through the tents that stood just
behind the soldiers and then, when they lowered them a second
time, they began to fall directly on the Durhams' line. One hit a
pile of ammunition and caused a small explosion; another disabled
a cannon; and several more hit the soldiers themselves and killed
several men, among them a man who had been slightly forward of
the line and who lay screaming on the ground with his stomach
torn out while his comrades stayed under cover in the trench. The
Durhams' own cannon were temporarily useless because the rebel
positions were much higher than theirs and so out of their range.

The rebel infantry and cavalry held off from an assault on the
garrison lines, leaving it up to Kyan's guns to do as much damage as
they could. Needham had already decided that it would be foolhardy
to launch an attack himself, and so the Durhams and the other units

that were under fire from the insurgent artillery had to pull back to a safer position, behind a ditch that had been left standing near the tents. The rebel leaders saw this happen and decided it was the moment to throw their infantry at the defenders.[31]

The infantry attack had actually already begun by this time at the fisheries. There the rebel right had assailed the garrison's defences, and they had fought their way into the streets of cabins. The cavalry had charged them, and they had counter-charged several times, and losses on both sides were already high. Some of the thatched roofs nearby had caught fire, and columns of smoke were beginnning to rise into the air and make the task of the defenders more difficult.[32]

This was the encouragement the rebel left and centre needed, and as they got ready to attack the strongest part of their enemy's defences they raised a huge cheer all along their line. Then, with the command to move forward from their officers, the 6,000 or 7,000 men who made up this part of the United Irish army began their attack. They had to cover a wide area of open ground before they could get close to the government lines, and as they did so, first at a steady walk, then a trot, then a full-blooded run, the troops were able to pour a tremendous concentration of both musket and cannon fire into their front lines. Scores of men fell early in the charge, and the troops kept up their fire steadily and made it practically impossible for them to get to the trenches. Eventually, with men falling in large numbers all along the line and with the thick cloud of smoke making everything confused, the rebels' offensive began to falter. Unit by unit the advance ground to a halt, and then the entire mass began to pull back, eventually withdrawing out of range of the muskets that were spitting such deadly fire at them from the trenches. They left the open ground littered with dead and dying men. This was the first time since 1 June that rebels from north Wexford had been driven back with heavy losses; and the soldiers, in contrast, secure behind their earthworks, had suffered hardly any casualties.

After they regrouped Perry prepared to send his men against the enemy's lines a second time. The column at the fisheries was by this time embroiled in a terrific struggle with the cavalry and infantry at the eastern end of the town and had managed to push

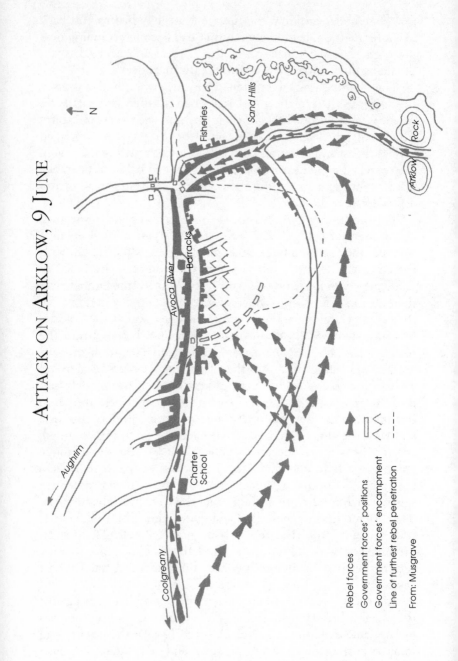

ATTACK ON ARKLOW, 9 JUNE

156

N

Aughrim

Coolgreany

Charter School

Avoca River

Barracks

Fisheries

Sand Hills

Arklow Rock

Rebel forces

Government forces' positions

Government forces' encampment

Line of furthest rebel penetration

From: Musgrave

all the way to a barricade that lay within sight of the bridge. The soldiers defended it resolutely, however, and after throwing themselves vainly at it several times, the rebels pulled back. Losses here were heavy too, although the cavalry also suffered heavily, losing several men, including John Knox Grogan, Cornelius's brother.

The second rebel charge of the Durham and Dumbarton sector of the garrison lines followed much the same pattern as the first. Once again the dense lines of rebels advanced across the open ground. Again they met concentrated musketry and cannon fire, and dozens of men were swept off their feet long before they could get to close quarters with the soldiers. Again their comrades pressed on with a courage that deeply impressed some of the government troops; but the effort was hopeless and eventually they lost the momentum of their charge and began to fall back to their own lines.

At some point in the battle, in spite of the tenaciousness of his men on the right, Needham's nerve almost failed him and he contemplated retreating to the north side of the bridge. However, he changed his mind when it became obvious that the rebels had no answer to the superior firepower of his men, and when it became clearer that the vulnerable eastern end of the defences was holding out too.

The rebels launched a further series of vigorous charges. These included further efforts to break through to the bridge at the fisheries and several attempts to overwhelm the Antrim barricade at the western end. Father Michael Murphy was killed while leading one of these, and at about the same time Esmond Kyan was hit by a cannon-ball and had the stump of his arm, amputated years before, torn off. Both losses were severe blows to the command structure, and, in a desperate move after this, one detachment of insurgents tried to outflank the Antrims on their right by crossing the marshy ground between the street and the river, but were caught in the open and driven back by deadly musket fire which inflicted heavy losses.

All along the line, in fact, the rebel efforts were frustrated at every turn. Again and again they charged, but with their gunpowder supply running low once more, their position was becoming increasingly untenable. Needham was under severe pressure also, but at about 8 or 9 p.m. the rebel officers decided to pull back altogether and to abandon the attempt to take the town. There had been at least four hours of intense fighting by that point, and all to no avail; even the detachment at the fisheries had begun to give ground by now. The retreat was orderly along most of the line, and the garrison did not try to take advantage of it, but as the units at the fisheries pulled back, the yeoman cavalry and dragoons charged at them and drove them out into the open country of the sandhills. There the retreating rebels were easy prey for the mounted soldiers, who ran them down with sabre and pistol and killed dozens as they tried desperately to escape, causing this entire sector of the rebel line to collapse. Fortunately for them, the rebel columns on Needham's right did not have to face a garrison counter-attack, since the infantry units remained under cover and the cavalry units that chased their comrades out into the sandhills did not wheel around and attack them.[33]

As darkess began to fall the full extent of the disaster became clear, and Perry and his officers had no option but to order a general retreat back to Gorey. The rebels had damaged a small part of the town and had caused about fifty casualties to the members of the garrison, but they had lost hundreds of men themselves. The exact cost of the battle is not clear, but the toll may have exceeded 500 dead and many hundreds more wounded, in addition to huge losses in weapons and ammunition.[34]

With night rapidly coming on, the officers tried to reform their army in the countryside just to the west of the town and to make an orderly retreat. They succeeded for the most part and managed to get dozens of the wounded away with them too, most of them on carts, but as they filed back towards Gorey they left scores of badly wounded men lying helplessly in the fields and ditches near the battle-lines.[35]

The defeat at Arklow was as severe as any the insurgents had yet suffered, and was at least as serious a setback as the disaster at New Ross four days earlier. At both ends of the county, therefore, the story was now the same: the rebels were unable to take a well-garrisoned town, and it must have been obvious to many of them that unless they were prepared to adopt the kind of guerrilla strategy advocated by Garrett Byrne, they would remain trapped within their own county until such time as the government was strong enough to invade it. Even the most optimistic of them must have realised that night that such a time was fast approaching.

Ironically, while the Wexford/Wicklow borderland was the scene of such a fateful clash, the day had passed relatively quietly in the central and southern parts of the county. What was left of the army at Carrickbyrne remained in camp throughout the day, awaiting the arrival of their new general. Father Philip Roche, for his part, probably spent the day travelling southwards from Gorey to Wexford.[36]

Six miles to their west, General Johnson stayed behind his fortifications for yet another day. That afternoon the soldiers executed more than a dozen men who had been captured and sentenced to die following the battle; all of them went to their deaths defiantly. The general also hanged a soldier who was convicted of looting; in this case he persuaded a rebel prisoner to conduct the execution on the promise of a pardon and release for himself. The man complied, but as he left the town a yeomanry officer followed him and shot him dead just outside the walls.[37]

In Wexford town the new rebel leadership was still settling in. Edward Roche issued yet another proclamation, this time declaring Hunter Gowan, Archibald Jacob, James Boyd and Hawtrey White to be outlaws, thereby empowering anyone who caught them to kill them with impunity. These four were more closely associated with government outrage than anyone else, and there were rumours that some of them had gone into hiding inside the county. The proclamation may have been in part a response to this, but it probably also met the need for revenge which more militant rebels felt at this point, and it undoubtedly diverted attention from the desperate situation in which the rebels generally now found themselves. In its language the proclamation reiterated the revolutionary republican tone of the previous day's document; it was addressed to 'the People of County Wexford' and purported to speak on behalf of 'we the people associated and united for the purpose of procuring our just rights'. It promised that the rebels would 'protect the persons and properties of those of all religious persuasions who have not oppressed us and are willing to join with heart and hand our glorious cause'. Should the outlaws be captured, it promised, they would be tried before a 'tribunal of the people'.[38] Again they were reaffirming the revolutionary idealism of the United Irishmen and reasserting their non-sectarian approach, but in stressing their former oppression they were perhaps taking an early step towards the denial of conspiracy and an assertion that the rising was no more than an effort on the part of the people to defend themselves against cruel injustice. In doing this Roche may have been subtly preparing the ground for a possible accommodation with the government.

Of course, neither Roche nor anyone else in or around Wexford or Enniscorthy knew of the disaster at Arklow as the day ended. At one point during the afternoon a rebel sympathiser had told one loyalist lady, Elizabeth Richards, that the rebels to their north had taken Arklow and had wiped out an army of 5,000 men that was on its way to relieve the town. Like other loyalists in the area, she was still unclear about what had happened even at New Ross and was certainly in no position to question the man's summation of events taking place north of the county boundary. From her viewpoint at least, the rebels were still very much in control of the situation.[39]

The rebel leaders who arrived back at Gorey Hill that night must have seen it very differently. As they gathered to rest for the night Perry and his staff surely realised full well what their position was. The options open to them were suddenly limited. As far as they could tell, there was still resistance in the midlands, and they are likely to have surmised that the Ulster United Irishmen, the most dedicated of them all, were still in the field. The only realistic options for them were either to readopt a defensive position and hope that the Ulstermen could carry the day and eventually break through to them, or, alternatively, to adopt the guerrilla approach proposed by Garrett Byrne two days before. This, however, would mean cutting down the size of the army and operating from the safety of the Wicklow mountains, and at this point most of the officers, Perry included, were not willing to abandon the conventional strategy and tactics from which they drew much of their self-respect and sense of legitimacy. But in spite of their brave attempt to confront the situation with resolution, few of the exhausted and demoralised men who tramped into Gorey that night could have had any illusions that the conventional phase of the rising had passed that day.

THE WAITING GAME
10–16 JUNE

THERE WAS REMARKABLE QUIET ON ALL FRONTS IN COUNTY Wexford on Sunday 10 June. The government side maintained its policy of containment and made no effort to follow up its recent successes with an offensive, and all around the perimeter of the county the various garrison commanders hemmed the rebels in. For the rebels the day was one for counting the cost. The new command structure was in place by now, but with reports of the defeat at Arklow spreading among them in the wake of the setback a few days before at New Ross, their predicament began to look ever more serious.

When dawn broke that day at Arklow, Needham realised that the rebels had retreated southwards, and he allowed his troops, most of whom had stood at arms all night, to leave their positions in order to get some rest. Instead of going to their quarters, however, many of them could not resist the temptation to range through the fields south of the town to look for wounded rebels. The place was littered with corpses, many of which had been ripped apart by cannon and cannister shot, and some of the soldiers amused themselves by mutilating those that were still intact. They killed any men they found still alive without hesitation. The body of Father Michael Murphy was among the scores of bodies that lay near the western barricade; it was near a cabin that had caught fire and part of it had been roasted. Tradition has it that some of the Ancient Britons (one of the regiments stationed in the town) recognised it as the body of an important rebel and by way of insulting it took some of the fat that had dripped from it and used it to polish their boots.

Like Johnson at New Ross four days earlier, Needham recognised the immediate necessity of disposing of the corpses. He formed burial brigades early in the day, and these dug mass graves at several places along the southern perimeter of the town and dumped cartloads of bodies into them. They threw the bodies they found in the sandhills into the nearby river, and many of these eventually floated out to sea. In the course of this operation several of the soldiers showed what one of their comrades later recalled as shocking disrespect to the remains of the dead, dragging many of them along the ground by the heels or tying cords about their necks and pulling them to the open pits.[1]

In the middle of the morning a small force of Antrim militia and dragoons came into the town from Rathdrum, expecting to find the rebels still nearby. By this time, however, Needham was very confident that they would not return, and he sent the detachment back after a few hours. In the meantime he ordered the entire garrison to assemble for inspection and thanked them for their efforts, being especially careful to acknowledge the efforts of the yeomanry who had defended the fisheries entrance. He and his garrison spent the rest of the day watching the countryside to their south, but the rebels showed no sign of returning.[2]

At Gorey, meanwhile, the rebels were trying as best they could to recover. They had already turned several buildings in the town into field hospitals and had placed scores of wounded men in them. Many of these men were badly injured, and some died before morning, including a lifelong friend of Miles Byrne named Owen Bruslaun. Esmond Kyan was among the severely wounded, and when morning came Perry sent him south to Wexford, where he might get better care.

A large part of the rebel army made it back to the camp by the middle of the day. They had managed to save much of their armaments, including the two precious cannon, but their supply of gunpowder was almost exhausted, and until they could get more from Wexford they could hardly consider any further offensive action.[3]

The situation of the rebels in the south of the county was little better. By this time Father Philip Roche had arrived in Wexford and conferred with Edward Roche and other officers. He celebrated mass during the morning and assured the congregation that they would eventually triumph, and he urged all to exercise

restraint and avoid atrocities. To many in the congregation,
though, the promises of success must have begun to ring hollow,
especially with news of Arklow coming in, and to moderates the
caution against atrocities would have sounded ominous.[4]

There was one military incident during the day. It was
insignificant in terms of casualties, but it boded very ill indeed for
the rebels. In the early hours of the morning the southern division,
which had now moved to Slieve Coilte, had noticed a small flotilla
of gunboats making its way down the River Barrow towards the
sea. Thomas Cloney took a detachment of men and tried to stop
the vessels before they could get too far downstream. He arrived at
the riverbank too late to stop two of the boats, but his men shot
the pilot of the third and forced her to pull into the bank. On
board they found some mail and newspapers, many of which gave
exaggerated accounts of government victories, but no arms. The
officially authorised versions of actions they had themselves been
involved in amused them; however, the general drift of the reports
served to confirm that the government had survived and that the
rebel movement had faltered badly over much of the country.[5]

The two gunboats that had evaded Cloney and his men
rounded Hook Head an hour or so after the skirmish and sailed
towards the mouth of Bannow Bay. When they got within range
of the village of Fethard, they began a bombardment and managed
to destroy several buildings and some fishing boats. At one point a
crowd of people who had been attending mass nearby gathered on
the shore and shouted defiance at them, preventing the captains
from landing any troops. The boats were forced to withdraw and
returned towards Waterford without doing any further damage.[6]
The sounds of the cannon, however, had been heard all over the
southern part of the county, including Wexford itself,[7] and rebel
leaders who listened to the distant booming must have recognised
it as a hint that they might soon have to face government forces
arriving from the sea. To local loyalist ears it was the first real sign
that help might be on the way.

There was one significant redeployment of rebel troops during
the day, a move which would have important consequences for
the position of loyalists in and around Wexford town. A battalion
of men which had been stationed in Wexford since the beginning

of the rising left and marched north to Vinegar Hill. The reason for this is not clear, but it appears to have been part of an effort on Edward Roche's part, in the aftermath of the defeat at Arklow, to shore up the rebel position in the northern theatre. It had the added advantage that it might bring some control to the Vinegar Hill camp; insurgents there had continued to execute several loyalists each day, and the arrival of the more disciplined body from Wexford did in fact put a stop to these atrocities, though it is uncertain whether that was a significant factor in the redeployment or not. By removing such a disciplined force from the town of Wexford, however, Roche was weakening the position of moderates there such as Harvey, Keogh and their supporters, and giving more militant elements such as those in league with Thomas Dixon an opportunity to pursue their own extremist agenda, even though at the time such a development could hardly have been predicted.[8]

In Dublin in the meantime Lake had something other than Wexford on his mind. He had learned of the successful defence of Arklow by now, but his attention was distracted by events in Ulster. As far as he knew at this juncture, the rebels there were still in control of large parts of Antrim and Down and General Nugent was struggling to keep the uprising from spreading beyond its initial core. For the time being, then, with the situation in so much of the country still uncertain and with their prowess in the open field already established at Tubberneering, there was no question of Lake risking a serious move against the Wexford rebels.[9] Besides, the reinforcements requested from England by Camden had still not arrived, and Lake was determined not to risk any major offensive in the south until they did so. His position in Dublin was now strong enough to justify such a cautious approach: he had a yeomanry garrison of 4,000 men in the capital[10] which negated any immediate danger from a revival of the midlands rebellion, and there was also the chain of strongpoints around Wexford which made a spread of the rebellion into neighbouring counties unlikely.

On Monday 11 June little changed. The rebel army at Gorey Hill began to recover to some extent from their shattering defeat.

Straggling bands which had lost touch with the main body had been returning to the camp for some time, and as they did so the leaders began to consider what their next move should be. Ammunition and gunpowder were still critically short, but during the day they decided to try to entice the government forces out from the entrenchments they occupied in Arklow so that they might meet them in the open country. During the afternoon Perry and the others discussed the idea of moving to a high point somewhere to their north, and by evening they had agreed to march the next day to Limerick Hill, a point much closer to Arklow but one from which it would be difficult to drive them.[11]

At about this time a worrying incident occurred in the town. Some rebels tried to force their way into the market house to kill some of the loyalist prisoners inside. Their principal target was Roger Owens, the Anglican clergyman from Camolin, who had a notorious record as a magistrate before the rising. In the end several other rebels, including Miles Byrne, intervened and persuaded their more bloodthirsty comrades to abandon the plan, but the episode demonstrated how volatile the situation was and how vulnerable the prisoners might be.[12]

Ten miles away at Arklow Needham continued to hold his ground. His men had still not completed the task of burying the dead, and by afternoon the stench of rotting flesh was noticeable all over the town and for several miles out into the countryside, where wounded rebels had hidden themselves in ditches and hedgerows and then died.[13] By evening most of this work was finished. (A female relative of Father Michael Murphy had arrived from the south and had taken his remains back to his home near Kilmuckridge, where she and some neighbours buried them.)[14]

As the day passed both Needham and Perry sent out patrols to probe each other's defences, and on a few occasions these detachments came within sight of each other. Both groups carefully avoided confrontation, however, and were satisfied to leave the ten-mile stretch between the two towns as a no-man's land for the time being. One of Needham's patrols did go to Coolgreany and arrest the owner of the public house in which the rebels had entertained themselves on the way to Arklow (this was enough for it to be suspected that he might be a rebel sympathiser), but apart from this and perhaps a few other arrests of suspected persons in or near the town, the troops remained very much on the defensive[15] and passed part of the afternoon in the main street hanging three rebels who had been captured during or shortly after the battle.[16] Others who were found in the surrounding countryside, particularly if they had wounds of any kind, were given less ceremony than this and were killed on the spot.[17]

Far to the south General Johnson and his garrison at New Ross continued to be equally cautious. This was the seventh day since they had fought off the rebels, and once more, apart from the occasional patrol which rode out to the west, they confined themselves to maintaining their fortifications and preparing themselves to withstand another assault on the town. Johnson was almost certainly aware of the rebel move to Slieve Coilte the day before, and he may have interpreted this as a preliminary to another attack, as he surely did their move that afternoon back northwards to Lacken Hill, just two miles north-east of the town.

Roche was in fact planning a second assault at this point. His chief handicap at this stage was his lack of firearms and ammunition, and since his army was smaller than Harvey's had been, this meant that success was almost impossible. He had to get a replenishment from somewhere, and so, at Thomas Cloney's suggestion, he decided he would send a small column of men to attack Borris House the next day. Borris, in south Carlow, was the seat of Thomas Kavanagh, a local landlord and a Catholic loyalist, and there was reason to believe that there was a store of muskets there. During the evening Roche sent a messenger to Vinegar Hill asking for a detachment of men to join in the attack. They agreed and consented to meet Cloney on the road to Borris during the morning. In all, Cloney would have about 1,000 men for the raid; it was a risky undertaking, but it was obvious that it was necessary if they were to have any chance of regaining the momentum.[18]

In and around Wexford town these developments were only vaguely known of, if at all. Men and women sympathetic to the rebel cause manned crossroads all day and all night, checking on everybody's movements, as they had done now for over a week.

Some of them made a point of mocking known loyalists as they passed, but other than that the town and its environs were largely peaceful.[19] The loyalist prisoners were in uncomfortable circumstances, but they were not in any immediate danger, and many loyalist families remained in their homes completely unmolested.

The rebel leadership in the town was nevertheless becoming increasingly anxious, and they spent the day watching and waiting. The danger of a sudden seaborne attack was becoming a more pressing concern in light of the incident at Fethard, and as a precaution they placed small outposts at Carne and Rastoonstown which might raise the alarm in the event of British vessels approaching the coast.[20]

Thomas Cloney and his column of a few hundred men left the Lacken Hill camp early in the morning of 12 June and took the road to Borris. Another column of about the same size marched out of Enniscorthy at about the same time to meet him on his route, and the two forces made a rendezvous somewhere in or near the Blackstairs and then headed across the Barrow valley directly for the little village that was their destination.

Borris was garrisoned by a small force of local yeoman cavalry and a detachment of about thirty Donegal militia. The officers in charge there learned of the rebel movements well before the attackers got close to the village, and they were prepared to meet them before they came within sight. The cavalry initially drew up outside the village, but, as the rebels appeared and it became clear how numerous they were, they quickly withdrew and fled back through the main street and on towards Kilkenny, leaving the Donegals to fend for themselves.

The rebels made their way through the village and laid siege to Kavanagh's house. The soldiers had barricaded themselves inside by sealing the ground floor completely and had taken up firing positions at the upstairs windows. Cloney had brought a cannon with him and began to use it on the walls, but after a time it became obvious that the piece was too small for the task and that the only hope they had of seizing the building was by mass assault. They launched several attacks in a vain effort to do this, but many of his men were hit by the musket fire from the windows long before they could get close to the walls. At one point Cloney made them push carts piled high with straw and mattresses before them as cover, but the bullets tore easily through the flimsy cover and killed several of them. Desperate attempts to set the doors and windows on fire also failed.

The struggle went on for several hours, but eventually Cloney realised it was hopeless and decided to withdraw before government reinforcements from the west might arrive. His men were angered at their failure and its high cost, and on the way back through the village several of them attacked an old man they suspected of telling the garrison of their approach. Cloney intervened just in time to save the man's life and managed to get his column clear of the village shortly before cavalry reinforcements arrived from Kilkenny. The cavalry made no effort to pursue the retreating rebels when they retook the place, and Cloney and his men made their way eastwards towards the Wexford border without hindrance.

Once inside their own county, the Lacken and Vinegar Hill units went their separate ways. Before they did so the Enniscorthy men took possession of the cannon that Cloney had brought with him that morning, insisting that their need of it was greater than that of their Lacken comrades. There was a tense stand-off between the two groups for a time, and in the end Cloney had to give in and return to his camp empty-handed. The raid had been a total failure and an expensive one, and practically all hope of a successful second attack on New Ross had now gone.[21]

The day went more smoothly for the northern rebels. They broke camp and were preparing to march to Limerick Hill at about the time that Cloney was setting out from Lacken for Borris. As they left Gorey, Perry had a detachment of trusted men take the loyalist prisoners out of the market house and march them south towards Wexford. The journey would take two days, but in light of the attempts by militant elements in the camp to take revenge on these men in recent days, the move seemed a wise one.[22]

The army itself split into two columns once it got outside the town. One, a group of about 300 men, moved directly north of the town and took up a position on the summit of Aske Hill, about eight miles due south of Arklow. From here they could watch for sudden movements by the garrison and offer at least some protection against a sudden attack on Gorey.[23] The main body, numbering perhaps 8,000, marched towards the north-west and reached Limerick Hill without incident. Here they were on a high point, just over six miles from Arklow, and had an excellent view of the country in all directions, including the land lying towards Arklow and Aske Hill, which they could see clearly across the broad valley to their east. Their hope was that Needham would now be tempted to come out from behind his fortifications and attack them; other than that, there was no chance of defeating him.[24]

Needham, however, showed no sign of taking the bait as the day passed. Instead he confined himself yet again to sending small mounted patrols out to his south, holding the rest of his army back in the town. One of these patrols went as far as the northern slope of Tara Hill, and another took Ignatius Redmond, the Coolgreany tavern-keeper, back to his village and released him, but none of them ventured further than that. However, they did keep up a fairly constant harassment of the countrypeople they encountered, and this caused a steady trickle of refugees to flee from the northernmost parishes of Wexford and to make their way towards the rebel camps further south, bringing with them as they went numerous atrocity tales.[25]

In Wexford town the rebel leaders were still watching for signs of naval vessels in the harbour and were still paying anxious attention to reports coming in from the distant camps. In the town and countryside around them the state of affairs was still fairly orderly. At one point in the day a band of rebels burst in on a dinner party at which several local loyalists were present and demanded to know the whereabouts of George Ogle.[26] Ogle was, in fact, long gone from the county, but the incident suggests that the level of frustration and anxiety was mounting among the rank and file in the southern part of the county, and the behaviour of certain elements was verging on the paranoid.

From the perspective of the rebel leaders in the town, the chances of a stunning victory in the field, the one thing that might stem this vengeful tide, continued to look very slight. To make matters worse, on this very day the Ulster rebels were decisively beaten at the Battle of Ballynahinch. The Wexford leaders would not be aware of this for a long time, but it meant that they were once again totally alone, and unless they could regain the lost initiative in dramatic fashion, it was inevitable that they would continue to be confined to their own county and eventually crushed. The only thing that could possibly save them now was a French landing, and while a small expeditionary force was in the early stages of preparation at Brest by this time, it would be weeks before it might be ready to sail. In the meantime the main French effort was concentrated in the Mediterranean, where Bonaparte's fleet was making steady headway in its journey to Egypt. Regardless of how hopeful the Wexford rebels might be that French vessels would appear off their coast, therefore, the longed-for French invasion was a phantom.

On 13 June the rebels at Lacken Hill and Limerick Hill waited in vain for the garrisons they faced to come out and attack them. The commanders of government forces stolidly refused to be drawn and simply held their ground and kept the rebel forces hemmed into their own county for yet another day.

Rebel frustration mounted. The force under Father Philip Roche remained at Lacken Hill throughout the day and made no further efforts to replenish their arms and ammunition. The disappointment at the failed raid on Borris was undoubtedly very great, and this probably accounts for the fact that desertions reached disastrous levels at this stage. The army had shrunk tremendously from the huge force Harvey had once commanded and may now have numbered no more than 1,000 or 2,000 men, and Thomas Cloney and others had to take up positions at the foot of the hill to prevent even more people from absconding. Those who did manage to escape either drifted back to their homes across the southern part of the county or—and this was increasingly common now—formed into small bands of marauders that began to pillage remote areas.[27]

The army on Limerick Hill sent patrols out towards Arklow, and on a few occasions they spotted some of Needham's cavalry detachments in the distance, but, as on the day before, they could never entice them to attack. Needham was absolutely determined to hold his ground and take no risks.

Here too there were ominous signs of an impending breakdown in rebel discipline. At one point during the day a rebel band marched south from Limerick Hill to the townland of Ballygullen, near the Carnew–Gorey road, and called by a farm owned by a family named Thumkin. The Thumkins were well-known loyalists, and two of them were alleged to have murdered Garrett Fennel, a popular local United Irishman, just before the rising. The rebels could find neither of the young men in question, but their father was at home, and they arrested him instead and marched him back towards Limerick Hill. As they approached the foot of the hill, a group of men on the slope recognised him. They rushed down the hill, threw themselves on the helpless old man and killed him on the road. He had not been involved in the killing of Fennel, but apparently at least some of the northern rebels were now prepared to lash out at anyone connected with the loyalist cause.[28]

In Wexford town in the meantime Edward Roche, Bagenal Harvey and several other leaders held a long and serious meeting about their situation. One of their concerns was the continued maintenance of order in the county: extremists in and around the town were still being restrained from committing acts of violence, and the Wexford town battalion at Vinegar Hill had put a complete halt to the execution of loyalists there for four days now; but the leaders were apparently concerned that this control might be lost. An even more significant objective may have been to lay the groundwork for a negotiated surrender; with the hopelessness of their position increasingly obvious and the arrival of French help uncertain, moderates like these were quick to move towards this option. But for the time being it was unclear how they might do this, and they appear to have made few firm decisions by the end of the meeting.[29]

For their part, some of the government commanders were considering a diplomatic initiative of their own by this stage— surprisingly so, given that things were going well for them militarily. The northern rebels were the first to know of this. Sometime during the day a lone horseman named John Tunks rode out to their camp from Arklow. After being allowed to pass through the rebel outposts, he announced to Perry and the other leaders on the hill that he had been sent south to negotiate for the release of Lord Kingsborough. The northern leaders accepted his word, and that afternoon they let him ride on southwards towards Wexford. When night fell he had still not reached his destination and probably slept somewhere in the central part of the county. The rebel leaders in Wexford town were still unaware of his approach, therefore, but officers in the northern camp now realised that diplomatic contacts of some kind were being made.[30]

The reason for this initiative is uncertain, but at this point Camden was still under the impression that the Ulster rebellion was a very serious problem, and he may have made the move in order to neutralise the threat from Wexford for the time. In the new circumstances that were developing in Ulster, however, Tunks's mission would take on a different significance, since the Wexford rebel leaders would be much more likely to negotiate when they became fully aware of their hopeless position.

By the evening of the 13th, then, the government's position was stronger than ever. Its ring of steel around County Wexford was holding firm and the rebels were unable to break out of it. It was now ten days since Johnson had arrived in New Ross, nine since Loftus had withdrawn to Tullow, and eight since Needham had reached Arklow, but for yet another day the commanders in charge of these positions had passed the time maintaining their fortifications, carrying out normal drills, and patrolling cautiously in the countryside between them and the rebel camps. Patience was the order of the day for government commanders, and this meant anxiety and frustration for their rebel counterparts in the hills a few miles to their east or south.

On Friday 14 June the rebel cause showed the first clear signs of collapsing internally when tensions among the various rebel factions in and around Wexford town finally began to manifest themselves in public. The two dozen or so loyalist prisoners and their guards who had been making their way southwards from Gorey for the past day and a half finally reached the town in the morning. Some Enniscorthy rebels had joined the guarding party *en route*, and when they took the men to their places of confinement they persuaded the jailers to release four of the

174

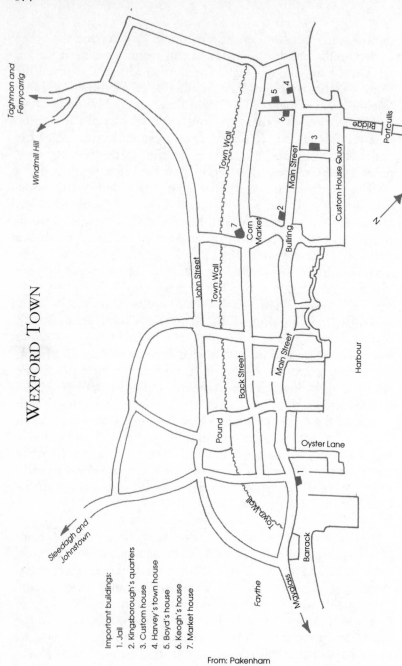

WEXFORD TOWN

Taghmon and
Ferrycarrig

Windmill Hill

Sleedagh and
Johnstown

Town Wall

John Street

Town Wall

Town Wall

Back Street

Pound

Main Street

Corn
Market

Bullring

Main Street

Custom House Quay

Harbour

Oyster Lane

Barrack

Faythe

Maudlins

Bridge

Portcullis

N

Important buildings:
1. Jail
2. Kingsborough's quarters
3. Custom house
4. Harvey's town house
5. Boyd's house
6. Keogh's house
7. Market house

From: Pakenham

Wexford loyalists to them in return. When they got hold of the four, they marched them back to Vinegar Hill and eventually put them all to death.[31] The fact that the more militant group from Enniscorthy could persuade the Wexford rebels to hand over these men suggests that there was already a shift in the balance between moderates and extremists in the rank and file in the county town.

John Tunks reached Wexford at some point in the day too. When he did so, he convinced the authorities to call a meeting of at least a dozen leading rebels and, significantly, other prominent townsmen. The fact that some non-rebels, even some loyalists, were included in the gathering indicates how anxious Keogh, Harvey and the others (Roche's whereabouts at this point is not clear) were to seize the opportunity to negotiate. In the meeting Tunks hinted that Lake might consider a negotiated settlement, and the rebel leaders accepted this in principle. The loyalist prisoners were their main bargaining counter now, and they evidently were very ready to use them.[32]

In the meantime, however, Captain Thomas Dixon, quiet for a week and a half since he had had the informer Murphy killed, was mounting a campaign of his own among more extreme elements on the streets. He organised a mob during the day which went out to Colonel Le Hunte's residence at Ardtramon to search for James Boyd. They failed to find Boyd, but did discover an orange-coloured screen, which they brought back into the town and presented in the streets as proof that Le Hunte was an active Orangeman. The crowd accepted the evidence and followed Dixon to the house where Le Hunte was being held, dragged him out into the street and were on the point of killing him when another party of rebels came up and rescued him. For the moment Dixon backed down and allowed the opposing party to take Le Hunte away to a safer place; nevertheless the sudden resurgence of his group was an ominous development.[33]

After talking with Tunks, the rebel leaders agreed to send a delegation to Lake and to open negotiations for surrender in return for the release of the prisoners. Somehow or other, perhaps by using threats, Dixon managed to convince them that he should be part of the delegation, and that afternoon a three-man mission, consisting of Dixon, Robert Carty and a North Cork militia officer set out for Arklow via Vinegar Hill. A few miles from the outskirts of Enniscorthy Dixon suddenly broke away from the other two men and rode on ahead of them. By the time they reached the camp he had apparently already rallied a large number of rebels to his side and had convinced them to prevent the other two men from proceeding any further. Dixon's supporters thereupon seized the officer and Carty and held them for the rest of the day and night, effectively destroying the mission and the first real chance the rebel leadership had had to avoid a final battle with the government. Edward Roche's role in all this is unclear, but he may have been at Vinegar Hill at this point himself and may even have co-operated with Dixon in his effort to terminate the diplomatic initiative.[34]

Meanwhile in the two main rebel camps the leaders were making an effort to regain the initiative. Father Philip Roche's army before New Ross was as hopelessly outgunned as ever, but he decided that he would launch an attack on the town in the next few days with or without additional weapons. That afternoon he sent word back across the southern part of the county that all available men should rally to the camp and prepare for an attack five days later, on 19 June. By this time he had clearly given up any chance of having the element of surprise on his side, a fact which gives this decision all the features of a desperate effort and one which was almost certainly doomed to failure.[35]

At Limerick Hill too the rebels were suffering from sagging morale. The Aske Hill detachment had been badly depleted by desertions over the previous few days, and the garrison there was reduced to barely more than a hundred men by this point. Similar desertions were probably taking place at Limerick Hill itself, and this may explain why Perry and his officers decided to send a large detachment towards the north-west that afternoon. This force went into the mountains and finally camped by evening on Mountpleasant, a low hill three miles beyond the Wicklow border, overlooking Loftus's outpost at Tinahely. Tinahely was without doubt a weak link in Lake's chain of garrisons, and the rebels' move may have been designed to test it. By nightfall the officers on Limerick Hill decided to move the entire army into the mountains near Tinahely, adopting thereby Garrett Byrne's strategy at last. At this stage none of them had any idea of the outcome of Tunks's mission, though it is possible that they were preparing to launch a guerrilla campaign in event of the negotiations leading to a surrender by their southern comrades.[36]

All this time the government forces still held their positions. Needham's patrols probed the countryside to their south as usual;[37] Loftus held his ground at Tullow; the small garrison at Newtownbarry kept a watchful eye on the Slaney corridor;[38] and Johnson anxiously watched the Lacken rebels from behind his trenches at New Ross. For all commanders, containment remained the only objective.

Lake was already preparing to bolster the garrisons around Wexford even further in preparation for a possible final assault. A few days before this, in spite of the fact that the situation was still serious in Ulster, he had sent dispatches to several commanders in the midlands and in Munster asking them to move in the direction of the south-eastern county. The messengers must have reached the three midland commanders he had in mind (Dundas, Eustace and Duff) on the 12th or 13th, and now, on the 14th, they finally reached Brigadier-General Sir John Moore at Fermoy.[39]

Lake's note asked Moore to march at once to Waterford and wait there for instructions from Johnson.[40] The journey would take at least three days, but in the meantime Dundas, Eustace and Duff would have begun their march too. By the evening of the 14th, then, Dublin Castle was almost ready to make its move against Wexford in spite of the Tunks mission. They were, however, waiting for two conditions to be fulfilled before launching the offensive: the first was the collapse of the Ulster rising, something which was by now taking place;[41] the second was the arrival of reinforcements from England to protect Dublin, and the expectation was that this would happen any day now.

Over the next two days the Wexford rebellion began to show even more serious signs of unravelling. The position of the moderate rebels in Wexford town declined markedly during Saturday 15 June. Robert Carty had returned to the town in the morning and at one point found Matthew Keogh meeting alone with Lord Kingsborough. He assumed that Keogh was plotting to surrender to Lake and publicly accused him of treachery, and the two erstwhile comrades almost came to blows. Keogh managed to extricate himself from the dilemma, but later in the day a crowd accosted him in the street and vilified him for his alleged treachery.[42] He realised at that point that he was in real physical danger and so went into hiding.

Thomas Dixon now seized his opportunity to gain the upper hand over the moderates. He organised a small band of his followers into a search party and went looking for Keogh. At one point the Dixonites forced their way into a meeting being held by one of the several committees that had been running the day-to-day affairs of the town and demanded that they hand over Keogh; their plan, they announced, was to shoot him as a traitor. Keogh was not to be found, but by evening Dixon and his group had taken control of the streets, and in the absence of the disciplined unit from the town that was still at Vinegar Hill, there was little prospect of the moderates wresting control back from them.[43]

The extremist cause was probably helped by the dearth of good news from the battlefront, owing to the continuing stalemates both to the north and west. At Lacken Hill Father Philip Roche persisted in his efforts to organise his army for the planned attack on New Ross, now only four days away, but the shortage of proper arms was a great problem and recruits were not coming into the camp in the numbers he had wished at all.[44] Meanwhile in the valley below the hill Johnson continued to hold his position and to watch him carefully.[45]

In the north of the county, however, there were some significant new developments and signs that the stalemate that had persisted since the battle at Arklow might soon end. During the morning Needham began to get reports of rebel camps forming to his west, in all likelihood in response to the march of the Limerick Hill camp out to Mountpleasant, which was completed during the day. He sent a detachment of several hundred cavalrymen out in that direction, and they returned to confirm that there was a rebel camp at Mountpleasant and another one at Ballymanus. Needham decided not to take any action in response to this news, preferring instead to hold his men behind their fortifications for the night, but he must have been concerned by the possibility that the rebels might be moving into the mountains to his west.[46]

At Tinahely itself in the meantime the tiny garrison had broken the defensive posture of larger goverment forces and had made a move against the rebels at Mountpleasant. That evening their cavalry rode out towards the hill and got within range of the insurgents. There was a brief exchange of fire, but neither side suffered significant casualties, and the cavalry eventually withdrew back into the village. The rebels made no effort to pursue them and settled down to spend a second night on the ridge, still seven miles to the north-west of their main camp and in an exposed position should Loftus suddenly move from Tullow against them. The soldiers of the garrison, for their part, had had an exilarating taste of offensive action, and their officers were anxious to try it again soon.[47]

At Dublin Castle Lake's position looked increasingly favourable with each passing hour. The day ended with no sign of the English reinforcements, but he realised that County Wexford was now the only part of the country still in open rebellion, and the preparations for the offensive against them was fully under way. The midlands units were getting ready to move towards Wexford, and Moore and his men had arrived at Clogheen, in south Tipperary, late in the evening. This left them barely more than a day's march from Waterford, and what they had seen of Tipperary by this time convinced them that there was no danger of rebellion breaking out in east Munster once they moved against Wexford.[48]

On 16 June, the fourth Saturday since the rebel mobilisation in Wexford, the government forces finally began to close in on the county. As Lake watched cautiously, Duff and Dundas made preparations for their journey down into the Barrow valley, from which they would turn eastwards to the county's borders, while Moore and his men continued their trek. They left Clogheen early in the day and by evening had reached Clonmel, putting them within an easy day's march of Waterford.[49] As the morning and afternoon passed, there still was no sign of the English reinforcements arriving in Dublin, and Lake was still determined to make no final move without them, but everything else had begun to fall into place.

The position of the rebels in Wexford deteriorated even further as the day passed. In the north of the county they did have some

cheering news. The Limerick Hill force finally completed its move
to Mountpleasant. They had by now spent four fruitless days at
Limerick Hill, and while they were leaving much of north
Wexford defenceless should government forces at Arklow go on
the offensive, they still held the small outpost at Aske Hill, a mile
to the north of Gorey, which would provide some protection
against Needham.[50] The last units got to Mountpleasant late in
the day and spread out on the little ridge above the village. As
evening came on, both the rebels and the heavily outnumbered
garrison held their ground and waited for the morning before
making any moves. A victory of some kind here might restore the
flagging rebel morale, but even the most optimistic of the leaders
must have realised that the prize itself would be rather small.[51]

At the camp on Lacken Hill there was no apparent
improvement in the rebels' circumstances. The army on the hill
remained depleted in men and ammunition and recruits, and new
supplies were still slow to arrive. Johnson was still taking no
chances, and although he had been in the town for almost two
weeks without going on the offensive (and it had been eleven days
now since the battle), he still merely watched the rebel camp from
a distance and awaited their next move. From dispatches,
however, he was undoubtedly aware of how hopeless the rebel
position now was.

Needham at Arklow was constantly in touch with Dublin, and
for the time being he occupied himself by dispatching groups of
captured rebels or suspected rebels as prisoners northwards; these
were mostly men his cavalry had captured in the countryside
south of the town. He was not averse to carrying out executions
on his own authority at this point in the war, and on this
particular day he had two men hanged as rebels. His yeomanry
still constituted a serious disciplinary problem and continued to
commit atrocities as a matter of course on their forays into the
country. During the afternoon he gave them a dire warning
against this, but they were itching to take revenge on their
enemies, real and imagined, and many of them could probably
sense the day of retribution approaching at this stage.[52]

To compound the troubles of the rebel leadership, the struggle
between the Keogh and Dixon factions in Wexford became even
more serious now. Keogh came out of hiding and attended a

committee meeting during the day, but Dixon and some of his followers found this out and forced their way into the room where the committee had gathered. Dixon pulled a pistol from his belt and tried to shoot Keogh in front of eveyone, but his shot missed, and Keogh's supporters managed to drive him and his followers out of the building. Keogh had narrowly escaped and his side had gained the upper hand for the time being, but the Dixonites were not overawed and were determined to take action to stop those they regarded as traitors to the cause at the next opportunity.[53]

That evening almost a thousand British troops sailed into Dublin harbour.[54] These would make the capital safe should there be any rebel resurgence in the midlands or elsewhere during Lake's absence, and as night fell he was finally ready to set out for the south and to co-ordinate the drive against Wexford himself.[55] The commander-in-chief was determined to enjoy the last act of the tragedy in person.

LAKE'S MOVE
17–20 JUNE

L AKE BEGAN HIS MOVE AGAINST WEXFORD THE NEXT MORNING, Sunday 17 June. His plan was to bring half a dozen columns up to the borders of the county during the next two days and to have them all ready to begin the attack on the 19th. The offensive itself would involve assaults from Arklow, Carnew, Newtownbarry and New Ross which would drive the rebels eastward and southward and then trap them in the central and south-eastern part of the county; there he would be able to deliver the final blow. The plan followed the general outlines of the one he had used two weeks earlier in the offensive that ended at Tubberneering, but now circumstances were very different, not least of all because he knew that the Wexfordmen were all alone in their resistance.[1]

The pieces fell into place for Lake during the day without any notable difficulties. Early in the morning Moore and his men broke camp at Clonmel and began their march across south-east Tipperary towards Waterford. Sir James Duff and his Limerick militia, the perpetrators of the Gibbet Rath massacre, began to move southwards at the same time through County Kildare, marching in the direction of Newtownbarry. In the meantime Lake himself had reached Baltinglass by late morning, and he and Dundas set out together that afternoon for Hacketstown. By evening Moore had reached Waterford, and a messenger was waiting for him with orders from Johnson instructing him to march to New Ross the following morning.[2] Duff had camped for the night by that point somewhere in south Kildare or north Carlow, and Dundas and Lake had already reached Hacketstown and were ready to push on to Carnew the next day. Lake dispatched a messenger to Loftus at Tullow and ordered him to join them at Carnew by the next evening.[3] One more day and all six columns, totalling about 10,000 men, would be poised on the borders of Wexford and ready at last to invade the defiant county.

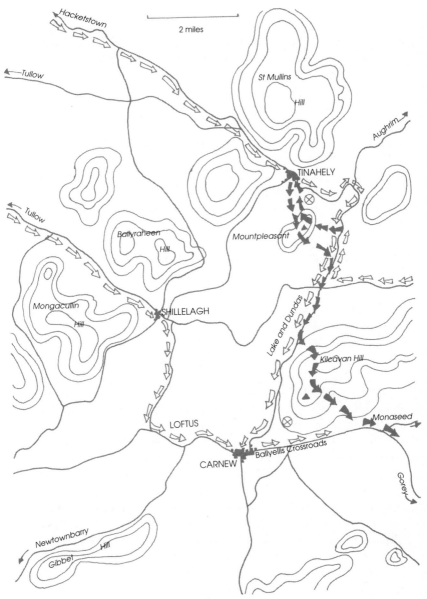

Hacketstown

Tullow

2 miles

St Mullins
Hill

Aughrim

TINAHELY

Tullow

Ballyraheen
Hill

Mountpleasant

Mongacullin
Hill

SHILLELAGH

Lake and Dundas

Kileavan Hill

LOFTUS

Monaseed

CARNEW   Ballyellis Crossroads

Gorey

Newtownbarry

Gibbet Hill

Government troops
Rebel troops
Battle sites
Rebel camps

THE CARNEW/TINAHELY AREA,
16 – 19 JUNE

The rebels made some movements of their own during the 17th, however, and these significantly altered the strategic challenge Lake faced. First of all, the Mountpleasant division suddenly attacked and captured Tinahely that morning. Loftus had sent a cavalry detachment under Lord Roden to reinforce the town just after dawn, but the rebels made their move just before they arrived. Part of the small garrison took up a defensive position a short distance to the south of the village when they realised that the rebel army was moving towards them. They put up only a token resistence, and after a small skirmish they pulled back into the town and then fled out along the road to Tullow, abandoning the place completely. Lord Roden and his cavalry met the garrison as they fled; they too turned about immediately and retreated back to Tullow with them.[4]

The engagement at Tinahely was a very minor affair compared with the battles the rebel army of north Wexford had already seen, but it did constitute a victory of a kind, and since it was the first one since Tubberneering it provided a small boost to morale. As soon as they got into the town some of the insurgents began to set its thatched cabins on fire; Tinahely was a well-known loyalist centre, and the action was probably a simple act of revenge, most likely initiated by the south Wicklow units. The column of smoke which rose from the burning town was visible for miles, and small bands of Wicklow and Kildare insurgents who had been hiding out in the hills nearby came out and joined the Mountpleasant camp as soon as they realised what had happened. Some of them were acquainted with the details of the rebel collapse in Dublin and the midlands and confirmed at last that the struggle elsewhere had completely failed. This was bitter but hardly surprising news for the leaders, but the new arrivals offered one ray of hope, a report that rumours of an imminent French landing were circulating in Dublin. This last revelation surely convinced men like Perry and Byrne that if they could hold out until the landing took place, the victory might yet be theirs.[5]

That evening, as they assessed their situation from the vantage-point of the south-west Wicklow hills, the northern rebels might have been forgiven for concluding that they were in a good position. Now that they had at last regained some momentum themselves, they are likely to have concluded that they might be able to entice garrisons in the hills around them to come out into the open and fight them on their own terms and to give them the victory in battle which they needed in order to breathe life back into the cause. There was another option at this stage, however, and given his arguments in the past, Garrett Byrne is almost certain to have spoken of it: an immediate retreat into the heart of the mountains and a patient wait there for the French landing. Even at this late stage, though, with little doubt remaining that they were the only county still in rebellion, the Wexford leaders appear to have insisted on maintaining the conventional strategy they had adopted from the beginning. They wanted to defend the frontiers of the county as if it were a sovereign state. In this scenario a major victory on the battlefield was the only thing that might give them the respite they needed to hold off the enemy until the French came.

Far to the south, meanwhile, the rebel leaders in central and southern Wexford had been involved in manoeuvrings of their own during the day. First of all, the battalion of rebels that had gone from Wexford to Vinegar Hill a week earlier now returned to their original base. These men rejoined the various companies that had been trying to keep control in Wexford on behalf of Matthew Keogh and the moderates. Not surprisingly, the executions recommenced on Vinegar Hill almost as soon as they left, but their arrival in Wexford later in the day gave Keogh the leverage he needed to regain control.[6] By afternoon, in fact, Keogh began to appear in public again, and to emphasise the point he even inspected a parade of rebels on the quay.[7] Then, to show his determination to safeguard the loyalist prisoners, he had about forty of them moved out of the jail and placed in the market house, where he thought they would be safer; these included the group that had been brought in from Gorey four days earlier. The prisoners were now housed in four places: the jail, the assembly rooms, the market house, and a prison ship in the harbour.[8]

Keogh's actions suggest that he was still hopeful of using the prisoners as a bargaining counter in future peace negotiations. Some of his comrades nevertheless still remained optimistic about their military prospects, at least on the surface. William Kearney told Elizabeth Richards that afternoon that a rebel army had

Dublin surrounded and cut off and that the capital would surrender to them in a matter of days. William Hatton announced to her later in the day that the second attack on New Ross was about to take place, and he assured her that this time it would succeed.[9]

The reality at Lacken Hill was rather different. Father Philip Roche was still preparing for his long-promised move, but his army was still small, and calls for men to join it from all over southern and central Wexford had gone largely unheeded; even Thomas Cloney spent this Sunday at home with his parents at Moneyhore.[10] If Roche's plan was to attack two days later, his prospects looked genuinely bleak at this stage.

The possibility of sectarian violence taking place in various parts of southern Wexford was still very real too. A number of rebels and their supporters were evidently expressing relief that Protestants were no longer in charge of the army and predicting that things would go better as a result. Who initiated these comments and which sections of the rebel body believed them is not clear, but in the struggle between the Keogh and the Dixon factions inside the town of Wexford they unquestionably helped the latter's cause.[11]

There may have been one other movement of rebel troops during the day. According to Edward Hay, a detachment of several hundred men left Vinegar Hill on the 17th and marched northwards as far as Ferns. His explanation for this is that this unit intended to attack Newtownbarry from that direction in the next day or two.[12] The claim is uncorroborated, and circumstances suggest that this group, while it may have been sent out by Edward Roche or another officer to attack Newtownbarry, is as likely to have been intended to keep Vinegar Hill in touch with the northern division which had now moved fully twenty-five miles away. With lines of communication becoming as extended as they were, and with the pressure on the rebel regime mounting internally and externally, Roche may have been anxious to keep in contact with his widely scattered forces and may well have ordered the deployment to guarantee this.

Monday 18 June was a cloudy day, the first indication that the extraordinarily warm and dry weather that had lasted since before the rising began was about to end—an ominous development at a critical time.[13] At Mountpleasant Perry and his officers began to discuss their situation early in the morning. They realised now that strong government forces were bearing down on them, and they renewed their old debate about strategy. Predictably, some of them, the Wicklowmen and some of the north Wexford men in particular, argued for moving into the mountains and the guerrilla strategy in anticipation of the French invasion. Others, mostly officers from central and southern Wexford in all likelihood, still wanted to concentrate on defending their home county and thus protect their property and families from the destruction that would inevitably result were they to allow the approaching soldiers easy access to it. In the end those in favour of the 'Wexford strategy' won yet again, and sometime in the morning the entire force abandoned Mountpleasant and marched two miles south to Kilcavan.[14] This was a much higher hill and was an excellent point from which to guard the north-western approaches to the county.

Lake and Dundas had by now mustered their men in Hacketstown for the march to Carnew, but rather than marching south-westwards to join Loftus at Tullow and then proceeding to Carnew together, they decided on the riskier strategy of going first to Tinahely and then turning south to Carnew from there. Loftus, it was agreed, would march to Carnew from Tullow directly and alone.

Both columns left at about the same time, and both made steady progress. By about midday the Hacketstown group reached the burned-out ruins of Tinahely, and from there they turned south and marched in the direction the rebels had just taken. After they had advanced a few miles Lake and Dundas could see the rebels camped on Kilcavan Hill, and they realised that they might block their own approach to Carnew. By this time Loftus was somewhere on the Tullow–Carnew road, and while they had an opportunity to trap the rebels between them now, by the same token the rebels might endanger either of them should they attack before they could complete their rendezvous.[15]

As it turned out, the insurgents had no intention of attacking, and when Lake and Dundas got close to the northern slope of Kilcavan Hill, Perry had his men form battle-lines and wait patiently for their opponents to make an assault on the hillside.

Perry was leaving the initiative up to the government's generals, hoping that he could finally use his pikemen in open ground if they were to attack.[16]

As this drama developed in the hills on the north-western border of the county, the other government forces were completing the last stages of their marches towards its western and south-western perimeter. Sir John Moore and his men had left Waterford early in the morning and had marched across southern Kilkenny without difficulty. Sometime before noon they made their way across the bridge over the Barrow and entered New Ross.[17] Now there were over 3,000 soldiers in New Ross, and since other units were to land on the coast of Shelburne barony in the next day or two, Johnson was finally in a good position to go on the offensive.[18] After maintaining a defensive posture for over two weeks in the cramped river town, this was surely welcome news to him.

Sir James Duff and his approximately 1,000 Limerick militiamen completed their march to Newtownbarry during the day too, and their arrival brought the garrison on the Slaney close to 2,000 men. This put them in an excellent position to push along the Slaney valley towards Enniscorthy and into the heart of County Wexford when the time came to move.[19]

At Arklow, in the meantime, Needham and his 2,000 men waited and watched the countryside to their south through the morning and afternoon, still waiting for the order to take the offensive.[20] The rebel garrison on Aske Hill had melted away completely by this point, and some of the men who had been stationed there and at Gorey had reassembled on Carrigrew Hill, much further south. The rebel defences in north-eastern Wexford were collapsing, therefore, and as the day advanced Needham almost certainly began to realise that the task of invading the area to his immediate south was becoming steadily easier.[21]

The task facing Lake, Dundas and Loftus on the north-western perimeter of the county that afternoon was a very different one. At some point Lake decided that he had to join up with Loftus before risking any move against the rebels on the hill above him, and so he and Dundas marched around the rebel camp and managed to reach the Tullow–Carnew road without any trouble. The rebels shifted their position as he moved and eventually found themselves facing directly west, with their enemy still moving to their left. By late afternoon their lines had come all the way around to the southern slope, and Lake and Dundas had managed to open the route into Carnew and make contact with Loftus. After that Lake felt bold enough to test the rebel resolve, and he formed a battle-line and began to move his men northward towards the slope of Kilcavan Hill. He hoped to entice them into charging at him and moved several cannon into place to goad them into doing this. The rebels had two cannon of their own, however, and a little powder, and they answered the barrage that Lake's gunners opened on them with salvos of their own.

After an hour or two of this stalemate, and with evening approaching, Lake decided that his tactic was not working, and so he pulled back most of his forces and moved them down into Carnew, where Loftus and his men were stationed. During the evening some rebel skirmishing parties came down off the hill, and several of the commander-in-chief's own patrols went out to meet them. For the next few hours these little bands fought fierce running battles in the fields and hedgerows between the town and the foot of the hill. Most of the fighting was by musket, and the rebels lost a considerable number of men as a result, including Hugh Byrne, Miles's brother, who was shot in the thigh and very severely wounded. When darkness came, the skirmishing finally stopped, but the rebels left a few small detachments in the valley below them to watch their enemy's camp during the night in case he should make any move. Among these men was Miles Byrne, who was part of a unit that took up position on the Carnew–Gorey road to watch for any attempt by the soldiers to slip past the hill and move on towards Gorey.[22]

Within County Wexford, meanwhile, events were approaching crisis point for the rebel leaders during this tense and ominous day. At Lacken Hill that evening Father Philip Roche was still trying to prepare for his attack on New Ross. He is unlikely to have been aware that Moore and his men had just reinforced the town even further, completely eliminating his chances of success, and it seems that he persisted in his plans even though his force was still very small and pitifully equipped.[23]

Keogh and Harvey and the other moderates remained very

much in control of the situation in Wexford town and, thanks to the battalions of local rebels, were managing to hold the upper hand against the Dixonites for yet another day. However, ugly rumours of impending sectarian violence continued to circulate and may even have intensified. As a gesture to the loyalists perhaps, William Kearney allowed the Rev. Roger Owens of Camolin to join his father and sister in their home at Summerseat for a few days. Given how notorious Owens was, this was a bold move on Kearney's part, and it was surely an act of defiance against Dixon and his followers.[24]

The immediate and overriding concern to the rebel leadership by this point was the military situation. Edward Roche, who may have been at Vinegar Hill at this stage, seems to have learned of the approach of government forces from the north during the day. In response, he ordered the detachment of several hundred men which had gone to Ferns the day before to move on to Camolin during the afternoon. By evening these men had formed a small camp on Carrigrew Hill, along with the fugitives from Aske Hill, and were now suitably positioned to form a vital communications link between Vinegar Hill and Kilcavan Hill.[25] Then, in a fatal move, sometime that afternoon or evening Roche and the other southern commanders sent a rider north to Kilcavan with orders for Perry and his men to retreat immediately to Vinegar Hill.[26] They had decided that the best course was to combine all rebel forces at a central strongpoint and thereby to force the government's columns to meet them in one huge battle. The plan had some merit. After all, victory, should it come, would set the government's scheme back for weeks, maybe months, and in the meantime the French might land or the Ulster rebels might seize the initiative. Many of the rebels on Kilcavan Hill, spoiling for a fight the next day with Lake and anxious to stay close to the safety of the Wicklow mountains, were, however, unlikely to have taken this view of their commanders' overall strategy.

The order to retreat reached Kilcavan Hill just before midnight. In spite of reservations they might have had, Perry and his aides complied immediately, and the entire army quickly collected its baggage and marched off the hill back in the direction of Gorey. Camp was broken in such a hurry that there was barely time to let the outposts in the fields to the south know of the move, and Miles Byrne's detachment only just got back to the hill in time to catch up with the rearguard.[27] In the burned-out shell of Carnew, in the meantime, Lake and his officers had no idea that this was happening, and during the rest of the night, as the rebels streamed eastward along the Carnew–Gorey road, most of his men slept undisturbed.

At this stage Lake had already worked out the finer details of his plan of attack on the rebel county, and the rebel force on the hill just to his north was a difficulty he had not expected. He had decided already that Needham and Loftus would move into the northern part of the county on the first day of the offensive, which was the next day, the 19th, and seize and hold the area north of a line from Carnew through Gorey to the sea. Moore and Johnson in the meantime would push out of New Ross and seize control of the south-western part of the county, that is the area to the south and east of Carrickbyrne. The forces at Newtownbarry were to remain where they were for the first day of the campaign, but were to be ready to move the day afterwards. Lake had already asked General Asgill at Kilkenny to transfer several of his detachments forward to Goresbridge and Borris as a reserve force should they be needed to bolster any part of his dragnet or to cut off retreating rebels.[28] All of these plans might have to be revised if he and his group could not either destroy the large rebel force on Kilcavan Hill or else drive them off the hill and push them back into County Wexford. Unwittingly, therefore, by pulling his northern army back from Kilcavan, Edward Roche had played right into Lake's hands.

An hour or so before dawn broke on 19 June, in one of the most extraordinary coincidences of the summer, it began to rain. This happened first at New Ross, but it spread across the entire county in the next few hours. It was the first rain to fall in weeks, and considering the significance some of the rebels had attached to the spell of unbroken weather, it boded ill for their cause.

One of the most immediate results of the deluge was that many of the rebel rank and file on Lacken Hill were forced to go down into the surrounding countryside and seek shelter in nearby farmhouses and barns. As a result, the camp was seriously depleted by dawn and contained no more than 400 men, although Father

Roche and many of his officers, Thomas Cloney among them, remained on the hill.[29] Whatever chance there was of a successful assault on the town below completely disappeared now as the rain damped the spirits of the shrunken army.

Down in the town Johnson, Eustace and Moore were also frustrated by the sudden change in the weather. Lake had asked them to make their move at first light, and their intention had been to drive quickly and decisively at Lacken in the early twilight. Now Johnson decided to wait until conditions improved.

The rain persisted, and at seven o'clock, now in broad daylight, it was still coming down heavily. Moore must have been especially concerned because Lord Dalhousie and a small reinforcement of troops that had just arrived from England was to move out from Duncannon Fort and make a rendezvous with him that afternoon at Foulkesmills, thereby securing control of Shelburne barony. If Dalhousie moved forward alone, he would be in danger of being cut off.[30]

Far to the north, in the Wicklow/Wexford borderland, the weather was still dry when dawn broke, and Lake's invasion of that part of the county was going ahead as planned. The retreating rebels reached Gorey sometime around dawn, and at about the same time Needham and his army moved out of Arklow and began their journey southwards along the road through Coolgreany.[31]

Loftus and Dundas stirred their troops before dawn at Carnew too and discovered to their amazement that the rebels had vanished from Kilcavan Hill during the night. Once they were satisfied that they had in fact moved eastwards, Loftus and his men marched unopposed as far as Craanford and halted there.[32] From that position they could support Needham should he encounter difficulties in his march on Gorey, and they could also prevent any attempt on the part of the rebels to drive into Wicklow between Gorey and Carnew.

In the first three or four hours of the day Needham's men advanced southwards very cautiously. They stopped in Coolgreany for several hours while scouts and outriders seached the countryside for rebel units. Then, at around seven o'clock, they recommenced their march and made their way towards Aske Hill and Gorey. The yeomen, who did much of the patrolling on either side of the road, began to terrorise the countrypeople they found, shooting several of the men and (establishing a pattern the soldiers would maintain for weeks) raping a number of the women.[33] A wave of panic spread before them now, and hundreds, even thousands, of people took to the roads and streamed southwards, away from the advancing soldiers.

The rebel army began to encounter these refugees early in their own retreat, and in a few hours the roads ahead of them were so choked with those fleeing south that it became difficult for them to keep order or make much headway. Their line of retreat was being blocked by their own people, and the problem got worse with each passing hour.[34]

Needham and his column reached Gorey at about 7 or 8 a.m. When they entered the town, they learned that the rebels had evacuated it only a short time before. They might have given chase to them and could perhaps have caught up with them with ease had they done so, but Lake's orders were to stay in the town for the rest of the day, and so, apart from sending out mounted patrols to reconnoitre the rebel rearguard as it moved, Needham paid no further attention to what was happening to the south. Instead he concentrated on settling his men into Gorey and searching the town for rebels. During the morning they went from house to house looking for anyone who might qualify as a suspect, and they had no hesitation in shooting any of these that they found.[35]

The rain stopped at New Ross at about the time Needham entered Gorey, and Johnson at last moved his army out. They marched directly towards Lacken and then split into three columns (under Moore, Eustace and Johnson himself) as they approached the hill. There was a dense fog over the valley as they moved, and the rebels did not spot them until they were quite close to the camp. Eventually Cloney saw them, and he roused Father Roche, who was still sleeping (perhaps drunk). They quickly realised that they were in no position to defend the hill against the sudden sortie, so they hurriedly made arrangements for a line of pikemen to form a temporary rearguard across the southern slope of the hill while the rest of the force made a hasty retreat eastwards.

The rebels got away cleanly, and the rearguard quietly evacuated their position too as the three columns of soldiers closed in. Behind them, however, they left most of their arms and supplies, Thomas Cloney not even having time to collect his horse. Johnson had envisioned Moore and Eustace outflanking the rebel camp to the right and left while he and his men drove directly at its centre, marching across open fields for the last half-mile or so. The three columns went ahead with this manoeuvre as planned, not realising until they finally got to the top of the hill that the rebels had slipped away.[36]

Within a very short time the news of the sudden offensive by Johnson was spreading through the countryside, and the hundreds, even thousands, of rebels who had spent the night in nearby houses began to come out and join the retreating column. The entire confused force stopped at Templenecro crossroads, two miles away from the hill, and the officers argued for a time over what they should do next. In the end they decided to make for Wexford town, a march of almost twenty miles which would take all day to complete, but the shock of the sudden attack was so great that they were convinced that this was the only safe thing to do. For his part, Johnson had expected them to rally at Carrickbyrne and planned on attacking them there. In undertaking the longer march, therefore, they probably saved themselves from complete destruction that morning.[37]

The government forces began to move eastwards themselves, once they had secured Lacken Hill. They separated briefly, Moore and Johnson taking different roads, but they met again at Old Ross and moved on together to Carrickbyrne. When they reached the hill and found it deserted, they realised that the rebel army had slipped out of their grasp for the present. Their instructions were not to go east of Carrickbyrne, and so, in keeping with Lake's orders, Johnson and Eustace returned to New Ross and prepared to move in the direction of Enniscorthy the next day, and Moore made his way southwards towards Foulkesmills.

Moore made good progress and halted at a demesne just west of the village before noon. Dalhousie had not yet arrived, and Moore therefore settled his men in camp on the demesne and waited. But as the afternoon wore on and there was no sign that the force from Duncannon was coming, he had to be satisfied to remain where he was for the night and hope that Dalhousie would catch up with him early on the following day.[38]

News of the government offensive had begun to spread eastwards rapidly during the morning and afternoon, and a panic as great as that breaking out in the north of the county gripped the countryside between New Ross and Wexford. Some of Moore's men, most notably his yeomanry units, had begun to commit atrocities as bad as those of their northern comrades early that morning; they killed at least sixty or seventy men they believed to be rebel stragglers in the parishes to the east of Lacken, many of them innocent bystanders, and they also raped several of the women who fell into their hands.[39] Streams of refugees began to choke the roads leading eastwards towards Wexford, and Philip Roche's army almost certainly found it as difficult to make steady progress in their retreat as did their northern comrades.

News of the sudden government offensive reached Wexford town itself quite early in the day. During the morning a horseman had galloped in with with a report of the attack on Lacken Hill, but Keogh, still in control of the town and apparently sceptical of the report, had him thrown in jail for stirring up trouble.[40] However, once Moore's men began to burn cabins in the country between Old Ross and Foulkesmills, the lookouts on Three Rocks could see the columns of smoke rising into the sky and their reports soon made their way into the town and confirmed the earlier news.[41]

The rebel leadership in the town began to panic. Edward Roche was somewhere to the north of the town at this stage, probably in the countryside to the south-east of Vinegar Hill, attempting to convince deserters to return and defend the camps.[42] In his absence, men like Keogh, Harvey and Kearney were in charge of Wexford's defences, and they may have anticipated putting up a stiff resistance to the forces approaching from the west; in preparation for this, Keogh ordered the outposts at Carne and Rastoonstown, several miles to the south, to pull back into the town to supplement the defences. Sometime during the day, however, reports came in that British battleships were cruising outside the harbour, and from that point on it was obvious that such resistance was hopeless; they could not possibly withstand a co-ordinated land and sea attack. The only thing to do now was to be cautious and hope for the chance to surrender peacefully.[43]

Edward Roche remained somewhere in the centre of the county throughout the day. From there he tried to co-ordinate the entire response to the invasion of the county, but in the confused circumstances that now prevailed this must have been difficult to do. In his absence from Wexford, and with Keogh's preoccupation with organising a defence, the extremist elements in the town suddenly had the opening they had for weeks been waiting for. Sometime during the afternoon Thomas Dixon and his wife (possibly accompanied by Edward Hay) rode across the bridge and disappeared into the Shelmalier countryside beyond. They returned later in the day at the head of a company of pikemen who carried a black flag in front of them emblazoned with the slogan 'Liberty or Death'. Dixon led the column into the town and along the quays and quartered them in the barracks for the night. Keogh and the other more moderate leaders were apparently distracted by events outside the town and paid little attention to this development, but Dixon was watching the situation carefully and had evidently decided already to take his personal revenge against loyalism, regardless of the outcome of the military struggle or of the effect his actions might have on the fate of others.[44]

The first day of Lake's invasion of County Wexford had been a stunning success. By nightfall his forces had completely seized the initiative and his generals were all exactly where he had intended them to be by that time. Moore was encamped securely at Foulkesmills, half-way between New Ross and Wexford and ready to push further eastwards in the morning; Johnson and Eustace were back at New Ross but ready to drive in the direction of Enniscorthy at dawn; Duff was ready to push towards Enniscorthy from Newtownbarry at the same time; and Needham at Gorey and Loftus just to his west at Craanford were set to push southwards in the general direction of Enniscorthy. Behind them all at Carnew, Lake himself was now ready to move into the rebellious county too.

The only hitch in the day's campaign was the failure of Lord Dalhousie to join Moore at Foulkesmills. Dalhousie had not landed as soon as Moore had expected, but for the present at least he still assumed that he was on his way and would make contact with him soon after dawn.

The two retreating rebel armies, in contrast, were in serious disarray and badly fatigued. The northern one had had no chance to rest during the day and by evening had marched well over fifteen miles in extremely difficult circumstances. They camped somewhere near Camolin that night, possibly on Carrigrew Hill; but with tremendous pressure on them by this stage, many of them may not have slept at all.[45] The southerners had pressed on towards Three Rocks all day and finally arrived at the western slope of the mountain by nightfall. The exhausted men stretched out on the rain-soaked summit to rest as well as they could for the night, and their general made his way down into Wexford town to meet with whatever leaders he could find there. What followed was a hastily convened council of war, made up of the town officers and Roche and some of his aides, which went on through much of the night. Eventually, they agreed to gather a new rebel army, which would include the Wexford town units, and to risk all in a confrontation with the government force approaching from the west. The combined force would amount to an army of 5,000 or 6,000 men and might be enough to turn the enemy back. What they expected the options to be after this had happened is not clear. As they left their meeting-place Father Roche and the other officers apparently gave little thought to the fact that they would be leaving the town in the hands of Thomas Dixon and his cronies once they had pulled the majority of the fighting men out of it.[46]

Lake's success continued unabated on 20 June, the second day of his invasion. At dawn Needham broke camp at Gorey and began his push southwards, with Oulart as his destination for the day; this move was intended to close off an important avenue of escape should the rebels try to pull back to Lake's left. As they marched along the road to Ballycanew his men had again rampaged through the countryside on either side of the road and committed horrible atrocities against the people they found.[47] Loftus, Duff and Dundas (accompanied still by Lake) also left their posts early in the morning and pushed on into the heart of the county. Duff reached Scarawalsh Bridge without difficulty. Loftus probably marched through Camolin to Ferns and made a rendezvous with Dundas and Lake there (they had probably come through the Slieveboy hills), and later in the day they all met with Duff at Scarawalsh and Lake gave orders for a large camp to be established on the demesne of Soloman Richards at Solsborough. The combined force numbered around 5,000 or 6,000 men, and they had wrested the entire northern third of the county from the rebels with very little effort. Besides that, the concentration of forces at the junction of the Bann and Slaney valleys ensured that rebels would now be unable to escape out into Carlow along the Slaney valley and guaranteed that they would have to retreat into the south-east of the county and be hopelessly trapped.[48]

The officers in the northern rebel army were aware of these troop movements during the day and struggled hard to keep ahead of them. Loftus's column must have come close to their rear several times, since he and his men were following a line of march that brought him to within a few miles of them. On a few occasions, in fact, skirmishers from each side came within range of each other, but the main rebel body continued to push its way along narrow winding roads towards Vinegar Hill and the government columns made no serious effort to stop them.[49]

The marching conditions remained atrocious for the rebels. The refugees were an even greater problem than they had been the day before, and they slowed progress to a snail's pace. As morning passed and the afternoon hours slipped by, though, it was probably clear to Perry and his officers that their enemies were going to postpone a final battle until at least the next day; they had the comfort of knowing that by that point they would have joined with Edward Roche and the forces of the south. In spite of the anger that many of them felt at being called away from Kilcavan, therefore, they may have felt quite confident that they could withstand their enemy in a pitched battle once they had received reinforcements and fresh supplies of arms and ammunition. What they could not have known was that, instead of being in place at Vinegar Hill, Roche was still roaming about the countryside between Enniscorthy and Wexford looking desperately for men to make the stand at Enniscorthy alongside him.

In the south of the county, in the meantime, the rebel position continued to deteriorate also. As soon as the day dawned Johnson and Eustace began their march along the road from New Ross towards Enniscorthy. They encountered no resistance, but many of their men ranged through the countryside on either side of the route and terrorised anyone they found. By the middle of the day they were close to Clonroche and were no more than a few hours march from the western outskirts of Enniscorthy, their destination for the day.[50]

Further to the south Moore made progress too, although in his case it was slower than anticipated. Dalhousie had still not arrived at dawn, and there was no sign of him as the morning hours passed. A few hours before noon Moore finally sent a cavalry unit southwards to Clonmines and Tintern in search of him, but they returned without hearing anything about him. (This, however, did not deter them from burning several more houses and spreading even more panic through the countryside during their journey.) Moore was supposed to go as far as Taghmon by evening, but when noon came and Dalhousie had still not arrived he felt obliged to remain where he was, at least for a time. After two or three more hours of waiting he finally gave up and decided to break camp and lead his column on to Taghmon. It was around 2 or 3 p.m. when his troops formed their marching lines. Just as they filed off from the demesne and began to move along the road towards the village of Foulkesmills they noticed a thick cloud of dust rising a mile or so ahead of them. They would not realise it for a few more minutes, but what was approaching them was a large rebel army that was determined to put a sudden stop to their advance.[51]

The force which Father Philip Roche led out towards the west that morning was a formidable one. His men were reinvigorated after recovering from their flight from Lacken and were determined to have revenge. They were primarily a force of pikemen, but they included several hundred gunsmen who would match some of the enemy's musketry, even if their powder was homemade and of low quality.[52]

The rebel vanguard was approaching Goff's Bridge when Moore realised what they were. The bridge spanned the Corock River, which ran into Bannow Bay and was quite narrow at this point and was at the bottom of a broad, shallow valley. The road the rebels were taking ran straight down to the bridge on its east side, while the road followed by Moore and his men passed through a crossroads about a quarter of a mile from it and then turned sharply to the left just before it. When Moore realised how large the approaching army was, he quickly halted his men at the crossroads and ordered his infantry to spread out in the fields on either side of the road; he had his gunners aim their cannon at the road itself and at the bridge.

The rebels were as surprised to find a government force drawn up to meet them when they came over the low hill just to the east of the bridge as Moore's men had been to see them. They began to spread out on either side of the road on the eastern slope of the valley as soon as they saw the soldiers, and in a hurried meeting Thomas Cloney persuaded Philip Roche to separate the several hundred gunsmen and to let them move forward to the bridge at once, where they could stop Moore from charging the other units before they were fully drawn up. As the rebel gunsmen moved down towards the bridge, Moore had about seventy of his riflemen move forward to harass them, and the soldiers opened fire on them as they crossed the stream at several points just to the north of the bridge. The rebels began to fire back, and both sides kept up steady gunfire as the main battle-lines formed on either side of them. Roche's army outnumbered Moore's by five or six to one, but the government force had at least three or four times as many guns as did the rebels, and they had the advantage of artillery. Unless the battle developed into a struggle at close quarters, therefore, the rebels had practically no hope of winning it.

The rebel strategy, forced on Roche, it seems, by Colclough and Cloney as much as being initiated by the commander himself, was to use their gunsmen to hold the centre but to throw the bulk of the pikemen out to the right and to swing completely around Moore's left flank and trap him. The rebel gunsmen were sustaining heavy losses in the exchange of fire from the outset of the battle, as their weapons were not nearly as effective as those of their opponents, but they nevertheless held their ground, and Colclough led his battalions off to the right and got as far as Haresmead crossroads, well beyond Moore's flank. Cloney's men followed them, and the rebel right threatened for a time to turn Moore's left from these positions. Their gunsmen, however, were by now under tremendous pressure from the devastating fire of the riflemen, and eventually they had to retreat back across the stream near the bridge and take up defensive positions there. Roche himself remained with this section of his army, but soon lost touch with what was happening in the fields and woods off to his right.

As the battle intensified Moore began to realise the danger he was in on his left, and in response he sent several light infantry units to meet Colclough's men in the fields and woods around the crossroads. A fierce struggle now developed on that sector of the battlefront, with especially intense fighting developing in a small wood nearby. For a time, in fact, the rebels pushed their opponents back, and there was a real possibility that they would begin to break. Moore saw this in time and move up behind them himself to stop what might easily have turned into a rout. His presence had a steadying effect on his men, and they began to fight more tenaciously. In the meantime Father Roche ordered several of the rebel pike units to cross the stream and to attack Moore's centre and right. The pikemen showed tremendous discipline in spite of the firepower ranged against them, including the two cannon. The concentrated rifle, musket and cannon fire eventually drove them back after several attempts, and in time Roche began to realise that he was unable to break through.

The fighting remained fierce off to the north, with both sides showing considerable courage and both losing large numbers of men. The greater firepower of the government forces began to tell, however, and after several hours' fighting it became obvious to Colclough, Cloney and Roche that it would be impossible to drive Moore from the field.

Eventually, at about 8 p.m., after a four-hour battle, the rebel units began to pull back. Their withdrawal was an organised affair, not a rout, and Moore made no move to follow them. Ironically, Dalhousie and his force of several hundred men finally arrived just as the rebels were disappearing in the distance. (Dalhousie had arrived later than expected at Duncannon and had spent much of the day making his way across Shelburne barony.) In the end the battle cost Moore close on 100 men. The rebel losses were more severe, and they may have left as many as 300 dead, many of them from the well-armed and highly disciplined Wexford town units. More importantly, perhaps, it now became very clear to Roche

and his fellow-commanders that it would be impossible to turn
back the government forces approaching from the west and that a
negotiated surrender was the only option open to them.[53]

Moore and Dalhousie still had time to reach Taghmon by
nightfall, but with the rebels somewhere in the countryside to
their east, they decided to take the safer course and set up camp
for the night at Foulkesmills.[54] The rebel leaders, in the meantime,
set their sights on Forth Mountain and decided to march to the
Three Rocks camp before stopping. They reached their
destination sometime around nightfall, and some of them almost
certainly made their way back into the town. When they arrived,
they found out that during their absence a tragedy of tremendous
proportions had taken place, and one which surely destroyed any
chance they had of receiving mercy from the government. Dixon
and his followers had taken over the prisons and in one of the
most callous acts of the war had murdered almost a hundred of the
loyalists.[55]

The circumstances surrounding the atrocity are, of course,
confused, but we can piece together at least part of the story. That
morning, when the last of the Wexford town units marched out
towards Three Rocks, the battalion of pikemen Dixon had
brought into the town from Shelmalier the day before had
remained behind in the barracks. This ensured that during the day
Dixon was in a position to overawe the rebel leaders who were
still in the town, including Matthew Keogh, William Kearney and
possibly Bagenal Harvey. By the early afternoon he had effectively
taken control of the streets, and at about the time the fighting
began at Foulkesmills he and his close associates, who may have
included Edward Hay, had assembled their followers on the quays
near the bridge.[56]

They held some kind of meeting or demonstration there and
decided to put the loyalist prisoners on trial. They then marched
down to the jail and either overpowered the guards or simply
persuaded them to let them have their way. They began the
process by setting up a panel of seven judges (in the format of a
court martial) to try the prisoners. Their henchmen then dragged
prisoners out of the jail, a few at a time, to be hurriedly questioned
and, in almost every case, sentenced to death. After that each

batch of prisoners was marched through the crowded streets to the bridge. There groups of pikemen forced them to kneel down, surrounded each of them, plunged their weapons into their sides, held them in the air for a time until they died, and then tossed their bodies over the parapet into the water.

The trials and executions went on for about three or four hours, ending at about the same time as the battle ten miles to the west. Dixon's followers were very thorough. When they were satisfied that they had condemned all their enemies in the jail, they went on to the market house and went through the same procedure with the prisoners there, and after that carried out a similar visitation of the prison ship in the harbour. The massacre was an opportunity for men of Dixon's type to take revenge on their worst enemies. Captain Cox of the Taghmon yeomanry was among those who died, as was Edward Turner, the man who had first brought news of the rising into Wexford on 27 May and who had been favoured by the moderate rebels.

By eight o'clock perhaps as many as ninety men had already died, and the killings only finally stopped when Edward Roche and his newly marshalled detachment arrived from the north and announced that all available men should march to Enniscorthy and defend Vinegar Hill against the government forces now converging on it. The prisoners who were already on the bridge awaiting execution were taken back to the jail, making what would have seemed to them a remarkable and providential escape.[57]

It is not clear where the moderate leaders were or what they were doing during the massacre on the bridge. They could hardly have agreed with the action, but in the absence of many of their most loyal units, they may have been forced to stay out of the way and to let Dixon and his allies to do their worst. From the point of view of the moderates, the terrible turn of events meant that the only worthwhile bargaining security they had, the safety of the prisoners, was now gone. Furthermore, now that such an unspeakable act had taken place under their very eyes, they surely also realised that it would be difficult for any of them to survive the final victory of the government forces.[58]

In the north of the county that final government victory was looking increasingly imminent by nightfall. At around sundown

Johnson and his column from New Ross reached the western outskirts of Enniscorthy at Bloomfield, a mile or so outside the town. The rebels on Vinegar Hill were still awaiting the arrival of their northern comrades, and Edward Roche was absent. Because of this, when the rebel officers on the hill heard of Johnson's approach, they had no alternative but to send several units out against him. William Barker led these men out and drew up a battle-line on a ridge outside the town, while Father Clinch and Father Kearns remained behind. Johnson's vanguard engaged them in a halfhearted battle for a time in the fading light, but since the general's instructions were to stop to the south-west of the town until the next morning, he held most of his units back and formed a camp once darkness began to fall. Both sides thereupon settled down to watch each other nervously for the rest of the night.[59]

Clinch and Kearns were now in a very difficult position. There still was no sign of the northern army when darkness fell, nor of Edward Roche and whatever force he had been able to muster. There was thus a real possibility that Johnson and his force, with only Barker's outnumbered and completely outgunned column to oppose him, would be able to seize the hill with ease as soon as dawn broke.

13

THE SLANEY'S RED WAVES
21–22 JUNE

THE REBELS OF NORTH COUNTY WEXFORD FINALLY REACHED Vinegar Hill and rescued Clinch and Kearns from their vulnerable position at about midnight on 20 June. They were exhausted from two days of difficult marching, and almost all of them lay down to sleep anywhere they could, some in the town, a few in the burned-out shells of cabins at the foot of the hill, but most on the hillside itself.[1] At about the same time Edward Roche was deciding to camp for the night with his detachment somewhere between Wexford and Enniscorthy, hoping to complete his march to Vinegar Hill when morning came. He knew that Enniscorthy was under severe pressure by this time, but he evidently concluded that the government forces would not move against it until sometime the following day. He was not aware just how close Johnson's and Lake's forces were at this point.[2]

Lake made the first preparations for his coming assault on Vinegar Hill before midnight. His main concern was to ensure that he co-ordinated his movements with Johnson, now four miles to his south-west, and with Needham, over eight miles away to his east. When he had time to assess the situation, he concluded that Needham needed to be more directly involved in the attack, and shortly before midnight he dispatched a messenger across country to Oulart with orders for him to lead his force to Solsborough immediately.[3] Lake appears to have sent word to Johnson at about the same time, instructing him to open an attack on the west side of the town just before dawn.[4] He would move against Vinegar Hill from the north at about the same time himself and intended that Needham would cover cover his left flank as he did so.

When Needham received the orders from Lake, he ordered his men to break camp at once and led them towards Solsborough, over the eight miles of winding roads, under cover of darkness. His army was encumbered by its sheer size and by the number of its baggage carts, but he reached Solsborough safely at about 2 a.m. and had his men spread out in fields next to the demesne.[5]

As soon as he got word of Needham's arrival, Lake ordered his officers to break camp and to move towards the northern slope of Vinegar Hill. Needham's men had had very little rest, but he ordered them to move off towards the left and to swing around the eastern flank of the hill as the other forces converged on it from north and west, and then to come all the way around to its south and cut off the rebel retreat. The plan was strategically sound, and since he now had a total of about 10,000 well-armed and well-supplied men at his command, Lake's chances of quick success seemed good, especially considering the fact that the rebels had little by way of numerical advantage, were completely exhausted, and were almost bereft of ammunition.

The long lines of soldiers marched out along the road from Solsborough to Enniscorthy, with Needham and his group moving off in the direction of Cooladine, at about 3 a.m. The main body kept to the road until they got to within about a mile of the hill. There the road forked, one branch running into the town between the riverbank and the western slope of Vinegar Hill, the other running off towards the south-east and passing about half a mile to its east. Duff and his men made their way along the road by the river; Dundas followed the branch that ran off to the left; and Loftus and his men began to advance towards the northern slope of the hill by going directly across the fields. Once within artillery range, all three columns stopped and waited while their gunners wheeled cannon into place and prepared to begin a barrage against the rebel positions above them.[6]

At Bloomfield Johnson and his gunners had by this time already opened an artillery barrage against the rebels under Barker (who was now joined by Kearns) on the ridge above them. The low booming sound of the cannonade awakened most of the camp on Vinegar Hill, and the various units that had scattered about the hill and town a few hours before stirred themselves and hundreds of them began to make their way towards the high ground on the east side of the river, followed by huge numbers of terrified refugees.[7]

The northern leaders were almost certainly aware of the presence of Johnson's army just to the west of the town before they went to sleep that night, but the sudden appearance of Lake's huge force in the dim light off to the north of the camp may have come as a surprise. The absence of Edward Roche and his battalions now became a serious concern, since his column was to have included hundreds of Shelmalier marksmen who might compensate somewhat for the lack of ammunition.

The troops from Solsborough opened an artillery barrage against the northern slopes of the hill at about four o'clock, and by that time their comrades on the western outskirts of the town were already putting severe pressure on the rebel defences there. Barker and Kearns had no answer to the cannonade Johnson had begun, and although they held their ground for a time in a musketry duel that spread along the ridge, their shortage of ammunition doomed them to retreat or destruction. Johnson's guns began to devastate parts of their line once they had found their range, and when Barker and Kearns finally heard the thunderous noise of Lake's opening artillery barrage from the northern side of the town they realised that they would have to pull back and resort to house-to-house fighting.[8]

The low booming sound of the artillery could be heard for miles that morning, and it awakened some of the loyalist prisoners in Wexford jail, among them George Taylor. Many of his fellow-prisoners continued to sleep, but Taylor realised what was happening and scratched the word 'Salvation' on one of the bars of his cell.[9]

The rebel leaders in Wexford town heard the low rumble too. It woke Edward Hay, and he immediately got up and made his way through the dark empty streets in search of the other officers. Eventually, in response to several desperate requests, Matthew Keogh called a meeting of the most important leaders. The group included Father Philip Roche and Thomas Cloney, who had not long before arrived back from the battle at Goff's Bridge, and also several 'prominent citizens' of the town. They gathered in Keogh's house in George's Street around dawn, and, with their position obviously hopeless, they agreed to ask Kingsborough to accept the surrender of the town. The militia colonel had already expressed a willingness to do this, and it seemed a sensible way of at least avoiding the destruction that would follow a siege.[10]

News of the meeting in George's Street soon spread, and a crowd gathered in the street outside Keogh's house. Keogh and the others eventually went out to them and asked that they approve the decision they had made by giving three cheers. They did so, and Keogh then, as a symbol of the transfer of power back to the old authorities, introduced Ebenezer Jacob to them as their mayor. Jacob announced that he gladly accepted his old office back.

Keogh then led the entire crowd down along the Main Street to the Bullring, where Kingsborough was still under house arrest. He entered and informed the colonel of their decision to surrender the town to him and asked him to be one of the delegates to Lake's camps. Kingsborough agreed to accept the surrender, but refused to be a delegate. Keogh and his fellow rebel officers had little choice but to agree, and accordingly they handed their swords over to him there and then.[11]

With Kingsborough refusing to ride out to meet Lake, the United Irish leaders still had to find a suitable delegation to do so. At about 8 a.m. they agreed among themselves that three delegations, each consisting of a rebel officer and a militia officer, would ride out towards the government camps. Robert Carty and a Captain Bourke were chosen to go out towards Moore's camp at Foulkesmills, Edward Hay and a Captain McManus would go towards Oulart (where they thought Needham was still camped), and Thomas Cloney and a Captain O'Hea would go towards Enniscorthy and find Lake himself. The emissaries all rode out shortly afterwards, and with them went the slim hopes Keogh and the other leaders had of a bloodless finale.[12]

The signs were indeed ominous. At about the time the emissaries set out on their journey the sound of a cannonade at Rosslare harbour, where several naval vessels had begun a barrage of the fort, could be heard. Clearly the government was determined to use massive force against the Wexford insurgents, from sea as well as from land.[13]

The struggle at Enniscorthy went on with great intensity as these manoeuvrings took place in Wexford, and by the time the delegations set out on their way the battle there was reaching its

Miles Byrne.

Main Street, Wexford, photographed almost a century after the Rising. The ancient street pattern has survived until modern times.

Chapel Lane, New Ross. One of the many narrow lanes in which the rebels suffered great losses.

Main Street, Arklow, looking westwards. The Antrim militia had its barricade at about this spot, and it was in front of it that some of the fiercest fighting took place.

The approach to Tinahely, looking northwards, at about the spot where the rebels overcame a small yeomanry force on 17 June.

Vinegar Hill, looking eastwards from the west bank of the river, half a mile north of the town. Lake' forces attacked from the left and foreground on 21 June.

The Slaney valley, looking northwards from the summit of Vinegar Hill. This was the vantage-point from which the rebels watched Lake advancing on them on 21 June.

Ballyellis, looking westwards towards Carnew. The rebels ambushed the Ancient Britons at this spot on 29 June. They lay concealed behind the wall on the right.

A view of the camp at Vinegar Hill before the battle.

Esmond Kyan.

The square at Hacketstown, where the north Wexford rebels tried and failed to overcome a small garrison on 26 June.

General Edward Roche.

Theobald Wolfe Tone. Although he played no part in the Wexford Rising, he was the outstanding Irish republican of the 1790s and the prime mover behind the series of republican revolts in 1798.

climax, making it unlikely that Lake would be anxious to negotiate at all by the time the emissaries got to him. He had stopped the artillery bombardment of the rebel positions as soon as daylight came in and began his general assault on the hill at about five or six o'clock. By then the rebels had spread out along the northern slope in response to the artillery fire, but had no way to respond to the bombardment, apart from the occasional and ineffective cannon shot of their own. In contrast, the government gunners had already done a lot of damage with explosive shells, and scores of men had already been killed by direct hits in the trenches that ran across the slope.[14] A detachment of rebel musketeers had formed a line near the foot of the hill, and these had been especially badly mauled. To make matters worse, thousands of refugees had crowded onto or near the hill, many of them staying close to relatives among the fighting men, and they made it very difficult for the various units to move about in response to the direction of the attack.[15] Moreover, as soon as it was clear daylight the northerners saw to their dismay that the Enniscorthy men had done nothing to fortify the hillside in the four weeks they had been in possession of it, and in a struggle against musketry and cannon this was a serious disadvantage.[16]

The rebel leaders themselves were aware of how desperate their situation was, and Perry told Garrett Byrne to ride southwards with a small escort in search of Edward Roche and his battalion of Shelmaliers not long after the cannonade began. Other than this, there was little else that Perry and his officers could do, except to deploy long lines of pikemen, to try to keep as much order in the camp as possible, and to encourage Barker and Kearns to hold out as long as they could at Bloomfield.[17] Even at this early stage many of them must have realised that they would eventually have to retreat, and their only hope was that Roche would arrive in time to give them the protection they so desperately needed once they abandoned the high ground. None of them could have anticipated that they would find themselves under such pressure so soon, and Roche's decision to call them back here must have seemed a dreadful mistake now.

Lake threw his forces at the rebel positions in earnest at about seven o'clock. At the same time Johnson attacked vigorously at Bloomfield and soon began to push Barker and Kearns back towards the town. Before long some of Johnson's units were within sight of the Duffry Gate, and the rebel defenders fell back towards the Market Square. There was some fierce street fighting in and near the square for the next hour or so, but eventually the rebel units withdrew from the east side of the town altogether and slipped back across the river. They regrouped there, and Kearns and Barker prepared to defend the bridge.[18]

The retreat to the east bank of the Slaney was so rapid in the end that the rebels abandoned a large group of wounded comrades who were lying in makeshift beds in the courthouse, even though most of these men were so badly injured that they had no hope of escaping without help. But by now the bridge was the most pressing concern for Kearns; should Johnson take it, he would be able to drive at the left flank of the army on Vinegar Hill or even swing around to the south and cut off their line of retreat along the road through Darby's Gap. If this happened, the entire rebel force might be destroyed; and with this a real possibility, there was little time for Kearns and Barker to worry about the courthouse.[19]

The battle for the bridge that now began was among the fiercest of the day. After they launched some counter-attacks Kearns and Barker consolidated their hold on its east end, and a stalemate developed as both sides charged and counter-charged along its length. The rebels held out, however, and prevented Johnson's units from gaining a foothold on the east bank of the river. Casualties were heavy on both sides as the fighting ebbed back and forth, and William Barker was among those badly wounded. His place was soon taken by Billy Byrne, who led a detachment of Wicklowmen down from the hill to buoy up the rebel defences and who fought even harder to hold the position.[20]

Inside the western section of the town, in the meantime, some of Johnson's men were conducting yet another appalling atrocity. Once they gained control of the Market Square, they discovered the rebel hospital and its wounded in the courthouse, and acting either on their own initiative or on orders from their officers, they surrounded the building and set it on fire. The action was a duplication of the destruction of the temporary rebel hospital at New Ross, and here once again the wounded men inside had no hope of escape. The flames soon engulfed the building, and the screams of the trapped occupants echoed through the nearby streets until they finally died away.[21]

The forces under Duff, Loftus and Dundas began their infantry assault on Vinegar Hill at about the time that Johnson's men reached the western end of the bridge. Duff's men pushed up the river side of the hill, Loftus and his men drove at the centre, and Dundas attacked on the left where a low ridge ran out eastwards. Lake remained with Dundas's column, and it was here that his breakthrough came. Hundreds of pikemen had spread out along the low shoulder opposite Dundas's position, and they launched at least one determined charge at his men. The soldiers managed to drive back these attacks and then launched a counter-attack, led by Colonel Wandsford, following which some of them gained a foothold on the top of the ridge. They quickly consolidated their hold here, making an assault on the main part of the hill from its east more feasible. Other units from Dundas's column soon followed Wandsford's men, and in a short time they were pushing the rebel pikemen back along the shoulder towards the top of the hill. With Johnson and Duff threatening their left, Loftus pressing heavily on their centre, and Dundas now driving in their right, the rebel leaders began to realise that their situation was hopeless.[22]

For Anthony Perry the continued failure of Edward Roche and his Shelmaliers to appear was the greatest disappointment of all. As his flanks began to give way and the pressure on the units holding the bridge mounted, the temptation to call for a retreat towards the south grew. Were the Shelmaliers to appear, they might be able to turn the tide and deliver the battlefield victory that was the entire reason for the retreat to Vinegar Hill in the first place, but in their continued absence the possibility of annihilation grew.

Perry and the other officers spread the order to retreat through the camp at about nine o'clock. The danger was that retreat could easily turn into a rout unless a proper rearguard action was carried out. The key to this was the units still holding Johnson's men at the bridge and the thick lines of pikemen still holding the northern and eastern slopes of the hill against Duff, Loftus and Dundas. Father Clinch was in command of these pikemen, and so the burden of protecting the army now fell to him and to Billy Byrne and Mogue Kearns. An added complication in this action was created by the presence of the thousands of terrified civilians who were huddled on the hilltop and who were in very great danger.

In the end the rebel leaders conducted the withdrawal with great skill. Clinch and his men fought a determined rearguard action which held up Duff, Dundas and Loftus just long enough for the main body to move down from the hilltop and make their way southwards along the road towards Darby's Gap. Kearns and Byrne managed to keep Johnson's men pinned down at the bridge while this movement took place, and they provided effective protection for the right flank of their retreating comrades.

Once the main body had travelled some distance to the south, the rearguards began to withdraw themselves. The units at the bridge got away cleanly, perhaps by backing up into the cabin suburbs to the south of the bridge, but Clinch's units came under heavy pressure. Lake had begun to throw the cavalry into the fray, and they caught up with some of the pikemen on the southern slope. Clinch remained with his men steadfastly, and he was killed when several of the mounted troops trapped him near the foot of the hill.[23]

Many of non-combatants were women, children and old people and could not move off as fast as the rebel army itself. By the time they got to the southern slope of the hill the rebels themselves were already well away and the cavalry, among them Lord Roden's men, were soon galloping in among their unarmed dependants. What followed was yet another merciless massacre of helpless civilians. The mounted troops chased down any men they found within a mile or so of the hill and killed them without mercy, regardless of whether they had been rebels or not. Many women and children died too, some of them slaughtered by the cavalrymen but many others perishing in the panic-stricken stampede that broke out; among them were several who were crushed under overturned carts.[24]

The rebel army itself completed its retreat relatively unscathed. Needham and his men, who were supposed to cut them off to the south, had not been able to reach Darby's Gap in time, perhaps because the route they took was so circuitous, or perhaps also because they had had little rest that night and were fatigued.

When the rebels got to Darby's Gap, they finally saw Edward Roche and his Shelmaliers approaching from the south. It was far too late for the commander-in-chief and his men to save the day (and the first Vinegar Hill rebels to meet them no doubt expressed their anger at their failure to come earlier), but just as they arrived Needham's vanguard was spotted approaching the gap from the east. Roche and his men immediately moved out to engage him, and from that point on they took on the role of rearguard for the entire retreating force. In the skirmishes which followed they drove Needham's units back repeatedly and saved the rebel army from possible devastation. Eventually Needham gave up the chase completely, and the rebels were thereafter able to march in surprisingly good order. Lake had achieved his goal for the day in capturing Vinegar Hill and Enniscorthy, but he had failed to do any serious damage to the opposing army.[25]

The truly decisive military events of the day took place further to the south. Sir John Moore and Lord Dalhousie probably could hear the distant sound of the battle at Enniscorthy as they roused their men at Foulkesmills that morning. They could not have known how the day was going, of course, and given the tough struggle they had had with the rebels the day before themselves, they may not have been all that confident of the outcome. Moore's orders had been to take up a position at Taghmon by this point; as soon as the combined force was ready, therefore, they marched out in the direction of the town, just three miles away.

They got there without incident an hour or so later, possibly at about 8 or 9 a.m. and therefore at about the time of the rebel retreat at Enniscorthy. Shortly after their arrival the lookouts spotted two men riding towards them from the direction of the Three Rocks, waving white flags. These were Carty and Bourke, and when they explained their purpose to the soldiers at the outposts they were allowed to go directly to Moore. They announced the surrender of Wexford to Kingsborough and informed him of the effort now going on to contact Lake.

Moore was uncertain what to do, but he decided he could make no moves without hearing from Lake, and so he asked Carty to return to the town and to ascertain the present position of Lake's forces. He insisted that Bourke should remain with him, however, and Carty, in no position to argue, rode back into the town alone.[26]

The emissaries riding northwards towards Enniscorthy had more eventful journeys. Hay and McManus learned that Needham was in Enniscorthy, not Oulart, as soon as they got to Castlebridge, and so they took the road towards Vinegar Hill through Darby's Gap.[27] Cloney and O'Hea had already parted from them and had gone towards Enniscorthy along the river road. Both parties met rebels retreating from Vinegar Hill early in their journey, and this slowed them down considerably, and on several occasions they had to explain what they were doing to angry and sceptical men, a few of whom even threatened to shoot them. What the reaction of Perry and the other officers was to the mission when they met Hay and McManus is not clear, but they must have been dismayed at the sudden surrender of the leaders in Wexford town, and men like Garrett Byrne, who almost certainly opposed the whole idea of a last stand in Wexford from the outset, must have been especially angered now. (Morgan Byrne held Hay and McManus as virtual prisoners for a time during their journey.)[28]

The two delegations eventually reached the outskirts of Enniscorthy. The battle was well over by the time either of them came within sight of Vinegar Hill, but Hay and Cloney both recalled in their memoirs that the sights that greeted them over the last mile or so of the journey were absolutely appalling. Bodies of men, women and children lay everywhere, along the road and in the fields on either side, many of them horribly mutilated, and the soldiers were still scouring the countryside for more victims.[29]

It was obvious to both pairs of men that they were in very real danger themselves. Hay and Cloney both realised this, and as they got close to the town they asked their companions to remove the greatcoats with which they had concealed their militia uniforms thus far. The tactic worked, and all four men successfully approached units of Duff's forces who were patrolling to the south of the town and managed to convince them that they should not be harmed. The soldiers initially held them on the east side of the river, but subsequently agreed to bring them to Lake, who had established himself in the heart of the town itself, on the west side.

The emissaries delivered their message about Kingsborough's acceptance of the surrender of the rebel leaders as soon as they reached Lake, but he gave no response and asked both Hay and Cloney to await one in his quarters. O'Hea and McManus parted company with the former rebels and joined their comrades. It was around midday when this first meeting took place, but as the afternoon slipped by Lake still gave no answer and Hay and Cloney were still waiting helplessly in his headquarters. At one point they even briefly ventured out into the streets, but several yeomen recognised them and threatened them. They withdrew to the relative safety of Lake's quarters after that and continued to wait.[30]

For his part, Lake was now in a position to dictate the situation, and he knew it. He had driven what appeared to him to be the main rebel army from the centre of the county and was master of its northern half; what was more, he had done so without much real effort. Lake might have been forgiven at this point for repeating the dictum of a certain Prussian general six years earlier in another context to the effect that what his men needed was whips rather than guns. As far as he knew, Moore and Dalhousie were enjoying similar success and could confidently be expected to have pushed rebel forces in the south of the county back towards Wexford town. With naval forces blockading Wexford harbour and with these advances on land, he knew he had the rebels trapped in the south-eastern quarter of the county. This was exactly as he had anticipated, and so he was under no pressure to parley with them. Perhaps because of this, or perhaps because of his anger at the rebuff the Tunks mission had received when the rebels were in a stronger position, he had now decided to punish them severely. Thus, with evening approaching, he still made no effort to respond to Hay and Cloney.

Unknown to Lake, however, there were dramatic developments taking place in the south of the county that would have a profound effect on his plans to snare the rebel forces the following day. During the afternoon, as he held his position at Enniscorthy and left the rebel delegates kicking their heels, Moore and Dalhousie had decided to move forward from Taghmon towards the Three Rocks. In doing this they were exceeding their orders, which were to stay at Taghmon, and their reason for taking this action is unclear. It is likely, though, that they were responding to the urgings of local loyalists such as James Boyd who were anxious on behalf of the prisoners in the town, perhaps because they had by now heard reports of the massacre on the bridge.[31]

Most of the northern rebels retreating from Vinegar Hill had made it as far as Ferrycarrig Bridge by the time Moore and Dalhousie left Taghmon, and the vast majority of them had gone into Wexford town in search of food. Roche and his Shelmaliers, who were not as badly off as many of their comrades, had set up a temporary camp on Windmill Hill. The Three Rocks, on the other hand, was only sparsely garrisoned.[32] As he approached the western slope of Forth Mountain, Moore sent a small detachment up to the summit to protect his right flank. There was a small rebel remnant on that end of the hill, but they fled as soon as they saw the soldiers coming, and the entire column was able to make its way unhindered along the narrow road on which the Meath militia had been annihilated four weeks earlier.[33]

Meanwhile in Wexford town there was tremendous confusion, and the rebels were in no state to resist this sudden advance by the government forces to their west. Harvey and Colclough had already realised how dangerous their situation was and decided to try to save themselves by slipping out of the town and making their way back to their homes. They had agreed to reunite later in the day and to make their way to the Saltee Islands where they might hide.[34] Keogh and several other southern leaders, on the other hand, insisted that Lake would accept their offer of a surrender and resolved to stay until the army arrived. In contrast, the officers from the north were less hopeful, and at least some of them had begun to toy with the idea of outflanking the approaching armies.[35]

The rebel rank and file was by now thronging the streets in search of food and trying to make sense out of the disaster that was befalling their cause. Some of them were anxious for revenge, and the situation of the remaining prisoners and of other loyalists in and around the town was very dangerous. Thus, when Robert Carty and a young militia officer set out for Moore's camp with news of Lake's whereabouts, a rebel from the northern army attacked them and shot the militiaman dead. Carty had to turn around and break his word to Moore.[36] Later on a number of rebels tried to break into Kingsborough's quarters near the Bullring and were only stopped from doing so when Anthony Perry appeared and ordered them to leave.[37] Ebenezer Jacob made every effort to impose order on the town, but in the midst of the fear and confusion that now prevailed the task was next to impossible, and there were probably many similar incidents that have gone unrecorded.

By midday the position of the loyalist prisoners had begun to change for the better. Just before noon their guards had let them move into the yard behind the jail, and at that point they had told them that the rebellion was collapsing. There were crowds of people in the street outside the building shouting abuse and making threats, and many of the prisoners were aware of how easily they might break in were the guards to withdraw. At about three o'clock, however, the entire guarding party suddenly handed their arms over to the prisoners and asked that they lock them up for safety in the cells. The loyalists complied and now took up defensive positions at the entrances to the building.[38]

In the meantime Thomas Dixon had arrived back in the town. He had returned alone, but the Shelmaliers, among whom he might expect to find some following, were still encamped on Windmill Hill with Edward Roche. Dixon managed to gather some supporters in the confusion, even though the Shelmaliers mostly remained aloof, and they began to make plans to kill the remaining prisoners.[39]

Sir John Moore and his army reached the eastern slope of Forth Mountain around this time. The Shelmaliers were still at Windmill Hill, and their outposts spotted Moore's men almost immediately and spread news of his appearance back into the town. There was no time to prepare a defence. Roche roused his men and led them down into the town, where he sought out several of the other northern officers, including Anthony Perry, Edward Fitzgerald, Garrett Byrne and Mogue Kearns. They held a quick meeting, at which the badly injured Esmond Kyan was also present, and agreed to rally as many of their units as they could and make a dash for the bridge and the open country beyond. Their hope was that, once out into Shelmalier and Ballaghkeen, they might have some chance of evading Lake's forces.

It was probably no more than half an hour, if that, between the time this meeting took place and the time Edward Roche and Perry led several thousand men, the bulk of the old northern army, across the bridge. Behind them in the town they left Father Philip Roche and Father John Murphy, as well as several thousand more rank and file who did not have a chance to join them. The two priests gathered as many units as they could, the total amounting to several thousand men also, and hurriedly made their exit from the town too, but, instead of going north over the bridge and following the other group, they decided to make their way southwards into the countryside of Bargy and Forth, taking roughly the same escape route that the town's garrison had taken on 30 May.[40]

Moore was watching the town from his vantage-point on Forth Mountain as all this took place, but he did not realise its significance. He saw the force that went over the bridge to the north, but he assumed they were refugees fleeing from the imminent fighting; he apparently saw nothing and knew nothing of the column that headed south.[41] It was a crucial error on his part. Because Lake had pulled Needham into the centre of the county, he had left a yawning gap in his dragnet along the east coast; and because he had moved forward to Forth Mountain so quickly, Moore had opened an equally wide gap between the mountain and the south coast. Two hurriedly marshalled rebel armies were now headed for these gaps, yet neither Lake nor Moore realised what was happening.

Not all the rebels fled from Wexford town, of course. Many, including the majority of the old southern army and thousands of refugees, stayed behind, either because they expected mercy from the soldiers or because they had no time to get away. Many of the southern leaders remained too, including Matthew Keogh, Robert Carty, William Kearney and John Kelly (who was still unable to move).[42] They still hoped for mercy from the government and expected that Kingsborough and Ebenezer Jacob would be able to secure it for them.

Staying behind for now also was Thomas Dixon, his wife and a small crowd of their followers. They gathered on Wexford Bridge, just as they had done the day before, and, according to one witness at least, began to make the same final preparations for mass executions as they had done on that occasion. With the cause clearly lost, Dixon was evidently determined to wipe out the captive loyalists before he left the town.[43]

From his position on the eastern slope of Forth Mountain Moore noticed that fires began to burn in several buildings inside the town. His fear now was that the rebels were resorting to a scorched-earth policy, and, in these circumstances, the safety of the prisoners he knew to be still inside the walls became his chief concern. He was hesitant to lead his men into the town, however, partly because this would be going too far beyond his orders, and also perhaps because he knew Lake wanted to take the town the next day himself. Several local loyalists, James Boyd and Henry Perceval among them, begged him to at least let them ride in and secure the prisoners, and eventually he agreed. At approximately 3 p.m. these two men took a detachment of about a dozen yeomen and made their way down into John Street and through the John's Lane Gate. There was no resistance to them as they passed, and in a matter of minutes they had reached the main street.[44]

Dixon and his followers were still at the bridge when the yeomanry got to John Street. Reports of the sudden appearance of the troops reached them quickly, and both Dixon and his wife mounted horses and galloped hurriedly northwards over the bridge. The rest of the crowd scattered by foot, most of them fleeing across the bridge too.[45]

Minutes later Boyd, Perceval and their men reached the quays. As they rode along they shouted out to any loyalists within earshot that they were rescued. They went straight to the jail to free the prisoners, but by the time they reached the building the prisoners were already coming out into the street. Members of their families and friends began to appear, and there were extraordinary scenes as they were reunited after a month-long separation. Someone rowed out to the prison ship in the harbour and began to ferry those prisoners back to the quays, and equally emotional reunions took place there.[46]

When it became clear to Moore and Dalhousie that there would be no opposition from rebels in the streets (one man did shoot at Boyd as he entered, but that was the only incident of its kind), they decided to send two detachments of troops in to guard the town for the night. The plan was still to let Lake be the one to take possession of the town, and these troops were merely a token force.[47]

Kingsborough now found himself in an odd position. The town had already been surrendered to him and most of the local rebels had given themselves up to him, but he was only a militia colonel, whereas the armies which were poised to move against the place the next day were commanded by regular army generals. Furthermore, if Lake's silence was anything to go by, they had no intention of accepting a peaceful surrender. The fact that several thousand rebels, including the entire north Wexford leadership, had evacuated the town with the intention of renewing the fight complicated matters even further. Most important of all, the fact that only one day earlier almost a hundred unarmed loyalists had been murdered in the town made it practically inevitable that the generals would want some kind of revenge. Kingsborough himself had been well treated during his captivity, however, and it seems that, in spite of these complications, he had made his mind up to try hard to persuade Lake and Moore to spare the town and the rebel leaders.

Others were less charitable in their outlook. As a portent of what was to come, that night bands of loyalists began to search the town for concealed rebels. By evening they had arrested dozens of men, and by midnight the jail was crammed with suspects. Keogh himself was spared this indignity and was placed under house arrest in his George's Street residence; Kelly too may have been put under guard in the place where he lay, still immobilised from his severe wound. Other former rebels hid as best they could, but many of them were discovered, dragged out into the street and hauled off to the prison.[48]

In Enniscorthy loyalist bands seached the town and surrounding countryside for hidden rebels too. They killed many of those they found. At one point a large group of loyalists discovered about fifty men hiding out in St John's Woods and shot every one of them.[49] The yeomanry that had made their way back into the county from Arklow via Gorey were heavily involved in these atrocities—making it clear what was to be expected once the old ruling class was in control of the county again.[50]

As a preliminary step in his move against Wexford town, Lake ordered Needham to move southwards and camp for the night at Ballinkeele demesne, the home of the Hays. This would place him half-way to Wexford and in a good position to cut off the rebels if they tried to retreat across the bridge. To cover his right flank, he sent Johnson southward along the west bank of the river with instructions to camp for the night a few miles from Wexford too, placing him in a good position to strike at the town from the north-west once the new day began. As for Dundas, Loftus and Duff, they were to remain with Lake himself at Enniscorthy for the night and were to form the main body of the army that would march on Wexford the next day.[51] What Lake did not know at this point, of course, was that most of the rebels had already evacuated Wexford town and that some of them were ten miles directly to his east at Peppard's Castle and would be behind him as soon as he moved south, while others were at Sleedagh demesne and about to slip past Moore's and Dalhousie's right flank.

The two rebel armies were in a good position now not only to evade Lake's net but even to strike out into other parts of the country. Lake had made sure that Asgill stood guard along the Barrow valley, so retreat in that direction might have been difficult, but the garrisons in north Wexford, south Wicklow and north Carlow were quite small by this time and would not have been able to prevent sizeable rebel forces from getting past them and reaching the mountains or driving out into the central plain. There was every possibility then that the rebels might maintain their struggle for a long time were they to decide to do so, even long enough to link up with a French invasion force that might still be weeks away. In this sense Lake was in a much poorer position that night than he realised, even though many of the rebels themselves were not aware of the larger picture.

Intense debates went on in both rebel camps during the night over what action to take on the following day. The lines of argument were broadly the same as they had been in most of the discussions of strategy that taken place over the previous weeks. Some wanted to push north beyond Wexford and to keep up the fight, while others refused to leave their native county and, now that the government had taken control of it, were willing to throw themselves on the mercy of the authorities rather than pursue what looked like a lost cause. At Peppard's Castle the entire leadership cadre, consisting of Perry, Fitzgerald, Garrett Byrne and Edward Roche, were in one mind on the matter and resolved to march northwards the next day. Hundreds, perhaps even thousands, of their rank and file disagreed, however, and these drifted away as the night passed. They had had enough of marching and campaigning and wanted to return home to their families. They were exhausted and disheartened and decided, one at a time or even in entire battalions, that the best course of action was to trust in the government's mercy. The leading officers could do little about this, and some of those who chose to leave were quite prominent themselves, including John Hay, who slipped away and rode to Ballinkeele, a decision he surely would not have made had he known that Needham's men were encamped there. When the night ended, the effect of these withdrawals became apparent and the army of 4,000 or 5,000 men that had escaped from Lake's clutches had been reduced to less than half that number.[52]

At Sleedagh the other rebel army was undergoing a similar crisis. There a fierce dispute broke out between Father Philip Roche and Father John Murphy as to the best course of action. Roche suggested that they all return to Wexford town and surrender. Murphy, on the other hand, argued that they should march out into the midlands and try to link up with rebel units holding out there, especially the coalminers of Castlecomer, and try to revive the failed rebellion. Ironically, the man who had been so opposed to a Wicklow strategy earlier on was now convinced that the only hope was to take the struggle outside County Wexford.

The argument between the captain and the general raged around the campfire for some time, and was intently followed by many of the men under their command. In the end, as dawn was approaching, and with no agreement in sight, Roche decided to abandon the camp altogether and return to Wexford and take a chance on Lake's clemency. None of the rank and file would agree to follow him, and so he rode out alone. In spite of their difference of opinion, Murphy and he wished each other well at their parting, and Murphy assured Roche that he could catch up with them later if he changed his mind.[53]

*

As soon as dawn broke the next morning, 22 June, Lake began to stir in Enniscorthy. He finally called Hay and Cloney to him and presented them with a written rejection of Kingsborough's note, pointing out quite simply that he would not treat with rebels. He then ordered Cloney to remain where he was and instructed Hay to ride south to Ballinkeele with Captain McManus. He was to join Needham there and to accompany him on to Wexford and deliver the response to the rebel leaders. Hay had no choice but to comply, and he and McManus rode out shortly afterwards and reached Ballinkeele an hour or so after dawn. By that time Lake was already beginning to move his men down along the road to Ferrycarrig, and Johnson was moving along the west bank of the river and planning to meet him near the bridge.[54]

Needham moved out in the direction of Wexford shortly after this. He made Hay ride alongside a detachment of the Ancient Britons that went on ahead of him as a vanguard, and when they arrived in the vicinity of Wexford, Captain Wynne, the Ancient Britons' commander, ordered him to go forward alone and reconnoitre the area around the bridge for him. He saw no sign of rebels and obediently returned with this information. Wynne then led the entire troop all the way to the northern end of the bridge, but discovered that the rebels had pulled down the temporary planking when they made their escape over it the evening before and that somebody had hauled up the portcullis in the middle. This held up the detachment for almost half an hour.

By the time they replaced the planks and shifted the portcullis they could see several ships burning near the quay. It must have been obvious to them by then that the rebels were no longer in control and that the loyalist backlash had already begun.[55]

Johnson and Lake had joined forces to the north-west of the town as Needham made his way towards Wexford, and they were approaching it from that direction when Wynne and Hay finally crossed the bridge. Meanwhile Moore had pulled back the troops he had sent into the streets for the night, leaving the town in the hands of Kingsborough, Jacob and the local yeomanry.[56]

Hay and Wynne sought out Kingsborough as soon as they reached the quays, and they eventually found him while Lake and his army were still some distance off to the north. Kingsborough gave them another note to take out to the commander-in-chief as soon as he learned what the latter's response to his first letter had been. This second communication assured him that he had already accepted the surrender of the town and that further action was unnecessary. The two men went out beyond the outskirts with the message and met Lake as he came in. It was a critical moment, for when he read this second note the commander-in-chief decided to spare the town.[57] The massacre and massive destruction of property that so many had expected would not take place after all; for the second time in the war, Wexford escaped being sacked.

By the middle of the morning Lake had joined Moore on Windmill Hill and had decided to keep the bulk of his forces stationed there. He sent some detachments into the town as a garrison and instructed Needham to march back north to Oulart as soon as he realised that his grip on the place was secure. With Moore and Johnson outside, he had detachments of soldiers conduct a thorough search of the town and the surrounding countryside for concealed rebels.[58]

The soldiers began their own campaign of terror in and around the town now, and while property was left unscathed, they made sure that scores of individuals suffered for the insurrection. They threw many of the men they arrested as suspected rebels into the jail along with those who had been there since the first wave of searches the evening before, and they started shooting others on sight. The particular policy depended very much on the whims of the officers conducting the searches. Many of the soldiers began to rape women in the countryside around the town during the afternoon, and by evening they had thoroughly terrorised the entire south-eastern region.[59] From her safe haven at Rathaspick Elizabeth Richards heard of many men being shot that afternoon near her home, and she could hear the screams of women who were being raped from her window during the evening. As a loyalist she was relieved that the rebellion was over, but from her entry in her diary that night it is clear that she regarded what was now being done to the local people, many of them completely innocent of involvement, with deep horror.[60]

Thousands of people went into hiding in various parts of the county as reports of these atrocities spread. Many hid in woodlands, hedges and ditches, and some even sought out sympathetic loyalist neighbours and tried to conceal themselves in their farmyards and gardens.[61] Lake issued a proclamation during the afternoon promising clemency for all rebels other than leaders, but most of them did not hear of this or, if they did, were unwilling to take the chance, and so as night began to fall huge numbers of them kept to their hiding-places.

The position of the rebel leaders who had decided to put their trust in the government was very bleak by this point. Matthew Keogh was kept under house arrest throughout the day, and John Kelly was brought into the jail. Father Philip Roche had arrived back in the town early in the morning and had ridden about in the streets unrecognised for some time. Eventually some yeomen realised who he was, and they dragged him from his horse and took him out to Windmill Hill, where they beat him beyond recognition. Then they brought him back into the town and threw him into the jail.[62]

The other prominent rebels were still at large. Cornelius Grogan was at home in Johnstown, hoping to remain free, but was too ill to escape.[63] Father Mogue Kearns, though wounded from the fighting in Enniscorthy, had managed to get away with a handful of followers and had made his way northwards towards the barony of Bantry.[64] Bagenal Harvey and John Henry Colclough were already on their way to the Saltee Islands. Colclough's young wife and infant child were with them, and they planned to find shelter in the cabin of one of Colclough's tenants who lived there. They were not aware of it at the time, but as they rowed across the open stretch of sea between the mainland and the islands somebody noticed them and passed the information back to the authorities in Wexford the following day.[65]

In spite of sparing the town and its population from total annihilation, and in spite of issuing a pardon to ordinary rebels who handed in their weapons, Lake decided to make some examples during his first afternoon in Wexford. He instituted a court martial and had two of the captured rebels put on trial. Neither of the rebels in question was especially prominent—he wanted to keep the bigger prizes for later—but the court found them both guilty of rebellion and condemned them to death. Then the soldiers took them to the bridge and hanged them.[66] These would be the first of many executions.

*

General Needham spent the afternoon making his way back to Oulart. His men had their own way of showing that they now had the upper hand. They shot several men they found hiding in the fields near the road and raped several women. Their victims included some milkmaids near Oulart village who were unfortunate enough to be working in the fields as they passed. The most notorious of the day's atrocities in the Oulart area took place outside McGawley's hotel. John McGawley, the owner's son, had been a rebel officer and was among those who left the Peppard's Castle camp in the early hours of the morning and set out for home. He was in the village when Needham got there and somebody informed the general of young McGawley's former position, adding that he had advocated that the rebel army set fire to Wexford before withdrawing from it the evening before. In an act of cruelty that typified his approach, Needham forced the innkeeper and his wife to come outside the building and watch as his soldiers hanged their son from the shafts of a cart.[67]

In the northern half of the county by this point scattered bands of yeomanry were conducting a reign of terror that at least rivalled the regime over which Lake and Needham were presiding further south. As news of the apparently total victory of government forces in the south spread northwards to Gorey and Arklow and the surrounding towns and villages, local yeomanry units started to venture far out into the countryside, determined to take their revenge on anyone they suspected of being a rebel or a rebel sympathiser. At the hamlet of Clogh, close to the Tubberneering battlefield, one of these detachments encountered a small band of rebels with whom they fought a short skirmish. Later they used this as a pretext to attack dozens of innocent countrypeople who had remained behind when the rebels fled the area or who had subsequently returned. Among their victims were a number of young women whom they raped and whose bellies they then ripped open. They left the mutilated bodies on the roadside, presumably as a message to their defeated enemies.[68]

The remnants of the two rebel armies that had escaped from Lake's net were making important moves of their own as the day passed. When morning came the force at Peppard's Castle, although depleted by desertions, set out on its march to the mountains. They eventually came close to the districts where government atrocities were taking place, and at one point they found the bodies of several of the violated and murdered women on the roadside. They were just a few miles south of Gorey when this happened, and even though they had planned on skirting by the town and heading straight for the mountains, they now changed course and made straight for it.

A group of yeomen spotted the rebel column as it approached the town along the Ballycanew road, and a small detachment of troops went out to meet it. The rebels, however, drove them back before them, and in a matter of minutes the small garrison in the town panicked and began to flee out along the road to Arklow. Before they left they took several prisoners out of the market house and, and as they had done a month before, shot them on the side of the street. As they left, riding two to a horse in many cases, scores of loyalist refugees who had fled from the town and returned twice already during the rebellion, also set out for Arklow to escape the rebels.[69]

A detachment of the rebel column gave chase to the fugitives as soon as it was realised that they had slipped out of the town. The garrison itself got away safely and reached Arklow unscathed, but the incensed rebels caught up with many of the refugees near Coolgreany. They set upon them without mercy and massacred almost fifty of them in the village, some quite brutally.[70] Then they returned to Gorey and rejoined the rest of the column on its march towards Croghan.

The rest of the journey was uneventful. Perry and his fellow-officers led the exhausted but determined men across the hills of north-west Wexford during the evening hours, and by nightfall they reached a place called the White Heaps at the foot of Croghan Mountain.[71] They had marched over twenty miles and had removed themselves completely out of Lake's reach; in fact Lake was still unaware of their existence as an organised force.

The column under Father Murphy conducted an equally impressive march that day and was well beyond Lake's grasp by evening too. They left Sleedagh shortly after Father Philip Roche rode off, and by the late morning they had reached Foulkesmills and passed over the fields that were still strewn with corpses from the battle of two days before. They spent the afternoon and early evening making their way northwards, passing by Carrickbyrne and Killann and pushing on towards the Scullogue Gap. They spotted an enemy cavalry patrol in the distance when they were near Killann, but the detachment fled from them almost immediately and they never came to blows. When they got through the Scullogue Gap later in the evening, they found a force of several hundred cavalry drawn up outside the little mountain village of Killedmond. This was perhaps one of Asgill's forward detachments. There was a short sharp battle, but the cavalry fled and left Murphy and his men in possession of the village. They burned much of it down, including a slated building the soldiers had used as a barracks, and with night coming on decided to camp on a low hill nearby until morning.[72] Like their comrades at Croghan, they too had marched well over twenty miles, and in their case too Lake was unaware that they were still in the field.

14

BREAKOUT
23–26 JUNE

LAKE SPENT 23 JUNE, THE FOURTH SATURDAY SINCE THE OUTBREAK of the Wexford rebellion, consolidating his grip on Wexford town and its vicinity. All the signs were that the rebellion was over now, and he had no idea that two small but determined rebel armies were marching away to his north and his west.[1] Of course, thousands of former rebels had not fled with the two insurgent columns and continued to conceal themselves wherever they could in and around the town throughout the day; these were now the most pressing concern for Lake.[2]

In the town itself the court martial took up the work it had left off the afternoon before. Among those put up for trial was John Hay, by far the most prominent rebel to appear before the court to date. He was accused of murdering John Boyd on the night the rebels first entered the town, and in the atmosphere that prevailed it was unlikely that he would get a fair hearing. After a short proceeding the seven officers found him guilty of murder and condemned him to death. He was brought to the bridge that afternoon and hanged.[3] His brother Edward may well have looked on.[4] Other rebel leaders who had been arrested could only bide their time and await their fate.

Quite a few prominent rebels remained at large. Incredibly, Edward Hay still roamed about the town quite freely and, in marked contrast to his executed brother, was not identified as an insurgent officer. Cornelius Grogan remained in seclusion at Johnstown, hoping that the storm would pass him by.[5] Thomas Cloney had evaded capture by Lake's men and hid in a barn owned by a yeoman named Rudd. At one point some soldiers came into the building looking for fodder for their horses, but they did not notice him and he escaped arrest once again.[6]

Of all the fugitives, the most remarkable case was that of John

Henry Colclough and Bagenal Harvey, both hidden by now on the Saltees. The news of their escape reached a Dr Waddy of Wexford town that morning. He informed Lake during the day and asked to lead a search party out to the islands to capture the two men. Lake agreed and let him have a schooner and a small party of soldiers for the task, and they set sail from Wexford quay in the middle of the afternoon. Waddy and his men would not be able to reach the Saltees until early the following day, but as they left Lake must have felt very confident that he was about to ferret out the last of the rebel leaders and complete his destruction of the United Irish movement.[7]

Far to the north and west the two small rebel armies were carrying on the campaign regardless of what was happening in south Wexford. During the day they began to make their way into the neighbouring counties in their effort to rekindle the rebellion in the midlands, and, for the time being at least, government forces in those districts were incapable of stopping them. In several ways the rebels were more formidable now than they had been for some time. They were far more mobile than they had been when they were more numerous, and they were more willing to adopt unconventional tactics. Furthermore, they exhibited all the determination of the committed militant core of the Wexford and south Wicklow United Irish movement and so were unlikely to give up after one or two setbacks. As the day passed, then, the greatest challenge to Lake was to his rear, even if he was still unaware of its existence.[8]

The column that had camped at Croghan for the night remained there throughout the morning. The leaders were discussing strategy, and they found it difficult to agree on details. Some wanted to remain where they were in order to give other detachments that had left Wexford town a chance to join them. There was particular concern about Father Kearns and his group, who were believed to have taken refuge in the woods to the west of Enniscorthy; many of the Wexford officers argued vehemently that they should wait for a few days and give him a chance to catch up with them. Garrett Byrne and the Wicklow leaders, however, were less patient, and they advocated that the entire force should move further into the mountains right away and not wait for Kearns, at least not in that exposed place. In the end Byrne's argument prevailed, and sometime in the afternoon, after they had shot some sheep on the nearby hills and eaten a meal of mutton, the first solid food many of them had had for three or four days, they broke camp and marched northwards down into the Ow valley.[9]

They went in the direction of Aughrim, a village only seven miles up the Avoca/Ow valley from Arklow. They saw little sign of government forces. Patrols were, in fact, riding out along the valley from Arklow as the afternoon passed, but none of them came close enough to skirmish and the rebels may not even have sighted them.[10] At one point, possibly before they left Croghan, a small detachment of yeomen from Carnew approached them from the west and fired a few artillery rounds in their direction. The cannonade did little damage, however, and the yeomen made no effort to follow it up with an infantry attack and withdrew after only a short time.[11]

The extreme caution shown by government forces in the Wexford/Wicklow borderland during this and several subsequent days was probably in part due to the fact that the commanders in Arklow and Carnew were still unclear as to the situation in southern Wexford and unaware of the strength and intentions of the rebels themselves. Moreover, the massacre at Coolgreany the day before must have terrified the small garrison. Not until the afternoon, when a loyalist prisoner who escaped from the rebel column made his way into the town, did they learn that the insurgents were moving on into the mountains and had no immediate plans to attack them.[12]

The insurgents reached Aughrim well before twilight and halted briefly in the village. Then they pushed north-westwards to Ballymanus, Garrett Byrne's home. They reached the abandoned farmstead by evening and decided to make a camp there for the night.[13] They were now about six miles inside County Wicklow and in a much less exposed position than they had been on Croghan. More importantly, they were in a good position to strike out into the hills and to rally to their side any scattered rebel bands left over from the earlier stage of the rebellion. They had lost many men through desertion at Peppard's Castle two days before, but they still numbered 1,000 or 2,000 determined troops, and, in addition, they were now in the heart of a mountainous terrain that Lake's forces, when they did make an effort to deal with them, might find very difficult indeed. That night the officers slept in the dwelling-house at Ballymanus, while the men bivouacked around the farmyard and in the out-buildings. The weather had become warm once again, making sleeping under the sky more comfortable. Should they find a means to replenish their supply of firearms and ammunition, this rebel force might prove very formidable indeed. In the days that were to come this would be their most pressing concern and would determine much of their strategy.

The rebel column that spent the night in the Blackstairs Mountains roused itself early in the day too. Unlike the Croghan group, they hurriedly abandoned their camp and pushed down into the Barrow valley, making for the Castlecomer plateau beyond it. Asgill had had substantial forces deployed in the villages along the Barrow during the first two days of Lake's offensive against Wexford, but he had pulled most of them back to Kilkenny by this time, and so much of the valley was virtually ungarrisoned, giving Father Murphy and his men the opening they needed. The only sizeable garrison they heard of at this stage was at Goresbridge, and this now became their immediate objective.[14]

When they got down into the bottom of the valley, they made straight for Goresbridge, where they knew they could cross the river into County Kilkenny. It was around the middle of the morning when they approached the village. There was a garrison of a few dragoons and two dozen Wexford militia in the place, and when they realised a rebel force was proceeding in their direction they drew up battle positions just to the east of the bridge. The rebel officers realised this when they came within sight of the village; they immediately split their force into three detachments, one of which advanced directly against the men defending the bridge (driving a stampeding herd of cattle before them as a battle tactic, as at Enniscorthy), while the other two crossed the river to the right and left of the bridge and made sweeping flanking movements designed to trap the small defending force. The

Rebel Movements, 22 June – 8 July

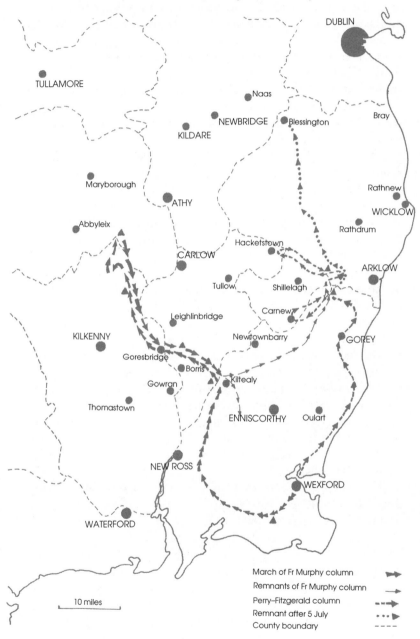

DUBLIN

TULLAMORE

Naas

NEWBRIDGE

Blessington

Bray

KILDARE

Maryborough

Rathnew

ATHY

WICKLOW

Abbyleix

Rathdrum

Hacketstown

CARLOW

ARKLOW

Tullow

Shillelagh

Leighlinbridge

Carnew

KILKENNY

Newtownbarry

GOREY

Goresbridge

Borris

Gowran

Kiltealy

Thomastown

ENNISCORTHY

Oulart

NEW ROSS

WEXFORD

WATERFORD

10 miles

March of Fr Murphy column
Remnants of Fr Murphy column
Perry–Fitzgerald column
Remnant after 5 July
County boundary

dragoons quickly realised how futile resistance was and fled out along the road towards Kilkenny. The militia were slower to retreat, and when they did begin to fall back they suddenly found themselves trapped just to the west of the village by the two rebel flanks. There were only twenty-six men in the unit, and they immediately threw down their arms and surrendered. The insurgents accepted this and made the men prisoners and took their guns and ammunition. Ironically, most of the new prisoners belonged to the Wexford militia.

The fleeing dragoons eventually reached Kilkenny and alerted Asgill. In response, the general formed a marching column of about 1,000 men and set out for Goresbridge. By this time, however, the rebels were already on their way out of the village and marching northwards towards Castlecomer. (They had made a quick but fruitless search for arms and had eventually taken several barrels of flour as their only booty.)[15]

Asgill realised when he got to Goresbridge that he had missed his chance to intercept them. He might have pursued them into the rolling country to his north and forced them to do battle somewhere to the south of Castlecomer that same day, but instead he took the more cautious course and withdrew back to Kilkenny. He did send mounted detachments northwards to follow the rebels and report on their movements as the day passed, but took no further offensive action against them. Like the commanders at Carnew and Arklow, therefore, he was apparently confused about what had happened to Lake's offensive and was very hesitant to attack a rebel force, numbering perhaps several thousand men, whose strength he did not know but whose reputation he obviously greatly feared.[16]

The rebels spent the rest of the day moving northwards along the Leinster ridge uninterrupted, driving ever closer to the coalmining districts of north Kilkenny. News of their approach spread before them that afternoon as they went, and hundreds of loyalists fled from their homes and sought shelter in Castlecomer.[17] By evening they were within a few miles of the town, but Father Murphy had no intention of attacking in the dark and so ordered his men to break off the march and camp for the night in the hills of the Leinster ridge.[18] Meanwhile in Castlecomer itself scores of frightened loyalists camped in the main street, and the garrison of about 200 yeomen stood at arms all night. Late in the evening Asgill sent another 100 men from Kilkenny to reinforce them (he evidently realised by this point what the immediate objective of the insurgents was), and the commanding officers issued guns to about a hundred loyalist supplementaries and asked them to join in the defence.[19]

The odds against Murphy's column were substantial at this stage. They numbered only around 1,000 or 2,000 badly armed and exhausted men (they had marched seventy miles in four days) and were about to throw themselves at a town defended by 400 well-fed, rested and well-armed men. The prize which they sought, a victory that would bring the coalminers out to join them, was nevertheless enough to justify the risk. As they passed the night on their hillside camp and ate the bread baked for them over open fires by their women companions[20] they may not have been fully aware of how well defended Castlecomer was, and they may have felt quite confident. Their greatest concern was almost certainly the fact that few of the inhabitants of the localities they had marched through during the day had chosen to join them.[21] They could only hope that this pattern would change drastically in the coming days.

Some thirty miles to the south-east of Father Murphy's camp, in the meantime, Lake was settling down for his third night in Wexford town. By this point Needham had almost certainly heard of rebel activity to his north from his post at Oulart, and Johnson must have received some reports of the actions at Killedmond and Goresbridge, since by now he was back in New Ross. Neither general may have realised the true significance of the news, however, and it is quite likely that at the end of the day they were still unaware of the real situation.

As soon as dawn broke on Sunday 24 June and he had celebrated mass Father Murphy and his men broke camp on the Leinster ridge. As they did so they discovered that during the night nine of the captured Wexford militiamen had been murdered. The culprits were most likely their former comrades, taking revenge now for endless tauntings over the previous weeks, but the rebel officers took no action to punish the killers.[22]

The column pushed on towards the little village of Doonane,

about four miles to the north-east of Castlecomer, where a detachment of coalminers were lying in wait to join them. There was a small garrison in the village, and in what amounted to a pathetic gesture of defiance the soldiers formed a battle-line outside when they learned the rebels were coming, but withdrew as soon as the column came within range and fled back along the road towards Castlecomer. Murphy and his men pushed on into the village and in a short time hundreds of coalminers from the locality joined them, most of them armed only with pikes and tools. It was a small victory but an important boost as they prepared to attack the much larger town to their south-west.[23]

It was still quite early in the morning when they resumed their march towards Castlecomer, but by that time Asgill was already on his way from Kilkenny with several hundred more troops. A lot would depend on who reached the place first. The rebels marched towards the town along the narrow country road that links it with Doonane. A few miles from Castlecomer they encountered a detachment of about sixty militiamen drawn up on the road ahead of them. The soldiers were surprised by their sudden appearance and tried to surrender, but in a moment of confusion one of their officers was killed by a rebel who was apparently uncertain of what was happening. The rest of the detachment then fled, taking their weapons with them and depriving the luckless insurgents of a valuable opportunity to acquire some more firearms.[24]

The rebels reached Castlecomer well ahead of Asgill. As they approached the town they split into two detachments. One of these crossed the River Dinen to attack on the northern side, while the other made its way towards the bridge at its eastern end. Father Murphy himself took command of the group attacking from the north, while Miles Byrne, now an important officer, was in charge of the assault on the bridge. Murphy's group had by far the easier task, since the road from the north ran straight into the heart of the town and this approach was relatively open. In contrast, the bridge which Byrne and his unit had to seize was quite narrow and was overlooked by several large stone houses, in the upper storeys of which soldiers were already stationed. Without artillery to help them, the task of storming these was bound to be very difficult.

Both detachments arrived at the edge of the town at about the same time and attacked almost immediately. Murphy's men managed to push their way in along the northern entrance quickly. As they did so many of cabins which lined the street caught fire (or were set on fire, it is not clear which), and the flames soon spread to much of the town. Byrne's men had some initial success and managed to make their way onto the bridge, but they were not able to dislodge the soldiers from the houses nearby and were soon pinned down behind the parapet and other adjacent cover. They lost several men while trying to storm the largest of the buildings, a house owned by Lady Butler, many of them dying in a vain attempt to set the front door on fire by pushing carts loaded with burning straw up against it; the tactic was a desperate one and no more successful now than it had been when Thomas Cloney's men tried it at Borris House two weeks before.

Eventually the house did catch fire, and the fate of the soldiers inside seemed to be decided. Some hurried negotiations took place, and the defenders agreed to give up if Father Murphy gave a written guarantee that they would not be harmed. At about that point, however, Asgill's advance guard got within range of the town and suddenly opened fire on the streets from outside it with musket and cannon. The rebels pulled back momentarily, long enough to allow the soldiers who had been under siege to escape to Asgill's lines; but then, in what amounted to a new phase of the struggle, the two small armies rearranged themselves and prepared for an open battle. Once again, however, Asgill's nerve failed him, and rather than push his advantage he decided not to risk an attack and began to pull his men back from the town, retreating along the road to Kilkenny and leaving the rebel column in undisputed possession.[25]

By the normal rules of war, the insurgent army had achieved a stunning victory. Castlecomer was a fair-sized town and had been well defended, while their own weapons had been very poor. Nevertheless, they had carried it by storm and had intimidated Asgill's army into retreating and leaving the coalmining districts in their hands. Unfortunately, the prize was not as great as they might have assumed. They took the opportunity to plunder the town of whatever supplies it contained, and acquired some valuable stocks of food, but they did not find much in the way of arms and ammunition, the one thing they desperately needed. In addition, very few new recruits joined them from the area. The much more formidable army which Murphy expected he might have by this point did not materialise, yet he and his men now found themselves over twenty miles from the western borders of Wexford and Wicklow and dangerously exposed should their luck not change. Even more ominously, they had lost many of their best fighting men in the attack.[26]

At this point they might well have turned back towards the east. It was about a day's forced march to the relative safety of the Blackstairs or Wicklow mountains, and they might be there by the following evening. Father Murphy and his officers resisted any temptation they felt to dash for the mountains, however, and decided that, if the coalmining areas of Kilkenny could not be counted on, perhaps the old United Irish strongholds in the midlands would still rally to the cause. Late in the afternoon, therefore, they led their battalions northwards in the direction of the border with Queen's County, pinning their hopes on making their way into County Kildare in the next day or two. By evening they were well inside Queen's County and only a few miles from Athy.[27] Murphy was already disappointed that rebels had not come to join him from Queen's County and Kildare, and by the time they stopped to make camp for the night on a low hill it was clear that none would. He and many of his officers were already thinking of turning about and heading back towards County Wexford the next day. He had led them on a heroic three-day march since leaving Sleedagh demesne, but he realised that further efforts might well be fruitless, and he evidently hoped that he might be able to rejoin the other column that had escaped from Wexford town three days earlier.

Forty miles to the east of Castlecomer, in the meantime, the other rebel column had been on the move too. During the morning hours, as Murphy and his men were storming Doonane and approaching Castlecomer, they had gone back down the valley to Aughrim. When they arrived there, they discovered that a government patrol had come into the village during the night and had massacred several civilians. They resisted the temptation to conduct a revenge attack on Arklow and stayed in Aughrim for much of the day to give small detachments of rebels from other parts of Wicklow a chance to join them. As the morning and afternoon passed, large numbers did in fact drift in, and even though these were poorly armed, they swelled their ranks considerably and made them more determined than ever to carry the fight to the enemy.[28]

They needed to replenish their supply of arms and ammunition, and sometime during the afternoon they agreed to move westwards and get in position to attack Hacketstown on the following day. The town was a relatively isolated government outpost, and its capture might have the twin advantage of providing new weapons and of eliminating a base from which government forces might operate in the hills.

Hacketstown was less than ten miles to the west of Aughrim, but the roads were narrow, hilly and winding and it took the rest of the day for the column to cover the distance, and evening was approaching by the time they got to within a mile or two of its outskirts. They stopped for the night somewhere in the hills just to its east and decided to attack early the next morning.[29] During all this time government patrols venturing out from surrounding towns kept their distance from them.[30] Hacketstown itself was garrisoned by a few hundred men, mostly yeomanry, and it is likely that as darkness fell that evening they did not realise an assault on the place was imminent.[31]

Meanwhile, far to the south in Wexford, Lake continued to hold the town and the surrounding area in a tight grip. A shipload of bread arrived from Dublin and alleviated the provisioning problem that had begun to develop.[32] The terror with which the ordinary inhabitants had come to regard Lake's troops did not subside, however, and thousands remained in hiding.[33] Even Sir John Moore, who rode southwards from the town in search of the rebels who had escaped in that direction (and whose whereabouts was still a mystery), could not persuade more than a handful of them to come out and accept pardons.[34]

Lake's campaign against the United Irish leadership went on unremittingly. A few of the leaders still remained at large, including Thomas Cloney and Edward Hay,[35] but during the day soldiers went out to Johnstown and arrested Cornelius Grogan, who now joined Father Philip Roche, Matthew Keogh and John Kelly in the jail.[36]

The court martial set about its work with more determination than usual that morning. In all, it tried a total of nine men before evening, among them Keogh and Roche. Keogh put up a strenuous defence, buttressed by appeals to his record during the rebel regime and by evidence from both Le Hunte and Kingsborough to the effect that he was no rebel but had simply taken on the task of governing the town to maintain law and order while the rebels held sway. This was not enough to convince the court, and the seven officers found him guilty of rebellion and sentenced him to be hanged the following day.

Father Roche had less support than Keogh. It is unclear if he attempted to make a similar argument, but his trial seems to have been much shorter and the verdict arrived at with far less deliberation. He too was condemned to hang the next morning. The other seven men received the same sentence.[37]

There was some extrajudicial violence during the day too. At one point some soldiers spotted a man named Maguire, a former rebel, making his way around the town in women's clothes. They gave him no trial, but simply dragged him down to the bridge and hanged him without ceremony.[38]

Two other leaders would join those languishing in the jail by nightfall, for sometime during the evening, about twenty-four hours after they had left Wexford, Waddy and the search-party that had gone in quest of Colclough and Harvey, returned with both men as their prisoners. It was an incredible end to a triumphant day for Lake. When the schooner put in at the quay, a large crowd gathered and accompanied the solders and their prisoners as they marched down the quayside to the jail. There the two commanders were thrown to join their former comrades, with whom they would await trial before the court martial. They could hardly have had any illusions about what the outcome would be.[39]

Later on Waddy and his companions related the story of how they had captured the two rebel generals. As they told it, they had reached the island at dawn that day and had searched the entire place, including a lonely tenant's cabin and a cave. They eventually found the fugitives, along with Colclough's wife and baby son, hiding in a well-concealed cave on one of the cliff faces, but they only did so by accident and as they were about to leave. Neither man offered any resistance, and they were arrested with ease.[40]

Lake's sweep of the rebel leadership now seemed complete. Only three days had passed since he first entered Wexford town, and only five days since he had entered the county itself. He may have been concerned about how long it was taking to entice the former rebel rank and file to accept the amnesty, and his mind must surely have turned to the continuing possibility of a French landing somewhere in the country, but, considering how serious the threat to the government had seeemed at one point, he must also have felt great satisfaction at the outright victory he appeared to have achieved. He was still unaware at this stage that the struggle was not quite over.

By the evening of the 24th, then, as the northern rebel column settled for the night outside Hacketstown and as their comrades camped just inside Queen's County, Lake had taken an important step in the liquidation of the rebel leadership, and the south Wexford loyalists must have watched with grim satisfaction as their political rivals faced destruction.

The next morning, 25 June, saw the government's campaign against the southern rebels reach its climax. Early in the day Matthew Keogh, Father Philip Roche and the seven other men condemned to die with them, prepared themselves for their executions. A crowd gathered around the bridge and in the streets leading to it well before eleven o'clock, the hour the hangings were to take place, and they watched silently, even sullenly, as the nine men were led out of the jail and taken along the main street towards the bridge.

There was a metal arch spanning the structure where it joined the quays, and the soldiers had decided to make this the gallows. They had thrown a rope across it and they decided to hang the nine men, one at a time, by hauling them by the neck from the ground.

Before dying Keogh prayed for a time with an Anglican minister and made a short speech declaring that he wanted to reform but not change the constitution, and also, somewhat incredibly, announcing that he had never been a United

Irishman. Father Roche met his death with less ceremony and no apologies; the rope snapped after he had been hauled up the first time, and he fell to the ground and regained consciousness and had to go through the ordeal a second time before dying. After each of the nine men died their bodies were lowered to the ground and mutilated by the soldiers before being tossed over the parapet into the water. Keogh's corpse was given especially vindictive treatment, perhaps because he was a Protestant rebel: his head was cut off, stuck on a pike and, after it was paraded about in the streets, put on a spike outside the courthouse where it would remain for months.[41]

Several other leaders were scheduled to stand trial that afternoon, but Lake decided to postpone the ritual for a day. Grogan, Harvey and Colclough passed the rest of the afternoon quietly in prison, therefore, and prepared themselves to go before the seven judges on the following day. Edward Hay, who remained at large, and Thomas Cloney, who was still hiding in Rudd's barn, continued to escape the government's clutches.[42] Most rank-and-file rebels were still in hiding too, still unwilling to trust the government's amnesty.

Meanwhile, as Roche and Keogh went to their deaths on Wexford Bridge, the tide was finally beginning to turn against the rebel columns that had been keeping up the fight outside the county to the north and west. Reports of the approach of Father Murphy and his men had evidently filtered northwards through Kildare and Queen's County during the previous evening and night. There was no time for the local garrisons to co-ordinate a response at that point, but during the night, as the rebels slept, several small columns of troops began to move southwards to meet them. One of these, a detachment of about 100 men from north Kildare, got as far as Athy, just a few miles from their camp, while a group of about 300 under a Major Matthews marched eastwards from Monasterevin and stopped at Doonane.

The commander of the detachment at Athy decided to attack the sleeping rebels under cover of darkness, in spite of the small size of his force. The rebels were exhausted at this point, and very badly armed, so his plan had some chance of success. It was foiled, however, by a local priest who learned of it and slipped out of the town during the night and warned them. Murphy had his men break camp at once, and they made their way southwards and reached the Leinster ridge again well before dawn.[43]

They crossed back into County Kilkenny early in the morning and made their way along the winding roads of the Castlecomer plateau during the rest of the day. The troops from Athy arrived too late at the site of their abandoned camp, but when they realised what had happened they began to follow the marching rebels at a distance. They did this for several hours until they encountered Matthews and his larger detachment from Monasterevin, and at that point the Athy unit broke off the pursuit and returned northward, leaving the fresher men to take it up.[44]

This set the pattern for the rest of the day, the rebels making their way back towards their crossing-point at Goresbridge, with Matthews and his men keeping pace with them. On several occasions Murphy wheeled his men about and tried to entice Matthews to attack him in the open fields, but each time the government troops held off. Matthews eventually did try an attack near Old Leighlin, but the rebels quickly sidestepped, and when he got to Leighlinbridge he led his men to the east bank of the river and marched southwards from there. These manoeuvrings show that he was anticipating the rebels' line of march and hoping to hit them on their flank as they turned eastwards themselves towards the Blackstairs once they got across the river.[45]

By the mid-afternoon Father Murphy and his men were under pressure from another direction too, since Asgill was on his way eastwards from Kilkenny with about 1,200 men and was in a good position to cut off the reteating column even before it could reach Goresbridge. Fortunately for the rebels, Asgill was yet again too late to stop them, and they got to Goresbridge ahead of him.

They were badly fatigued by this point, but rather than stay in the ungarrisoned town for the night they pushed on across the Barrow and headed eastwards towards the Scullogue Gap. The pass was still twelve miles away when night began to fall, and this convinced Murphy and his officers to make their camp on a low hill called Kilcumney, about a mile east of the town.[46] They had marched almost twenty miles in the course of the day, having now covered a total of almost a hundred miles in five days, and this alone, apart from the battles they had fought during that time, was enough to weaken them. The shortage of food and the failure of the people of the midlands to join them must have caused serious demoralisation too. For committed United Irishmen, such as most of these no doubt were, a retreat into the mountains and the adoption of guerrilla tactics until a French landing took place was the only option left, and they camped for the night with this in mind. Many of them fell fast asleep, and few of them suspected that, as they rested, Asgill from the west and Matthews from the north continued to move ever closer to them.

The day proved almost as dispiriting for their comrades in the northern column. They began the attack on Hacketstown, on which they pinned so much hope, early in the morning. The garrison, which consisted of about 200 soldiers, most of them infantry, had come to realise an attack was imminent, and their commander drew them up in a battle-line to the east of the entrance as the rebels approached from the direction of Aughrim. The rebel officers split their forces into three detachments as they came close to the enemy line. One crossed the Derreen River, which ran parallel to the road and to its right, and moved around to the garrison's left. The other made its way across several fields to the rebel left and threatened the defenders' right, and a third drove straight ahead along the road.

When the central detachment came close to the infantry along the road, they began a musketry duel with them. Many of the Kildare and Wicklow rebels (most notably Michael Dwyer and William Reynolds and their men) were especially prominent at this stage (perhaps because they still had some ammunition), and the rebel ranks seem to have shown real determination in pushing forward in the face of the garrison's fire. The government cavalry began a retreat back into the town shortly after the battle began and then fled out along the western road towards Clonmore. The infantry offered some resistance for a time, but eventually followed the example of the mounted units and pulled back into the town. They could not get cleanly away as the cavalry had done and therefore had to take up defensive positions in the town itself.

Like a lot of plantation towns in the Leinster chain (most strikingly Newtownbarry), Hacketstown consisted of an elongated central square with small streets of cabins running out of it. The square was dominated by a few buildings, including the barracks, the Protestant church and the rectory of the local Anglican minister named McGee. The most important of these was the barracks, and it was there that most of the troops now fled. The building had a thatched roof, which would normally be a weak point, but it was large, it commanded the entire square, and it had an earthwork on its exposed side; furthermore, its windows and doors were well barricaded. In a matter of minutes the soldiers were at firing positions at all of its access points, and several armed loyalists placed themselves at the windows of the rectory also.

The rebels heavily outnumbered their enemies, but they had fewer firearms and once again had to attack fortified buildings without artillery and with little gunpowder. They threw themselves at the barracks almost as soon as they got inside the town, but were caught in the open square amid deadly musket fire, and many of them lost their lives in completely futile attempts to take the place by storm. In scenes remarkably like those played out at Castlecomer on the previous day, and at Borris two weeks before, they adopted every tactic they could think of to dislodge the soldiers, including that of advancing behind carts loaded with straw and mattresses. The bullets penetrated these, and none of the attackers could get close enough to the building to set its roof on fire. The efforts went on for hours, and scores of men died in the attempt, but all to no avail, and by midday they seemed no closer to taking the building than they had been when they first attacked it.

Some of the shots which had been hitting the rebels had been coming from McGee's house, and at about midday some of them turned their attention to this building and tried to force their way into it. The defenders were well fortified here too, and once again many men were killed in the effort to carry the house by storm and others lost their lives as they tried to advance behind mobile barricades such as loaded carts. They persisted for several hours and only stopped when the losses became too heavy and the cause too obviously futile to justify further attacks.

Sometime in the afternoon, probably around three or four o'clock, the rebel officers called off the attack. Much of the town was in ruins by that time since fires had caught hold on the streets of cabins, but the soldiers showed no sign of running out of ammunition and the fires were having no effect on them. The rebels remained long enough to bury their dead, of which there were perhaps around a hundred, and they then retreated along the road on which they had arrived in the morning, and made their way back into the south Wicklow hills. As soon as they had gone the garrison left the barracks and made their way as quickly as they could towards Tullow, taking all of their equipment with them. The rebels had managed to drive them out of Hacketstown, therefore, but they had failed in their primary purpose, namely the acquisition of arms, and had lost many valuable men in the effort.[47]

The defeat was a major setback. Somewhere to the east of the town the insurgents divided into two columns, one of which marched northwards towards Donard, while the other, composed mostly of Wexford and south Wickow men, made its way back to Croghan and camped there once again before nightfall.[48] For the moment at least, then, the Wexfordmen and south Wicklowmen had returned to the policy of waiting for Kearns's battalion and other lost units (including, no doubt, Father Murphy's) to join them; then, perhaps, they could push back into the sanctuary of the mountains. The force which headed northwards towards Donard that night may well have been designed as a magnet for bands still holding out in Kildare and Meath.

The rebel cause continued to unravel on the following day, Tuesday 26 June. When dawn broke that morning, there were thick patches of fog in low-lying areas all over south Leinster. This made it impossible for the column camped on Kilcumney Hill to see what was happening in the countryside around them as they awoke.[49] By that time the two columns of government troops that had chased them the day before had come to within a mile or so of the hill—Matthews with his 300 men to its north and Asgill with his 1,200 its west. In addition, in a move that may not have been co-ordinated with Asgill and Matthews, at least one cavalry detachment from Wexford itself was making its way westward through the Scullogue Gap.[50]

As they awoke, the rebel officers remained ignorant of this set of developments. To their horror, though, they discovered that the

Castlecomer miners had decamped during the night and had taken dozens of the best guns with them, leaving them even more poorly equipped than they had been when they began the long march into the midlands.[51]

Once the camp was fully astir, Father Murphy sent small patrols out into the foggy morning in several directions to scout out the enemy's position. They returned in a very short time with the alarming news that at least three government columns were almost on top of them, one in the north, one in the west and a third approaching from the Scullogue Gap. The fog was still hiding them, and the rank and file only realised how dangerous their situation was when some of Asgill's cannon suddenly opened fire on the hill.

The insurgents were heavily outgunned and outmanoeuvred, and their numerical advantage was slight by now. Retreat was the only viable option. Father Murphy pulled them back to another hill about a mile to the east almost at once, and at that point the fog began to lift. For a short while the officers considered making a stand on this ridge, but soon changed their minds and ordered a retreat eastward towards the pass. The men and women of the column began to move almost immediately and travelled across the ten miles or so between the hill and the mountains in a state verging on panic. They met the cavalry that had come down from the Scullogue Gap along the way and drove them off without difficulty, but Matthews and Asgill kept up a hot pursuit from the other direction and harassed their rear at every oppotunity. A small rebel rearguard consisting of the few well-armed marksmen tried as hard as it could to hold the soldiers off, and when the majority of the insurgents got into the Scullogue Gap they were still able to protect them. Several of the sharpshooters took up positions on the rocky slopes of the pass and kept up a steady fire on the approaching soldiers. At this point Matthews and Asgill broke off their pursuit, perhaps because of the firepower directed against them, or maybe because they were satisfied to drive the rebel army back into Wexford once again. Once they were safely inside the gap, the rebels were able to rest for a while and wait for their scattered comrades to return before resuming their march.[52]

The whole retreat had been a very confused affair. Many units had become separated from the main body, and these only rejoined it piecemeal over the next hour or two. Among those who were missing once the column began to reassemble in the pass was Father Murphy himself. At first the other officers seem to have paid little attention to this and expected the priest and the men who were with him to appear in a short while. But as time passed and he still failed to appear, they became concerned and perplexed. They waited for him for a considerable time, but eventually realised they had to move for themselves and gave up all hope of his returning.[53] They could only conclude that he had been killed or captured, and the decision to move on without the man who had led them so courageously and for so long must have been exceedingly difficult.

The disappearance of Father Murphy is a mystery. It seems that he and a comrade had become separated from the rest of the men in the confusion of the flight. For reasons that are unclear, however, rather than crossing the mountains and trying to rejoin the column once it got through the Scullogue Gap, the two of them decided to make their way northwards along the western slope in the direction of Tullow, turning their backs on whatever was left of the army. Murphy had relatives in this area and knew the mountains well and probably expected to escape by hiding out in safe houses until the worst of the government's campaign of retribution passed.[54] The failure of the effort to rally the Kilkenny coalminers and the old United Irish units of the midlands was apparently all the proof he needed that there was no hope.

In the Scullogue Gap in the meantime the survivors of the column milled about in confusion. The majority of them, disheartened perhaps by the loss of their leader, now wanted to scatter and make their way to various hiding-places in the Wexford plains below them. Among these sanctuaries was Killoughram Woods, which lay just five miles away and were clearly visible from where they stood. A group of a few hundred argued against this course, though, and agreed with Miles Byrne, who suggested that they strike out across north Wexford and try to reach the Wicklow mountains, where other units were probably operating, including the column that had left Wexford town on 21 June. The assumption that a French force was on its way to Ireland lay behind this thinking.[55]

In the end most of the men opted to take their chances in County Wexford and to end their involvement in the struggle. In small groups and even as isolated individuals they spent the rest of the afternoon and evening making their way towards their home parishes, where they would try to make contact with their families and eventually rebuild their lives. When evening came, most of them would have covered only a small part of the journey home, and it is likely that they spent the night concealed in scores of hiding-places across the barony of Bantry.[56]

The few hundred men and women who remained with Miles Byrne followed him northwards, along the eastern slopes of the mountains, towards Wicklow. The journey to Monaseed would take them all of seven days, and they can hardly have gone much more than five miles by nightfall on that first day. Subsequently they would travel across the most remote stretches of country, avoiding all villages and towns. They had several badly wounded men with them, including Byrne's brother, Hugh, and they had to carry these on the handful of carts they had managed to hold onto. The women who accompanied them were also accommodated on the carts as far as possible.[57]

The troops who had driven Father Murphy's force across south Carlow withdrew westwards to their normal stations on the other side of the Barrow that afternoon and evening, leaving it up to Lake and the armies inside Wexford to finish off the rebels. As they did so, though, they perpetrated one of the worst massacres of the entire rebellion in the parishes of south Carlow, an area which up to now had been little involved in the rising. Some of this killing may have begun as early as that morning, while the troops were pursuing the rebel column. As had happened in so many similar instances elsewhere, the soldiers took to killing any men they found in the area on the grounds that they might be rebels. The slaughter went on through much of the day, and in several instances the soldiers forced their way into farmhouses and indiscriminately shot and bayoneted both women and men. By the end of the day they had put almost 200 people to death, including, no doubt, some fugitive rebels, but including also large numbers of completely innocent people. By evening scores of columns of smoke marked the swathe of killing and arson that they had spread across the valley.[58]

The rebel army on the Wexford/Wicklow border passed 26 June in relative tranquillity. They remained in camp at the White Heaps throughout the morning and afternoon and were content to use the day to recuperate from the defeat at Hacketstown. Their numbers were even more seriously depleted at this stage, and the entire column barely exceeded a thousand men.[59]

A few miles to their east at Arklow, however, the situation of the garrison had changed significantly. Over the past week it had consisted of only a few hundred men under the command of a mere captain. A reinforcement of several hundred militiamen under Lieutenant-Colonel O'Hara arrived from the north during the day, transforming it into a force that might conduct offensive actions in the days ahead.[60] All that was required now was for Lake to comprehend the exact nature of the situation in the region for this and other garrisons to take the initiative once more. For the moment, however, all was quiet in the area around Arklow, and local commanders who were aware of the rebel assault on Hacketsown maintained a cautious approach to the enemy, whom they knew to be holding out somewhere in the hills near them.

As for Lake, his attention was still occupied by the campaign against the south Wexford United Irish leadership, and he may still not have realised what was happening in Wicklow and Carlow at this late stage. The highlight of the day was the court-martialing of several more rebel officers, the most important of them being Cornelius Grogan. As a longstanding political enemy of local loyalists he was an even more important prize than men like Philip Roche and Matthew Keogh, even if he had played a less significant role in the rebellion than had either of them.

His trial turned out to be a lively affair. He argued that he had been forced to take part by his tenantry and claimed that, apart from supplying the town of Wexford with provisions, he had taken little part. He adamantly denied that he participated in any battles. His defence was so tenacious, in fact, that the trial lasted through the entire afternoon, and when evening came the judges consented to postpone the rest of the proceedings until the next morning. Some of those who stood trial with Grogan, including Edward Freyne, were dispatched more summarily, however, and he and several other lesser United men were sentenced to be hanged the next morning at the bridge, regardless of the fact that Grogan's fate was as yet uncertain.[61]

Thomas Cloney remained in hiding, reasoning (correctly, it would seem) that there would be no clemency for officers who had been as prominent as he. His place of concealment was less secure than it had been a day or two before, since for some reason Archibald Jacob had come to suspect that Rudd was hiding someone, and accordingly he and a group of yeomen had conducted hurried searches of the place already. Rudd realised that Jacob would be back in the next day or two to search the place more thoroughly, and so that afternoon he gave Cloney an old yeoman uniform and a horse and helped him to make an unobtrusive exit from the town. By nightfall the fugitive had made his way northwards into the countryside near Moneyhore and was hiding in the cabin of one of his father's tenants.[62]

With the court martials and executions proceeding apace, Lake was beginning to give some thought to moving back to Dublin himself. As commander-in-chief for Ireland his proper place was in the capital, and his immediate task was to delegate the command of County Wexford to a subordinate. Word arrived during the day that General Hunter and a substantial force of British troops was on its way from the Channel Islands to Duncannon and would land at Wexford in a day or two. Hunter was clearly the man to take over the county and conduct the remaining trials of the rebels.

As for Lake's other generals, most of these were still in and around Wexford town, although their deployment to other parts of the country was now under way. Moore, who had impressed Lake considerably and was becoming an increasingly important figure, was encamped at Taghmon and keeping a close eye on the southern third of the county.[63] Needham was still at Oulart, and from there watched developments along the east coast, and Duff was still with Lake in Wexford. Johnson began his trek back to his original post at Mallow during the afternoon of this particular day;

this, along with Lake's consideration of his own move, suggests that he was thinking of readying the defences of the island at large against what he surely expected would be the next phase of the struggle—a French invasion.

15

THE CAMP AT THE WHITE HEAPS
27 JUNE – 5 JULY

ON WEDNESDAY 27 JUNE LAKE FINALLY GOT HIS CHANCE TO leave Wexford. That morning General Hunter arrived at the head of two British regiments, and the commander-in-chief wasted no time in placing him in charge of the entire county and making plans to set out by sea for Dublin himself. It had been ten days exactly since he had left the capital for the south, and now he was returning in triumph. He was still unaware that significant rebel forces had eluded him on the 21st and remained a threat to government outposts in other parts of south Leinster.

General Hunter was not aware of this either, but as soon as he arrived he decided to deploy his forces throughout the county in such a way that they would be in a good position to deal with the rebels on the Wicklow border when the time came. His plan was to concentrate most of his units in the south of the county; the largest group would remain under his own command at Wexford town, with another large force under Moore at Taghmon and a sizeable garrison under Eustace at New Ross. He decided to send fairly substantial forces northwards too; thus Duff would move to Newtownbarry and Needham to Gorey. In addition, he decided to send one of his own trusted officers, Colonel Grose, to Enniscorthy and to have Colonel L'Estrange take up position in Ferns.[1] Once it was completed, this disposition would place substantial garrisons in place in a ring of towns around the entire area of south Wicklow and north Wexford, and it would only be a matter of time before they became aware of the location and strength of the rebel column at Croghan. After that the insurgents were bound to come under far more severe pressure than they had experienced thus far.

*

The rebel column itself seems to have been unaware of the changes taking place to their south, and they passed the day uneventfully at the White Heaps camp, still waiting for Kearns and Murphy and their men to join them. They saw no sign of government forces in either direction from the mountain and continued to rest, to nurse their wounded, and to replenish their food supply from the flocks of sheep on the nearby hills.[2]

Miles Byrne and his few hundred followers, meanwhile, were still making their way painstakingly across the north-western region of the county. At this stage they were probably somewhere close to the River Slaney between Enniscorthy and Newtownbarry, but they had a long journey ahead of them still before they could hope to reach the Wicklow border and augment the Croghan force.[3]

In Wexford town Generals Lake and Hunter spent most of the day dealing with the United Irish leaders. Cornelius Grogan's court martial resumed early and lasted until around midday. In the end the rebel commissar received a conviction and death sentence, which was to be carried out on the bridge the next morning. His pleadings that he had taken no part in any battles were effectively demolished by the evidence presented by several witnesses who swore to have seen him riding out to New Ross on the day of the battle there and returning again that evening.[4]

The court also heard the cases against Patrick Prendergast and Bagenal Harvey. Like Grogan, Harvey put up a spirited defence, protesting that he was forced to take the role he did. The effort was in vain, however, and by evening he had received the same verdict and sentence as the rest: death by hanging the next morning.[5] Of the entire southern leadership, in fact, only Colclough and a few others remained to be dealt with by this point, and Colclough's trial was to take place the next day. Sometime before evening he appealed to some loyalists he knew to get him help, but this was to no avail and by nightfall it must have been clear to him that he would soon follow Harvey and Grogan to the gallows.[6]

The government's campaign of vengeance reached its climax the next day, the 28th. Just before noon Harvey, Grogan and

Prendergast went to the gallows on the bridge together as the usual crowds watched silently. Grogan was brave to the last, but Harvey's nerve failed him and he tried to delay the moment of his execution as long as he could. When the sentences were finally carried out, the soldiers threw Prendergast's body into the water (after they had stripped and mutilated it), but, as they had done with Matthew Keogh's corpse, they cut the heads off the bodies of Grogan and Harvey and paraded them around the town on pikes. Afterwards they fixed them on spikes alongside Keogh's head outside the courthouse.[7] Protestant rebels were clearly to be made a special example of.

Colclough went on trial that afternoon. In spite of his best efforts, he too was condemned to die, and his execution was set for the same evening. His young wife went to the officers in charge and requested that after the hanging her husband's body should be handed over to her and not treated like the others. They agreed to the request, and that evening, after he too had been hanged from the infamous metal arch, his widow took his body home to Ballyteige and had it buried.[8]

One other high-ranking officer of the United Irish army, John Kelly of Killann, was executed on Wexford Bridge during the days of Lake's court martials, but the precise date of his trial and execution is not known. (It may in fact have taken place in the days shortly after Lake captured the town.) The sentence, if sentence there ever was, was carried out with particular brutality in this case. Kelly's wound was still so serious that he could not walk, and he had to be carried to the gallows in a cart. After he was hanged the soldiers cut off his head, but instead of displaying it on the courthouse they kicked it about the streets, including the street where his sister lived. The young woman had the misfortune to come to the window at one point and was confronted with the spectacle.[9]

Other executions would take place in Wexford over the coming months and years, but they would be less frequent and far less spectacular. Incredibly, Edward Hay was still at large on the 28th and would remain so. Thomas Cloney was still hiding in the cabin near Moneyhore, and he too was secure for the time being; Father Kearns had abandoned his hideout in Killoughram Woods and had joined him there by this time.[10] Ironically, Captain

Thomas Dixon's whereabouts was completely unknown. Popular legend would later have it that he made his escape to America and lived there peacefully for the rest of his life. Thus the one southern rebel 'leader' who deserved severe punishment had vanished without a trace.

As all this took place the rebel army at Croghan waited in vain for their comrades from the south for the third day in succession. Yet again the morning and afternoon passed without any sign that Father Kearns and his men or other units from the heart of County Wexford might join them.[11] Further north, meanwhile, in the western districts of Wicklow, other columns were biding their time too, including the large one which had taken part in the attack on Hacketstown. Both groups evidently believed that there was still the chance of a French landing and that they would get no mercy from the government were they to surrender. Besides, given the nature of the terrain that they now occupied, the chances of conducting a successful guerrilla campaign until the French did come must have seemed promising.

The military situation to their south finally began to change during the day as Hunter carried out his redeployments. Sometime during the afternoon Duff and his force arrived in Newtownbarry, Needham reached Gorey, and Grose moved up to Enniscorthy. The new Enniscorthy garrison was now in a good position to relay communications from the northern outposts to Hunter.[12] Garbled accounts of the activities of the Croghan rebels must have been filtering quite far south by this time, and Needham and Duff were undoubtedly aware of them by evening.

The most pressing task facing Needham and Duff once they got to their new posts was the need to bring the local yeomanry under some kind of control; until they could do this there was little chance of dealing with the rebels. These units had been terrorising the north Wexford and south Wicklow countryside for a week now, and tales of their brutality were commonplace in the parishes all around Gorey. Many units were involved in atrocities, but the worst accounts were associated with Hunter Gowan and his band of followers. This group, soon to be known as the 'Black Mob', had killed many men they suspected of involvement in the rising, including one man whom they murdered in his bed in front of his wife. On another occasion they shot a father and his two sons with the rest of their family looking on.[13]

In one of the most unfortunate incidents of the week, Father John Redmond, the curate of Camolin and a close acquaintance of Lord Mountnorris, found himself accused of involvement in the rebel attack on Camolin Park that had taken place on the first night of the rising. He rode into Gorey and was attacked by several yeomen as he passed down the main street. They kicked and punched him brutally and accused him of being a rebel officer. He admitted he was present at the attack on Mountnorris's house, but insisted he was trying to stop the insurgents from setting the house on fire. In spite of his pleas, however, his accusers threw him into the market house with several other prisoners and threatened to take their revenge on him in time.[14]

One of the inevitable results of this campaign of terror was that many bands of former rebels in north Wexford refused to accept the government's amnesty. Instead they continued to hide out in copses and ditches all over that part of the county and fled as soon as government troops came within sight of them. The Camolin cavalry spotted a band of men near Ballydaniel Bridge, just ouside their home village, on this particular afternoon (the 28th) and tried to entice them to give themselves up. The men made no effort to respond to them, however, and fled across a bog and into some woods in the distance as soon as they saw the cavalrymen.[15]

Many groups of fugitive rebels also remained hidden in south Wexford. Sir John Moore took a detachment of troops and ventured into the parishes to the south of Taghmon during the afternoon, but found that very few former rebels would come out and accept pardons. Terror was still the order of the day, and fear and distrust of the government still had a firm grip on former rebels and innocent non-combatants alike.[16]

On Friday 29 June the greater part of County Wexford remained fairly quiet. Now that the principal executions were over, the day passed without notable incident in Wexford town itself. Hunter was concentrating his attention on the administrative and military challenges ahead of him, though for the moment he was not ready to take the initiative, and since the hundreds of former rebels still refused to accept the amnesty, the need to persuade them to come out into the open remained one of his main concerns.

On the Wicklow border the rebel column stayed in camp for the fourth day in succession. There was still no sign of government forces making any moves against them, and they were prepared to continue to wait for Kearns or Murphy to join them. They did not realise at this stage that Father Kearns's battalion had practically dissolved and that neither he nor Cloney were in a position to give them significant reinforcements. They were also not aware of the disaster that had befallen Father Murphy's force and the fact that Miles Byrne and his small column were moving steadily towards them and were now barely more than a day's march away; by sticking to their plan of avoiding villages and exposed countryside, this remarkable group had remained unscathed now through four days of very difficult travelling.

Meanwhile in the main towns of north Wexford, north Carlow and south Wicklow the government forces were consolidating their position and learning more about the rebel camp at Croghan. Duff at Newtownbarry, Needham at Gorey and O'Hara at Arklow were the principal figures involved, and they passed the day gathering as much information as they could and passing it on to Hunter at Wexford and (in the case of O'Hara certainly) northwards to Lake, who was by now back in Dublin Castle.

Needham was especially anxious to find out what was happening in the hills to his north, and that evening he decided to send some yeomen who were familiar with the countryside around Croghan out to reconnoitre the rebel camp. He selected none other than Hunter Gowan and his unit for the task, and he asked them to wait until darkness fell and then to ride out as far as Croghan or as close to it as they could get and to assess the strength of the rebel force there.[17]

Gowan's patrol left Gorey at about 1 a.m. on 30 June, a fateful day as it would turn out. They made their way across the north-western parishes of the county without incident and eventually reached Tinnebaun Hill, a ridge overlooking the rebel camp. When they climbed to the top of the ridge, they had an excellent view of the rebel positions in the broad valley below them, and they watched the camp for a while without the rebel sentries ever suspecting their presence. Then they rode quietly back down the southern slope and made their way into Gorey. In their report to Needham later in the morning they claimed that the rebels were exposed and that they were not a formidable force. This convinced Needham that he could deal with the Croghan rebels unaided.[18]

What Gowan and his men did not know was that the the rebel leaders were considering making a move of their own at that very time. They were perhaps becoming aware of the fact that government forces were mustering all around them and that they would eventually be attacked. They realised that their only hope of holding out in this area was to somehow acquire fresh supplies of ammunition, and in spite of the dismal failure to do this in the attack on Hacketstown, they had agreed before nightfall that they would break camp and conduct a sudden attack on Carnew, eight miles to the south-west, the next day. Carnew was the only town near them that did not have a substantial garrison (there were only about fifty men stationed there),[19] and since they had destroyed a large part of it earlier in the rebellion, they apparently assumed they might have a reasonable chance of overwhelming the defenders and seizing their equipment.

The officers began to muster their men for the march shortly after dawn—about the same time that Gowan was reporting on his expedition to Needham in Gorey. The entire force, along with the carts bearing the wounded and the women followers, began to make their way westwards along the hilly, winding roads that led to Carnew while it was still quite early. Their route took them straight to the village of Monaseed, where they stopped briefly and talked with the keeper of the village inn. Then they pushed on towards Carnew, which was still about three miles away.[20]

Shortly after they left Monaseed a local loyalist made a frantic ride into Gorey and warned Needham of what was happening. The general, who had seriously underestimated the strength of the rebels because of Gowan's report, called up about 200 cavalrymen and sent them west immediately with orders to attack the rebels on the march. The cavalry included some yeomen, but it was made up mostly of members of the Ancient Britons, a regiment that was already infamous for its brutality in the area.[21]

The mounted detachment rode to Monaseed first and got as

much information as they could from the innkeeper, who was a loyalist, as it turned out, and who reported that the rebel officers had complained of their near-total lack of ammunition. Heartened by this news, they rode on along the road towards Carnew, anxious to catch their enemies by surprise from behind.[22]

The rebels were not to be taken by surprise, however. Their scouts saw the cavalry approaching from the direction of Monaseed when the main part of the column was in the townland of Ballyellis, about two miles from Carnew, the last townland before the Wicklow border. Warning of the imminent attack passed along the column quickly, and as soon as they realised what was about to happen the rebel officers tried to organise a defensive action. There was a boggy field across the ditch to their left and a high ditch on their right, between the two of which their men might be caught. Their only hope was to trap the cavalry in this vice instead, and they used the few minutes they had before the arrival of the cavalry to set up an ambush. The carts with the women and wounded were near the front of the column, and they had these placed on two roads that branched off, one to the west and the other to the south, just ahead of them. These would make do as barricades should the cavalry reach them. Then they had the main body of the column scramble across the high ditch and take up positions behind it.

There was a bend in the road between the approaching cavalry and the rebels at this point, and the Ancient Britons did not see what was now taking place ahead of them. When they finally rounded the bend, the entire rebel force was already out of sight behind the ditch, and even the carts had been moved sufficiently far back along the Carnew road as to be invisible. As they came parallel to the ditch, then, the mounted troops had no idea that hundreds of rebels, pikemen and gunsmen alike, lay in wait for them.[23]

The rebel musketeers opened fire when the soldiers were well inside the trap. The opening volleys devastated the troops and threw them into complete confusion. Moments later the pike units swept across the ditch, some at a point opposite the soldiers, others further back along the road towards Monaseed. The gunsmen and pikemen closest to the Ancient Britons stormed into their ranks with fierce determination, while the group in their rear closed off any chance they had of escaping back in the direction in which they came.

The soldiers had no chance. Many of them were pulled or shot from their horses and killed on the road; others tried to escape across the ditch and into the boggy ground to the south of the road. Many of these did manage to get away, but rebel units gave chase and caught up with several of them before they could run very far. They showed them no mercy. A few of those who had been in the front ranks of the column got as far as the carts on the road to Carnew and succeeded in making their way around them and escaping to the town. Another group, consisting mainly of the various yeomanry corps that had been towards the rear of the column, never actually entered the rebel trap, but held back when the shooting started and remained at a distance throughout the fighting. The Ancient Britons, however, were caught completely off guard by the insurgents.

Later rebel accounts of the Battle of Ballyellis, as it would be called, claimed that over sixty soldiers died that morning. The real figure was closer to thirty. But even this was a stunning and unexpected defeat for the government side. The yeomanry units that had never taken part in the battle eventually wheeled about and retreated back to Gorey with news of the disaster; they were joined in their flight by the scores of Ancient Britons who had gone into the trap but had somehow escaped.[24]

Once their enemies had vanished, the rebel column was able to reform and their leaders could assess the extent of their victory. They had acquired some weapons and ammunition, but hardly enough to make a significant difference to their situation. They had also captured some horses, although most of these were badly wounded and could hardly be of much use. The skirmish was nonetheless a victory—and they were badly in need of victories at this point. One rebel later recalled that at the moment the fighting began they were 'burning for revenge' against the soldiers, and the fight certainly gave them the chance to satisfy this ambition.

The sense of uplift provided by the engagement is illustrated by a moment of levity the men allowed themselves when it was over. According to one eyewitness account, they took great amusement from watching as one of their comrades sounded the reteat on a captured bugle and the riderless horses scattered through the fields tried desperately to fall into line.[25] The uncoordinated prancing of the animals reminded them, it seems, that their enemies were not invulnerable and that there might still be hope for a victorious end to their struggle.

The chief objective of the march had, of course, been to attack Carnew, and so at around midday, with their resolve stiffened, they moved on towards the town. All hope of attacking the place by surprise was now gone. The noise of the battle itself would have been sufficient warning for the garrison, but the three or four soldiers who had escaped in that direction certainly confirmed for them that an an attack was imminent. By the time the first rebel units appeared on the eastern outskirts of the town the approximately fifty soldiers had already barricaded themselves into one of the few slated buildings left, a brewery which the insurgents had chosen not to destroy on 8 June. Dislodging them would be difficult now.

The rebels opened an attack on the brewery almost as soon as they arrived in the town. The soldiers were well armed and in a good position, and so, just as the rebels had already done at Hacketstown and just as their comrades had done at Castlecomer, they tried desperately to dislodge them by using loaded carts as cover. The effort went on for an hour or so, but yet again it ended in failure. The fire coming from the building was too concentrated and too deadly to allow the critical breakthrough, and after some time it became obvious that the task was hopeless.

After about an hour they called off the attack, and Perry and the other officers led the column out of the town and made their way to the summit of Kilcavan Hill. They made a camp for the night there, just as they had done in rather different circumstances twice before, and waited for morning before moving again. The effort to replenish their arms had largely ended in failure, but they nevertheless had the satisfaction of inflicting a stinging defeat on their enemies, and their morale was undoubtedly raised for the first time in several days.[26]

Needham first heard of the defeat at Ballyellis when the remnant of the cavalry force brought news of the ambush to him at Gorey that afternoon. In the evening he sent the Camolin cavalry out to reconnoitre the battle site, and they returned with confirmation of the carnage and also with the news that the rebel column was encamped in the hills beyond Carnew.[27] This particular piece of information no doubt relieved Needham, since it meant that they were not contemplating an attack on his own position, but nevertheless the events of the day suggested that his enemy was far more formidable than Gowan had claimed and must have convinced him that it would take a considerable effort to drive them from their present position.

As Needham pondered these latest developments some of his yeomanry were taking revenge for the defeat at Ballyellis in their own way. A group of them went to the market house and dragged the unfortunate Father John Redmond out into the street. They held a brief and possibly mock court martial of the helpless man and found him guilty of treason for his alleged part in the attack on Lord Mountnorris's house. They sentenced him to death and hanged him immediately in the main street. According to one account of the atrocity, Lord Mountnorris himself strode up to the priest's lifeless body as it hung from the rope and fired a brace of pistols into it.[28] Even former moderate loyalists like Mountnorris were now fully committed to the 'White Terror'. Indeed, in the circumstances of the time, moderate loyalists were becoming fewer in number with each passing day.

In contrast to the district between Gorey and Carnew, the rest of the county saw few dramatic developments on 30 June. At Newtownbarry, Ferns and Enniscorthy, Duff, L'Estrange and Grose continued to hold their respective positions and to learn what they could of the situation in the surrounding countryside. Eustace at New Ross and Moore at Taghmon did the same. Hunter himself remained in Wexford town, trying to garner what information he could about the condition of the country to his north. Everywhere, though, the former rebels continued to shy away from coming into contact with the troops, largely because local loyalists were keeping up their campaign of retribution.

In a few instances bands of fugitive rebels began to fight back against the yeomanry, and this soon led to the emergence of full-scale banditry in certain districts. The rebel groups that had taken refuge in woodland areas were especially prominent in this regard, among them the men hiding out in Killoughram. In most cases such groups consisted of army deserters as well as former rebels, and many of them were of a quite motley character. They were, however, frequently the only form of protection standing between the local population and the yeomanry's terror campaign. Thus at Killoughram at about this point in the summer some of the fugitives, already being referred to as the 'Babes in the Wood' by some, attacked a yeomanry patrol that had been terrorising people near the woods. They captured several of the soldiers in the ambush, dragged them inside the forest and shot them all dead.[29] It is not clear if this gesture had any real effect in deterring the yeomanry. Certainly all the indications are that law and order generally had broken down in many districts, and banditry was often accompanied by simple brigandage, where desperadoes from both sides attacked vulnerable people in the various localities regardless of their political opinions, thereby making life almost intolerable for a people who had already suffered a great deal from the effects of war.[30]

On Sunday 1 July the rebels who had devastated the Ancient Britons at Ballyellis remained in the hills above Carnew, watching for signs of a more serious foray against them. Needham was at this stage still puzzled about their strength and whereabouts, but was too frightened by the previous day's disaster to take any chances. He was satisfied to send a small reconnoitring patrol out to his west to find out what they could about the insurgents' location. The patrol rode as far as Ballyellis, where they collected some of the corpses from the battle, but they could learn little concerning the rebels themselves. The local people were either elusive or unco-operative, and by late afternoon they had to return to Gorey with their gruesome cargo and with the report that the rebels had disappeared.[31]

In spite of this frustration, however, Needham's position did improve a little during the day. Yet another sizeable force of government troops, the Gordon Highlanders, commanded by the Marquis of Huntly, arrived at Arklow from the north, making the garrison much more formidable. There was little chance now that the rebels could take serious offensive action, and between Duff at

Newtownbarry, L'Estrange at Ferns, Needham at Gorey, Huntly at Arklow and Grose at Enniscorthy a dragnet was already in place that could eventually trap them in their borderland stronghold. In addition, the small outpost at Carnew had apparently survived the attack of the day before and had maintained its advanced position. For the time being all these garrisons simply held their ground and watched the countryside to their north and west carefully for any signs that the rebels were on the move.

As for the rebels, they spent the entire day in their new camp on the summit of Kilcavan Hill. Why they stayed there is unclear, but presumably they were still mystified by the failure of the other columns to join them and were hoping against hope that they might still arrive from Carlow or Wicklow, if not from Wexford itself.

Meanwhile far to the south the loyalists continued to consolidate their grip on the county. The spate of atrocities in the area around Wexford town began to diminish by this time, although thousands of former rebels still remained in hiding. One loyalist woman received a surprise visit from her husband, an officer with the Wexford militia under Asgill at Kilkenny. She was hiding over twenty men in and around their farmyard, and at one point in the day she brought them out and introduced them to her husband. Beforehand she had asked him to pledge that he would not betray them, and he kept his word. The scene that followed was extraordinary. The militia officer conversed kindly with the men who had been his enemies, and they assured him that they were proud of the struggle they had put up. It was clear to both husband and wife that they were unbowed in defeat and completely unconvinced that the government would honour any promises made to them.[32]

If the reign of terror had subsided a little around Wexford town, however, it remained intense in the parishes around New Ross. There the local yeomanry continued to conduct terrible atrocities against all those whom they suspected of involvement in the rising, and they showed no sign of letting up. Sir John Moore wrote disparagingly of these outrages in his diary that evening and condemned the yeomanry as being worse than the rebels ever were; however, there was little he could do about it.[33]

*

On Monday 2 July the rebel column at Kilcavan finally moved. They broke camp early in the day and marched westwards across the Fitzwilliam estate towards the village of Shillelagh. The estate was in the heart of loyalist south-west Wicklow and was dotted with the large farmhouses of Fitzwilliam's middlemen. There is at least one claim that they captured several local loyalists on this march and put them to death. The allegation is not corroborated, but, given the fierce loyalism of the area and the fearsome reputation of its yeomanry, it is quite likely that these killings did take place.[34]

The rebels saw no sign of government forces until they were just outside Shillelagh. Then they observed a column of yeoman cavalry and infantry, about 150 men in all, drawn up to oppose them. They continued to advance undaunted, and the cavalry fled as soon as they got close to them. The infantry held its ground.

Rather than attack them directly, the rebel officers led their men off to the right and made for the slope of a high hill called Ballyraheen, about a quarter of a mile away. The yeomen reacted slowly to the move and only tried to beat the rebels to the hill when they realised what was happening. But they were too late: Perry and his officers were already drawing up a battle-line along the steep slope when they reached it.

The yeomanry commanders were two local middlemen named Chamney and Nixon. They might have withdrawn to the village at this point and sent dispatches to Carnew or Tullow for reinforcements, but they chose instead to charge the rebel line. The rebels defended their position with musket fire once the soldiers got close to them and then swept down the hill in a determined pike charge. The yeomen were driven back quickly and with great loss, perhaps dozens of men killed, among them the two captains. What was left of the force fled from the bottom of the hill to Captain Chamney's house, which lay nearby, and once inside they barricaded the doors and windows and made ready for a siege.[35]

The quick victory on the hill had no doubt yielded the rebels more arms and ammunition, and they might have withdrawn back towards the mountains with this prize and felt that the day had been well spent. However, the remnant of the yeomanry barricaded into Chamney's house was too tantalising a target for them to ignore, and instead of moving back towards the east they decided to try to dislodge them. And so, once again, as at Borris, Hacketstown and Carnew, they attacked a fortified slated house defended by well-armed soldiers. Predictably, their attempts to carry the building by frontal assault failed in a hail of bullets which felled many of their best men; and predictably also, they then resorted to the use of mattresses and loaded carts as cover, and this only resulted in more needless deaths.

The efforts went on for several hours and became especially destructive once evening fell. By that stage a nearby house had caught fire, and this gave the defenders plenty of light to pick off their attackers from a distance. Eventually, with midnight approaching and their losses already substantial, Perry and his officers decided to call off the attack. When they had all their men in formation, they led them back eastwards, but rather than stopping for the night at Kilcavan, they pushed on all the way to Croghan, almost ten miles away, and made camp at their familiar site, the White Heaps.[36] The three-day expedition to the west had yielded two victories in the open field and some much-needed new weapons, but had been expensive in loss of life, and their inability to storm well-barricaded buildings was underlined forcefully.

Government commanders in County Wexford and in other parts of south Leinster had remained completely unaware of what was taking place around Shillelagh as the day passed. Huntly sent patrols out along the Ow valley from Arklow several times during the day, but they learned little about the rebels. Needham too sent out several scouting parties. One of these was led by Lord Mountnorris and went as far as Limerick Hill. They saw no sign of the rebels either, and so, like Huntly, Needham knew no more of their whereabouts when the day ended than he did when it began.[37] Duff at Newtownbarry and L'Estrange at Ferns were probably equally puzzled.

Hunter continued to focus his attention on the south of the county in spite of the stand-off that had developed in the north. This was a natural decison for him, given the importance Lake had attached to the area. He therefore spent the day continuing to reassert government authority in the countryside and, through Moore and others, tried to bring some order to what was still a chaotic situation. In a telling comment, Moore noted in his diary that evening that the yeomanry were still on the rampage in the south-west of the county and that things were still so unstable that should the French land, it would be impossible to hold the country.[38] If this was the perspective of a general who was stationed in a relative undisturbed place like Taghmon, the foreboding of men such as Huntly, Duff and Needham, whose bailiwick was still effectively a war zone, can well be imagined.

The other side of this story, of course, is that the rebel leaders probably did continue to hold fast to the hope that the French were on their way and that conditions were still ripe for the quick spread of rebellion to the rest of the country once they landed. It would be another two weeks before even the small expeditionary force that the French government was preparing at Brest would be ready to sail, but as long as the expectation of an imminent invasion remained, the mountain chain that ran from Wicklow down into the Wexford/Carlow borderland retained great strategic significance: it could, after all, become the springboard from which the rebel effort on behalf of the French cause would come. It is virtually certain that there was continued tension between those rebel officers who wanted to move north into the sanctuary of the mountains without further delay and to avoid the risk of being caught by a sudden government offensive, and those who still held to the view that they should give more time to the lost columns that still might want to join them from points to their south and west. As they settled for the night at the White Heaps, therefore, this argument seems to have been debated anew; it may explain their amazing reluctance to leave Wexford territory. In the end it would be their undoing.

On the following day, 3 July, Miles Byrne and his little column of men and women finally reached Monaseed after a journey of seven days. They were exhausted from the march, and many of the wounded they had brought with them were in poor condition. Byrne's own brother, Hugh, was among these, but he was able to walk unaided by this time. The men and women of the band scattered to their homes as soon as they arrived and tried to find their families. In many cases parents, brothers and sisters had gone to stay with relatives or friends some distance away, and it took time to track them down. Miles Byrne discovered that his mother and sister were staying at Buckstown House; ironically, this was the home of the owner of the brewery in Carnew which had been used by the garrison there as its citadel two days before. The young rebel officer had an emotional reunion with his family and finally got a chance to rest and recover a little from his ordeal.

The members of Byrne's column gradually learned of the fate of the other rebel column during the day. They heard some of the details of the battles that had taken place at Ballyellis and Ballyraheen, and by evening they knew that the column was encamped at Croghan, just four miles to the north-west. Byrne and a few others called their old comrades together once again and made preparations to go to Croghan the next day. Many of them were willing to follow him, but quite a few were so demoralised that they chose to stay near Monaseed or nearby hamlets and take their chances with the amnesty. This probably left no more than one or two hundred men available for the trek northwards the next morning, but Byrne's spirits remained high.[39]

At Croghan in the meantime the rebel leaders had at last received reliable reports that Father Mogue Kearns and Thomas Cloney were holding out with some men in Killoughram Woods. They must have learned this from a straggler who had made his way to Croghan that day. They could not have been certain that the report was true, but it was sufficient to prevent them from going on into the Wicklow mountains at this point, and Garrett Byrne and Edward Fitzgerald persuaded the other officers to let them take a small band of trusted men and to ride southwards during the coming night to find Kearns and Cloney. They were convinced that they could persuade both men to come and join them on the Wicklow border.

As the day wore on there were still no signs that any of the government forces in the region were moving against them, and they therefore decided that the camp would remain where it was until Fitzgerald and Byrne returned. At around twilight the two men mounted good horses and set out in the gathering darkness on their journey south. Killoughram was over twenty-five miles away, and so the risks involved in the mission were very great.[40]

*

Meanwhile in Wexford town General Hunter was mulling over recent reports that rebel columns were still intact and active in the north of the county. Similar reports had no doubt been arriving for some time, but their frequency and urgency were increasing. He concluded on the basis of what he was hearing that the stories were exaggerations and that the rebel force mentioned in the dispatches was merely a straggling band. Moore, who was getting similar information by this point, was less optimistic, however, and tried, but failed, to convince Hunter of the danger.[41] This was partly why Needham, Huntly, Grose, L'Estrange and Duff still got no orders to move against the rebels and spent the day patrolling in the immediate vicinity of their positions and dispatching captured rebels and suspects to Dublin.[42] In Dublin Castle Lake was becoming well acquainted with the news of the rebel forces still in the field in Wicklow, and he was less inclined to be complacent about it.

On the following day, 4 July, after considering the situation carefully, Lake finally took the initiative. He sent instructions to Huntly and Needham to move against the rebel forces to their west and north as soon as possible. Accordingly, Needham spent the day drawing up a plan of attack. By the afternoon he had the details worked out: Huntly would march up the Ow valley and cross Croghan and attack the White Heaps camp (where he now knew the rebels were stationed) from the north; Duff would march from Newtownbarry to Carnew and then move against the rebels from the west, cutting off their line of retreat through the Wicklow Gap; L'Estrange would move due north from Ferns and approach them from the direction of Hollyfort; and Needham himself would move against them from the south-east. If all went according to plan, the rebel column would have almost no hope of escape. Needham had decided (perhaps on Lake's urging) to make his moves the following morning, and he and the other commanders were thus able to spend almost the entire day preparing their men for the attack.[43]

The rebels were completely unaware that this grand assault was being planned, and they spent most of the day waiting to see what outcome the mission to Killoughram would have. Fitzgerald and

Byrne would presumably have reached their destination around dawn and would have to wait for nightfall again before venturing back towards the camp. As they bided their time a large detachment left the camp and made its way around to the northern slope of Croghan and burned a cluster of wooden huts that stood unoccupied there. These structures had been built during a gold rush several years before, and the leaders evidently feared that the troops might use them as shelter at some point in the future. The raiding party returned to camp that afternoon, by which time Miles Byrne and his band had arrived.[44]

The reunion of the remnants of the two columns that had escaped from Wexford town two weeks before must have been an emotional one, although its details have gone unrecorded. Now the Croghan group finally learned of the fate of their comrades, including, no doubt, the details of the campaign into Kilkenny, the attack on Castlecomer and, most mystifying and disconcerting of all, the desperate battle at Kilcumney on 26 June and the disappearance of Father John Murphy. Byrne and his men already knew of many of the activities of the Croghan force over the previous two weeks, but now they also learned of the perilous mission to Killoughram. They all had no option but to spend the rest of the day and the night waiting for the return of Fitzgerald, Garrett Byrne and, they hoped, Father Mogue Kearns and Thomas Cloney.

Anthony Perry decided to take the opportunity to pay a quick visit to his home at Perrymount that night;[45] his decison to do so suggests that he and the other officers had resolved to lead their force into the heart of the Wicklow mountains as soon as Fitzgerald and Byrne returned and were not expecting to be back in County Wexford for quite some time.

Nobody at the Croghan camp had any idea at this stage how the mission to Killoughram had fared. Later they would learn that Fitzgerald and Byrne had made their way safely to the woods by dawn of that day. They eventually came across some of the bandits that were hiding out there, and these men informed them that Cloney and Kearns were in Moneyhore. One of the outlaws agreed to go and tell the two former rebel leaders of the presence of Fitzgerald and Byrne and of their request that they go with them to join the army at Croghan. When the messenger found them, Kearns readily agreed to come, but Cloney refused. (In his own version of the event, he claims that his father and sisters pleaded with him not to go.) By evening Kearns had joined the two riders in the woods, and when night fell they set off on the return journey to Croghan, leaving Cloney behind to fend for himself.[46] But as the three rode back that night Needham and the other government commanders were already in the early stages of their co-ordinated attack on the White Heaps.

Needham's plan was to have all of the columns involved in the attack move towards Croghan during the night and to be near the rebel camp by dawn. Accordingly, he ordered each of the commanders to move his men out of their post shortly after midnight.[47] Huntly led his Highlanders out towards Aughrim so as to be ready to make his way up the northern face of Croghan before first light; Duff and his column made their way to Carnew without incident and by dawn were ready to approach Croghan from the direction of Annagh Hill; L'Estrange gathered his smaller force around midnight too and led them slowly northwards towards Craanford. Needham himself moved out with the largest of the four columns, about 2,000 men, around midnight and pushed on towards Limerick Hill, and then from there moved directly from the south towards the White Heaps.[48]

As the four columns closed in on the White Heaps, the rebels were getting ready to move themselves. Shortly after midnight Anthony Perry returned from Inch. Then, an hour or so later and not long before dawn, Fitzgerald, Byrne and Father Kearns reached the camp.[49] The entire north Wexford United Irish leadership, except for Fathers John and Michael Murphy, were now back together. In the dim dawn light as they greeted each other after a separation of two weeks, their resolution must surely have been strengthened. They had already agreed to delay their march into the safety of the mountains no longer; as soon as the daylight became brighter they would make straight for the Wicklow Gap, two miles to their north-west, and from there they could move deep into the mountains. Once into that wild terrain they would be very hard to tie down and might survive for weeks or even months as a mobile light infantry force. In the midst of the handshakes and congratulations and pledges to fight on fiercely, they did not realise that even then the net was closing around them from all sides.

*

When dawn did finally break on 5 July, there was a dense fog lying all across the broad valley around the White Heaps; it had rained during the night, and now, in the warmth of the summer morning, banks of mist were forming over the wet ground. The rebel officers got their camp moving quickly, and the entire force, consisting of about 1,000 men, set out through the mist across the rolling, heathery hills towards the pass that led into Wicklow. They had marched about a mile through the fog when the morning silence was suddenly shattered by a deafening volley of musketry fired from directly in front of them. As it turned out, Duff's men had managed to range themselves directly across their route towards the Wicklow Gap. The soldiers did not expect to encounter the rebels at that point and had actually fired the volley in panic when they heard the sound of marching men approaching them. The shots did little damage to the rebels, but they were undoubtedly as surprised by the encounter as Duff's men had been, and as they could not tell how large the government force ahead of them was, their officers wheeled them about and led them southwards and away from the danger. The sun came up as they marched south and began to burn off the fog. Once the air had cleared, Perry and the other officers could make out Duff's force behind them, but they could not at that time see any other government units and assumed that Duff was alone. Duff made no effort to catch up with them, however, even keeping his cavalry well back from their rearguard, and merely followed them steadily at a distance. Perry and his aides soon began to suspect that he was driving them into a trap, but they could not tell where it was set.

In reality, of course, the rebels had inadvertently foiled Needham's original plan. At this point Huntly and his men were already climbing to the top of Croghan, and once they reached the summit they would realise that the rebels had departed. Needham and his group were moving towards the now abandoned camp at White Heaps too and would not realise what had happened for some time. L'Estrange was somewhere on the road between Camolin and Craanford.

The main chance the rebels had of still escaping through the

Wicklow Gap was to attack Duff and overwhelm him before the other sections of the net closed on them. Sensing this, they turned around and tried to do so at a place called Ballygullen, four miles south of the White Heaps and about a mile north of Craanford. Ballygullen consisted of gently rolling fields and high hedgerows, and here the pikemen and handful of gunsmen might have a chance against the 1,000 troops that Duff could throw at them. Bands of rebel musketeers spread out along the high ditches on either side of the road, with pike units interspersed among them and behind them, and waited for Duff's men to attack them.

In the circumstances, with Huntly, Needham and L'Estrange still on their way, Duff might have held off and simply waited for the others to arrive. However, he may have realised that the plan had been upset somewhat by the fact that the rebels had left their camp (and at about this time Needham was in fact trying to adjust his original strategy to account for this new development), and he may also have assumed that he was strong enough himself to break the rebels there and then. For whatever reason, the Limerick commander decided that he would seize the rebel gauntlet and attack before Needham and the others came up.

The battle that ensued was short but fierce. Duff made the first move by sending his cavalry straight at the rebel lines. When they got within musket range, the rebel gunsmen opened fire with what ammunition they had left and brought several of them down. Those who succeeded in reaching the hedgerows where the pikemen were waiting were stopped and driven back with considerable loss. Chastened by this experience, Duff kept his mounted troops behind the lines for the rest of the struggle and relied instead on his infantry. As a result, a confused battle developed in the fields of Ballygullen that involved several intense musketry exchanges interspersed with pike and bayonet charges by either side. Nobody could make the decisive breakthrough, however, and after about half an hour the fields on either side of the road were littered with dead and dying men. The failure to break the stalemate was especially disconcerting for the rebel leaders, and when news was relayed to them by their scouts that more government troops were approaching from the east and south their situation suddenly began to look desperate.

The rebel position, however, was not completely hopeless at

this stage. Because they had moved, they had unwittingly taken Huntly and the Highlanders out of the game, and instead of columns coming at them from all four points of the compass, they had only three to deal with, one to their north, one to their south, and one to their east. The rebel officers saw that their only hope was to slip through the gaps in the closing net before it was too late. They decided to split their column into three detachments, to evade the governments troops separately, and to join forces again later on in the day and make their way across the border into Wicklow at some point to the west of their present position.[50]

There was little time to work out the finer details of the plan. With Duff still very close to them, one part of the column (which included Miles Byrne and his band) split off and made their way westwards towards the hills above Carnew. The remainder split into two other detachments, and these proceeded southwards, both managing to slip past L'Estrange and his men. Duff was himself confused about what was happening now (he may have known less about the whereabouts of Needham and L'Estrange than the rebels did at this stage), and he held his ground as his enemy pulled back. Eventually all three government columns met at Craanford, but by that time the rebels were well away.

For reasons that are not clear (perhaps he wanted to wait for Huntly), Needham decided not to give chase, and so the three insurgent detachments made rapid progress and in an hour or so were miles away from their erstwhile pursuers. Miles Byrne's group made their way safely out into the hills near Carnew, while the other two pushed on southwards and rejoined each other by the time they reached Camolin, three miles away. They stopped in the village for a short while and happened to encounter the Anglican Dean of Ferns, a man named Brown, whom they took captive, perhaps thinking they might need a hostage. From there they marched on to their oldest campsite, Carrigrew Hill, and when they reached the summit and realised that they were not being followed, they released their prisoner.[51]

The rebel force that gathered on top of Carrigrew Hill probably numbered no more than about 1,000 men, if that. Most of the officers were with this detachment, and they now had to consider what their next step should be. After delaying their escape into the mountains for so long, many of them must have

been bitterly disappointed that they had been foiled in the
attempt and had been pushed back into the heart of north
Wexford where it seemed certain that they would eventually be
surrounded and destroyed. Edward Fitzgerald, who seems to have
wielded increasing authority among the men as time went on,
took the initiative at this point and addressed the ranks. He told
them that they were free to scatter to their homes, but that
anyone who wished to join him and the other leaders in a dash
towards the mountains was welcome to do so. Some of the men,
exhausted and demoralised, elected to abandon the cause and to
return home. Nevertheless, in spite of the difficulties they so
obviously faced, most of them made the decision to stay with their
leaders and strike out for the mountains once again.

The scouts who had been watching the surrounding
countryside while these matters were being debated, suddenly
noticed a cavalry force approaching from the direction of Ferns.
Dean Brown had alerted the garrison there, and now they were
racing to the hill to cut them off. Many of those who had chosen
to make for their homes had already made their way down the
slopes of the hill, and many others now rushed down to escape
before the soldiers came up. Fitzgerald and the other officers and
their group rushed down the northern slope and past Donovan's
House, their headquarters on the morning of Tubberneering, and
fled out into the countryside beyond. The cavalry did not realise
this, and the main body thus got away safely. A different fate was
in store for the men who were trying to escape to their homes.
The approaching soldiers spotted them as they came down the
slopes and pursued them through the fields for much of the rest of
the day. They showed no quarter when they caught up with any of
them, and by the end of the day had killed many of them.
Incredibly, Fitzgerald and his little column of dedicated men
travelled the ten miles or so to the Wicklow border without being
caught. They reached their destination after dark, crossing the
county boundary somewhere between Carnew and Croghan.[52]

In the meantime the third detachment had remained in hiding
in the hills near Carnew all day, waiting for the others to join
them. Fitzgerald and his group did not know of their exact
location, however, and stole quietly past them in the darkness
without either group realising the other was nearby. Miles Byrne's

men realised what had happened well before dawn. His disappointment must have been great, but he and his men decided to follow them and to try to catch up with them during the night. Sometime before dawn on 6 July, therefore, the last rebel column slipped out of County Wexford. It was exactly forty days since bands of Wexford United Irishmen had first begun to mobilise, and now, with the departure of this group, the fighting inside the county itself was coming to an end.[53] But while the rebellion in Wexford was now over, the Wexford United Irishmen were far from finally defeated.

THE FINAL CONCLAVE
6–15 JULY

THE REBEL COLUMN UNDER FITZGERALD AND HIS FELLOW-OFFICERS marched well beyond the Wicklow border before stopping in the pre-dawn hours of 6 July, and they finally camped for the night somewhere in southern part of the county. During the night the officers discussed their next moves. Garrett Byrne and Edward Fitzgerald were now taking most of the initiative and the other chiefs (Perry, Kearns, Kyan and Roche) seem to have been deferring to their judgment. The safe course at this point would have been to hold out in the mountains until the French landed. The signs were that all hope of open resistance in the counties of south Leinster and the midlands was gone, and the mountains at least provided shelter and food (in the form of the huge flocks of sheep that dotted their slopes). At some point in the discussions, however (and this may have had its beginnings in the debates at Croghan over the previous two weeks), the idea of striking out across the central plain and trying to link up with the Ulster rebels was proposed. The Ulster rebels had been crushed for several weeks, and there was little or no hope of their reviving, but the Wexford and Wicklow rebels did not realise this.

After a debate that at times became very heated, they finally decided that they would spend several days collecting as many recruits as they could from the mountains of Wicklow and then set out across the midlands, picking up any scattered bands of diehard rebels that they might come across in Kildare and Meath, and make their way to Down and Antrim. They could hold out there, in the real heartland of the United Irish movement, and be ready to go on the offensive beside their Ulster comrades when the French troops arrived.

The adoption of this Ulster strategy angered several groups in the camp. Some were so opposed to it that they decided to leave the column altogether and to stay in the mountains. Among them was Michael Dwyer. Before morning he and a band of followers left and made their way northwards, eventually reaching Glenmalure and setting up a new base of operations there.

The main column broke camp after dawn and went on into the mountains by way of Aughrim and Ballymanus. They halted briefly at Garrett Byrne's house in Ballymanus and discovered that in the two weeks since they had last camped there government patrols from Arklow or Rathdrum had reduced it to a charred ruin. They moved on in the afternoon and made their way into the heart of the mountains. Joseph Holt, who knew the terrain very well, was their principal guide, and by the end of the day they were probably at the headwaters of the Ow river, near the foot of Lugnaquillia, and well beyond the reach of any government detachments.[1]

Miles Byrne and his column had less good fortune. They too had travelled some distance into Wicklow after crossing the border in the pre-dawn hours, but they could not find the larger force and eventually decided to break up and look for shelter for the night in the townlands around Kilpipe. One of Byrne's own sisters lived nearby at Ballintemple, and he made his way there and went to sleep in a stable. The hope was to reassemble in the morning and continue the journey northwards.[2]

Disaster struck, however. Just after dawn a cavalry patrol, probably from Arklow, suddenly appeared in the area around Kilpipe and began to search for the rebels (somebody must have passed information on their whereabouts to Arklow during the night). They found several of the men and shot them on the spot. Byrne and a few others narrowly escaped detection and got away unnoticed, but the column was now scattered and disoriented. After several hours of searching the soldiers rode back to their base. When it was safe, most of the men came out of their hiding-places, and after a few hours those that had survived gathered together to continue the march. But by this point they had fallen far behind the other group, and their chances of catching up with them soon were slight. Besides that, they may now have numbered less than a hundred men, and so they had to move much more cautiously.

Later in the day they were delayed yet again when another

cavalry patrol spotted them. At the time they were on the top of a small hill, and the cavalry rode part of the way up the slope as if preparing to attack them. Byrne and his men drew up a small line of battle in response, but the cavalry pulled back at the last moment and retreated and disappeared into the countryside. (On the way they noticed a wounded rebel lying in a cornfield who had somehow become separated from the rest; they shot him dead as soon as they saw him.) No other government troops appeared for the rest of the day, but it would be very difficult for what was left of the column to regain the time they had lost, and by the end of the day they were probably somewhere near the village of Aughrim, almost a full day's march behind the larger column.[3]

Byrne and his exhausted men finally reached Glenmalure at the end of the next day, the 8th. They found Michael Dwyer and his band there. Dwyer surely had some idea of the whereabouts of the main column (although Byrne claims in his memoirs that he did not), but Byrne elected to stay with Dwyer rather than try to catch up with them in the next day or two. Byrne and his men were probably happy to join Dwyer and to turn down the chance of participating in the risky march to Ulster.[4]

We know little about the movements of the main group of rebels over the next few days. They probably made their way directly northwards on 7 July, and would have been somewhere close to Hollywood by that evening. We know that they reached Borleas demesne, near Blessington, by evening on the 8th. By this time they had collected a large number of new recruits from the valleys of Wicklow, raising their strength to perhaps 1,000 or 2,000 men.[5]

They decided at this point to make contact with the handful of Kildare rebels under William Aylmer who were still holding out in Timahoe Bog. These men had been passing back and forth between the bog and the Wicklow mountains for several weeks, and it may have been some of them who persuaded the rebels from Wexford and Wicklow to come out across Kildare and join them and then move on towards Ulster from there.[6] The march would be a diversion, but they might pick up more recruits and they could attack the odd isolated government oupost and seize more weapons. The chance of acquiring arms and ammunition was certainly tantalising by this stage, since their serviceable firearms were even fewer in number than a week before, and their ammunition, apart from whatever the new Wicklow recruits brought, must have been very nearly exhausted.

The prospect of going out into open country yet again after finally reaching the haven of the mountains must have shaken the resolve of many of the rank and file. That evening Father Mogue Kearns gave them all a stirring address, assuring them of the wisdom of the course they were now taking and urging them on to one final effort.[7] Then they settled down for the night, having prepared all in readiness to leave their mountain sanctuary behind as soon as daylight came.

As for the band that had taken shelter in Glenmalure, they remained in their hiding-place and ventured out very little over this and the next few days. The garrison commanders at Arklow and Rathdrum probably knew of their presence in the area, but they either did not consider them to be of any great significance or they were so frightened of them that they did not dare venture near them for the time being. They were content, therefore, to hold their own positions and to send out the occasional patrol until higher-ranking commanders decided when and how to deal with them.

General Lake, who had taken himself out of the Wexford campaign a week earlier, now became the key figure in the government's response. He was as confused as anyone about the position of the rebels by this stage, but he had come to realise that there was still resistance of some kind in County Wicklow, and on 8 July, as the main rebel body camped at Borleas, he made his way southwards to Arklow and prepared to co-ordinate the campaign. As soon as he got to Arklow he made contact with Needham, Moore and Hunter.

Duff was seriously ill by this point, and Lake relieved him of any role in the campaign. He ordered Needham to move northwards to Rathdrum with about half of his force, leaving the rest in Gorey as a reserve, so he could strike out at the glens. Moore was to be the linch-pin, however. Lake began by promoting him to the rank of major-general, a clear recognition of the vital role he had played up to this point, and then he ordered him to march north in the next day or two and take command of all of the forces then in Arklow and Carnew. He was to follow this up with a sweep northwards along the western slopes of the Wicklow mountains to trap the rebels in the glens. After that a simple sweeping movement into the heart of the glens would put a complete end to the insurgent forces.[8]

On the night of the 8th, still at Taghmon, Moore summarised Lake's plan in his diary and noted his promotion and the quiet state of south Wexford with some satisfaction. A reinforcement was to arrive the following day from Waterford, and once it was in place he would be ready to leave for Enniscorthy, Carnew and the mountains beyond. It is clear from his comments that he was very confident that a few more days would see the final end of the struggle.

The rebels at Blessington were now in a difficult position. There were small bands in various parts of Kildare that were ready to join them, but the country to their west and north was dotted with well-armed government garrisons of various sizes, any one of which might effectively oppose them. In the smaller villages these often amounted to no more than a few dozen yeomen, but in the larger towns there were often detachments of 100 or 200 militiamen. Naas, just ten miles to the west of Blessington, had almost 1,000 men, and there were substantial garrisons beyond that at Kildare, Newbridge and Edenderry. There was a chain of strongpoints further north too, including a substantial force under General Wemys at Drogheda, and another under Major-General Meyrick at Navan. The large garrison at Maryborough might be a factor also should the rebels have initial success,[9] and Dublin itself had combined yeomanry, militia and regular army forces numbering several thousand men. The journey to Ulster would bring the rebel column well within the range of many of these concentrations, and so they would have to pick their routes carefully and yet move quickly so as to be in Ulster before their intentions became too widely known. In the circumstances, it was extraordinary that they even decided to risk the trek.

They made their way down from the hills near Blessington and crossed the county boundary into Kildare early the next morning, 9 July. Rather than heading directly for Naas, which would have been the shortest route to Timahoe and Aylmer's hideout, they swung south-westwards towards the more lightly guarded towns of Ballymore Eustace and Kilcullen. They encountered no opposition, but at Kilcullen they learned that a small escort of soldiers had just passed through on their way to Newbridge with a keg of gunpowder. Garrett Byrne immediately set off along the Newbridge road with a small party of mounted men in pursuit of the escort and its powder and caught up with them in a short time. The soldiers were taken completely by surprise and put up no resistance. Byrne and his men soon returned to the main column, complete with powder. The barrel was smaller than they had hoped, but it was an important addition to their supplies.

When they resumed their march, they passed to the west of both Newbridge and Naas. They still encountered no opposition, and by evening were somewhere in the central part of the county; they stopped around twilight and camped for the night when they found a suitable place. By this point their presence must have been known of in several Kildare towns, but it is possible that they were still mistaken for a straggling party of Kildare rebels, several of whom had been seen in the countryside over the previous weeks, and so there may not have been a general alarm about their presence yet.[10]

Moore was making his way northwards through County Wexford during the same day. He set out with his column, a force of close to 2,000 men, very early in the morning and reached Enniscorthy well before midday. He had stopped there to rest his men and sent a dispatch to Lake, who was moving south himself and was now at Ferns. Lake responded with a request that they make a rendezvous at Ferns the following day. This gave Moore time to explore Enniscorthy and to survey the appalling destruction caused by the two fierce battles that had been fought there. Most of the town was a charred ruin, and the stench of death was everywhere. He climbed Vinegar Hill and was shocked by the smell from the hundreds of rotting bodies that lay half-buried in the shallow soil on its slopes. Here, for the first time, he got a vivid impression of how truly terrible this war had been.[11]

*

On 10 July the rebel column in central Kildare broke camp early in the morning once again and marched on northwards towards Timahoe. They still encountered no resistance, and it seems that the garrisons to their west at Edenderry and to their east at Naas remained confused about their exact whereabouts throughout the day. That afternoon they reached the banks of the Grand Canal at Robertstown and met one of Aylmer's men, who told them that they should meet with the Timahoe rebels at Prosperous, about three miles to the east. They swung back in that direction, and Aylmer was indeed waiting for them when they arrived.

At this point they might have worked out the plans for the final push to Ulster. It was a three or four days' march away, and since they had already captured a new supply of powder there was a reasonable chance that they might reach their destination in safety. However, Aylmer was not yet ready to set out. Instead he suggested that they make a quick diversion and attack the small town of Clonard, which was about fifteen miles away to the west, just across the border in south-west Meath. It is quite likely that Aylmer claimed that there was a stock of arms there and that it could be captured with ease.[12] It is notable also that Mogue Kearns had served as a curate there and may have had his own reasons for encouraging such a move.[13] Byrne, Fitzgerald and the other officers were persuaded by their arguments, and so the entire force changed direction, headed westward and reached Timahoe by evening and camped there for the night, ten miles from Clonard.[14]

Far to the south, in the meantime, Moore and Lake spent the day closing in on the Wicklow mountains. Moore had marched out of Enniscorthy at 4 a.m. He halted briefly at Scarawalsh, placed a detachment of the Meath militia on the bridge as a garrison and ordered another unit to ride up the river to hold the equally important bridge at Ballycarney. After this he pushed on to Ferns with the bulk of his force, arriving there while it was still early morning. Then he and Lake marched northwards together to Carnew, probably taking the narrow road that passes through the Slieveboy hills.

They reached the ruined town by evening without any trouble

and stopped there for the night. They were now at the south-western edge of the mountains and poised for the final phase of the operation against what they thought was the main haunt of the rebels.[15]

In Glenmalure, meanwhile, Michael Dwyer, Miles Byrne and their men were still biding their time. They had no idea now of where the larger column was, but probably surmised that it was somewhere in the midlands on its way towards Ulster. They had spent five days in the glen, and there was still no sign of government forces approaching them. This gave them a chance to recover from the ordeals of the previous weeks and to prepare for the assault on their sanctuary that they must have realised was coming sooner or later.[16]

On the morning of 11 July the rebels at Timahoe delayed their departure for Clonard for several hours for reasons that are not clear. There may have been renewed arguing about the wisdom of the diversion; certainly subsequent events would show that at least some of the Wicklow officers, Joseph Holt in particular, had serious objections to the attack. It was close to midday by the time they finally marched out towards the west, and reports of their intentions reached the commander of the tiny garrison at Clonard long before their arrival. The commander in question was a Captain Tyrrell, who was also the High Sheriff of Meath. He had barely twenty men in the town (including two of his own sons), but he sent a dispatch to Kinnegad, three miles further west, asking for help right away and drew his meagre force up outside the village in a small battle-line.

Tyrrell realised he was heavily outnumbered as soon as the rebels appeared, and so he hurriedly withdrew his men to a barracks inside the village where he knew they could hold out for a time. The building was perfect for defence. It was sturdy, it was roofed with slate, it was flanked by courtyards on either side, and there was a small tower at the end of one of them. He placed several men in the tower, and the rest took up positions at the windows of the barracks itself.

Any temptation the insurgent leaders felt to withdraw once the garrison had taken up firing positions in the barracks was

Midlands, Scene of Final Campaign of Wexford Rebels, 9 – 15 July

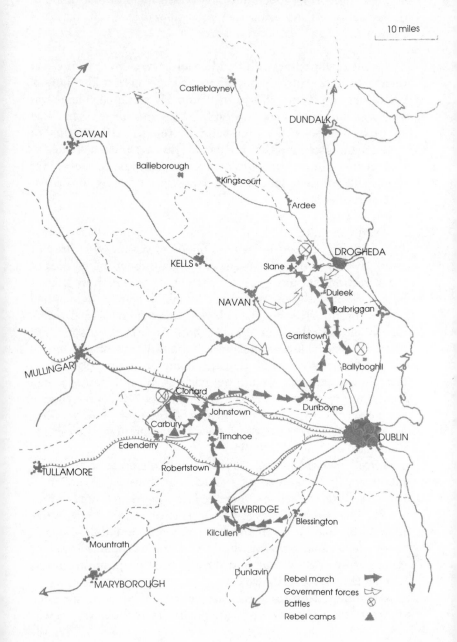

10 miles

Castleblayney

DUNDALK

CAVAN

Bailieborough

Kingscourt

Ardee

KELLS

Slane

DROGHEDA

Duleek

NAVAN

Balbriggan

Garristown

MULLINGAR

Ballyboghil

Clonard

Johnstown

Carbury

Dunboyne

Timahoe

Edenderry

DUBLIN

TULLAMORE

Robertstown

NEWBRIDGE

Blessington

Kilcullen

Mountrath

Dunlavin

MARYBOROUGH

Rebel march

Government forces

Battles

Rebel camps

overcome by the enthusiasm of the Kildaremen for the attack. One of them, a man named Farrell, opened the assault by leading a cavalry charge against the building. The more experienced Wexford and Wicklow rebels could hardly have approved of such a move. As soon as the attackers got within range of the tower and barracks the soldiers inside unleashed a volley which swept several of them from their horses, including Farrell himself. The rest soon fell back, and the leaders did not attempt to use their mounted units again in the action, but brought the infantry up to the front and threw them at the stronghold.

This tactic worked no better. Groups of rebels made their way around the building and tried to surround it. Some of them crept along a wall which flanked one of the courtyards, and these managed to pin down the men stationed in the turret, and a few even got into its ground floor and tried to force their way up the stairs inside. Another group broke into a garden that lay beside one of the courtyards and tried to launch an attack on the defenders in the barracks from there. Yet another group made their way to the western edge of the village, where they took possession of the bridge across which reinforcements from the west would have to come. In spite of these sensible deployments, the soldiers inside the barracks could not be budged, and they kept up a steady harassing fire on all the rebel detachments, including those holding the bridge. Those inside the turret did eventually lose their struggle when the structure caught fire, but even this did little to shake the resolve of the men in the barracks.

The battle raged on in this way for several hours, but eventually, with no sign of any headway being made and with the arrival of reinforcements likely, the rebels began to slacken their efforts. The first group to give up were those on the bridge. They had lost several men from the gunfire coming from the barracks and eventually withdrew altogether from their position. Not long afterwards the groups that had overwhelmed the turret and invaded the courtyard beside it pulled back too.

At about this time a government reinforcement of just under thirty men arrived from Kinnegad. Now that the bridge was no longer in rebel hands, they were able to link up with Tyrrell and his men. The fight continued until almost 6 p.m., but it was clear by then what the outcome would be, and the rebel leaders finally called on their men to disengage and to pull back.

One account puts the number of insurgents killed in the action at one hundred men. This is probably an exaggeration, but given the nature of the struggle, it is likely that their casualties were quite high. They retreated back across the border into County Kildare without anything to show for the effort except for their losses and the fact that their supply of powder, so vital if the march to Ulster was to have any chance of success, was almost exhausted. By nightfall they had reached the little village of Carbury, a few miles to the south-east of Clonard and camped on a small hill nearby.[17]

The failure to take Clonard was a devastating blow to the midlands campaign, and many of the rank and file were deeply angered by the serious reverse they had suffered. During the evening a dispute arose between those who now wanted to return to the safety of the mountains and those who advocated pressing on regardless. Joseph Holt emerged as the main spokesman for the idea of returning to the mountains, but most of the other officers were for staying in the midlands. During the night the debate broke down, and Holt stormed out of the camp, determined to make his own way back to the mountains, taking a sizeable band of Wicklowmen with him. Many of Aylmer's followers also left the camp during the night, and as dawn approached the column had been reduced to something over 1,000 men at most, the majority of them from Wexford.[18] To make matters worse, their ammunition was low once again, and reports of their presence were already spreading through the entire midlands region. Even the most optimistic of them must have realised that there was little chance of reaching Ulster now.

As the rebel cause suffered this severe reverse on the Kildare/Meath border, the government's campaign in southern and western Wicklow went ahead as planned. In the morning Moore had set out along the dangerous winding road running north from Carnew and had reached the burned-out ruins of Hacketstown by midday. Lake followed behind him all morning, and from Hacketstown they then pushed on together to a place called the Gap. By this time they had heard that there were some rebels holding out in the Glen of Imaal. It was late in the afternoon when they reached the Gap, and they decided to camp there for the night and to push into the Glen the next day. By nightfall they were getting reports that the rebels had crossed out of Imaal and into Glenmalure and that others were stationed on the high ridges around Seven Churches. A column of government troops, mostly Fermanagh militia under Colonel Campbell, was moving southwards along the north-western slope of the mountains in their direction and had already passed Donard. Lake realised that Campbell was in a good position to cut off the rebels should they try to escape in that direction, and he sent out a rider to make contact with Campbell during the night to ensure that he held his position. Any rebels that were taking refuge in the mountains were now hoplessly surrounded.

That night as the rebels licked their wounds at Carbury, and as Holt and his men made their way across Kildare towards the mountains, Moore and Lake worked out the details of their final assault. They decided that Lord Huntly would move northwards from Arklow to Rathdrum and send patrols probing up towards the mouth of Glenmalure. Colonel Campbell, now at Ballinclay, would march up to the Wicklow Gap and take up a position at the head of the glen. Lake would lead a column of troops over the ridge into the glen and take up a position at Greenane, where he would effectively close off its mouth. Meanwhile Moore and his men would leave the roads altogether and drag two cannon up the south-western rim of the glen and stop there for the night. On the following day, the 13th, they would all push into the heart of the glen. The rebels would be trapped inside and would have little chance of escape. If all went well, the rising would be finally over in less than forty-eight hours.[19]

At dawn on the morning of the 12th, as Lake and Moore got ready to break camp and move into Glenmalure, what was left of the rebel column at Carbury Hill broke camp too and began to march north-eastwards across the northern edge of the Bog of Allen towards the Meath border and, fifty miles beyond it, Ulster.

They had only travelled a short distance and were eating a hurried meal at a place called Rynville when the rearguard noticed several cavalry detachments approaching from the south. The cavalry in question was commanded by Colonel Gough and had ridden all the way from Edenderry that morning. The rebels resumed their march, with Gough's men following them but staying out of range for the time being. All the rebels were on horseback at this stage, in most cases two per animal, and so they were able to travel at a brisk pace.

When they came close to Kilcock, yet another group of Kildaremen broke away. They fled in the direction of the village and scattered. The rest of the force, numbering perhaps under 1,000 men, continued to make steady progress, though with Gough still hovering behind them at a distance. At around midday they crossed over the Grand Canal at Johnstown Bridge and were once again inside County Meath. Gough's cavalry cut off any stragglers they came across, and on a few occasions the rebel rearguard had to fight small skirmishes with them, but they still managed to avoid a pitched battle against a force that was fresher, better armed and almost as numerous.

After they crossed into Meath the rebels turned eastwards and passed through Summerhill and several other small villages, evidently in the faint hope of picking up recruits from what had been the United Irish stronghold on the southern fringes of the county. They had little success, but by evening they were approaching Dunboyne and had still managed to keep out of Gough's clutches, and thus far no other government forces had appeared. Just at the edge of darkness Gough finally called his men off and withdrew back towards Edenderry. He was assuming it would seem, that the concentrated forces of Dublin and the towns around it could now easily deal with what remained of the rebels. Whatever his reasoning, his withdrawal gave the rebels the respite they needed and the chance to make a camp and rest their exhausted horses for the night.[20]

Whether they realised it or not, news of the approach of the insurgents was spreading fast by this time. The garrisons around south Meath, Dublin and Louth knew of their march and were already preparing to deal with them the following day. Word of their march had also been carried into Dublin by midnight, and to the garrisons at Drogheda and Navan.[21] By the end of the 12th, therefore, yet another net was about to close on them.

Meanwhile, far to the south of the rolling farmland of Meath, the net woven by Lake and Moore was closing on the rebels in Glenmalure. It rained heavily in the mountains that morning, but

Moore began his push towards the southern rim of the glen early in the day and made good progress in spite of the conditions. By midday he had reached the top of the ridge and had a sweeping view of the long, canyon-like valley in which he assumed the rebels were sheltering. Because of the extreme wet, wind and cold, he decided to overstep his instructions for the day and ordered his men to make their way down the side of the valley and into the heart of the ravine. It was evening when he got to the bottom, and he decided to push his way towards the head of the valley before darkness. Apart from a single sighting of a small number of people on the mountainside above him, (he assumed these to be local inhabitants), he saw no sign of rebels. He could only conclude that they had either eluded him or that they had never been there in the first place.[22]

When dawn broke on 13 July, the rebels at Dunboyne began their march again. It was clear by now that the former rebels of south Meath were not going to join them, and so they now turned due north, towards the Ulster border. They saw no sign of government forces throughout the morning, and at around midday they stopped on Garristown Hill, near the Meath/Dublin border and less than ten miles from County Louth; Ulster was now barely more than thirty miles away. Unknown to them, however, a force of about 1,000 men under General Meyers was approaching from the direction of Dublin, and at the same time his messengers were on the way to Navan and Drogheda with instructions for the commanders there to close in on the rebels from the north-west and north-east.

General Wemys and his men left Drogheda early in the afternoon and took the road to the village of Duleek, a few miles to the south-west of Garristown, and Meyrick and his column moved down to Tara Hill from Navan and then marched eastwards to meet him. The plan was for Wemys and Meyrick to meet before the rebels had had a chance to reach the Boyne and to trap them as they approached the river.[23]

By sheer luck the rebels were about three miles to the north of Duleek by the time Wemys got there. He saw them in the distance as soon as he got into the village, but decided not to give chase and risk a pitched battle. Instead he marched slowly towards Slane and met Meyrick in the late evening at a place called Black Lion. By that time the rebel column was well out of sight and had already crossed to the north side of the Boyne, and as night approached Wemys and Meyrick made their way by different routes towards Slane and crossed the Boyne themselves.[24] The rebels had by now already advanced several miles into County Louth. None of their officers seems to have realised that they were being followed, and they decided to halt for the night where they were.[25]

Meyrick and Wemys could have attacked the rebel camp during the night, and had they done so they might well have devastated them. They decided to take no action, however, perhaps because they were confident that they could catch up with the rebels the next day, and they established a camp for themselves a few miles to the south of the rebel position. At some point in the night the rebels learned of their presence, but they remained where they were themselves while darkness lasted. They were afraid, nevertheless, that a move might be made against them during the night, and so the entire column remained awake, as did the government troops just to their south.

In Wicklow Sir John Moore and General Lake had spent the day on a futile search for the rebels who had evaded them the day before. In the morning they made a rendezvous in the glen and they met briefly with Colonel Forster and Lord Huntly on the ridge at Seven Churches later in the day. They now had information that there were some rebels on Blackmoor Hill, several miles to the north, near Blessington. Moore left the valley late in the afternoon, and Lake took his two cannon and pushed on over the mountains towards Blessington, evidently to investigate this report. He found no evidence of the rebels' presence, however, and by evening none of the commanders in the area had any idea where the insurgent bands had gone.[26]

The real whereabouts at this stage of the several hundred rebels who had, according to Miles Byrne, sought refuge in Glenmalure is something of a mystery. They may have scattered over several mountains and valleys far to the north and west of the Wicklow Gap and Glenmalure at this point, or maybe they were concentrated somewhere to the east of Blessington (although not at Blackmoor) as the reports said. Holt and his group had been on their way back to the mountains for two days now, and it is quite possible that they can be identified as the assemblage on Blackmoor Hill. Incredibly, Byrne's memoirs say nothing of these days and make no mention whatever of Moore's sally into the glen, which suggests that he and Dwyer had vacated their original hiding-place by the time Moore and Lake approached it, and so never knew of the brief expedition against them.

On the early morning of 14 July, the ninth anniversary of the fall of the Bastille, the position of the main rebel force encamped inside County Louth had begun to look bleak. No contemporary account of the stand-off mentions the weather, but if the rain which soaked Moore and his men on the mountains on the 13th was by now falling in Meath and Louth too, then the rebels must have been badly affected by it. Unlike the soldiers, who were rested, well fed and properly clothed, they were now in a terrible state. Their supply of food had been meagre for a long time, their clothes were little more than rags, and most of them had not shaved or had their hair cut for weeks. Their long matted hair and beards and ragged attire, along with the gaunt look many of them surely had from hunger and exhaustion, must have made them a pathetic sight.[27] A soaking from rain in the exposed countryside could only have added to their misery.

Amazingly, though, their spirits were high. The fact that they had managed to get across the Boyne and were within a day's ride of Ulster may explain this. In addition, the fear they seemed to instil in the government forces once they were in the open country may have led then to believe that nothing could stop them from joining the Ulster rebels now. The fact that it was Bastille Day must surely have heartened the more committed republicans among them too.

When dawn broke, several of the officers addressed the men. They spoke of how disappointed they were that the people of Meath had not rallied to them, but they pledged themselves to fight on regardless. The men cheered in response. As one of them would recall years later, 'They were now in a state of desperation, yet they were more cool and steady than they had been at any previous time.' After the speeches they mounted their horses and began to push their way northwards towards Ardee, with Meyrick and Wemys following them. Both commanders realised that their infantry had no hope of keeping pace with the mounted rebels, and so they sent several hundred cavalry ahead to harass them. Many times in the rebellion the insurgents had successfully fought off cavalry units, but now, exhausted and badly outgunned, they found themselves unable to hold off the pursuing units, and their rearguard came under heavy pressure.

After an hour or more of desperate efforts on the part of the rearguard to fight off the pursuers, Fitzgerald and Byrne decided make a stand. They chose a spot in a townland called Knightstown, where there was a broad stretch of bog with a narrow strip of dry land running through it. They assumed that pikemen could defend this causeway against cavalry and that after a few charges the soldiers might give up, giving them the chance to press on through County Louth.

The cavalry officers recognised the tactic as soon as they got to the edge of the bog and saw the rebels drawn up with pikes at the ready. They ordered at least one charge, which the pikemen easily beat back, but they then waited for the rest of their column to move up so that the infantry and artillery could be brought into the battle. At around eleven o'clock these arrived, and Meyrick ordered his gunners to level their cannon at the rebel ranks massed across the bog in front of him. When they unleashed their deadly grapeshot, several of the rebels fell, many of them killed. Some of their officers were hit too, including Edward Fitzgerald, who stayed on his feet but was covered in blood.

Garrett Byrne now took charge and shouted to the men to make for some high ground to the west of the bog. He realised that they were in a dangerous situation and yelled out that they should all escape as best they could after they had made the crossing. Moments later the rank and file plunged their horses into the marsh and began to struggle across the soaking ground.

Many succeeded in reaching the other side and broke out into the hedgerows and thickets that lay beyond. Dozens more made slower progress and were still in the bog when the soldiers reached it. The cavalry had charged along the dry causeway as soon as the flight began and cut many men down there and on the edge of the marsh. The infantry made their way into the bog itself and killed anyone they caught up with. Most of the rebels managed to escape, however, and in small bands or even as isolated individuals they got away towards the west. The final toll from the engagement is uncertain, but close on a hundred men may have died, although all the senior officers survived the fighting. The soldiers suffered very few casualties. In a matter of an hour or two, therefore, all hope of reaching Ulster was gone, and now several hundred men were left to try to find a way of eluding their pursuers in open, flat countryside.[28]

Amazingly, several groups of rebels managed to reassemble and form smaller and more compact bands once they had made their escape. One of these rode north-westwards towards County Cavan and eventually reached Kingscourt by the end of the day. Another went due north towards Ardee, and yet another succeeded in returning southwards. The first two bands were quite small, twenty or thirty men to each it would seem, but the group which turned southwards numbered several hundred men and included Garrett Byrne, Edward Fitzgerald and Esmond Kyan. (Anthony Perry, Father Mogue Kearns and William Aylmer made their way westward and lost touch with the larger groups.) Riding two to a horse, they made their way safely to the Boyne once again and crossed at a point a short distance downstream from Slane, this time with the Wicklow mountains as their goal.[29] With astonishing determination they had evidently resolved to try to get back to their safe haven and adopt the guerrilla option initiated by Dwyer, Miles Byrne and Holt.

From the Boyne they galloped southwards towards Garristown Hill. General Meyers, who had pulled back to the capital on the previous day once it was clear that the rebels had circumvented both Wemys and Meyrick, had now returned and had established himself in Slane. His place in north County Dublin had been taken by a small force of infantry and cavalry, about 200 men in all, under the command of a Highland officer named Gordon. Gordon and his men had left Balbriggan at about 1 p.m. and had just settled themselves to the east of Garristown at about 4 p.m. when a scout noticed the rebels crossing the hill. Gordon was too far to the east to intercept them, but began to follow them southwards.[29]

The rebels soon realised they were being pursued yet again.

The pattern was now familiar to them, although the danger must have seemed even more pressing since their numbers were so few and they were only lightly armed and their horses could have had but little strength left.

The chase lasted for almost three hours. Gordon's cavalry got far ahead of his infantry and the rebels pushed somewhat to the east, so that instead of heading directly south or even south-west in the direction of the mountains, they were being driven deep inside County Dublin and directly towards the capital. If this were to continue, they were, in the end, bound to be trapped hopelessly.

At about 7 p.m., one of the leaders, perhaps Garrett Byrne, made the decision to turn about and make what he must have known would be a desperate last stand. At this point the head of the column was approaching the little crossroads hamlet of Ballyboghil in north central County Dublin. Outside the village there was a field on the right of the road which sloped gently up from it, and Byrne ordered his men to cross the hedgerow and form a battle-line at its top. As they did so they dismounted and chased their horses away. They were a dreadful sight now. To their gaunt and ragged appearance was added the signs of exhaustion and desperation. Nevertheless, Edward Fitzgerald turned to them and somehow summoned up a stirring parting message, remembered years later by one of the men who heard him as 'Men! We stood faithful together as long as we could. Each of us must now do the best we can for ourselves. Farewell.'

Moments later Gordon's cavalry, about one hundred in number, arrived and spread out across the lower part of the field. Then an officer yelled the command to charge, and the troops thundered their way up the slope towards the rebels. The rebels had never given ground to cavalry before, but now, frightened and demoralised, they began to break ranks, perhaps even before the shock of the charge came fully to bear on them. Some held their ground for a time and fought the mounted troops fiercely once they were among them, but even they soon broke and fled.

It was now a mad scramble to escape. Men ran headlong towards the hedges and ditches around the field with the mounted soldiers in pursuit. Somehow dozens of them managed to climb into the surrounding fields and fanned out in groups of two and three or singly and hid where they could. Many concealed themselves in the high barley and wheat; others hid in copses and hedgerows. Some simply ran as far and as fast as they could. By the time twilight came most of them had somehow escaped, and the cavalrymen were satisfied to round up the approximately two hundred horses that they had let go.[30]

Some of the insurgents were bolder and made their way southwards during the night, Byrne, Fitzgerald, Roche and Kyan among them. They got to the banks of the Royal Canal before dawn and managed to swim across unnoticed. They crossed the Liffey in the same way a few hours later, and by then they could see the dark beckoning mass of the Wicklow mountains in the distance.[31] After fifty days they were finally and totally beaten, and their only hope was to hide out in the mountains and escape the bayonets of their enemies.

And so in this way the great Wexford rebellion came to a close. Over the next several weeks more of the insurgent leaders would pay with their lives for the part they had played. Anthony Perry and Father Mogue Kearns tried to travel together southwards through the midlands, but were captured in County Kildare and taken to Edenderry and hanged.[32] Esmond Kyan decided to surrender himself to the government at the end of the month; he was taken to Wexford and executed on the bridge.[33] Billy Byrne was arrested later in the summer and charged with various atrocities and hanged outside Wicklow.[34] Father John Murphy and a companion were captured in County Carlow and hanged at Tullow.[35] Walter Devereux of Carrigmenan, one of those accused of having been involved in the Scullabogue massacre, was captured in Cork as he tried to make his way to America and suffered the same fate there.[36]

Resistance of a kind lasted for a time in a few isolated places. A remnant of the fugitives who had taken refuge in Killoughram Woods eventually formed an outlaw gang led by an old rebel named James Corcoran; they continued to operate on either side of the Blackstairs until the spring of 1804, when they were eventually hunted down and killed.[37] Michael Dwyer, the Wicklow rebel, held out in his native mountains with a handful of followers almost as long, finally surrendering in 1803.[38] Other

Wexford rebels continued to hide out for several years either in their own county or in Dublin, where several hundred of them were living in safe houses shortly after the rising.[39]

There were, no doubt, people who wanted to see a renewed attempt at rebellion, but for the vast majority of the Wexford United Irishmen this was not the case. In August, when the French landed a token force on the west coast, there was no reaction in Wexford; and in 1803, when Robert Emmet tried to lead a second rebellion in Dublin, there was little or no response from the county.[40]

Some prominent rebels were lucky enough to be arrested after the worst of the 'White Terror' had passed or to escape arrest altogether. Garrett Byrne, Edward Fitzgerald, Edward Roche and Thomas Cloney all surrendered in the late summer after negotiating terms with the government. Roche, the man who came closest to being the true leader of the Wexfordmen, died in prison a year later, perhaps by his own hand. Fitzgerald and Byrne were exiled and settled together in a small town not far from Hamburg, where they both lived on into the second decade of the new century.[41] Cloney was perhaps the most fortunate of them all. He surrendered at Enniscorthy late in the summer and was sent a prisoner to Fort William in the Scottish Highlands.[42] He was back in Ireland by 1803 and had some contact with Robert Emmet, but took no direct part in his rebellion.[43] A few years later he leased a farm in Carlow, and this became his home. For years thereafter he was watched very carefully by local magistrates, but he channelled his energies into politics and was locally prominent in O'Connell's Emancipation campaign.[44] He wrote his memoirs in the early 1830s and lived on into the fifth decade of the century.

Edward Hay, the rebel director of armaments, escaped arrest completely. As early as 1802 he was travelling about the county collecting material for a book on the rebellion which was published in the following year. Considering how critical it was of the ultra-loyalist element which had come to the fore by that point, this was one of the bravest things he did, even if he was careful to distance himself from the movement in the text.

Miles Byrne, the eighteen-year-old from Monaseed, avoided arrest too. He went into hiding for a time in the Wicklow mountains, but then moved to Dublin and lived among the fugitive Wexford population there. He got involved in Emmet's conspiracy in 1802–3, and it was he who arranged for a meeting between Emmet and Thomas Cloney on the green at Harold's Cross one evening. He was disappointed at the total failure of the rising in 1803, and soon afterwards stowed away on an American ship in the harbour and made his way to France.[45] He spent the rest of his life there, and after a distinguished military career he retired to Paris, where as an old man in the 1850s he wrote his memoirs. He finally died in 1862, having never once returned to Ireland.[46]

The bitterness that the entire decade of the 1790s and the summer of '98 in particular sowed in County Wexford lasted a long time. Ultra-loyalism thrived in the first decade or two of the new century, with men like Hunter Gowan, Hawtrey White and Archibald Hamilton Jacob very much to the fore in it. Gowan died early in the century, after living through a bitter family dispute,[47] and White was discredited as an alarmist within a few years and fades out of the historical record well before 1805.[48] Jacob, on the other hand, was still writing warnings of imminent rebellion to the Castle authorities from his vantage-point in Enniscorthy as late as 1814, and he was among many local loyalists who had by that time established the tradition of marching to the summit of Vinegar Hill every year on the anniversary of the battle and burning a liberty tree there. On several occasions these celebrations ended in destructive violence in the town.[49] In New Ross too local loyalists held a march every year well into the new century to celebrate their victory in the battle of 5 June. This too often ended in violence.[50]

In time, however, the county recovered from the trauma of its brutal civil war. The towns that had born scars of battle for years were rebuilt, and few signs of the huge fires that had swept away whole streets could be seen. The economy recovered too, and as the rebel generation grew into middle age and beyond Wexford became notable once again as one of the more prosperous and more peaceful counties in Ireland. The fact that there was a significant exodus of Protestants from the county to Canada in the first few decades of the new century may in part account for the decline of sectarian tensions over those decades too.[51] The liberal faction regained control of county politics as early as 1807 and never lost their grip thereafter.[52] The county did not suffer to any notable degree in the Great Famine, and for that reason perhaps the radical republicanism that emerged in the mid and late nineteenth century was never very strong there.

The memory of 1798, however, remained very much alive in Wexford throughout the nineteenth century, and it has persisted into the twentieth. There was a rash of monument-building in the late nineteeth and early twentieth century that left physical reminders of the struggle scattered across much of the county, and local nationalists sponsored commemorations of the event in 1898, 1938 and 1948, and there are plans to hold large celebrations in 1998 to mark the bicentennial.

In 1969 Thomas Pakenham suggested that the ghost of '98 was about to be laid at last. It was tempting to suggest this at a time when Ireland had enjoyed almost half a century of relative peace. The events of the next two decades would prove him wrong. Perhaps what we need to do is learn to live with our ghosts—to confront them, to get to know them, to try to understand why they have haunted us so. For the historian the job is to tell the story of this tragedy as objectively as he or she can, no more and no less, accepting all the while that we all have our prejudices, but being determined nevertheless to be honest about them. The pain of the past will not go away, but maybe we can somehow come to live with it, just as we can somehow come to live with one another, even though, inevitably, we will haunt one another too.

NOTES AND REFERENCES

ABBREVIATIONS

DDA	Dublin Diocesan Archives
NAI	National Archives of Ireland
NLI	National Library of Ireland
OP	Outrage Papers (NAI)
PRO, HO	Public Record Office, London: Home Office Papers
RIA	Royal Irish Academy
RP	Rebellion Papers (NAI)
SOC	State of the Country Papers (NAI)
TCD	Trinity College, Dublin

Preface (pp. xiii–xv)

1. Thomas Pakenham, *The Year of Liberty: the story of the great Irish rebellion of 1798* (London, 1969).
2. Colm Toibín, 'New Ways of Killing Your Father', *London Review of Books*, 18 Nov. 1993, p. 3.
3. Charles Dickson, *The Wexford Rising in 1798: its causes and course* (Tralee, 1955).
4. Sir Richard Musgrave, *Memoirs of the Different Rebellions in Ireland* (London, 1801).
5. Marianne Elliott, *Partners in Revolution: the United Irishmen and France* (London, 1982); L. M. Cullen, 'The 1798 Rebellion in Wexford: United Irish organisation, membership, leadership' in Kevin Whelan (ed.), *Wexford: History and Society: interdisciplinary essays on the history of an Irish county* (Dublin, 1987), pp. 248–95; Kevin Whelan, 'Politicisation in County Wexford and the Origins of the 1798 Rebellion' in David Dickson and Hugh Gough, *Ireland and the French Revolution* (Dublin, 1990), pp. 156–78; Nancy Curtin, *The United Irishmen: popular politics in Ulster and Dublin, 1791–1798* (Oxford, 1994).
6. Nicholas Furlong, *Father John Murphy of Boolavogue, 1753–1798* (Dublin, 1991).

Chapter 1: Prelude: 14 July 1789 – 25 May 1798 (pp. 1–11)
 1. Cullen, *Recollections*, p. 76.
 2. Powell, 'Economic Factor', p. 145.
 3. Dickson, *Wexford Rising*, p. 251. Smyth claims that Irish was not necessarily a 'brake' to politicisation (see *Men of No Property*, pp. 31–2).
 4. Cullen, 'Emergence', p. 213.
 5. Whelan, 'Politicisation', pp. 156–7.
 6. Johnston, *Eighteenth Century*, pp. 132–63.
 7. Whelan, 'Politicisation', p. 167; Smyth, *Men of No Property*, pp. 178–80.
 8. Whelan, 'Politicisation', p. 3; *Parl. Reg.*, xvi (1791) p. viii.
 9. Whelan, 'Politicisation', p. 158; Furlong, *Murphy*, p. 15.
10. *Parl. Reg.*, xvii (1792), pp. 37–8, 127–8, 189, 240, 282.
11. Foster, *Modern Ireland*, p. 261.
12. Whelan, 'Politicisation', pp. 168.
13. Bartlett 'End to Moral Economy', pp. 51–3; Hay, *Insurrection*, pp. 21–7; Smyth, *Men of No Property*, pp. 102–5.
14. Johnston, *Eighteenth Century*, p. 185.
15. Elliott, *Partners in Revolution*, pp. 95–6; Smyth, *Men of No Property*, pp. 157–62.
16. Elliott, *Partners in Revolution*, pp. 71–2; Smyth, *Men of No Property*, p. 21.
17. Foster, *Modern Ireland*, p. 275.
18. Dickson, *Wexford Rising*, p. 11. The payroll for the Castletown corps is extant (see Genealogical Office, Dublin, MS 620).
19. Elliott, *Partners in Revolution*, pp. 109–23; Pakenham, *Year of Liberty*, pp. 17–19.
20. There was considerable sympathy for the invaders, at least in the northern parishes of the county (see Byrne, *Memoirs*, i, pp. 3–5).
21. NAI, RP 620/30/103, 620/30/226, 620/30/232, 620/31/39, 620/31/101, 620/33/44, 620/33/124, 620/34/20; NAI, SOC 1016/49, 3191; Lecky, *Ireland*, iv, pp. 48–52, 78–9; Byrne, *Memoirs*, i, p. 7; Cullen '1798', p. 275.
22. Powell 'Economic Factor', pp. 151–4.
23. Whelan 'Politicisation', pp. 159–60; Cullen, '1798 in Wexford', pp. 263–8.
24. Powell 'Economic Factor', pp. 154–5; Hay *Insurrection*, pp. 52–3. A copy of this proclamation is in NAI, OP 990/35, signed by George Ogle among others.
25. Lecky, *Ireland*, x, pp. 252–8.
26. Ibid., pp. 227–31.
27. Ibid., pp. 263–4; Cullen, '1798 in Wexford', p. 249.

28. Elliott, *Partners in Revolution*, pp.194–5.
29. Lecky *Ireland*, iv, p. 213. Wicklow magistrates were especially watchful of communications between suspects in Wicklow and in Wexford (see NAI, RP 620/3/51/1, 620/36/105).
30. Cullen, '1798 in Wexford', p. 268; Whelan, 'Role of the Catholic Priest', pp. 298–301; Furlong, *Murphy*, pp. 31–3.
31. Cullen, '1798 in Wexford', pp. 263–8.
32. Hay, *Insurrection*, pp. 57–71; Gordon, *Rebellion*, pp. 55–9.
33. Cullen, '1798 in Wexford', pp. 263–7, 276.
34. Graham, 'Union of Power', pp. 251–3; see also PRO, HO 100/77/44–6.
35. Lecky, *Ireland*, iv, pp. 299–333.
36. Graham, 'Union of Power', pp. 253–4.
37. Pakenham, *Year of Liberty*, pp. 107–21.
38. In north Carlow, for example, the United Irishmen only learned of the imminent mobilisation late on 24 May (see Farrell, *Carlow*, p. 82).
39. Cullen, '1798 in Wexford', p. 269.
40. Ibid., pp. 282–3.
41. For a very meticulous reconstruction of the Wexford leadership see Cullen, '1798 in Wexford', pp. 277–85; for more detailed biographical information on individual officers see Dickson, *Wexford Rising*, pp. 187–214; for a detailed discussion of Wexford Catholic society in general see Whelan, 'Catholic Community', pp. 129–70. The comfortable circumstances of one of these families, the Furlongs of Templescoby, is clear from their father's will of 1819, abstracted in NLI, Ainsworth MS 43; several of these families are also listed in the Catholic Qualification Rolls (see NAI, 2/446/52/).
42. Cullen, '1798 in Wexford', pp. 285–6; Whelan, 'Role of the Catholic Priest', pp. 297–315.
43. Cullen '1798 in Wexford', p. 282.
44. Elliott, *Partners in Revolution*, pp. 24–6, 367–8; Whelan, 'Politicisation', p. 169.
45. Whelan, 'Role of the Catholic Priest', p. 297; Furlong, *Murphy*, pp. 27–8.
46. Whelan, 'Politicisation', pp. 169–70.
47. Ibid., pp. 161–2.
48. Ibid., pp. 1–4.
49. Ibid., pp. 5–6; Furlong, *Murphy*, p. 48. On Jacob's background see Jacob, *Historical and Genealogical Narrative*.
50. Dickson, *Wexford Rising*, pp. 35–42; Furlong, *Murphy*, pp. 38–42.
51. See note 34 above.

52. NAI, RP 620/3/32/6, 620/37/141.
53. Pakenham, *Year of Liberty*, p. 145; Dickson, *Wexford Rising*, p. 43.
54. NAI, RP 620/37/141; Byrne, *Memoirs*, i, pp. 25–7.
55. Pakenham, *Year of Liberty*, pp. 113–16.
56. Furlong, *Murphy*, p. 48.

Chapter 2: Outbreak: Noon, 26 May – 8 a.m., 27 May (pp. 12–27)
1. News of the rising had reached Kilcormick early in the morning on 26 May, but it may have got there as early as the afternoon of the 25th (see Cullen, *Recollections*, pp. 7–8).
2. Musgrave, *Rebellions*, i, p. 404.
3. Wheeler, *War*, pp. 82–3.
4. Cullen, *Recollections*, p. 8.
5. Ibid., p. 288; Hay, *Insurrection*, pp. 77–80.
6. Cullen, *Recollections*, p. 282; Hay, *Insurrection*, p. 80.
7. Dickson, *Wexford Rising*, p. 44.
8. Byrne, *Memoirs*, i, pp. 27–9.
9. Cullen, '1798 in Wexford', p. 282.
10. Hay, *Insurrection*, p. 80.
11. Ibid.; Cullen, *Recollections*, p. 12.
12. Hay, *Insurrection*, p. 79.
13. Musgrave, *Rebellions*, i, p. 329. This signal fire is also mentioned in the ballad 'Boolavogue'.
14. Cullen, '1798 in Wexford', p. 270, 290.
15. Historians of the rebellion in Wexford have understated the importance of arms stockpiles as the reason for raids on houses (see Dickson, *Wexford Rising*, p. 57).
16. Whelan, 'Religious Factor', p. 72 .
17. Musgrave, *Rebellions*, i, pp. 404–5; Wheeler, *War*, p. 83.
18. Barber Recollections, p. 3; Musgrave, *Rebellions*, i, p. 411; Taylor, *Rebellions*, p. 32.
19. Musgrave, *Rebellions*, i, p. 410; Taylor, *Rebellions*, p. 30.
20. Musgrave, *Rebellions*, ii, pp. 338–40; Taylor, *Rebellions*, pp. 30–2; Lecky, *Ireland*, iv, p. 336. Turner was among those magistrates who signed the memorial proclaiming sixteen north Wexford parishes to be in a state of rebellion in November 1797 (see NAI, OP 990/35).
21. Miles Byrne and some comrades reached Camolin early the next morning. It is clear from his account that the village was in the hands of rebels or rebel sympathisers already (see Byrne, *Memoirs*, ii, p. 32); for corroboration of a rebel seizure of the village on 27 May see Wheeler, *War*, p. 86.

22. The Camolin cavalry was in Ferns (see Wheeler, *War*, p. 85).
23. Musgrave, *Rebellions*, i, p. 414; Wheeler, *War*, p. 86. There is great confusion about this attack. In some accounts it is claimed that the Kilcormick rebels carried it out—an impossible task if they conducted all the raids attributed to them that night and still got to Oulart by dawn (see Kavanagh, *Popular History*, pp. 98–9; Furlong, *Murphy*, p. 53); in others the claim is made that the raid occurred a day later, on 28 May (see Cullen, '1798 in Wexford', pp. 289–90).
24. Taylor, *Rebellions*, p. 32; Gordon, *Rebellion*, p. 90; Dickson, *Wexford Rising*, p. 39.
25. Musgrave, *Rebellions*, i, p. 418; Dickson, *Wexford Rising*, p. 67. Kavanagh claims, probably erroneously, that Murphy's neighbours persuaded him to go to Kilthomas (see *Popular History*, p. 103).
26. Whelan, 'Religious Factor', pp. 72–3.
27. Sunset was at 8.05 p.m. (see *Kalendar Compiled by John Watson Stewart for the Year of Our Lord 1798* (Dublin, 1798), p. 21).
28. See Cullen, '1798 in Wexford', p. 281; Whelan, 'Role of the Catholic Priest', p. 308. For an interpretation which sees his involvement as fortuitous see Furlong, *Murphy*, pp. 44–7.
29. Cullen, *Recollections*, pp. 9–10; Kavanagh, *Popular History*, pp. 97–9; Wheeler, *War*, pp. 83–4; Gordon, *Rebellion*, p. 89; Taylor, *Rebellions*, p. 26; Furlong, *Murphy*, pp. 48–50.
30. Musgrave, *Rebellions*, i, p. 406; ii, pp. 329–37.
31. This attack may have involved the band from Kilcormick, but given that they attacked at least three houses in their own parish between sunset and dawn (and managed to get to Oulart by dawn), it is likely that a separate band was involved here.
32. Taylor, *Rebellions*, p. 28.
33. Musgrave, *Rebellions*, i, pp. 407–8; Gordon, *Rebellion*, p. 89; Furlong, *Murphy*, p. 53.
34. Musgrave, *Rebellions*, i, pp. 413–14.
35. Ibid., ii, p. 335.
36. Cullen, *Recollections*, pp. 11–12; Musgrave, *Rebellions*, i, pp. 408–10; ii, pp. 333–4; Taylor, *Rebellions*, p. 28; Dickson, *Wexford Rising*, p. 57. Burrowes's wife was a Clifford of Castle Annesley, a local landed family (see Genealogical Office, Dublin, MS 142, p. 59).
37. Cullen's informant (*Recollections*, p. 11), who was not actually present, suggests that the Kilcormick band carried out the attack but the affidavit of an eyewitness, Burrowes's son, indicates that rebels were gathering near the house very early in the evening, long before the Kilcormick group could have got there (see Musgrave, *Rebellions*, ii, p. 333).

38. Kyan's wherabouts at this point is a mystery. There is no mention that I can find of his being arrested during these days, but we first encounter him as a prisoner in Gorey's market house on 4 June at the time of its second evacuation by government troops (see Byrne, *Memoirs*, p. 76). This suggests that he was brought there sometime after the first evacuation and repossession of the town on 28–29 May, when all the prisoners were shot (see Gordon, *Rebellion*, pp. 106–7).

39. Cullen, *Recollections*, p. 12.

40. Ibid. For an especially convincing discussion of the significance of Ballinamonabeg see Cullen, '1798 in Wexford', p. 291.

41. Hay, *Insurrection*, p. 81; Cullen, '1798 in Wexford', p. 294.

42. Kavanagh, *Popular History*, p. 101; Cullen, '1798 in Wexford', p. 293.

43. Cullen, *Recollections*, pp. 10–11.

44. Hay, *Insurrection*, p. 81.

45. Cullen, *Recollections*, pp. 12–13.

46. NAI, RP 620/37/177; Musgrave, *Rebellions*, i, p. 419; Hay, *Insurrection*, 81; Kavanagh, *Popular History*, p. 99.

47. Cullen, *Recollections*, p. 13.

48. Hay, *Insurrection*, p. 82; Kavanagh, *Popular History*, p. 291.

49. Cullen, *Recollections*, p. 14.

50. In the Camolin Cavalry Detail Book it is recorded that the weapons were 'distributed to improper persons' on 26–27 May (see Wheeler, *War*, p. 86). Kavanagh claims that the house was burned (*Popular History*, p. 302).

51. Edward Sinnott's whereabouts at this point and throughout the rising is a mystery.

52. Graham, 'Union of Power', p. 251.

53. Cullen, *Recollections*, p. 13; Musgrave, *Rebellions*, i, pp. 406, 414.

54. Wheeler, *War*, p. 83.

55. Musgrave, *Rebellions*, i, p. 405.

56. He was commander of the Scarawalsh infantry (see RIA, Haliday Pamphlets, no. 768, p. 88).

57. Wheeler, *War*, p. 83.

58. The logical place for a rendezvous would have been Solsborough, the residence of Solomon Richards, near which the road from The Harrow joined the road from Scarawalsh to Enniscorthy.

59. Musgrave, *Rebellions*, i, p. 409.

60. Wheeler, *War*, pp. 83–4. The entry in the Detail Book simply states that the rumours of attacks and killings were 'found to be true'.

61. Cullen, *Recollections*, pp. 9–10; Kavanagh, *Popular History*, pp. 97–9; Wheeler, *War*, pp. 83–4; Gordon, *Rebellion*, p. 89; Taylor, *Rebellion*, p. 26.

62. Jones, *Narrative*, p. 69; Hancock, *Principles*, p. 66.
63. Wheeler, *War*, p. 85; Gordon, *Rebellion*, p. 92; Taylor, *Rebellions*, p. 32.
64. Haughton Narrative, NLI, MS 1576; Wheeler, *War*, p. 86; Musgrave, *Rebellions*, i, pp. 405–6. Some rebel accounts suggest that the chapel was burned before the rising (see Cullen, *Recollections*, p. 9).
65. Byrne, *Memoirs*, i, p. 25.
66. Wheeler, *War*, pp. 85–6; Gordon, *Rebellion*, p. 89; Musgrave, *Rebellions*, i, p. 406; Kavanagh, *Popular History*, pp. 101–2.
67. Musgrave, *Rebellions*, p. 406; Taylor, *Rebellions*, p. 30.
68. Wheeler, *War*, p. 85.
69. Ibid., pp. 85–6.
70. Kavanagh, *Popular History*, p. 103; Taylor, *Rebellions*, p. 32; Gordon, *Rebellion*, p. 90.
71. Musgrave, *Rebellions*, ii, p. 339.
72. Kavanagh, *Popular History*, pp. 100–1; Musgrave, *Rebellions*, i, pp. 414–15; Taylor, *Rebellions*, p. 29; Gordon, *Rebellion*, p. 90.

Chapter 3: First Blood: 8 a.m.–midnight, 27 May (pp. 28–44)

1. Miles Byrne (who was not present) gives Murphy a very prominent role at this stage (see *Memoirs*, i, pp. 34–5), and Cullen's informant suggests that Morgan Byrne and Sparks carried much influence (see *Recollections* pp. 12–13).
2. Musgrave, *Rebellions*, i, pp. 414–15; Cullen, *Recollections*, pp. 12–13.
3. Cullen, *Recollections*, p. 13.
4. Musgrave, *Rebellions*, i, p. 415.
5. Ibid., pp. 415–16.
6. Ibid., p. 415.
7. Cullen, *Recollections*, p. 13; Gordon, *Rebellion*, p. 91.
8. Musgrave, *Rebellions*, i, pp. 416–17; ii, pp. 336–7; Taylor, *Rebellions*, p. 32.
9. It is difficult to tell the precise time of White's departure northward, but it seems likely that he was still only a few miles north of Oulart as late as 3 p.m. that afternoon.
10. Hay says he arrived 'early on this morning' (*Insurrection*, p. 81) and since he reported that attacks were already taking place around Newfort, this would suggest it was possibly as early as 6 a.m. but hardly later than 8 a.m.
11. Hay, *Insurrection*, p. 81.
12. Cullen, *Recollections*, p. 13.
13. Kavanagh, *Popular History*, p. 99; Musgrave, *Rebellions*, i, p. 419; Hay, *Insurrection*, p. 81; Wheeler, *War*, p. 165; Taylor, *Rebellions*, p. 33; Jones, *Narrative*, p. 70; Jackson, *Narrative*, p. 12.

14. Taylor, *Rebellions*, p. 33.
15. Jones, *Narrative*, p. 70.
16. There is no evidence for their precise route but this is the most likely one.
17. Taylor, *Rebellions*, p. 32.
18. Gordon, *Rebellion*, p. 90; Taylor, *Rebellions*, p. 32; Wheeler, *War*, pp. 85–6; Kavanagh, *Popular History*, pp. 101–4.
19. Dickson, *Wexford Rising*, p. 67.
20. There is at least no mention of them taking part in any other actions that day.
21. Wheeler, *War*, p. 86.
22. Cullen, *Recollections*, pp.13–14.
23. Ibid.; TCD, Cullen Manuscripts, MS 1472/1.
24. Hay, *Insurrection*, pp. 81–2; Croker, *Researches*, p. 348.
25. Wheeler, *War*, p. 165.
26. Hay, *Insurrection*, p. 84.
27. Ibid., p. 82.
28. Ibid.
29. See p. 22 above.
30. Cullen, *Recollections*, pp. 19–20.
31. Cullen claims 1,000 (*Recollections*, p. 14), while Kavanagh claims 3,000 (*Popular History*, p. 102).
32. Cullen, *Recollections*, p. 17; Kavanagh, *Popular History*, p. 104.
33. Cullen, *Popular History*, pp. 16–17.
34. Maxwell, *History*, p. 93.
35. Cullen, *Recollections*, p. 17.
36. For the best accounts of the battle see ibid., pp. 17–19; Kavanagh, *Popular History*, pp. 104–7; Hay, *Insurrection*, pp. 82–4; Jones, *Narrative*, pp. 70–2; Taylor, *Rebellions*, p. 33; Musgrave, *Rebellions*, i, pp. 420–1; Furlong, *Murphy*, pp. 58–9. Foote's own account is in NAI, RP 620/37/177.
37. Kavanagh, *Popular History*, p. 108. Cullen's informant claimed a rebel straggler wounded Le Hunte with a pike (*Recollections*, p. 20).
38. Hay, *Insurrection*, p. 84.
39. Dickson, *Wexford Rising*, p. 66.
40. Ibid., p. 91; Gordon, *Rebellion*, p. 92; Taylor, *Rebellions*, p. 34.
41. There is no mention of any disturbances in the accounts that have survived.
42. See pp. 33–4 above.
43. Handcock, *Principles of Peace*, p. 67.
44. Jackson, *Narrative*, p. 13; Wheeler, *War*, p. 86–7; Taylor, *Rebellions*, 34; Croker, *Researches*, p. 348.

45. Pakenham, *Year of Liberty*, pp. 158–68.
46. Dickson, *Revolt in the North*, pp. 123–4.

Chapter 4: The Battle for Enniscorthy: 28 May (pp. 45–58)
 1. Miles Byrne says they left at 7 a.m. (see *Memoirs*, p. 37).
 2. Byrne seems to have travelled south to join the rebels with a few
    comrades separately from other Monaseed recruits, and he may
    have caught up with the main army shortly after they left
    Camolin (see *Memoirs*, p. 32).
 3. Hay, *Insurrection*, p. 91; Gordon, *Rebellion*, p. 92; Furlong,
    Murphy, pp. 63–4.
 4. The number of guns captured at Camolin Park is uncertain.
    According to the Camolin Cavalry Detail Book, barely more
    than a hundred were stored there for the purposes of supplying
    the yeomanry (see Wheeler, *War*, p. 81), but there are claims
    that they seized as many as 800 firearms (see Cullen, '1798 in
    Wexford', p. 290).
 5. According to Snowe, this retreat took place on the day before
    (see Snowe, *Statement*, p. 5).
 6. See NAI, SOC 30/191 for an example of his alarmist reports to
    Dublin Castle before the rebellion broke out.
 7. Pakenham, *Year of Liberty*, p. 155. There is one claim that some of them
    defecated in the palace (see 'Notes on Joly Copy of Hay', NLI, MS).
 8. Handcock, *Principles of Peace*, pp. 63–4.
 9. Byrne, *Memoirs*, i, pp. 37–8; Handcock, *Principles of Peace*, pp.
    68–9; Jones, *Narrative*, p. 72; Snowe, *Statement*, p. 5; Dickson,
    Wexford Rising, pp. 68–9. For other information on Quaker
    experiences in the rebellion in Wexford see Jacob Poole's
    Journal, NLI MS 8737(3); Haughton Narrative, NLI MS 1576.
10. Handcock, *Principles of Peace*, pp. 68–9.
11. Kavanagh, *Popular History*, pp. 108–9; Dickson, *Wexford Rising*, p. 69.
12. There is some evidence of a rebel concentration at Ballyorril for
    a day or so before this (see Lett, 'Diary', p. 119), but it seems that
    units from more northerly parts of the county came to the hill
    only at this time (see Byrne, *Memoirs*, i, p. 38).
13. There is no concrete evidence of this, but the movements of the
    rebel forces up to this point suggest it.
14. NAI, RP 620/37/234; Byrne, *Memoirs*, i, p. 42. Philip Hay later
    claimed they numbered 10,000 or 12,000 by this stage (see NAI,
    RP 620/56/98).
15. Snowe, *Statement*, pp. 5–6; Musgrave, *Rebellions*, i, 428–31.
16. Hay, *Insurrection*, p. 90.

17. Their subsequent behaviour suggests this (see p. 54 below).
18. This is obvious in Snowe's own account (see *Statement*, p. 6).
19. Ibid., p. 8.
20. Ibid., pp. 7–9.
21. Byrne, *Memoirs*, i, pp. 42–3. No account of the battle actually mentions the leaders conferring on this strategy, but the circumstances of their battle strongly suggest they did.
22. Musgrave, *Rebellions*, i, pp. 432–3.
23. NAI, RP 620/56/98; Byrne, *Memoirs*, i, p. 43.
24. Jones, *Narrative*, pp. 73–4.
25. Ibid., pp. 74–5; Snowe, *Statement*, pp. 8–9.
26. Jones, *Narrative*, p. 76.
27. Ibid., pp. 76–7; Dickson, *Wexford Rising*, p. 72.
28. Jones, *Narrative*, pp. 77–8; Gordon, *Rebellion*, pp. 93–5.
29. Musgrave, *Rebellions*, i, pp. 435–6.
30. Gordon, *Rebellion*, pp. 94–5; see also NLI, MS 25004; NAI, RP 620/56/98; Furlong, *Murphy*, pp. 67–8.
31. Snowe, *Statement*, pp. 12–14; Gordon, *Rebellion*, p. 95; Jones, *Narrative*, p. 78; Musgrave, *Rebellion*, i, p. 438; Hay, *Insurrection*, p. 93.
32. Jackson, *Narrative*, p, 14. Hay claims that Archibald Jacob fled the town early in the battle (see *Insurrection*, p. 93).
33. Snowe, *Statement* pp. 13–14; Gordon, *Rebellion*, pp. 95–6; Musgrave, *Rebellions*, i, pp. 438–9; Jackson, *Narrative*, p. 14; Byrne, *Memoirs*, i, p. 44.
34. Byrne, *Memoirs*, pp. 45–6; Kavanagh, *Popular History*, pp. 114–15.
35. See NAI, RP 620/6/70/28; TCD, Madden MS 873, f 804; DDA, Caulfield–Troy Correspondence, 30 Sept., 7 Oct., 1799; Barber Recollections, p. 9.
36 Lett, 'Diary', pp. 120–2.
37. The best summaries of the battle are in NLI, MS 25004; Jones, *Narrative*, pp. 72–7; Taylor, *Rebellions*, pp. 37–8; Lett, 'Diary', pp. 120–1; Barber Recollections, pp. 5–8; Musgrave, *Rebellions*, i, pp. 439–41; ii, pp. 343, 346–7; Dickson, *Wexford Rising*, pp. 73–4.
38. Enniscorthy had several prominent United Irish officers (see p. 60), and the cabin-burning and subsequent developments indicate that the town's population in general was sympathetic to the rebel cause.
39. Musgrave, *Rebellions*, i, p. 488.
40. See NAI, RP 620/56/98; Musgrave claims 500 rebels were killed (see *Rebellions*, i, p. 437).
41. NAI, RP 620/56/98; Musgrave, *Rebellions*, i, p. 441.
42. Byrne, *Memoirs*, i, p. 45.

43. Hay, *Insurrection*, pp. 95–6, 99; Musgrave, *Rebellions*, i, p. 476.
44. Jackson, *Narrative*, p. 13.
45. Byrne claims 100 dead on each side (*Memoirs*, i, pp. 45–6), but Musgrave (*Rebellions*, i, p. 437) claims 74 troops and over 500 rebels.
46. Hay, *Insurrection*, p. 95.
47. See p. 2 above.
48. Hay, *Insurrection*, p. 95; Jackson, *Narrative*, p. 15.
49. Jackson, *Narrative*, p. 15.
50. Wheeler, *War*, pp. 86–7.
51. Ibid., p. 87; Gordon, *Rebellion*, pp. 103–5.
52. For biographical details on Perry see Dickson, *Wexford Rising*, p. 194. On Garrett and William Michael Byrne see TCD, Madden MS 873, ff. 304–7.
53. There is no direct reference to rebel mobilisation in northern parishes on this date, but the arrival of bands from the borderland area in the camp the next day suggests that it was taking place on the 27th (see p. 59 below).
54. Cloney, *Narrative*, pp. 15–16, 238. Furlong concludes that Kearns most likely joined at Ballyorrill Hill that morning (see *Murphy*, p. 66).
55. Given the strong liberal tradition of this area and its close connections to the political wing of the United Irishmen, it is more likely that there was confusion between political and military figures here than anywhere else in the county (see Cullen, '1798 in Wexford', pp. 281–2).
56. See p. 83 below.
57. Alexander, *Narrative*, pp. 30–1.
58. Ibid., p. 30.

Chapter 5: The Road to Wexford Town: 29 May (pp. 59–69)

1. Byrne, *Memoirs*, i, p. 47; Kavanagh, *Popular History*, p. 115.
2. Cloney, *Narrative*, pp. 238.
3. Ibid., pp. 238–9, 268.
4. See Dickson, *Wexford Rising*, pp. 198–203.
5. Cloney, *Narrative*, pp. 16–17, 239–41; Byrne, *Memoirs*, i, pp. 47–8; Dickson, *Wexford Rising*, p. 75.
6. Byrne, *Memoirs*, i, p. 46; Maxwell, *History*, p. 97.
7. See p. 4 above.
8. Byrne, *Memoirs*, i, pp. 48–9.
9. Ibid., pp. 53–4.
10. Hay, *Insurrection*, p. 100–1; Dickson, *Wexford Rising*, pp. 76–8.
11. Musgrave, *Rebellions*, i, pp. 445–9.
12. TCD, Madden MS 873, f. 802; Cloney, *Narrative*, p. 239.

13. Cloney, *Narrative*, pp. 239–41; NLI, MS 25004.
14. Byrne, *Memoirs*, i, pp. 48–9, 53; Hay, *Insurrection*, p. 101; Kavanagh, *Popular History*, p. 115; Dickson, *Wexford Rising*, p. 76.
15. Graham, 'Union of Power', p. 251.
16. Hay, *Insurrection*, p. 101.
17. Byrne, *Memoirs*, i, pp. 52–3.
18. Hay, *Insurrection*, pp. 96–7; Wheeler, *War*, p. 167; Jackson, *Narrative*, p. 15; Taylor, *Rebellions*, p. 39; Gordon, *Rebellion*, p. 99; Musgrave, *Rebellions*, i, p. 472.
19. Hay, *Insurrection*, p. 96.
20. Ibid.
21. Wheeler, *War*, pp. 166–7; Hay, *Insurrection*, pp. 96–7.
22. Hay, *Insurrection*, p. 97; Jackson, *Narrative*, p. 15. For evidence of the cost to individuals of the destruction of cabins near the wall see NAI, RP 620/61/69.
23. Hay, *Insurrection*, p. 97.
24. Ibid., pp. 103–4; Wheeler, *War*, p. 167.
25. Hay, *Insurrection*, p. 97.
26. Cullen, '1798 in Wexford', p. 261.
27. Hay, *Insurrection*, pp. 97–8.
28. Ibid., p. 98.
29. Ibid., pp. 98–9; Taylor, *Rebellions*, p. 38; Gordon, *Rebellion*, pp. 97–8.
30. Cloney, *Narrative*, pp. 18–9; Byrne, *Memoirs*, i, p. 53; Hay, *Insurrection*, pp. 101–2; Kavanagh, *Popular History*, p. 115.
31. Byrne suggests he was not a hostage, but his behaviour subsequently and the attitude of rank-and-file rebels to him indicates that he had become alienated at this stage (see *Memoirs*, pp. 53–4).
32. Hay, *Insurrection*, pp. 102–3.
33. Byrne, *Rebellions*, i, p. 46.
34. No source mentions any concentration of them here.
35. Cloney, *Narrative*, p. 20; Byrne, *Memoirs*, i, p. 54; Kavanagh, *Popular History*, pp. 115–17. William Barker took command of the camp on Vineger Hill (see Furlong, *Murphy*, p. 74).
36. Wheeler, *War*, p. 167.
37. Ibid., p. 94.
38. Gordon, *Rebellion*, p. 106.
39. Alexander, *Narrative*, pp. 30–1.
40. Pakenham, *Year of Liberty*, pp. 163–4.
41. Hay, *Insurrection*, p. 105; Gordon, *Rebellion*, p. 99; Musgrave, *Rebellions*, i, pp. 472–3.

42. Hay, *Insurrection*, pp. 105–6; Gordon, *Rebellion*, p. 100; Musgrave, *Rebellions*, i, p. 473.

Chapter 6: Ruse de Guerre: 30 May (pp. 70–85)

1. It is unclear how much daylight had come in at this stage, but the column appears to have approached the hill before sunrise, as it was still dark when they passed through Taghmon.
2. Dickson, *Wexford Rising*, p. 80.
3. The distribution of the rebel units on the mountain is not specified in any source, but given that their main concern was Wexford town, this is likely to have been their pattern of encampment.
4. Taylor, *Rebellions*, p. 39; Musgrave, *Rebellions*, i, p. 472.
5. Cloney, pp. 20–1. Here Cloney suggests that none of the officers wanted to take responsibility, but given his tendency to deny the existence of an organised United Irish movement in the county, this can be dismissed as a falsehood (see Cullen, '1798 in Wexford', p. 256).
6. Cloney, *Narrative*, p. 21.
7. Hay, *Insurrection*, p. 105.
8. Cloney, *Narrative*, pp. 21–2; Hay, *Insurrection*, pp. 105–6; Byrne, *Memoirs*, i, pp. 55–6; Musgrave, *Rebellions*, i, pp. 473–4; Taylor, *Rebellions*, pp. 39–40; Kavanagh, *Popular History*, p. 117. For Fawcett's own account see NAI, RP 620/38/11, and for Maxwell's see PRO, HO 100/77/29–32.
9. Musgrave, *Rebellions*, i, p. 475. For reaction of a fellow-officer in Cork at the time see NAI, RP 620/37/234).
10. Taylor, *Rebellions*, p. 38.
11. Hay, *Insurrection*, p. 107; Jackson, *Narrative*, p. 17; Byrne, *Memoirs*, i, p. 56; Dickson, *Wexford Rising*, p. 228.
12. Since he lived in John Street, Dick Monk probably did not see the attack on the bridge, but Keogh, a Protestant and a resident of George's Street, was likely to have witnessed it.
13. Hay, *Insurrection*, p. 106.
14. Cloney, *Narrative*, p. 22.
15. Dickson, *Wexford Rising*, p. 82.
16. The rebel units on the summit of Forth Mountain may have seen them earlier than this, but the units at the foot of the hill could not have done so.
17. PRO, HO 100/77/29–32; Cloney, *Narrative*, p. 23; ; Byrne, *Memoirs*, i, p. 56; Taylor, *Rebellions*, p. 46; Gordon, *Rebellion*, pp. 100–1; Musgrave, *Rebellions*, i, p. 476; Kavanagh, *Popular History*, pp. 125–6; Dickson, *Wexford Rising*, pp. 82, 228–9.

18. Hay, *Insurrection*, p. 107.
19. Ibid., p. 117.
20. Cloney does say that he approached Fitzgerald for advice just before the attack on the Meath militia (see *Narrative*, p. 20–1).
21. Hay, *Insurrection*, p. 118.
22. Snowe, *Statement*, pp. 16–17; Gordon, *Rebellion*, p. 101.
23. In his own account of the day he asserts that he was not (see PRO, HO 100/77/29–32).
24. PRO, HO 100/77/29–32; Hay, *Insurrection*, pp. 107–8; Musgrave, *Rebellion*, i, pp. 478–9.
25. Hay, *Insurrection*, p. 108.
26. Ibid., pp. 108–9; Taylor, *Rebellions*, p. 41; Gordon, *Rebellion*, pp. 101–2; Jackson, *Narrative*, p. 16; Dickson, *Wexford Rising*, p. 83.
27. Hay, *Insurrection*, pp. 109–10; Musgrave, *Rebellions*, i, p. 481.
28. Byrne, *Memoirs*, i, p. 57; Cloney, *Narrative*, pp. 23–4; Taylor, *Rebellions*, p. 41; Gordon, *Rebellion*, p. 102; Jackson, *Narrative*, p. 16; Dickson, *Wexford Rising*, p. 229.
29. Cloney, *Narrative*, p. 24.
30. Hay, *Insurrection*, p. 111; Byrne, *Memoirs*, i, p. 57; Cloney, *Narrative*, pp. 23–4.
31. Hay, *Insurrection*, p. 118.
32. Snowe does not mention encountering any problems (see *Statement*, pp. 16–17).
33. Taylor, *Rebellions*, pp. 41–2; Hay, *Insurrection*, p. 111.
34. Hay, *Insurrection*, pp. 111–12.
35. Ibid., pp. 112–13; Cloney, *Narrative*, p. 24; Taylor, *Rebellions*, p. 24; Kavanagh, *Popular History*, p. 130. Jones claims they did a great deal of damage (see *Narrative*, p. 59).
36. Jackson, *Narrative*, p. 17; Dickson, *Wexford Rising*, p. 229.
37. Byrne, *Memoirs*, i, pp. 58–9; Cloney, *Narrative*, pp. 24–5.
38. Jackson, *Narrative*, pp. 20–1.
39. Byrne, *Memoirs*, i, p. 59; Taylor, *Rebellions*, p. 42; Gordon, *Rebellion*, p. 102; Jackson, *Narrative*, p. 18.
40. Jackson, *Narrative*, pp. 20–1; Dickson, *Wexford Rising*, p. 88.
41. Cloney, *Narrative*, p. 24.
42. Snowe, *Statement*, pp. 16–18.
43. Musgrave, *Rebellions*, i, p. 482; Gordon, *Rebellion*, p. 102; Hay, *Insurrection*, p. 120.
44. Hay, *Insurrection*, pp. 120–1.
45. Musgrave, *Rebellions*, i, pp. 482–3.
46. Byrne, *Memoirs*, i, pp. 58–9; Cloney, *Narrative*, p. 22; Jackson, *Narrative*, p. 16.

47. Hay, *Insurrection*, pp. 114–15; Taylor, *Rebellions*, p. 42; Kavanagh, *Popular History*, p. 130. Dickson claims that this happened on 4 June (see *Wexford Rising*, p. 88).
48 Alexander, *Narrative*, pp. 31–2.
49. Wheeler, *War*, pp. 94–5.
50. Hay, *Insurrection*, p. 121.

Chapter 7: First Reverses: 31 May – 1 June (pp. 86–100)
 1 Hay, *Insurrection*, p. 121.
  2. Byrne, *Memoirs*, i, p. 59; Hay, *Insurrection*, p. 121; Lecky, *Ireland*, iv, p. 367; Dickson, *Wexford Rising*, p. 89.
  3. Byrne, *Memoirs*, i, p. 62; Hay, *Insurrection*, p. 130; Lecky, *Ireland*, iv, p. 372.
  4. Hay, *Insurrection*, p. 121.
  5. No source specifically mentions Colclough's departure from Barrystown or arrival in Wexford, but he seems to have been in the town by that afternoon.
  6. Byrne, *Memoirs*, i, p. 59; Hay, *Insurrection*, p. 121; Kavanagh, *Popular History*, p. 131.
  7. Musgrave, *Rebellions*, i, p. 485; Taylor, *Rebellions*, pp. 42–3; Dickson, *Wexford Rising*, p. 90.
  8. Furlong has continued the tradition of regarding Father John Murphy as the commander of the northern army (see *Murphy*, pp. 91–2), but there is evidence from contemporary sources that Edward Roche was its general (see NAI, RP 620/39/184, 620/56/98).
  9. Cloney, *Narrative*, pp. 29–30; Byrne, *Memoirs*, i, pp. 59–60; Lecky, Ireland, iv, p. 369; Dickson, *Wexford Rising*, pp. 89–90. See also Furlong, *Murphy*, pp. 87–90, for a vivid reconstruction of these debates.
10. Byrne, *Memoirs*, i, p. 62; Hay, *Insurrection*, pp. 124–5; Lecky, *Ireland*, iv, p. 368.
11. Pakenham has nonetheless chosen to use this term (see *Year of Liberty*, p. 276).
12. There is no mention in any source of any form of government being established for the county *per se*. It seems reasonable to conclude, therefore, that the camps were *de facto* seats of government for all but Wexford town.
13. Byrne, *Memoirs*, i, p. 65; Cloney, *Narrative*, p. 29; Taylor, *Rebellions*, pp. 43–4; Hay, *Insurrection*, p. 122; Musgrave, *Rebellions*, i, p. 489; Kavanagh, *Popular History*, pp. 132–3.
14. Hay, *Insurrection*, pp. 125–6.
15. Cloney, *Narrative*, p. 30.

16. Hay, *Insurrection*, p. 122; Byrne, *Memoirs*, i, p. 63; Cloney, *Narrative*, p. 29; Taylor, *Rebellions*, p. 43; Kavanagh, *Popular History*, p. 132.
17. Alexander, *Narrative*, p. 32.
18. Musgrave, *Rebellions*, i, p. 486 .
19. Pakenham, *Year of Liberty*, p. 180.
20. Ibid., pp. 180–1.
21. Gordon, *Rebellion*, p. 114; Musgrave, *Rebellions*, i, p. 489.
22. Pakenham, *Year of Liberty*, p. 181.
23. Musgrave, *Rebellion*, i, p. 489.
24. Walpole reached Carnew on 2 June, suggesting that he was in south Kildare a day earlier (see Musgrave, *Rebellions*, i, p. 490).
25. Musgrave, *Rebellions*, i, p. 486.
26. Wheeler, *War*, pp. 100–1.
27. On Lake's mood at this point see PRO, HO 100/77/3.
28. Express riders could probably have covered the distance from Dublin to Arklow in a day with ease (see p. 120 for an example).
29. Wheeler, *War*, p. 103.
30. Byrne, *Memoirs*, i, p. 64.
31. Musgrave, *Rebellions*, i, p. 486.
32. Ibid., p. 487; Taylor, *Rebellions*, p. 45.
33. Byrne, *Memoirs*, i, p. 64.
34. Ibid., pp. 64–5; Gordon, *Rebellion*, pp. 108–9; Taylor, *Rebellions*, p. 45; Musgrave, *Rebellions*, i, pp. 486–7.
35. Byrne, *Memoirs*, i, pp. 65–6; Gordon, *Rebellion*, p. 109; Taylor, *Rebellions*, p. 96.
36. Byrne, *Memoirs*, i, p. 67.
37. Hay, *Insurrection*, p. 138. Perry had joined the camp that morning (see Furlong, *Murphy*, p. 94).
38. Hay, *Insurrection*, p. 138.
39. Wheeler, *War*, pp. 104–5.
40. Ibid., p. 105.
41. Ibid., pp. 105–6; Gordon, *Rebellion*, pp. 111–13; Taylor, *Rebellions*, pp. 47–8; Musgrave, *Rebellions*, i, pp. 488–9; Hay, *Insurrection*, pp. 138–9; Lecky, *Ireland*, iv, p. 384; Dickson, *Wexford Rising*, pp. 98–100.
42. Cloney, *Narrative*, p. 30.
43. Hay, *Insurrection*, pp. 140–2; Taylor, *Rebellions*, p. 43.
44. Wheeler, *War*, p. 106.
45. Castle officials learned that reinforcements would soon be on their way from England at about this point (see Camden to Portland, 1 June 1798, PRO, HO 100/77/1, 2, 5–7).
46. NLI, La Touche Papers, MS 3151, pp. 27–8.
47. Lake to Camden, 1 June 1798, PRO, HO 100/77/3.

48. Hay, *Insurrection*, pp. 130–1.
49. Byrne, *Memoirs*, i, pp. 61–2.
50. Hay, *Insurrection*, pp. 130–2; Whelan, 'Wexford Republic', pp. 19–22.
51. Byrne, *Memoirs*, i, p. 60; Lecky, *Ireland*, iv, p. 372.
52. Hay, *Insurrection*, p. 125.
53. Byrne, *Memoirs*, i, p. 61
54. Barber Recollections, pp. 13–15.
55. Richards Diary, pp. 16–17.

Chapter 8: Walpole's Horse and Walpole's Foot: 2–4 June (pp. 101–120)
1. Musgrave, *Rebellions*, i, pp. 489–90.
2. Ibid., p. 490; Gordon, *Rebellion*, p. 114.
3. Musgrave, *Rebellions*, p. 492.
4. Alexander, *Narrative*, pp. 35–8.
5. Ibid., p. 38.
6. Byrne, *Memoirs*, i, p. 67.
7. Alexander mentions a small uprising near Glenmore around this time (see *Narrative*, pp. 35–6).
8. Hay, *Insurrection*, p. 141.
9. Ibid., pp. 141–2.
10. PRO, HO 100/77/21–2.
11. PRO, HO 100/77/19.
12. PRO, HO 100/77/13–16.
13. The exact campsite is unknown, but they were very close to the town early the next morning (see Alexander, *Narrative*, p. 37).
14. Musgrave, *Rebellions*, i, p. 490–1.
15. Cloney, *Narrative*, p. 33.
16. Byrne, *Memoirs*, i, p. 68.
17. Ibid., pp. 68–9.
18. Alexander, *Narrative*, pp. 38–40; Musgrave, *Rebellions*, i, p. 491.
19. Musgrave, *Rebellions*, i, p. 490.
20. Ibid., pp. 490–1.
21. Wheeler, *War*, p. 108.
22. Ibid., pp. 108–9.
23. Byrne, *Memoirs*, i, pp. 68–72.
24. Musgrave, *Rebellions*, i, p. 492; Dickson, *Wexford Rising*, pp. 237–40.
25. Musgrave, *Rebellions*, i, pp. 491–2. For evidence of Camden's confidence that night see PRO, HO 100/77/25–8.
26. Byrne, *Memoirs*, i, p. 72; Gordon, *Rebellion*, p. 114; Wheeler, *War*, pp. 109–10. Richard Donovan, the proprietor of Ballymore House, claimed £75 in compensation for damage done by the

rebels after the rising, but received only £31 (see NLI, Ainsworth MS 98, p. 984).

27. Hay, *Insurrection*, p. 142.
28. Ibid., pp. 143–5; Jackson, *Narrative*, p. 27.
29. Hay, *Insurrection*, pp. 145–6; Jackson, *Narrative*, p. 27.
30. Byrne, *Memoirs*, i, p. 72; Gordon, *Rebellion*, p. 114.
31. Rebel units were still forming in Wexford town for the attack on New Ross late on the 3rd (see Wheeler, *War*, pp. 357–8).
32. Musgrave, *Rebellions*, i, pp. 492–3.
33. Byrne claims they had no videttes out (see *Memoirs*, i, p. 73), but Dickson's source claims otherwise (see *Wexford Rising*, p. 103), as does Maxwell's (see *Rebellion*, i, pp. 110–11).
34. Musgrave, *Rebellions*, i, p. 493; Maxwell, *Rebellion*, p. 109.
35. Maxwell, *Rebellion*, pp. 109–10; Musgrave, *Rebellions*, i, pp. 493–4.
36. Jones, *Narrative*, pp. 91–2; Musgrave, *Rebellions*, i, p. 494; Maxwell, *Rebellion*, p. 110. Miles Byrne (*Memoirs*, i, p. 73) was with the rebel vanguard of 300 men and claims that they encountered Walpole's column already drawn up to meet them at a turn in the road; however, it is likely that Byrne was not aware that smaller rebel parties were already in places like the rock, and that he was mistaken in claiming that Walpole was not actually ambushed.
37. Musgrave, *Rebellions*, i, p. 493.
38. Maxwell, *Rebellion*, p. 110.
39. The best accounts of the battle itself are Byrne, *Memoirs*, i, p. 73; Maxwell, *Rebellion*, pp. 110–12; Gordon, *Rebellion*, pp. 114–15; Musgrave, *Rebellions*, i, pp. 493–6; Jones, *Narrative*, pp. 91–4; Wheeler, *War*, p. 110; Dickson, *Wexford Rising*, pp. 237–8, 240; Furlong, *Murphy*, pp. 97–100.
40. For Loftus's own version see NAI, RP 620/38/49.
41. Gordon, *Rebellion*, pp. 115–16; Musgrave, *Rebellions*, i, p.496; Dickson, *Wexford Rising*, p. 240.
42. Byrne, *Memoirs*, i, pp. 75–6; Musgrave, *Rebellions*, i, pp. 496–7; Wheeler, *War*, pp. 110–11; Jones, *Narrative*, p. 93.
43. Byrne, *Memoirs*, i, p. 76.
44. Ibid., pp. 76–7; Musgrave, *Rebellions*, i, pp. 498–500.
45. Hay, *Insurrection*, p. 148; Cloney, *Narrative*, p. 33; Dickson, *Wexford Rising*, pp. 109–10.
46. Musgrave, *Rebellions*, i, p. 503; Hay, *Insurrection*, pp. 148–9.
47. Alexander gives a very vivid account of the confusion between the two front lines that evening (see *Narrative*, pp. 48–53).
48. Wheeler, *War*, p. 111; Gordon, *Rebellion*, pp. 125–6.
49. Gordon, *Rebellion*, p. 116.
50. Whelan, 'Religious Factor', p. 73. Musgrave (*Rebellions*, i, p. 517)

and Taylor (*Rebellions*, p. 52) claim that the round-up of Protestants began on 1 June.

51. Maxwell, *Rebellion*, p. 112 For despondent reaction to Walpole's death in the Castle see PRO, HO 100/77/33, 35, 36.
52. PRO, HO 100/77/39–42.

Chapter 9: The Gateways of Ross: 5–6 June (pp. 121–142)

1. Musgrave claims that 30,000 rebels attacked New Ross (*Rebellion*, i, p. 505), but Dickson claims that the total rebel numbers in County Wexford could not have exceeded 30,000 (*Wexford Rising*, p. 34).
2. Cloney, *Narrative*, p. 44; Musgrave, *Rebellions*, i, p. 526.
3. Hay, *Insurrection*, p. 149; Cloney, *Narrative*, pp. 33–4.
4. Alexander, *Narrative*, p. 70; Musgrave, *Rebellions*, i, pp. 504–5; Cloney, *Narrative*, pp. 34–5; Hay, *Insurrection*, pp. 149–50.
5. There is no record of their strategic discussions, but from the circumstances it seems very likely that this formation was agreed upon beforehand.
6. Cloney, *Narrative*, p. 35.
7. Alexander, *Narrative*, pp. 89–90; Musgrave, *Rebellions*, i, pp. 511–12.
8. Alexander, *Narrative*, pp. 69–70.
9. Ibid., pp. 41–6.
10. The withdrawal of Colclough and his units is alluded to only indirectly by both Cloney and Hay, perhaps out of respect for the Colclough name at the time of their writing, but there is little doubt that he and his men did abandon the battle at its outset (see Hay, *Insurrection*, pp. 150–1; Cloney, *Narrative*, p. 37).
11. Alexander, *Narrative*, pp. 70–1; Hay, *Insurrection*, pp. 150–1; Cloney, *Narrative*, pp. 35–8.
12. Alexander, *Narrative*, p. 72; Cloney, *Narrative*, p. 38; Hay, *Insurrection*, p. 151.
13. Cloney, *Narrative*, p. 37; Musgrave *Rebellions*, i, pp. 505–6.
14. Cloney, *Narrative*, pp. 37–8.
15. Alexander, *Narrative*, pp. 73–6; Cloney, *Narrative*, pp. 38–9; Hay, *Insurrection*, pp. 151–2.
16. Cloney, *Narrative*, p. 39.
17. Alexander, *Narrative*, p. 74.
18. Musgrave, *Rebellions*, i, p. 507; Cloney, *Narrative*, p. 38; Alexander, *Narrative*, pp. 74–5.
19. Alexander, *Narrative*, pp. 75–6; Musgrave, *Rebellions*, i, p. 507.
20. Dickson, *Wexford Rising*, p. 113; Vesey to Camden, 5 June 1798 PRO, HO 100/77/82–3.

21. Alexander, *Narrative*, pp. 79–80; Musgrave, *Rebellions*, i, p. 507; Cloney, *Narrative*, pp. 38–9.
22. Alexander, *Narrative*, p. 80.
23. Ibid., p. 56.
24. Ibid., p. 76.
25. Ibid., p. 60. The fighting in South Street does not seem to have been nearly as intense as in the streets near the esatern wall of the town.
26. Ibid., pp. 55–6.
27. Neville Steet has a sharp hill near its northern end which would have hidden most of it from anyone stationed at the gate.
28. From Alexander's account, it seems that large areas of the town caught fire in a short period of time (see *Narrative*, pp. 75–6).
29. Cloney, *Narrative*, p. 39.
30. Alexander noticed how ineffective their powder was when he observed them firing in Mary Street (see *Narrative*, p. 56).
31. Musgrave, *Rebellions*, i, pp. 511–12.
32. Cloney, *Narrative*, p. 39.
33. Musgrave, *Rebellions*, i, p. 508; Alexander, *Narrative*, p. 80.
34. Alexander describes this post as a rebel strongpoint, held by men firing from its windows (see *Narrative*, pp. 81–2), but in other sources it is described as a hospital (see Cloney, *Narrative*, p. 44), which is a more plausible use.
35. Alexander, *Narrative*, pp. 80–1.
36. Cloney says: 'It was quite disheartening to behold the smallness of our numbers, yet the few who remained seemed to prefer death to the abandonment of a victory' (see *Narrative*, p. 40).
37. The timing of the counter-attack is uncertain, but considering the speed with which Johnson appears to have retaken the town and the time at which the fighting ended, noon or at most an hour or so afterwards would seem the most likely time.
38. Cloney, *Narrative*, p. 40; Hay, *Insurrection*, p. 154.
39. Alexander, *Narrative*, p. 82.
40. Ibid., pp. 84–5; Cloney, *Narrative*, p. 40; Hay, *Insurrection*, p. 152.
41. Hay, *Insurrection*, p. 154.
42. Cloney, *Narrative*, p. 40.
43. Ibid.
44. Musgrave, *Rebellions*, i, p. 510–11.
45. This may even be an exaggeration, as Cloney could barely get forty men for his last attack (see *Narrative*, p. 40).
46. The total death toll may include many non-combatants and has been estimated to have been as high as 2,000 on the 'rebel' side

(see Hay, *Insurrection*, p. 154–5; Alexander, *Narrative* , pp. 85–6).

47. Alexander, *Narrative*, p. 85.
48 Cloney, *Narrative*, pp. 41–3.
49. Ibid., p. 158; Gordon, *Rebellion*, p. 121; Dickson, *Wexford Rising*, p. 120.
50. The timing is important. If the massacre took place at 9 a.m. (see Dickson, *Wexford Rising*, p. 120), then it probably preceded the worst of the government atrocities at New Ross, including the burning of the hospital. If it took place later, then it followed them.
51. For details of massacre see NLI, Court Martial Papers, MS 17795 (1–7); TCD, Madden Papers, MS 873, f. 451; NLI, Musgrave Papers, MS 4156; Musgrave, *Rebellions*, i, pp. 525–7.
52. Cloney, *Narrative*, p. 44; Hay, *Insurrection*, pp. 156–8.
53. Richards Diary, pp. 19–20. Jackson does not seem to have heard the news on the 5th (see *Narrative*, p. 31).
54. Alexander, *Narrative*, pp. 90–2.
55. Cloney, *Narrative*, p. 43.
56. Byrne, *Memoirs*, i, p. 84.
57. Ibid., pp. 84–5.
58. Ibid., p. 94.
59. Taylor, *Rebellions*, p. 52.
60. Gordon, *Rebellion*, p. 127; Wheeler, *War*, p. 111.
61. Wheeler, *War*, pp. 111–12; see also PRO, HO 100/77/44–6.
62. Taylor, *Rebellions*, p. 51; Gordon, *Rebellion*, p. 116; Dickson, *Wexford Rising*, p. 238. For details of troop strength in the various garrisons see PRO, HO 100/77/52–3.
63. Hay, *Insurrection*, p. 180; Wheeler, *War*, p. 116; Musgrave, *Rebellions*, pp. 538–9; Gordon, *Rebellion*, p. 127.
64. Byrne, *Memoirs*, i, pp. 85–6.
65. Hay, *Insurrection*, pp. 159–61; Cloney, *Narrative*, pp. 44–5; Musgrave, *Rebellions*, i, p. 532.
66. PRO, HO 100/74/6, 100/77/50–1.
67. Alexander, *Narrative*, pp. 92–3.
68. Ibid., pp. 96–9 .
69. PRO, HO 100/77/52–3, 54, 66–70, 72.

Chapter 10: A Forest of Pikes: 7–9 June (pp. 143–161)
  1. No source provides the details of this transfer of power, but Roche's activities then and in subsequent days suggest that he had effectively become commander-in-chief.
  2. Byrne, *Memoirs*, i, p. 94; Musgrave, *Rebellions*, i, p. 533. Furlong (see *Murphy*, pp. 108–10) regards Roche as less important than this.

3. Hay, *Insurrection*, pp. 162–3; Dunne, 'Popular Ballads', p. 151.

4. Cloney, *Narrative*, p. 45.

5. Jackson, *Narrative*, pp. 31–2.

6. Byrne, *Memoirs*, i, pp. 86–7.

7. Ibid., pp. 88–90.

8. Ibid., pp. 91–3. Furlong (*Murphy*, p. 106) claims that a bitter dispute broke out between Father John Murphy and Father Michael Murphy at this point.

9. Alexander, *Narrative*, pp. 97–9.

10. Musgrave, *Rebellions*, i, p. 539; Wheeler, *War*, pp. 116–17.

11. Gordon, *Rebellion*, pp. 127–8.

12. Dickson, *Wexford Rising*, pp. 240–1.

13. PRO, HO 100/77/52–3.

14. Byrne, *Memoirs*, i, pp. 89–90.

15. Ibid., pp. 93–5; Hay, *Insurrection*, pp. 179–80.

16. Musgrave, *Rebellions*, ii, pp. 398–9; Taylor, *Rebellions*, pp. 176–8.

17. Furlong, *Murphy*, p. 113.

18. Byrne, *Memoirs*, i, pp. 93–4.

19. Hay, *Insurrection*, p. 180; Wheeler, *War*, pp. 117–18; Musgrave, *Rebellions*, i, p. 539; Gordon, *Rebellion*, pp. 27–9; Dickson, *Wexford Rising*, pp. 241–2.

20. Alexander, *Narrative*, p. 99.

21. Pakenham, *Year of Liberty*, p. 216.

22. Taylor, *Rebellions*, p. 88; Byrne, *Memoirs*, i, pp. 98–9.

23. Cullen, *Recollections*, p. 23.

24. Several sources suggest that he remained in Castletown (see Taylor, *Rebellions*, p. 97; Kavanagh, *Popular History*, p. 186; Furlong, *Murphy*, pp. 113, 188), but Miles Byrne claims that he was at Arklow and played a prominent role; his account, I think, suggests that Murphy arrived later and was greeted with enthusiasm by the ranks (see *Memoirs*, i, p. 102).

25. Cullen, *Recollections*, pp. 22–3, 25–7; Byrne, *Memoirs*, i, p. 99; Dickson, *Wexford Rising*, p. 134.

26. Wheeler, *War*, p. 119.

27. Ibid., pp. 118–19; Gordon, *Rebellion*, p. 129; Musgrave, *Rebellions*, i, pp. 541–2; Byrne, *Memoirs*, i, pp. 130–1; Dickson, *Wexford Rising*, p. 241.

28. Cullen, *Recollections*, pp. 23–4.

29. Byrne, *Memoirs*, i, pp. 99–100.

30. Ibid., p. 99; Musgrave, *Rebellions*, i, p. 545.

31. Byrne, *Memoirs*, i, pp. 99, 104. Cullen's informant does not mention an opening artillery barrage (see *Recollections*, p. 24).

32. Byrne, *Memoirs*, i, pp. 99–100; Taylor, *Rebellions*, p. 91.
33. NAI, RP 620/56/98; Herndon Letter, NLI MS 21586. The best accounts of the battle itself are Byrne, *Memoirs*, i, pp. 101–4; Cullen, *Recollections*, pp. 24–5; Musgrave, *Rebellions*, i, pp. 542–5; Wheeler, *War*, pp. 119–20; Dickson, *Wexford Rising*, pp. 242–4; Herndon Letter, NLI MS 21586; Philip Hay Account, NAI, RP 620/56/98.
34. Musgrave (*Rebellions*, i, p. 545) claims that 1,000 rebels were killed, while Byrne only admits that losses were 'considerable', with hundreds wounded (*Memoirs*, i, p. 108).
35. Byrne, *Memoirs*, i, pp. 107–8.
36. See pp. 163–4 below.
37. Alexander, *Narrative*, pp. 94–6.
38. Taylor, *Rebellions*, p. 83; Hay, *Insurrection*, p. 173.
39. Richards Diary, pp. 23–4.

Chapter 11: The Waiting Game: 10–16 June (pp. 162–181)
1. Dickson, *Wexford Rising*, pp. 244–5; Wheeler, *War*, p. 120. A loyalist later claimed that Murphy had a letter advocating the slaughter of Protestants in his pocket (see NLI, Musgrave Letters, MS 4156, pp. 47–8).
2. Wheeler, *War*, pp. 120–1.
3. Cullen, *Recollections*, p. 27; Byrne, *Memoirs*, i, pp. 107–9.
4. Musgrave, *Rebellions*, i, p. 576.
5. Cloney, *Narrative*, pp. 45–6; Hay, *Insurrection*, pp. 173–4.
6. Hay, *Insurrection*, p. 188; Musgrave, *Rebellions*, i, pp. 523–4. For accounts of this incident by Johnson and the gunboat commander see NAI, RP 620/38/135.
7. Richards Diary, p. 23.
8. Hay, *Insurrection*, p. 186. For details of some executions on Vinegar Hill see TCD, Madden Papers, MS 873, f. 800, 803, 873, and NLI, Court Martial Papers, MS 17795 (1–7), and for evidence of tensions between some Wexford town rebels and Dixon see NLI, Musgrave Letters, MS 4156, pp. 67–70.
9. PRO, HO 100/77/114–18, 120–2; Pakenham, *Year of Liberty*, pp. 227–8.
10. PRO, HO 100/77/148–52.
11. Byrne, *Memoirs*, i, p. 109; Cullen, *Recollections*, pp. 27–8.
12. Byrne, *Memoirs*, i, pp. 110–11.
13. Wheeler, *War*, pp. 138–9; Dickson, *Wexford Rising*, p. 245.
14. Dickson, *Wexford Rising*, p. 132.
15. Wheeler, *War*, pp. 138–9.
16. Dickson, *Wexford Rising*, p. 245.

17. Cullen, *Recollections*, pp. 27–8.
18. Cloney, *Narrative*, pp. 47–8.
19. Richards Diary, pp. 24–5.
20. Hay, *Insurrection*, pp. 188–9.
21. Ibid., pp. 189–90; Cloney, *Narrative*, pp. 48–50.
22. Byrne, *Memoirs*, i, p. 111.
23. Dickson claims this happened on 16 June (see *Wexford Rising*, p. 139), but it makes more sense in strategic terms on 12 June.
24. Byrne, *Memoirs*, i, p. 109.
25. Wheeler, *War*, p. 139.
26. Richards Diary, p. 26.
27. Cloney, *Narrative*, pp. 51–2.
28. Byrne, *Memoirs*, i, pp. 112–13.
29. Hay, *Insurrection*, pp. 191–2.
30. Ibid., pp. 191–2. Curiously, Byrne makes no mention of Tunks.
31. Ibid., p. 194.
32. Ibid., pp. 193–4.
33. Ibid., p. 193; see also NLI, Musgrave Letters, MS 4156, pp. 55–7.
34. Hay, *Insurrection*, pp. 194–5.
35. Richards Diary, pp. 24–5.
36. Byrne, *Memoirs*, i, p. 113; Cullen, *Recollections*, p. 28.
37. Wheeler, *War*, p. 140.
38. Hay (*Insurrection*, pp. 164–5, 185–6) claims that one patrol from Newtownbarry killed a mentally retarded youth near Scarawalsh Bridge.
39. See p. 182 below.
40. Moore, *Diary*, p. 294.
41. Pakenham, *Year of Liberty*, pp. 230–1.
42. Musgrave, *Rebellions*, i, pp. 573–4.
43. Ibid., p. 475.
44. Cloney, *Narrative*, p. 52. The problem of recruitment is apparent from the small size of the Lacken army a few days later (see pp. 191–2 below).
45. Alexander, *Narrative*, p. 100.
46. Wheeler, *War*, pp. 140–1.
47. Byrne, *Memoirs*, i, p. 113.
48. Moore, *Diary*, pp. 294–5.
49. Ibid., p. 295.
50. Hay, *Insurrection*, p. 189.
51. Byrne, *Memoirs*, i, p. 113; Cullen, *Recollections*, p. 28.
52. Wheeler, *War*, pp. 141–2.
53. Musgrave, *Rebellions*, i, p. 475.

54. Pakenham, *Year of Liberty*, pp. 248–9.
55. PRO, HO 100/77/157.

Chapter 12: Lake's Move: 17–20 June (pp. 182–204)
  1. Wheeler, *War*, p. 142. For an example of the government's confident mood see PRO, HO 100/77/163, 165.
  2. Moore, *Diary*, p. 295.
  3. Musgrave, *Rebellions*, ii, p. 4.
  4. Byrne, *Memoirs*, i, pp. 113–14; Cullen, *Recollections*, p. 29; Gordon, *Rebellion*, pp. 135–6; Jones, *Narrative*, p. 149.
  5. Byrne, *Memoirs*, i, pp. 115–18; see also Keogh, 'Fr John Martin', pp. 225–46. Holt provides us with a glimpse of life among the rebel bands that had been holding out in the Wicklow mountains during these weeks (see *Memoirs*, pp. 41–4).
  6. Hay, *Insurrection*, p. 199.
  7. Croker, *Researches*, p. 365.
  8. Taylor, *Rebellions*, p. 184.
  9. Richards Diary, pp. 30–1.
 10. Cloney, *Narrative*, pp. 52–4.
 11. Musgrave, *Rebellions*, i, pp. 577–8.
 12. Hay, *Insurrection*, p. 200.
 13. Richards Diary, p. 32.
 14. Byrne, *Memoirs*, i, p. 119.
 15. Gordon, *Rebellion*, p. 136.
 16. Byrne, *Memoirs*, i, p. 119; Cullen, *Recollections*, p. 29.
 17. Moore, *Diary*, p. 295.
 18. Ibid., p. 296. See p. 192 below.
 19. Musgrave, *Rebellions*, ii, p. 5.
 20. Wheeler, *War*, pp. 146–7.
 21. Dickson, *Wexford Rising*, p. 139.
 22. PRO, HO 100/77/170; Gordon, *Rebellion*, p. 136; Cullen, *Recollections*, p. 29; Byrne, *Memoirs*, i, pp. 119–20; Furlong, *Murphy*, p. 124.
 23. Cloney, *Narrative*, p. 54.
 24. Croker, *Researches*, p. 340.
 25. Hay (*Insurrection*, p. 200) mistakenly says they met rebels retreating from Mountpleasant.
 26. Byrne, *Memoirs*, i, p. 120; Cullen, *Recollections*, p. 29. Furlong implicates Fitzgerald too in this decision (see *Murphy*, p. 125).
 27. Byrne, *Memoirs*, i, pp. 120–1.
 28. Musgrave, *Rebellions*, ii, pp. 1–3; Furlong, *Murphy*, pp. 127–8. For an example of loyalist confidence see NLI, Tottenham Letters, pos. 4937 (16 June 1798).

29. Cloney, *Narrative*, p. 54.
30. Moore, *Diary*, p. 295.
31. Wheeler, *War*, p. 147; Dickson, *Wexford Rising*, p. 245.
32. Musgrave, *Rebellions*, ii, p. 1.
33. Byrne, *Memoirs*, i, pp. 121–2; Dickson, *Wexford Rising*, p. 245.
34. Byrne, *Memoirs*, i, p. 122.
35. Dickson, *Wexford Rising*, pp. 245–6.
36. Cloney, *Narrative*, pp. 54–6; Alexander, *Narrative*, pp. 100–1; Moore, *Diary*, p. 295. For evidence of the poor state of the rebel supplies see NLI, Elmes Letters, pos. 8361 (8 July 1798).
37. Cloney, *Narrative*, pp. 56–7; Moore, *Diary*, p. 295.
38. Moore, *Diary*, p. 296; Hay, *Insurrection*, p. 203.
39. Moore, *Diary*, p. 295. One loyalist source suggests that there were only twenty deaths in the battle and aftermath (see NLI, Elmes Letters, pos. 8361 (8 July 1798)).
40. Wheeler, *War*, p. 183.
41. Hay, *Insurrection*, p. 204.
42. Ibid., p. 203.
43. Ibid., p. 204.
44. NLI, Musgrave Letters, MS 4156, pp. 75–6; Hay, *Insurrection*, p. 207; Wheeler, *War*, p. 184.
45. Cullen, *Recollections*, pp. 29–30; Byrne, *Memoirs*, i, p. 121.
46. Cloney, *Narrative*, pp. 56–7; Hay, *Insurrection*, pp. 204–6.
47. Wheeler, *War*, pp. 148–9; Cullen, *Recollections*, p. 33; Dickson, *Wexford Rising*, p. 246.
48. Musgrave, *Rebellions*, ii, pp. 5–6.
49. Byrne, *Memoirs*, i, p. 123.
50. Musgrave, *Rebellions*, ii, p. 5; Alexander, *Narrative*, p. 102.
51. Moore, *Diary*, p. 296.
52. Cloney, *Narrative*, pp. 57–8.
53. Ibid., pp. 58–60; Moore, *Diary*, pp. 296–8; Jones, *Narrative*, pp. 119–20. For rebel casualties see NLI, Elmes Letters, pos. 8361 (8 July 1798), and for evidence of confused reporting of the battle to the government see PRO, HO 100/77/82, 174. A nearby loyalist family, Goffs of Horetown House (hence Goff's Bridge) lost a great deal of property because of this battle (see NLI, Goff Letters, MS 9765, no. 75).
54. Moore, *Diary*, p. 298.
55. Cloney, *Narrative*, p. 60.
56. Wheeler, *War*, pp. 185–6. For more evidence of Thomas Dixon's involvement see letter by Father James Dixon, his cousin, NAI RP 620/39/184.

57. Veritas, *Vindication*, pp. 11–14; DDA, Caulfield–Troy Correspondence, 31 July 1798; Taylor, *Rebellions*, pp. 187–91; Wheeler, *War*, pp. 187–9; Jackson, *Narrative*, pp. 32–5; Musgrave, *Rebellions*, ii, pp. 16–28; Hay, *Insurrection*, pp. 211–25; NLI, Musgrave Letters, MS 9765, pp. 45–6; Whelan, 'Politicisation', p. 175.
58. Veritas, *Vindication*, p.13; Hay, *Insurrection*, p. 216.
59. Byrne, *Memoirs*, i, p. 124; Musgrave, *Rebellions*, ii, p. 5. Furlong claims that Father John Murphy was already at Vinegar Hill with an advance unit by this time (see *Murphy*, p. 126), but I suspect that he was not.

Chapter 13: The Slaney's Red Waves: 21–22 June (pp. 205–228)
   1. Cullen, *Recollections*, p. 35.
   2. There is no direct reference to Roche camping to the south of Enniscorthy that night, but his departure from Wexford Bridge at 8 p.m. and his failure to reach Enniscorthy suggest so.
   3. Dickson, *Wexford Rising*, p. 246.
   4. There is no direct reference to this contact, but the timing of Johnson's action the next morning suggests it happened (see p. 206 below). For Lake's own summary of the battle see PRO, HO 100/77/177.
   5. Jones, *Narrative*, pp. 52–3; Dickson, *Wexford Rising*, p. 246.
   6. Jones, *Narrative*, p. 53; Dickson, *Wexford Rising*, pp. 246–7; Musgrave, *Rebellions*, ii, p. 6.
   7. Cullen, *Recollections*, pp. 74–5; Musgrave, *Rebellions*, ii, pp. 11a–12a.
   8. Cullen, *Recollections*, p. 35; Musgrave, *Rebellions*, ii, pp. 11a–12a.
   9. Taylor, *Rebellions*, p. 191.
  10. Hay, *Insurrection*, pp. 228–30; Cloney, *Narrative*, p. 62.
  11. Hay, *Insurrection*, p. 231; Cloney, *Narrative*, pp. 65–6; Wheeler, *War*, pp. 189–90.
  12. Hay, *Insurrection*, p. 230; Cloney, *Narrative*, p. 66.
  13. Wheeler, *War*, p. 189.
  14. Musgrave, *Rebellions*, ii, p. 6–7.
  15. Ibid., p. 6.
  16. Byrne, *Memoirs*, i, p. 127.
  17. Cullen, *Recollections*, pp. 35–6.
  18. Musgrave, *Rebellions*, ii, pp. 11a–12a.
  19. See p. 211 below.
  20. Byrne, *Memoirs*, i, pp. 129–30; Cullen, *Recollections*, pp. 36–7.
  21. Byrne, *Memoirs*, i, p. 130.
  22. Musgrave, *Rebellions*, ii, pp. 6–7. For an anonymous but detailed account of the battle see NLI, MS 25004.

23. Musgrave, *Rebellions*, ii, pp. 7–8; Cullen, *Recollections*, p. 37; Byrne, *Memoirs*, i, pp. 129–30; Dickson, *Wexford Rising*, p. 247. For a list of captured ordnance etc. see PRO, HO 100/77/190.

24. Dickson, *Wexford Rising*, pp. 248–9.

25. Cullen, *Recollections*, pp. 37–8; Byrne, *Memoirs*, i, pp. 133–4.

26. Moore, *Diary*, p. 298; Hay, *Insurrection*, p. 236.

27. Hay, *Insurrection*, pp. 232–4.

28. Cloney, *Narrative*, p. 66; Hay, *Insurrection*, p. 234.

29. Cloney, *Narrative*, pp. 68–9; Hay, *Insurrection*, p. 234.

30. Cloney, *Narrative*, p. 69; Hay, *Insurrection*, p. 235.

31. Moore, *Diary*, p. 298.

32. Byrne, *Memoirs*, i, pp. 134–5; Hay, *Insurrection*, pp. 236–7.

33. Moore, *Diary*, p. 298.

34. Byrne, *Memoirs*, i, p. 138.

35. Byrne (*Memoirs*, i, p. 129) says they had begun to discuss this before leaving Vinegar Hill.

36. Hay, *Insurrection*, p. 239.

37. Ibid., p. 237; Wheeler, *War*, p. 191. Caulfield claims that he spent the entire day with Kingsborough so as to protect him (see DDA, Caulfield–Troy Correspondence, 31 July 1798).

38. Jackson, *Narrative*, p. 36.

39. Wheeler, *War*, p. 191.

40. Byrne, *Memoirs*, i, pp. 143–4; Hay, *Insurrection*, p. 240. Furlong suggests that Perry and the others essentially abandoned John Murphy and Philip Roche (see *Murphy*, p. 138), but given the panic which broke out that afternoon, their separate departures may have been accidental.

41. Moore, *Diary*, p. 299.

42. Byrne (*Memoirs*, i, p. 138) describes him as being 'dangerously ill' at this point.

43. Wheeler, *War*, p. 199.

44. Moore, *Diary*, p. 299; Musgrave, *Rebellions*, ii, pp. 36–7.

45. Wheeler, *War*, p. 191.

46. Musgrave, *Rebellions*, ii, p. 37; Jackson, *Narrative*, pp. 37–8; Taylor, *Rebellions*, pp. 191–2.

47. Moore, *Diary*, p. 299; Musgrave, *Rebellions*, ii, pp. 40–1.

48. Taylor, *Rebellions*, pp. 193, 241–2.

49. Musgrave, *Rebellions*, ii, p. 51.

50. Gordon, *Rebellion*, pp. 155–6.

51. Dickson, *Wexford Rising*, p. 249; Musgrave, *Rebellions*, ii, pp. 40–1.

52. Byrne, *Memoirs*, i, pp. 187–8; Cullen, *Recollections*, p. 42.

53. Byrne, *Memoirs*, i, pp. 151–2; Furlong, *Murphy*, pp. 139–40.

54. Cloney, *Narrative*, pp. 71–3; Hay, *Insurrection*, pp. 242–3. For official copy of Lake's note see NAI, RP 620/38/218.
55. Hay, *Insurrection*, pp. 243–4.
56. Moore, *Diary*, p. 299.
57. Hay, *Insurrection*, pp. 244–5.
58. Moore, *Diary*, p. 299; Dickson, *Wexford Rising*, p. 249.
59. Hay, *Insurrection*, pp. 246–7.
60. Richards Diary, p. 38.
61. Croker, *Researches*, p. 376.
62. Hay, *Insurrection*, p. 245.
63. Ibid., p. 250.
64. See pp. 229–30 below.
65. See p. 230 below.
66. Jackson, *Narrative*, p. 73. Cloney claims that Lake had a rebel infirmary, with fifty-seven men inside, burned down once he entered the town; but he is the only one to make such a claim (see *Narrative*, p. 218; Furlong, *Murphy*, p. 190).
67. Hay, *Insurrection*, p. 246; Cullen, *Recollections*, pp. 37–40; Dickson, *Wexford Rising*, p. 249.
68. Byrne, *Memoirs*, i, pp. 188–9; Cullen, *Recollections*, p. 42; Wheeler, *War*, pp. 201–2.
69. Byrne, *Memoirs*, i, pp. 187–9; Cullen, *Recollections*, p. 47; Gordon, *Rebellion*, p. 157; Wheeler, *War*, p. 202.
70. Byrne, *Memoirs*, i, p. 189; Gordon, *Rebellion*, pp. 157–8; Musgrave, *Rebellions*, ii, pp. 422–4.
71. Byrne, *Memoirs*, i, p. 189.
72. Ibid., pp. 154–5; Furlong, *Murphy*, pp. 140–2.

Chapter 14: Breakout: 23–26 June (pp. 229–252)
1. Moore, *Diary*, p. 299.
2. Hay, *Insurrection*, p. 250; Musgrave, *Rebellions*, ii, p. 43.
3. Significantly, Hay makes no mention of his brother's execution.
4. Hay, *Insurrection*, p. 250.
5. Ibid., pp. 249– 50.
6. Cloney, *Narrative*, pp. 75–6.
7. Musgrave, *Rebellions*, ii, p. 44.
8. Moore (*Diary*, p. 299) suggests this was still the case on the 25th.
9. Byrne, *Memoirs*, i, p. 194.
10. Cullen, *Recollections*, p. 42.
11. Byrne, *Memoirs*, i, p. 194; Hay, *Insurrection*, pp. 157–8.
12. Wheeler, *War*, pp. 202–3.
13. Cullen, *Recollections*, p. 42; Holt, *Memoirs*, pp. 53– 9.

14. Byrne, *Memoirs*, i, p. 155.
15. Ibid., pp. 155–6; Gordon, *Rebellion*, p. 165; Musgrave, *Rebellions*, ii, pp. 73–5; Furlong, *Murphy*, pp. 142–3.
16. Musgrave, *Rebellions*, ii, pp. 75–8. Asgill had fought in America and was arrested there as a spy on one occasion (see TCD, Madden Papers, MS 873 f. 439).
17. Musgrave, *Rebellions*, ii, p. 79; Gordon, *Rebellion*, p. 166.
18. Byrne, *Memoirs*, i, p. 156. This camp was in the townland of Baunreagh (see Furlong, *Murphy*, p. 143).
19. Musgrave, *Rebellions*, ii, p. 79.
20. Byrne, *Memoirs*, i, pp. 156–7.
21. Ibid., p. 158.
22. Ibid. There was a hurried but halfhearted investigation of this (see Furlong, *Murphy*, p. 144).
23. Byrne, *Memoirs*, i, p. 158–9.
24. Ibid., pp. 160–1; Gordon, *Rebellion*, p. 166. As at New Ross, a rebel emissary was shot by the guards at the opening of this battle (see Furlong, *Murphy*, p. 148).
25. Byrne, *Memoirs*, i, pp. 161–5; Hay, *Insurrection*, pp. 257–9; Gordon, *Rebellion*, pp. 166–7.
26. Byrne, *Memoirs*, i, p. 163.
27. Ibid., pp. 166–7; Furlong, *Murphy*, p. 152.
28. Hay (*Insurrection*, pp. 258–9) speaks of Perry's group as going to such places as Donard and Blessington and then returning to Ballymanus; he was probably confusing them with Wicklow rebels that were moving south to join Perry.
29. Jones, *Narrative*, pp. 151–2.
30. Wheeler, *War*, p. 203.
31. Jones, *Narrative*, p. 152.
32. Jackson, *Narrative*, p. 73.
33. Croker, *Researches*, p. 380.
34. Moore, *Diary*, p. 300.
35. Cloney, *Narrative*, p. 76.
36. Hay, *Insurrection*, p. 250.
37. Jackson, *Narrative*, pp. 74–5; Musgrave, *Rebellions*, ii, pp. 41–3; Hay, *Insurrection*, p. 250.
38. Jackson, *Narrative*, p. 73.
39. Hay, *Insurrection*, p. 250; Musgrave, *Rebellions*, ii, p. 44. For an account by the ship's captain see NAI, RP 620/56/114.
40. Musgrave, *Rebellions*, ii, pp. 44–6.
41. Hay, *Insurrection*, pp. 250–1; Musgrave, *Rebellions*, ii, p. 43.
42. Cloney (*Narrative*, pp. 76–7) was hiding under a bed in which a

woman who had just given birth was lying.

43. Musgrave, *Rebellions*, ii, pp. 86–7.

44. Ibid., p. 87.

45. Byrne, *Memoirs*, i, pp. 167–8; Hay, *Insurrection*, p. 257; Musgrave, *Rebellions*, ii, pp. 87–8.

46. Byrne, *Memoirs*, i, p. 168; Gordon, *Rebellion*, pp. 167–8; Furlong, *Murphy*, p. 155.

47. Cullen, *Recollections*, p. 43; Hay, *Rebellion*, pp. 259–60; Gordon, *Rebellion*, p. 169; Jones, *Narrative*, pp. 152–3; Musgrave, *Rebellions*, ii, pp. 50–2.

48. Cullen, *Recollections*, p. 43; Hay, *Insurrection*, p. 260. Both Hay and Cullen claim that the rebels moved northwards, but subsequent dispositions suggest that one column moved east.

49. Byrne, *Memoirs*, i, p. 170.

50. Gordon, *Rebellion*, p. 168.

51. Byrne, *Memoirs*, i, p. 169.

52. Byrne, *Memoirs*, i, pp. 169–70; Cloney, *Narrative*, pp. 83–4; Hay, *Insurrection*, pp. 257–8; Gordon, *Rebellion*, p. 168; Musgrave, *Rebellions*, ii, pp. 88–9.

53. Byrne, *Memoirs*, i, p. 171; Cloney, *Narrative*, pp. 86–7.

54. Mac Suibhne, *Carlow*, pp.66–70. Furlong regards this as an accidental separation (see *Murphy*, p. 156).

55. Byrne, *Memoirs*, i, p. 172; Cloney, *Narrative*, p. 87; Hay, *Insurrection*, p. 258.

56. Gordon, *Rebellion*, p. 258.

57. Byrne, *Memoirs*, i, pp. 173–4.

58. Ibid., p. 171; Cloney, *Narrative*, pp. 84–6; Hay, *Insurrection*, p. 258. Musgrave (*Rebellions*, ii, p. 89) and Gordon (*Rebellion*, pp. 168–9) both suggest that the victims were rebels.

59. Cullen, *Recollections*, p. 43.

60. Wheeler, *War*, p. 206.

61. Jackson, *Narrative*, pp. 80–1; Hay, *Insurrection*, p. 253.

62. Cloney, *Narrative*, pp. 78–9.

63. Moore, *Diary*, p. 300.

Chapter 15: The Camp at the White Heaps: 27 June – 5 July
    (pp. 253–277)

  1. Moore, *Diary*, pp. 300–1. The authorities in Dublin Castle only learned of the rebel camp at Croghan at this point (27 June) (see PRO, HO 100/77/198).

  2. Cullen, *Recollections*, p. 43; Byrne, *Memoirs*, i, p. 197.

  3. Byrne, *Memoirs*, i, p. 174.

4. TCD, Grogan Papers, MS 11077(1–4); Jackson, *Narrative*, p. 81. Grogan's estate was confiscated by the crown (see NAI, RP 620/56/117, 620/77/73A).
5. Jackson, *Narrative*, pp. 83–4.
6. Croker, *Researches*, p. 379. For evidence of how determined the authorities were to eliminate Colclough see TCD, Hacket Deposition, MS 24555(36).
7. Jackson, *Narrative*, pp. 84–5.
8. Ibid., pp. 86–8.
9. NLI, MS 4157, p. 31.
10. Cloney, *Narrative*, p. 88.
11. Cullen, *Recollections*, p. 43.
12. Hay, *Insurrection*, pp. 253–4.
13. Ibid., p. 253.
14. Ibid., pp. 266– 8; Wheeler, *War*, p. 208; Gordon, *Rebellion*, pp. 185– 6.
15. Wheeler, *War*, p. 209.
16. Moore, *Diary*, p. 302. It was on this day that Cornwallis wrote an elaborate condemnation of the conduct of the troops (see PRO, HO 100/77/200–1).
17. Musgrave, *Rebellions*, p. 53.
18. Ibid., p. 53–4.
19. Ibid., p. 55.
20. Cullen, *Recollections*, p. 43.
21. Gordon, *Rebellion*, p. 172.
22. Ibid., p. 172–3.
23. Cullen, *Recollections*, p. 43.
24. Ibid., pp. 43–6; Holt, *Memoirs*, pp. 76–86. There was a French *émigré* among the dead (see TCD, Madden Papers, MS 873 f. 248).
25. Cullen, *Recollections*, p. 45.
26. Ibid., p. 46; Gordon, *Rebellion*, p. 173; Musgrave, *Rebellions*, ii, p. 55.
27. Wheeler, *War*, p. 216.
28. Gahan, 'Black Mob and Babes in the Wood', p. 95. On 1 July Needham had a member of the Esmonde family, local Catholic landlords, but loyalists, put on trial by court martial in Gorey (see NAI, RP 620/3/26/6).
29. Gahan, 'Black Mob and Babes in the Wood', p. 97.
30. Ibid., pp. 97–8.
31. Wheeler, *War*, p. 216.
32. Croker, *Researches*, pp. 380–1.
33. Moore, *Diary*, p. 303.
34. Musgrave, *Rebellions*, ii, p. 55. Musgrave displays confusion about the sequence of events here.

35. Cullen, *Recollections*, p. 47; Byrne, *Memoirs*, i, p. 202; Hay, *Insurrection*, pp. 261–2; Gordon, *Rebellion*, p. 174; Musgrave, *Rebellions*, ii, pp. 55–6. Musgrave claims that there were 72 killed, while Hay claims that the figure was 19.
36. Cullen, *Recollections*, pp. 47–8; Byrne, *Memoirs*, i, pp. 202–3.
37. Wheeler, *War*, pp. 216–17.
38. Moore, *Diary*, pp. 302–3.
39. Byrne, *Memoirs*, i, pp. 174–9.
40. Cullen, *Recollections*, p. 48.
41. Moore, *Diary*, p. 303.
42. Wheeler, *War*, p. 217.
43. Ibid., pp. 217–18; Musgrave, *Rebellions*, ii, p. 56.
44. Byrne, *Memoirs*, i, pp. 179–80, 204.
45. Ibid., p. 204.
46. Cloney, *Narrative*, pp. 88–91; Cullen, *Recollections*, p. 48.
47. Wheeler, *War*, p. 218.
48. Cullen, *Recollections*, p. 48.
49. Ibid.
50. Ibid., pp. 48–9; Byrne, *Memoirs*, i, pp. 205–10.
51. Cullen, *Recollections*, pp. 49–50.
52. Ibid., p. 50.
53. Byrne, *Memoirs*, i, pp. 210–11.

Chapter 16: The Final Conclave: 6–15 July (pp. 278–300)
1. Cullen *Recollections*, p. 53.
2. Byrne, *Memoirs*, i, pp. 213–15.
3. Ibid., pp. 215–17.
4. Ibid., p. 219.
5. Cullen, *Recollections*, p. 53. Holt's account of the backdrop to the gathering at Borleas is quite convoluted and, I think, unreliable (see *Memoirs*, pp. 92–4).
6. Musgrave (*Rebellions*, ii, p. 66) claims that Michael Reynolds of Kildare convinced them to do this.
7. Cullen, *Recollections*, p. 53.
8. Moore, *Diary*, p. 304. For Cornwallis's perspective on the rebel threat at this date see PRO, HO 100/77/214–19.
9. See pp. 289–90 below.
10. Cullen, *Recollections*, pp. 53–4.
11. Moore, *Diary*, pp. 304–5.
12. Cullen, *Recollections*, p. 54. Holt confirms this (see *Memoirs*, p. 191).
13. Whelan, 'Role of the Catholic Priest', p. 305.
14. Cullen, *Recollections*, p. 54.

15. Moore, *Diary*, p. 305.
16. Byrne is remarkably silent about these days (see *Memoirs*, ii, pp. 219–20).
17. Cullen, *Recollections*, pp. 54–5; Gordon, *Rebellion*, pp. 176–7; Musgrave, *Rebellions*, ii, pp. 66–9; Holt, *Memoirs*, pp. 102–9.
18. Cullen, *Recollections*, pp. 55–6. Holt's account of his own leave-taking is rather different (see *Memoirs*, pp. 109–19).
19. Moore, *Diary*, p. 305.
20. Cullen, *Recollections*, pp. 56–7.
21. Ibid., p. 67.
22. Moore, *Diary*, pp. 305–6.
23. Cullen, *Recollections*, p. 67.
24. Ibid., pp. 67–8.
25. Cullen, *Recollections*, p. 57.
26. Moore, *Diary*, p. 306.
27. Cullen, *Recollections*, p. 54.
28. Ibid., pp. 57–9. The government would not realise that they had finally broken the rebels for another three days (see PRO, HO 100/77/24850).
29. Cullen, *Recollections*, pp. 68–9.
30. Ibid., pp. 59–60, 71–2.
31. Ibid., pp. 76–7.
32. Ibid., p. 98; Dickson, *Wexford Rising*, pp. 194, 203.
33. Cullen, *Recollections*, pp. 78–9; Hay, *Insurrection*, p. 270.
34. Byrne, *Memoirs*, i, pp. 241–2. See NLI MS 9760 for evidence given against him by Biddy Dolan of Carnew, *alias* Croppy Biddy, against him.
35. Furlong, *Murphy*, pp. 159–63.
36. Hay, *Insurrection*, pp. 285–6.
37. Cullen, *Recollections*, pp. 110–11.
38. For the best account of his life as a bandit see Dickson, *Dwyer*.
39. Byrne, *Memoirs*, i, p. 243; Cullen, *Recollections*, p. 81.
40. Byrne, *Memoirs*, i, pp. 284–5.
41. Cullen, *Recollections*, pp. 77–8.
42. Cloney, *Narrative*, pp. 99–170; Joyce, *Cloney*, pp. 38–41.
43. Joyce, *Cloney*, pp. 42–6; Byrne, *Memoirs*, i, pp. 261–2.
44. Joyce, *Cloney*, pp. 47–56.
45. Byrne, *Memoirs*, i, pp. 241–333.
46. Ibid., ii, passim.
47. See D. Akenson, *The Orangeman: The Life and Times of Ogle Gowan* (Toronto, 1986), for a slightly fictionalised history of the Gowan family during and after 1798.

48. Hay, *Insurrection*, pp. 278–9.
49. NAI, SOC 1382/75, 1382/81, 1561/32.
50. Ibid., 1091/86.
51 See Elliott, 'Emigration from South Leinster' in Whelan (ed.), *Wexford*, p. 422; for discussion of sectarian legacy see Dunne, 'Popular Ballads', pp. 148–52.
52. Cloney, *Narrative*, pp. 179–80.

BIBLIOGRAPHY

MANUSCRIPT SOURCES: IRELAND

Dublin Diocesan Archives
   Troy Papers

Genealogical Office
   Meyler Papers
   Kavanagh Papers
   MS 620 Castletown Payroll
   MS 142 Clifford Will

Registry of Deeds
   Deed Abstract 508–242–330088

Royal Irish Academy
   Haliday Pamphlets

National Archives, Dublin
   1A 52 76 Catholic Qualification Rolls Index, Leinster
   Customs and Excise Papers (Administration), no. 79
   Frazer Manuscripts
   Military Records
   MS 3092 Test Book
   MS 1/1–4 Wills (Charitable Donations)
   Officials Papers
   Outrage Papers 990/35
   Rebellion Papers 620/3–61
   State of the Country Papers 1016/49, 3191
   State Prisoners' Petitions

National Library of Ireland
   MS 25004 Account of 1798 (anon.)
   MS 673   Bennet Notes
   MS 2495   Bloomfield Papers
   MS 4574   Caulfield Letters
   MS 24555 Colclough Papers

MS 17795	Court Martial Records
MS 9760	Cullen Papers
Mic pos. 6486	Diary of Elizabeth Richards
Mic pos. 8361	Elmes Letters
MS 11077	Grogan Papers
MS 9765	Goff Letters
MS 24555	Hacket Deposition
MS 1576	Haughton Narrative
MS 21586	Herndon Letters
MS 8737(3)	Jacob Poole's Journal
MS 3151	La Touche Letters
MS 59–203	Lake Papers
Mic pos. 7665	List of persons who suffered losses in 1798
MS 4156/7	Musgrave Letters
MS 22459	'Newfoundland in 1798' (C. Byrne)
MS 22124	Pat Rossiter Legend
MS 24441	Redmond Letters

Mic pos. 4937 Tottenham Letters
Ainsworth Transcripts Vol. 4, no. 98 p. 984 (Donovan)
'Joly Copy' of Hay's *History* 'A few observations on Mr Hay's exaggerated account of the insurrection in County Wexford'

Trinity College, Dublin
MS 1182	Commissary General's Letter Book
MS 1472	Cullen Manuscripts
MS 870	Courts Martial
MS 873	Madden Manuscripts
MS 871	Musgrave Papers
MS 869	Sirr Papers

Public Record Office of Northern Ireland
| T3048/C/18 | McPeake Papers |

University College, Dublin
| MS 577 | Irish Folklore Commission Records |

Wexford County Library
Recollections of Jane Barber

Manuscript Sources: Britain

British Library
  Add. MSS

Hampshire Public Record Office (Portsmouth)
  Wallop Papers

Public Record Office
  Home Office Papers 100
  Quit Rent Papers
  Militia Muster Rolls and Pay Lists

Primary Printed

Alexander, John, *A Succint Narrative of the Rise and Progress of the Rebellion in the County of Wexford, especially in the vicinity of Ross* (Dublin, 1800)

An Irish Country Gentleman, *Causes of the Popular Discontents in Ireland* (London, 1804)

An Irish Emigrant, *The Causes of the Rebellion in Ireland, disclosed in an address to the people of England* (London, n.d.)

Anon., *State of the Country in the autumn of 1798* (London, 1798)

Anon., *The Trial of W. M. Byrne for high treason* (Dublin, 1798)

Anon., *Standing Orders for the Yeomanry Corps of Ireland* (Dublin, 1798)

Anon., *A List of the Counties of Ireland and the respective Yeomanry Corps in each County according to their precedence established by lot on the 1st of June, 1798* (Dublin, 1798)

Anon. [Edward Hay?], *Authentic Detail of the Extravagant and Inconsistent Conduct of Sir Richard Musgrave* (n.p., n.d.)

Anon., *An Impartial Narrative of the Most Important Engagements which took place between His Majesty's Forces and the Rebels during the Irish Rebellion, 1798* (Dublin, 1799)

Anon., *An Account of the late Insurrection in Ireland, in which is laid open the secret correspondence between the United Irish and the French government, between Lord Edward Fitzgerald, Mr Arthur O'Connor, James Quigley and others, together with a short history of the principal battles between the king's forces and the insurgents* (London, 1799)

Anon., *A History of the Irish Rebellion in the year 1798* (Dublin, 1799)

Anon., *Observations on the Reply of the Right Reverend Doctor Caulfield, Roman Catholick Bishop, and of the Roman Catholick Clergy of Wexford, to the Misrepresentations of Sir Richard Musgrave* (Dublin, 1802)

A Wexford Freeholder, *Observations on Edward Hay's 'History of the Insurrection in the County of Wexford, A.D. 1798'* (n.p., n.d.)

Barrington, Jonah, *Personal Sketches of his Own Times* (London, 1827)

——*Rise and Fall of the Irish Nation* (Dublin, 1833)

Byrne, Miles, *Memoirs*, 2 vols (2nd ed., Dublin, 1906)

Caulfield, James, *The Reply of the Right Reverend Dr Caulfield, Roman Catholick Bishop, and of the Roman Catholick Clergy of Wexford to the Misrepresentations of Sir Richard Musgrave* (Dublin, 1801)

Chartres, Rev., *Vinegar Hill, a poem* (Dublin, 1802)

Cloney, Thomas. *A Personal Narrative of those Transactions in the County of Wexford, in which the author was engaged, during the awful period of 1798* (Dublin, 1832)

Cooper, George, *Letters on the Irish Nation: written during a visit to that kingdom in the autumn of the year 1799* (London, 1801)

Corish, P. J. (ed.), 'Bishop Caulfield's *Relatio Status*', *Archivium Hibernicum*, xxxviii (1966), pp. 103–13

Cornwallis, Marquis, *Correspondence of Charles, 1st Marquis Cornwallis* (London, 1859)

Croker, T. C., *Researches in the South of Ireland illustrative of the scenery, architectural remains, and the manners and superstitions of the peasantry. With an appendix containing a private narrative of the rebellion of 1798* (London, 1824)

Crone, John S., *A Concise Dictionary of Irish Biography* (Dublin, 1937)

Cullen, Luke, *'98 in Wicklow and Wexford* (Wexford, 1938)

——*Personal Recollections of Wexford and Wicklow Insurgents of 1798* (Enniscorthy, 1959)

de Latocnaye, *A Frenchman's Walk through Ireland, 1796–7* (Dublin, 1917)

Devereux, James Edward, *Observations on the Factions which have Ruled Ireland, on the Calumnies thrown upon the People of that Country, and of the Justice, Expediency and Necessity of restoring to the Catholics their Political Rights* (London, 1801)

Edwards, R. D., 'The Minute Book of the Catholic Committee, 1773–92', *Archivium Hibernicum*, ix (1942), pp. 3–172

Emmet, T. A. and R., *Memoirs* (New York, 1915)

Farrell, William (ed. R. J. McHugh), *Carlow in '98: the autobiography of William Farrell of Carlow* (Dublin, 1949)

Fletcher, Hon. Justice, *Charge of the Hon. Justice Fletcher to the Grand Jury of the Co. Wexford at the summer assizes of 1814* (Belfast, 1814)

Flood, W. H. Grattan (ed), 'The Diocesan Manuscripts of Ferns during the Rule of Bishop Sweetman', *Archivium Hibernicum*, ii (1913), pp. 100–5

Frazer, R., *Statistical Survey of the County Wexford* (Dublin, 1807)

Goff, Dinah, *Divine Protection through Extraordinary Dangers experienced by Jacob and Elizabeth Goff and their Family during the Irish Rebellion of 1798* (London, 1857)

Gordon, Rev. James Bentley, *A History of Ireland from the earliest accounts to the accomplishment of the Union with Great Britain in 1801* (Dublin, 1805)

———*History of the Rebellion in Ireland in the year 1798* (Dublin, 1801)

———*Mr Gordon's Vindication of his 'History of the Rebellion in Ireland', in answer to the objections formed against it by Sir Richard Musgrave, Bart., and others* (Dublin, 1802)

[Handcock, G.], 'Reminiscences of a Fugitive Loyalist in 1798', *English Historical Review*, i (1886), pp. 536–44

Handcock, Thomas, *The Principles of Peace exemplified in the Conduct of the Society of Friends in Ireland during the Rebellion of 1798* (London, 1825)

Haughton, Joseph, *Narration of Events during the Irish Rebellion of 1798* (n.p., n.d.)

Hay, Edward, *History of the Insurrection of the County of Wexford, A.D.1798* (Dublin, 1803)

Hibernicus, *Memoirs of an Irishman, now in America, containing an account of the principal events of his life* (Pittsburgh, 1828)

Holmes, George, *Sketches of some of the Southern Counties of Ireland collected during a tour in the autumn of 1797, in a series of letters* (London, 1801)

Holt, Joseph, *Memoirs* (London, 1838)

Jackson, Charles, *A Narrative of the Sufferings and Escapes of Charles Jackson, late resident of Wexford in Ireland, including an account by way of a journal of several barbarous atrocities committed in June 1798 by the Irish rebels* (Dublin, 1798)

Jacob, Archibald Hamilton, and John H. Glascott, *An Historical and Genealogical Narrative of the Families of Jacob* (Dublin, 1875)

Jones, John, *Impartial Narrative of the Most Important Engagements which took place between His Majesty's Forces and the Rebels during the Irish Rebellion, 1798* (Dublin, 1798)

Kennedy, Patrick, *Legends of Mount Leinster* (repr., Enniscorthy, 1989)

Knox, Alexander, *Essays on the Political Circumstances of Ireland written during the administration of Earl Camden* (London, 1799)

Kingston, George, Earl of, *A Narrative of the Proceedings of the Commissioners of Suffering Loyalists in the Case of Capt. Philip Hay* (Dublin, 1808)

Lett, Barbara Newton (ed. Rev. J. Ranson), 'A '98 Diary', *The Past*, iv–vi (1948–50), pp. 117–49

Lewis, Samuel, *A Topographical Dictionary of Ireland*, 2 vols (Dublin, 1837)

Longfield, Ada K., *The Shapland Carew Papers* (Dublin, 1946)

MacNeven, W. J., *Pieces of Irish History* (New York, 1806)

Mac Cuarta, Brian, 'Matthew de Renzy's Letters on Irish Affairs', *Analecta Hibernica*, xxxiv (1987), pp. 107–82

MacDonagh, T., *The Viceroy's Postbag* (London, 1904)

MacLaren, Archibald, 'A Minute Description of the Battles of Gorey, Arklow and Vinegar Hill; together with the movements of the army through the Wicklow mountains' in Charles Dickson, *The Wexford Rising in 1798: its causes and course* (Tralee, 1955), pp. 239–49

——*A Genuine Account of the Capture and Death of Lord Edward Fitzgerald. An Impartial Description of the Battles of Dunboyne, Naas, Hacketstown, Tara Hill, Kildare, Owlart, Gorey, Arklow, Vinegar Hill, etc.* (Bristol, 1799)

Moore, Sir John, *The Diary of Sir John Moore*, ed. Sir J. F. Maurice, 2 vols (London, 1904)

Musgrave, Sir Richard, *Memoirs of the Different Rebellions in Ireland* (Dublin, 1801)

[——]*A Concise Account of the Material Events and Atrocities which occurred in the Present Rebellion, by Veridicus* (Dublin, 1799)

O'Byrne, E. (ed.), *The Convert Rolls* (Dublin, 1983)

Parnell, William, *An Inquiry into the Causes of the Popular Discontents in Ireland, by an Irish country gentleman* (London, 1804)

Roche, Jordan, *A Statement and Observations on Cases that occurred in the Counties of Cork, Wexford, and Wicklow, particularly during the last campaigns* (Dublin, 1799)

Snowe, William, *Statement of Transactions at Enniscorthy on 28 May (1798)* (Dublin, 1801)

Stewart, John W., *The Kalendar compiled by John Watson Stewart for the year 1798* (Dublin, 1798)

Taylor, George, *An History of the Rise, Progress and Suppression of the Rebellion in the County of Wexford, in the year 1798, to which is annexed the author's account of his captivity and merciful deliverance* (Dublin, 1800; repr. Dublin, 1829)

——*The Monitor, nos i–iii, giving an account of the sufferings, persecutions, tortures, and cruel deaths, of near forty persons, who were taken prisoners by the rebels* (Wexford, 1799)

———Teeling, C. H., *The History of the Irish Rebellion of 1798: a personal narrative* (Glasgow, 1828)

Tone, T. W., *Life of Theobald Wolf Tone, written by himself and continued by his son; with his political writings and fragments of his diary* (Washington, 1826)

———*Proceedings of a Military Court held in Dublin Barracks* (Dublin, 1798)

Van Brock, F. W., 'A Memoir of 1798', *Irish Sword*, ix (1969–70), pp. 192–206

Veridicus, *see* Musgrave

Veritas, *The State of His Majesty's Subjects in Ireland professing the Catholic Religion* (Dublin, 1799)

Veritas, *A Vindication of the Roman Catholic Clergy of the Town of Wexford during the late unhappy rebellion from the groundless charges and illiberal insinuations of an anonymous writer signed Verax* (Dublin, 1798)

Wakefield, Edward, *Account of Ireland, Statistical and Political* (London, 1812)

Wheeler, H. F. B., and A. M. Broadley, *The War in Wexford: an account of the rebellion in the south of Ireland in 1798, told from original documents* (London, 1910)

Young, Arthur, *A Tour in Ireland*, 2 vols (London, 1780)

NEWSPAPERS/JOURNALS

Annual Register, or a view of the history, politics and literature for the year
Dublin Gazette
Faulkner's Dublin Journal
Irish Magazine and monthly asylum for neglected biography (ed. Watty Cox)
Irish Independent
New Ross Standard
The People
Walker's Hibernian Magazine
Wexford Herald

PARLIAMENTARY RECORDS

Parliamentary Register, or the History of the Proceedings and Debates of the House of Commons of Ireland, vol. xvii, pp. 425–6, 458–9, 489

Reports of the Secret Committees of Lords and Commons with the Addresses of both Houses to His Excellency the Lord Lieutenant (Dublin, 1797)

Report from the Committee of Secrecy of the House of Commons of Ireland (Dublin, 1798)

Report from the Secret Committee of the House of Commons and the House of Lords, with an appendix (Dublin, 1798)

Report from the Committee of Secrecy relating to Seditious Societies, etc. Reported by Mr Secretary Dundas (15 March 1799)

Commissioners for Inquiring into the Losses Sustained by such of His Majesty's Loyal Subjects as have suffered by the Rebellion (Wexford list) (*Journal of the House of Commons of Ireland*, vol. xix (1800), pt 2, appendix)

SECONDARY SOURCES

Anon., *Irish Rebellions, No. 11: The United Irishmen* (London, 1866)

Bartlett, T., 'An End to Moral Economy: the Irish militia disturbances of 1793', *Past and Present*, no. 99 (1983), pp. 41–64

———'Indiscipline and Disaffection in the Armed Forces in Ireland in the 1790s' in Corish (ed.), *Radicals, Rebels and Establishments*, pp. 115–34

———'An Officer's Memoir of Wexford in 1798', *Journal of the Wexford Historical Society*, xii (1988–9), pp. 72–85

———The Origins and Progress of the Catholic Question, 1690–1800' in Power and Whelan (ed.), *Endurance and Emergence*, pp. 1–19

———'Indiscipline and Disaffection in the French and Irish Armies during the Revolutionary Period' in Dickson and Gough (ed.), *Ireland and the French Revolution*, pp. 179–201

———*The Fall and Rise of the Irish Nation: the Catholic question, 1690–1830* (Dublin, 1992)

———and D. W. Hayton, *Penal Era and Golden Age: essays in Irish history, 1690–1800*, (Belfast, 1979)

Beames, M., *Peasants and Power: the Whiteboy movements and their control in pre-Famine Ireland* (Brighton, 1983)

———'Peasant Movements: Ireland, 1785–1795', *Journal of Peasant Studies*, ii (1975), pp. 502–6

Beckett, J. C., *The Making of Modern Ireland* (London, 1966)

Brady, J. (ed.), *Catholics and Catholicism in the Eighteenth-Century Press* (Maynooth, 1965)

Brockliss, L. W. B., and P. Ferté. 'Irish Clerics in France in the Seventeenth and Eighteenth Centuries: a statistical study', *Proceedings of the Royal Irish Academy*, lxxxvii, 9 (1987), pp. 527–72

Brown, B. (and K. Whelan), 'The Brown Families of County Wexford' in Whelan (ed.), *Wexford: History and Society*, pp. 446–89

Burns, R. E., 'The Irish Popery Laws: a study in eighteenth-century legislation and behavior', *Review of Politics*, xxiv (1962), pp. 485–508

Butler, T., *A Parish and its People: history of Carrick-on-Bannow* (Wellington Bridge, 1985)

Canning, A. S. G., *Revolted Ireland, 1798 and 1803* (London, 1886)

Canny, N. P., *Kingdom and Colony: Ireland in the Atlantic world, 1500–1800* (Johns Hopkins U.P., 1988)

Christianson, Gale E., 'Secret Societies and Agrarian Societies in Ireland, 1790–1840', *Agricultural History*, xlvi (1972), pp. 369–82

Clark, S., and J. S. Donnelly (ed.), *Irish Peasants: violence and political unrest, 1780–1914* (Manchester, 1983)

Cloney, S., 'The Cloney Families of County Wexford' in Whelan (ed.), *Wexford: History and Society*, pp. 316–41

Comerford, R. V., *et al.* (ed.), *Religion, Conflict and Coexistence in Ireland: essays presented to Monsignor Patrick J. Corish* (Dublin, 1990)

Comoradh '98, *The French Revolution and Wexford* (Enniscorthy, 1989)

Connolly, M. T., 'The Agricultural Pattern in County Wexford' in M. J. Gardiner and P. Ryan (ed.), *National Soil Survey of Ireland: soils of County Wexford* (Dublin, 1964)

Connolly, S. J., *Priests and People in Pre-Famine Ireland* (New York, 1982)

———'Violence and Order in the Eighteenth Century' in P. Flanagan, P. Ferguson, and K. Whelan (ed.), *Rural Ireland, 1600–1900* (Dublin, 1987), pp. 42–61

———*Religion, Law, and Power: the making of Protestant Ireland, 1690–1760* (Oxford, 1992)

Corish, P. J., *The Catholic Community in the Seventeenth and Eighteenth Centuries* (Dublin, 1981)

———*The Irish Catholic Experience: a historical survey* (Dublin, 1985)

———(ed.), *Radicals, Rebels and Establishments* (Belfast, 1985)

———Two Centuries of Catholicism in County Wexford' in Whelan, *Wexford: History and Society*, pp. 222–47

Corkery, D., *The Hidden Ireland* (Dublin, 1925)

Cronin, S., *Irish Nationalism: a history of its roots and ideology* (New York, 1981)

Cullen, L. M., *Anglo-Irish Trade, 1660–1800* (Manchester, 1968)

———*An Economic History of Ireland since 1660* (London, 1976)

———'Eighteenth-Century Flour-Milling in Ireland', *Irish Economic and Social History*, iv (1977), pp. 5–25

———*The Emergence of Modern Ireland* (London, 1981)

———'The 1798 Rebellion in its Eighteenth-Century context' in Corish (ed.), *Radicals, Rebels and Establishments*, pp. 91–113

———The 1798 Rebellion in Wexford: United Irish organisation, membership and leadership' in Whelan (ed.), *Wexford: History and Society*, pp. 248–95

———*The Hidden Ireland: reassessment of a concept* (Dublin, 1988)

———'The Political Structures of the Defenders' in Dickson and Gough (ed.), *Ireland and the French Revolution*, pp. 117–38

———Late Eighteenth-Century Politicisation in Ireland: problems in its study and its French links' in P. Bergeron and L. M. Cullen, *Cultures et pratiques politiques en France et en Irlande, XVIe–XVIIIe siècle* (Paris, 1990), pp. 137–58

———'The Internal Politics of the United Irishmen' in Dickson *et al.* (ed.), *The United Irishmen* (Dublin, 1993), pp. 176–96

Curtin, N., 'The Transformation of the United Irishmen into a Mass-Based Organisation, 1794–96', *Irish Historical Studies*, xxxiv(1985), pp. 463–92

———'Symbols and Rituals of the United Irish Mobilisation' in Dickson and Gough (ed.), *Ireland the French Revolution*, pp. 68–82

———'The United Irish Organisation in Ulster, 1795–8' in Dickson *et al.* (ed.), *The United Irishmen*, pp. 209–21

———*The United Irishmen: popular politics in Ulster and Dublin, 1791–1798* (Oxford, 1994)

Daly, M. E., and D. Dickson (ed.), *The Origins of Popular Literacy in Ireland* (Dublin, 1990)

de Vál, S., 'Éirí Amach Beag na bliana 1793', *The Past*, xvi (1988), pp. 59–60

Dickson, C., *The Life of Michael Dwyer, with some account of his companions* (Dublin, 1944)

———The Battle of Vinegar Hill', *Irish Sword*, i (1949), pp. 293–5

———*The Wexford Rising in 1798: its causes and course* (Tralee, 1955)

———*Revolt in the North: Antrim and Down in 1798* (Dublin, 1960)

Dickson, D., 'Middlemen' in Bartlett and Hayton (ed.), *Penal Era and Golden Age*, pp. 162–85

———*New foundations: Ireland, 1660–1800* (Dublin, 1987)

————D. Keogh, and K. Whelan (ed.), *The United Irishmen: republicanism, radicalism and rebellion* (Dublin, 1993)

————and H. Gough (ed.), *Ireland and the French Revolution* (Dublin, 1990)

Donnelly, J. S., 'Propagating the Cause of the United Irishmen', *Studies*, lix (1981), pp. 5–23

Duggan, M., 'County Carlow, 1791–1801' (M.A. thesis, UCD, 1969)

Dunne, T., *Theobald Wolfe Tone: colonial outsider* (Cork, 1982)

————'Popular Ballads, Revolutionary Rhetoric and Politicisation' in Dickson and Gough (ed.), *Ireland and the French Revolution*, pp. 139–55

Elliott, M., 'The Origins and Transformation of Early Irish Republicanism', *International Review of Social History*, xxiii (1978), pp. 405–28

————'Irish Republicanism in England: the first phase, 1797–9' in Bartlett and Hayton (ed.), *Penal Era and Golden Age*, pp. 204–21

————*Partners in Revolution: the United Irishmen and France* (London, 1982)

————'Emigration from South Leinster' in Whelan (ed.), *Wexford: History and Society.*

————*Wolfe Tone: prophet of Irish independence* (New Haven, 1989)

Faolain, T., *Blood on the Harp: Irish rebel history in ballad* (Troy, New York, 1983)

Fitzpatrick, A. J., 'The Economic Effects of the French Revolutionary and Napoleonic Wars on Ireland' (Ph.D. thesis, Manchester Univ., 1973)

Fitzpatrick, W. J., *The Sham Squire and the Informers of 1798* (Dublin, 1866)

Flanagan, T., *The Year of the French* (London, 1979)

Forde, F., *Maritime Arklow* (Dún Laoghaire, 1988)

Froude, J. A., *The English in Ireland in the Eighteenth Century* (London, 1874)

Furlong, N., 'Life in Wexford Port, 1600–1800' in Whelan (ed.), *Wexford: History and Society*, pp. 150–72

————*Father John Murphy of Boolavogue, 1753–1798* (Dublin, 1991)

Gahan, D., 'The Estate System of County Wexford, 1641–1876' in Whelan (ed.), *Wexford: History and Society*, pp. 201–21

———— Religion and Land Tenure in Eighteenth-Century Ireland: tenancy in the south-east' in Comerford *et al.* (ed.), *Religion, Conflict and Coexistence in Ireland*, pp. 99–117

————'The"Black Mob" and the "Babes in the Wood" : Wexford in the wake of the rebellion, 1798–1806', *Journal of the Wexford Historical Society*, xiii (1990–1), pp. 92–110

Garvin, T., 'Defenders, Ribbonmen and Others: underground political networks in pre-Famine Ireland', *Past and Present*, no. 96 (1982), pp. 133–55

Gibbon, P., 'The Origin of the Orange Order and the United Irishmen', *Economy and Society*, i (1970), pp. 135–63

Godechot, J., *La Grande Nation: l'expansion revolutionnaire de la France dans le monde de 1789 à 1799* (Paris, 1956)

——*France and the Atlantic Revolution of the Eighteenth Century* (New York, 1965)

Goodhall, D., 'All the Cooking That Could Be Used: a Co. Wexford election in 1745', *The Past*, xii (1978), pp. 3–22

—— 'The Dixon Family of Castlebridge', *Irish Genealogist*, vi, 5 (1984), pp. 629–41

Gough, H., 'The French Revolution and Ireland' in Dickson and Gough (ed.), *Ireland the French Revolution*, pp. 1–13

Graham, T., ' "An Union of Power"? The United Irish Organisation' in Dickson *et al.* (ed.), *The United Irishmen*, pp. 244–55

Griffin, W. D., 'The Forces of the Crown in Ireland, 1798' in G. L. Vincitorio (ed.), *Crisis in the Great Republic: essays presented to Ross J. S. Hoffmann* (New York, 1969)

——'The Green and the Black: Ireland's Catholic hierarchy confronts the rebellion of 1798', *Proceedings of the Consortium on Revolutionary Europe*, xiv (1984), pp. 419, 445–8

Guillon, E., *La France et l'Irlande pendant la Revolution* (Paris, 1888)

——*La France et l'Irlande sous le Directoire* (Paris, 1888)

Harwood, P., *History of the Irish Rebellion of 1798* (London, 1844)

Hayes, R., *Ireland and Irishmen in the French Revolution* (London, 1932)

——*The Last Invasion of Ireland* (Dublin, 1937)

——'Priests in the Independence Movement', *Irish Ecclesiastical Record*, 5th ser., lxvi (1945), pp. 258–70

Hayes-McCoy, G. A.. 'The Wexford Yeomanry and Miles Byrne', *An Cosantóir*, viii (1948), pp. 3–10

——*Irish Battles* (London, 1969)

——'The Irish Pike: additional notes on its history', *Galway Archaeological Society Journal*, xxi (1920), pp. 44–50

——'The Topography of a Battlefield: Arklow 1798', *Irish Sword*, i (1949–50), pp. 51–6

——'The Red Coat and the Green', *Studies*, xxxii (1943), pp. 396–408

Hechter, M., *Internal Colonialism: the Celtic fringe in British national development* (1975)

Hill, J. R., 'Religious Toleration and the Relaxation of the Penal Laws:

an imperial perspective, 1763–1780', *Archivium Hibernicum* (1989), pp. 98–109

Jacob, R., *The Rise of the United Irishmen, 1791–1794* (London, 1937)

Jeffreys, W. H., 'The Furlongs of County Wexford', *Old Wexford Society Journal*, vi (1976–7), pp. 73–80

Johnson, J. H., 'The "Two Irelands" at the Beginning of the Nineteenth Century' in N. Stephens and R. E. Glasscock (ed.), *Irish Geographical Studies* (Belfast, 1970), pp. 224–41

Johnston, E. M., *Great Britain and Ireland, 1760–1800* (London, 1963)

———— *Ireland in the Eighteenth Century* (Dublin, 1974)

Jones, E. H. S., *An Invasion That Failed: the French expedition to Ireland, 1796* (Oxford, 1950)

Joyce, J., *General Thomas Cloney—a Wexford rebel of 1798* (Dublin, 1988)

Kavanagh, P. F., *A Popular History of the Insurrection of 1798* (Dublin, 1920)

Kehoe, L., *Glynn, 1789–1989* (Wexford, 1989)

Kelly, J., 'The Parliamentary Reform Movement of the 1780s and the Catholic Question', *Archivium Hibernicum* (1988), pp. 95–117

Kennedy, W. P., 'The Irish Jacobins', *Studia Hibernica*, xiv (1976), pp. 109–21

Kenny, C., 'The Exclusion of Catholics from the Legal Profession in Ireland, 1537–1829', *Irish Historical Studies*, xxv (1987), pp. 337–57

Keogh, D., 'Fr John Martin: an Augustinian friar and the rebellion of 1798', *Analecta Augustiniana*, li (1988), pp. 225–46

————'The Catholic Church, Archbishop Troy and Radicalism, 1791–3' in Dickson *et al.* (ed.), *The United Irishmen*, pp. 124–34

————' "The Most Dangerous Villain in Society": Fr John Martin's mission to the United Irishmen of Wicklow in 1798', *Eighteenth-Century Ireland*, vii (1992), pp. 115–35

————*The French Disease: the Catholic Church and radicalism in Ireland, 1790–1800* (Dublin, 1993)

Lecky, W. E. H., *A History of Ireland in the Eighteenth Century*, vol. iv (London, 1892)

Leighton, C. D. M., *Catholicism in a Protestant Kingdom: a study of the Irish ancien régime* (Dublin, 1994)

McAnally, Sir H., *The Irish Militia, 1793–1816: a social and military study* (Dublin, 1949)

MacDermot, F., *Theobald Wolfe Tone: a biographical study* (London, 1939)

————'The Church and Ninety–Eight in Ireland', *Today*, iii (1938), pp. 41–4

McDowell, R. B., 'The United Irishmen of Dublin, 1791–4', *Bull. Ir. Comm. Hist. Sc.*, no. 1 (1939)

———'United Irish Plans of Parliamentary Reform: select documents', *Irish Historical Studies*, iii (1942), pp. 39–59

———*Irish Public Opinion, 1750–1800* (London, 1944)

———'Proceedings of the Dublin Society of United Irishmen', *Analecta Hibernica*, xvii (1949), pp. 3–143

———'The Personnel of the Dublin Society of United Irishmen, 1791–4', *Irish Historical Studies*, ii (1940–1), pp, 12–53

———'The Fitzwilliam Episode', *Irish Historical Studies*, xvi (1966), pp. 115–30

———*Public Opinion and Government Policy in Ireland, 1801–1846* (London, 1952)

——*Ireland in the Age of Imperialism and Revolution, 1760–1801* (Oxford, 1979)

McEleavey, O., *Tithes: their history, with a review of the system in Ireland* (Belfast, 1911)

Mackesy, P., *Statesmen at War: the strategy of overthrow, 1798–9* (London, 1974)

MacGrath, K., 'Two Wexford Priests in 1798', *Irish Ecclesiastical Record*, 5th ser., lxx (1948), pp. 1092–8

McSkimmin, S., *Annals of Ulster, 1790–1798* (Belfast, 1849)

———*A History of the Irish Rebellion* (Belfast, 1853)

Mac Suibhne, P., *A History of Clonegal Parish* (Carlow, 1970)

———*'98 in Carlow* (Carlow, 1974)

Madden, R. R., *Down and Antrim in '98* (Dublin, n.d.)

———*The United Irishmen: their lives and times*, 4 vols (Dublin, 1857)

———*Literary Remains of the United Irishmen of 1798* (London, 1887)

Maxwell, W. H., *History of the Irish Rebellion in 1798* (London, 1845)

Miller, D., 'The Armagh Troubles, 1784–95' in Clark and Donnelly (ed.), *Irish Peasants*, pp. 155–91

Moody, T. W., 'The Political Ideas of the United Irishmen', *Ireland Today*, iii, 1 (1938), pp. 15–25

——— and W. E. Vaughan (ed.), *A New History of Ireland*, vol iv: *Eighteenth-Century Ireland, 1691–1800* (Oxford, 1986)

Moore, Thomas, *The Life and Death of Lord Edward Fitzgerald* (London, 1832)

Morton, R. G., 'The Rise of the Yeomanry', *Irish Sword*, vii (1966–7), pp. 58–64

Murphy, C., 'The Wexford Catholic Community in the Later Seventeenth Century' in Comerford *et al.* (ed.), *Religion, Conflict and Coexistence*, pp. 99–117

Murphy, H., *Families of County Wexford* (Dublin, 1986)

O'Brien, George, *The Economic History of Ireland in the Eighteenth Century* (Dublin, 1918)

O'Brien, Gerard, *Parliament, Politics and People: essays in eighteenth-century Irish history* (Dublin, 1989)

O'Brien, J., *British Brutality in Ireland* (Cork, 1989)

O'Connell, M. R., *Irish Politics and Social Conflict in the Age of the American Revolution* (Philadelphia, 1965)

O'Flaherty, E., 'Ecclesiastical Politics and the Dismantling of the Penal Laws in Ireland, 1774–82', *Irish Historical Studies*, xxvi (1988), pp. 33–50

————'The Catholic Convention and Anglo-Irish Politics, 1791–3', *Archivium Hibernicum*, xi (1985), pp. 14–35

Ogle, T. A., *The Irish Militia Officer*, (Dublin, 1893)

O'Keeffe, T., 'The 1898 Efforts to Celebrate the United Irishmen: the '98 centennial', *Éire–Ireland*, xxiii (1988), pp. 104–15

O'Kelly, P., *General History of the Rebellion of 1798* (Dublin, 1842)

Ó Snodaigh, P., 'Notes on the Volunteers, Militia, Yeomanry and Orangemen of County Wexford', *The Past*, xiv (1983), pp. 5–48

————'Class and the Irish Volunteers', *Irish Sword*, xvi (1986), pp. 165–84

Ó Tuathail, P., 'Wicklow Traditions of 1798', *Bealoideas: the Journal of the Folklore of Ireland Society*, v (1935), pp. 154–88

Pakenham, T., *The Year of Liberty: the story of the great Irish rebellion of 1798* (London, 1969)

Palmer, R. R., *The Age of the Democratic Revolutions: a political history of Europe and America, 1760–1800*, 2 vols (Princeton, 1958–64)

Palmer, S., *Police and Protest in England and Ireland, 1780–1850* (Cambridge, 1988)

Perkin, H., *The Structured Crowd* (1981)

Philpin, C. (ed.), *Nationalism and Popular Protest in Ireland* (Cambridge, 1987)

Plowden, F., *An Historical Review of the State of Ireland, from the invasion of that country under Henry II to its union with Great Britain* (London, 1803)

Powell, T., 'The Background to the Wexford Rebellion, 1790–8', (M.A. thesis, UCD, 1970)

————'An Economic Factor in the Wexford Rebellion of 1798', *Studia Hibernica*, xvi (1976), pp. 140–57

Power, T. P., *Land, Politics and Society in Eighteenth-Century Tipperary* (Oxford, 1993)

————and K. Whelan (ed.), *Endurance and emergence: Catholics in Ireland in the Eighteenth-Century* (Dublin, 1989)

Rodger, R. B., *The War of the Second Coalition: a strategic commentary* (Oxford, 1964)

Ronan, M. V., 'Priests in the Independence Movement, 1796–8', *Irish Ecclesiastical Record*, 5th ser., lviii (1946), pp. 95–103

St Mark, J. J., 'Matilda and William Tone in Washington DC after 1798', *Éire–Ireland*, xxii (1987), pp. 4–10

————'The Oswald Mission to Ireland from America: 20 February to 8 June 1793', *Éire–Ireland*, xxiii (1988), pp. 25–38

Savage, J., *'98 and '48: the modern revolutionary history and literature of Ireland* (New York, 1884)

Senior, H., *Orangeism in Britain and Ireland* (London, 1966)

Sheedy, K., *Upon the Mercy of the Government* (Dublin, 1988)

Shennan, J. H., *Liberty and Order in Early Modern Europe: the subject and the state, 1650–1800* (New York, 1986)

Simms, S., *Rev. James O'Coigly, United Irishman* (Belfast, 1937)

Smith, A. W., 'Irish Rebels and English Radicals, 1798–1820', *Past and Present*, no. 7 (1955), pp. 78–85

Smyth, J., *The Men of No Property: Irish radicals and popular politics in the late eighteenth century* (London, 1992)

Stewart, A. T. Q., 'A Stable and Unseen Power: Dr William Drennan and the origins of the United Irishmen' in J. Bossy *et al.* (ed.), *Essays presented to Michael Roberts* (Belfast, 1976), pp. 80–92

Stoddart, P., 'Counter-Insurgency and Defence in Ireland, 1790–1805' (D.Phil. thesis, Oxford Univ., 1972)

Sullivan, J. J., *The Education of Irish Catholics, 1782–1831* (Ph.D. thesis, QUB, 1959)

Swords, L., *The Green Cockade: the Irish in the French Revolution, 1789–1815* (Dublin, 1989)

Wall, M., *The Penal Laws, 1691–1760* (Dundalk, 1960)

————'The United Irish Movement' in J. L. McCracken (ed.), *Historical Studies, V* (London, 1965), pp. 122–40

————The Rise of a Catholic Middle Class in Eighteenth-Century Ireland', *Irish Historical Studies*, xi (1958), pp. 91–115

————'The Decline of the Irish Language', in B. Ó Cuív (ed.), *A View of the Irish Language* (Dublin, 1969), pp. 81–90

————*Catholic Ireland in the Eighteenth Century: the collected essays of Maureen Wall* (Dublin, 1989)

Wells, R., *Insurrection: the British experience, 1795–1803* (Gloucester, 1983)

Whelan, K., 'A Geography of Society and Culture in Ireland since 1800' (Ph.D. thesis, UCD, 1981)

————'The Catholic Parish, the Catholic Chapel and Village

Development in Ireland', *Irish Geography*, xvi (1983), pp. 1–16

——'The Catholic Church in County Tipperary, 1600–1900' in W. Nolan and T. McGrath (ed.) *Tipperary: History and Society* (Dublin, 1985), pp. 212–55

——'The Religious Factor in the 1798 Rebellion in County Wexford' in P. Flanagan, P. Ferguson and K. Whelan (ed.), *Rural Ireland, 1600–1900* (Dublin, 1987), pp. 62–85

——*A History of Newbawn* (Newbawn, 1986)

——(ed.), *Wexford: History and Society: interdisciplinary essays in the history of an Irish county* (Dublin, 1987)

——'The Role of the Catholic Priest in the 1798 Rebellion in County Wexford' in Whelan (ed.), *Wexford: History and Society*, pp. 296–315

——'The Regional Impact of Irish Catholicism, 1700–1850' in W. J. Smyth and K. Whelan (ed.), *Common Ground: essays on the historical geography of Ireland presented to T. Jones Hughes* (Cork, 1988), pp. 253–77

——'The Devereux Family of Carrigmenan' in L. Kehoe, *Glynn, 1789–1989*, (Wexford, 1989), pp. 35–46

——'Politicisation in County Wexford and the Origins of the 1798 Rebellion' in Dickson and Gough (ed.), *Ireland and the French Revolution*, pp. 156–78

——'The Catholic Community in Eighteenth-Century County Wexford' in Power and Whelan (ed.), *Endurance and emergence*, pp. 129–70

——Catholics, Politicisation and the 1798 Rebellion' in R. Ó Muirí (ed.), *Irish Church History Today* (Armagh, 1990), pp. 63–84

——'Catholic Mobilisation, 1750–1850' in P. Bergeron and L. M. Cullen (ed.), *Cultures et pratiques politiques en France et en Irlande, XVIe–XVIIe siècle* (Paris, 1990), pp. 235–58

——'The United Irishmen, the Enlightenment and Popular Culture' in Dickson *et al.* (ed.), *The United Irishmen*, pp. 269–98

Williams, G. A., *Artisans and Sans Culottes: popular movements in France and Britain during the French Revolution* (London, 1968)

Wynne, G., 'Atlantic Perspectives: a review essay', *Canadian Historical Review*, lxix (Sept. 1988), pp. 340–51

Zimmermann, G., *Songs of Irish Rebellion: political street ballads and rebel songs, 1780–1900* (Dublin, 1967)

INDEX